RITES OF PASSAGE
AT $100,000+

RITES OF PASSAGE
AT $100,000+

*...the insider's guide to
absolutely everything about
executive job-changing.*

JOHN LUCHT

THE VICEROY PRESS

NEW YORK

Designers: Spencer Drate and Ed Burke
Project Editor: Sally Arbuthnot

Library of Congress Cataloging-in-Publication Data

Lucht, John, 1933–
Rites of passage at $100,000+ : the insider's
  guide to absolutely everything about executive
  job-changing.

  Bibliography: p.
  Includes index.
  1. Executives—United States—Recruiting.
  2. Job hunting—United States. I. Title.
HD38.25.U6L83   1988   658.4'09   87-50459
ISBN 0-942785-07-X

"This is what I tell my friends."

John Lucht

CONTENTS

vii

RITES OF PASSAGE
AT $100,000+

How Do They Do It?

Graduate from a fine college. Acquire advanced degrees. And doggedly climb the corporate pyramid.

Chances are you still won't find out how the elite, upwardly-mobile executives move...seemingly at will...from company to company, gathering responsibility, job satisfaction, pay, perks, prestige, and power.

The upward-movers stay long enough in a company to prove their ability. They're building a resume that says, "Outstanding progress." And as long as they're on the fast track, they stay right where they are.

But when they're blocked in their current company, they *move* rather than forego their personal agendas.

They've programmed themselves to reach the top. When blocked at company A, they move swiftly and gracefully to company B, where they have an open opportunity to go all the way. And if stymied, they're not stumped. They just move neatly and quickly again, maintaining career momentum...not foundering, not falling behind.

Of course moving up isn't the only reason for moving out. Sometimes quality-of-life can be improved by the right job change. The upward-movers aren't any more willing to be ground down than to be held back. If circumstances become unreasonable, it's time to move before they become untenable.

And once again the right opportunity seems to be right at hand.

How do they do it?

Rites of Passage

For the past 17 years, I've been an executive recruiter filling high-level positions for some of America's leading corporations. Day after day, year after year, I've observed...and brokered...those pivotal company-to-company transitions that launch a fast-rising career into higher orbit, and that restore momentum when a senior executive is underutilized or fired. Amazing, isn't it, how many of the most successful executives have lost their jobs *at least* once.

What I've observed is that a very few exceptionally fast-rising and self-secure executives...maybe the top ½ of 1%...seem to have a virtuoso mastery of the job-changing process, which they continually use to their advantage. Exceptionally able in doing their job, they're just as able when it comes to changing jobs.

They deliberately attract the attention of the top executive recruiters... something I want you to do, too. As a result, they're periodically told about attractive opportunities, most of which they turn down. That is, until there's something really worth moving for. Then they snap into action, and win out over tough competition. They don't move often. But when they do, their career surges ahead.

Even when they refuse to look at something a recruiter proposes, they still build up future career momentum. The recruiter who called them realizes once again how secure and fast-rising they are with their current employer, so he resolves to offer them an even higher-level opportunity next time.

And yet, successful as these executives are in handling recruiters, they also know when it serves their self-interest to ignore the recruiters entirely. Then they go straight to potential employers...something you should also do under the right circumstances.

Indeed, it's their remarkably sure sense of *their own self-interest*, and how very differently it should be pursued under similar-appearing circumstances, that makes these special executives as impressive in the management of their careers as in the handling of their business responsibilities.

These able and observant men and women have mastered the art of job-changing at the advanced level, which I've arbitrarily defined as approaching and exceeding $100,000. At six-figures, the rules and methods for job-changing are different than at lower levels. There are more initiatives executives can take, more contacts and opportunities to be explored. But also more pitfalls and more misinformation.

So you and I are about to do something we saw years ago in Sociology class. Remember the "primitive societies" that took their "initiates" aside and gave them a cram course in what they ought to know for future well-being? They got life's practical knowledge once-and-for-all-in-a-hurry, instead of painfully by trial-and-error over the next 20 years. And of course, they also got some secrets that presumably they'd never find out, unless an insider told them. "Rites of Passage" is what the professor called that process, and you and I are about to go through a modern-day version of the same idea.

What I've done is to collect all the advanced-level job-changing wisdom I've picked up over the past 17 years from the executives who do it best. And to that I've added a dimension of behind-the-scenes information on the executive recruiting industry which even they haven't had access to.

The result is a comprehensive cram course in changing jobs, which is as informative and helpful as I can possibly make it. It's *Rites of Passage*, updated and upscaled for you...an old idea in a new time and place.

> **But before we go any further,**
> **let's look at one of the most important benefits of**
> **knowing how to change jobs advantageously.**
>
> **It's the self-confidence to push for faster**
> **advancement right where you are.**

Realizing that you can move efficiently if and when you decide to do so, you'll feel a lot freer to have periodic frank discussions with your current superiors, letting them know that you feel ready to step ahead, and drawing out their unvarnished reactions to your self-appraisal.

There's truth in the old saying, "The squeaking wheel gets the grease." The person who's doing an excellent job and has the self-confidence to ask about the company's tentative timetable for his own promotion is much more likely to get the next higher-echelon position that opens up, than his equally-fine but silent co-worker. The reason:

> "We felt we *had* to do something for Frank pretty soon, or we might lose him."

And the person whose career is marked by a *series* of fully-deserved but sooner-than-his-superiors-might-have-preferred promotions is the one who winds up "at a surprisingly young age" in the corner office. By that time his equally-able, hardworking, and loyal co-workers have stopped asking, "What's he got that I haven't?" It's obvious:

> "He's just got more on the ball. Why, he's moving up through the organization like a shot! He's just what you call a 'fast-track' sort

of guy. He's going places. Mark my words, someday he'll be president of this company!''

Momentum is its own reward.

Momentum is also a self-fulfilling prophecy. By this time Frank's superiors have not only stopped holding back his progress to accommodate their own, they've begun sponsoring him for even quicker promotions. Knowing their fast-moving subordinate is already attracting upper-management attention for his rapid progress, his current superiors extol him to *their* superiors.

Frank's bosses can't be faulted for not recognizing an exceptional talent when they see one...and certainly not for petty jealousy. So they cheer him along, either as an ideal replacement ready now to take their job so they can move up, or if that's not possible, as an ideal candidate for a higher-level position somewhere else in the company:

> "He's ready for more responsibility right now. Unfortunately, I just don't have it for him, unless you want to give him my job. He could handle it!''

Frank's current supervisor, Steve Steady, is being shrewd, not stupid, when he talks like that. The reply he gets proves it:

> "Certainly not, Steve. We can't give him your spot. You're doing a great job right where you are. In fact, one of your many fine talents is your ability to recognize and help groom the future leaders of this company. You stand out like a beacon in contrast to some of the other old guys around here who'd feel threatened by a young superstar like Frank. That's why we like to put our up-and-comers through your department...to get your solid knowledge of the business, without holding them back and dampening their enthusiasm. Incidentally, Frank speaks well of you too, Steve. He'll probably be giving *you* some promotions as the years go by!''

That's the way it works. Once career momentum takes hold, it builds and builds. And, ironically, having the solid self-confidence that comes from knowing there are plenty of attractive opportunities for you outside your current company *encourages you to press for maximum progress where you are.*

But please...no blackmail!

Don't misunderstand. I'm not talking about actually interviewing for an outside job, getting an offer, confronting your employer, and eliciting a counteroffer that pushes you ahead where you are. That's a bad idea. It's blackmail. And even if you get by with it once or twice... "three strikes and you're out." Nobody likes a blackmailer. And no one earmarks him for the future presidency of the company.

In fact, after a pivotal executive is "saved" by a counter-offer, he's usually not looked upon in quite the same favorable way. Instead of being slated for important future positions, he tends to be left out of organizational planning. Or he's categorized as an *alternate*:

> "Well, *if Al's still with us*, we could *also* consider him for that job."

No, don't come in with an outside offer you hope your company will meet or beat. It serves you right if they just wave goodbye, and you're headed for a job and a company you don't really want.

Instead, take this approach. Tell your boss:

> YOU: "Got a call today from an executive recruiter, who was looking for a Vice President—Marketing for a $150 million specialty foods company. I told him I wasn't interested, but I'd call back with some suggestions. He didn't name the company. Who do you think it might be?"

> HE: "Maybe Calico Country. They're about that size and they just put in a new President. Maybe she's reorganizing. Who called you?"

> YOU: "A guy I know, Hunter Probe, at Randall Radley Associates. I like it here, and I haven't personally been interested in anything he's had so far. But I've pointed him toward some other people, so he keeps calling. Remember my friend Carol Stevens? I mentioned her to Hunter, and that's how she moved to Farm House Foods as Marketing VP, which was a big jump for her."

> HE: "I didn't know you knew anyone at Randall Radley Associates. How'd you meet Hunter Probe?"

YOU: "Oh, he just called one day last fall. He was looking for a head of Brand Management at Conglomerated Foods, and some people mentioned my name. I told him I like this company, and he'd have to come up with a lot bigger job than that to attract me away. However, they were offering a bushel of money...about $20,000 more than I'm making now, even after that big raise you pushed through for me in January."

HE: "You never told *me* any of this!"

YOU: "I didn't see any need to, Bill. I knew you were doing everything you could to fix the salary situation. No point in trying to put pressure on you. What I'm really hoping, is for you to get Phil's job when he retires next summer, so maybe I can have your job."

HE: "*You and three other people*! And all of them have been in this division a lot longer than you have. But I must admit, George, you're doing *excellent* work. You've got our attention, and we're planning a great future for you. In fact, when Alex signed off on your raise, he told me that you're..."

Now you've got the right idea. You can't whack a relationship into place with a sledge hammer. You're likely to shatter it. An occasional gentle tap on the shoulder will do far more good...and less harm... than one big dramatic hit.

> ## It's almost never too late for the right move.
>
> ## And it's possible to look outside, without risking the job you have.

Let's go back to Frank's boss, Steve Steady, the older fellow whose department the company likes to put its "young superstars" through... to get his "solid knowledge of the business, without holding them back and dampening their enthusiasm." Obviously the company likes him a lot better than it does "some of the other old guys around here who'd feel threatened by a young superstar like Frank." In fact, it sounds like those other "old guys" are on thin ice.

But is Steve happy? Is he enjoying enough status, and making enough money, to justify relegating himself to "unsung hero"? He's got job security. But does he have job satisfaction?

Maybe not. Maybe somewhere under Steve's 25-years-with-the-company tie clasp beats the heart of a striver, who still wants the challenge, recognition, and rewards he deserves. Maybe Steve secretly yearns to be more than just a reliable upper-middle-manager, who's also a mentor to upwardly-mobile young "superstars"...protégés who, even after they leave Steve's department, still call him for basic knowledge they've progressed too fast to acquire.

Whether he realizes it or not, Steve's actually in quite a good position to pursue advancement outside his current company. True, he's 52 years old. But he's also more comfortably established and more mobile than a younger man. His pension is fully vested. His home is almost paid for. And his youngest child graduates from college nine weeks from tomorrow.

Steve can afford to take risks he wouldn't have earlier. What's more, his degree of risk in moving is even less than it might seem. Since he's no longer on the "fast track," his compensation isn't particularly high. Even if Steve encounters bad luck in the first outside job he takes, he can surely duplicate what he earns now in *some* subsequent position. And knowing Steve's ability and commitment, he *won't fail*!

Moreover, the outside world will be receptive to Steve. He's an excellent administrative business generalist, and he has a consummate knowledge of his industry, gained in one of its most respected companies.

Chances are, one of the smaller and younger companies in Steve's field can greatly profit from his experience. And he'll probably come in at a much higher echelon than he occupies in the huge conglomerate he works for now. Certainly he'll be a member of the Management Committee, and probably in time he'll be on the Board of Directors. And because his wise counsel will be heard at the highest level of the company...as it's not and never will be where he is...Steve will surely be more respected, more influential, and proportionally higher-paid than in his current company. Best of all, a dynamic, youthful company may provide an interesting equity opportunity that Steve could never hope for where he is.

Steve's problem, however, is to find out what specific opportunities may exist for him outside his current company *without letting his employer know he's looking*. He certainly shouldn't jeopardize his comfortable, secure job, just to look for outside opportunities, which may never materialize or may, after interviewing and investigation, turn out to be no better than what he has.

Fortunately, Steve can safely look outside if he wants to. In fact, he can do so very aggressively, while minimizing any risk that his current employer will find out. How to do so is one of the many matters you and I will cover in detail before we part company at the end of this book.

**For some executives, even a lateral move
can be attractive...**

and sometimes a counteroffer should be accepted.

Let's look in on Steve Steady's 54-year-old brother Stan, who runs a large out-of-the-mainstream department in an altogether different company. Unlike Steve, Stan is a specialist. And he's already running just about as big an operation in his specialty as he's likely to find anywhere else. Even so, outside opportunity beckons.

Aided by a leading executive recruiting firm, the Chief Operating Officer of a large conglomerate directly competitive with Stan's present company is talking to Stan. He wants Stan to come over and do for Next-Co the very same job he's done brilliantly for the past 11 years at Current Corporation.

The incentive to switch: Considerably higher compensation for our one-company taken-for-granted executive...about 15% more than industry-average pay for his job, whereas Stan's now making 25% less than industry-average. That's actually a 53% improvement in cash, plus a company car, which Stan doesn't have now.

Should he accept? He'd be a fool not to. In fact, Stan resigned yesterday afternoon.

But his boss, shocked and upset, asked him "not to say anything about this to anyone else for 24 hours, and until you and I have talked again." Obviously, there's a counteroffer in the wind.

Usually it's a big mistake for any upwardly-mobile executive to forego a leap-ahead opportunity and stay where he is in response to a counteroffer. But Stan may be an exception.

As a specialist, Stan's now at the top of his field...heading his function at one of the largest conglomerates. He's gone about as far as he can reasonably expect to go. Unfortunately, for that reason, and because his superiors have assumed that no outside company would ever identify and grab Stan, Current Corporation has been neglecting his compensation. Now that Stan has resigned to join Next-Co, his superiors are suddenly waking up. Stan's boss is talking to his boss:

> "Face it, Harry, we've been getting by with murder. We knew Stan loved the company, and loved that little department he's built. We figured he'd never try to leave, and we never imagined that anyone would swoop in here looking for him. So we haven't been paying him what he's worth. He'll be getting $115,000, plus a car, plus stock options at Next-Co. And you know what we've been paying him? $75,150, straight salary!"

> "If we have to replace Stan, we'll probably have to come up with about the same money they're offering which, with the car, comes to more than $120,000. And it'll cost us an extra $30,000 to $40,000 just to hire a recruiter to look for somebody."

> "Therefore, I say let's hit Stan with a base of $115,000, and no car, since we have a policy against cars. But let's also throw in a VP title, which will qualify him for stock options and Level II incentives. And maybe we should dress up that tacky little office he has. If I know Stan, he's probably as hungry for some recognition as he is for money. We've got the best guy in the industry! Let's at least *try* to keep him."

Well, Stan, under your unusual circumstances, maybe they're coming up with a counteroffer you should seriously consider. You'd only be

Director of Physical Distribution at Next-Co, and in either company you probably can't look forward to a seat in the Boardroom. It's too bad your superiors didn't "get religion" sooner. But now that they realize you're visible to the outside world, they're not going to be so casual about your "care-and-feeding" again. You love the department you've built. Maybe you should stay.

Obviously, Stan, your superiors don't even suspect that *you drew yourself* to the attention of the executive recruiting community.

And we won't tell them. Congratulations. Mission accomplished!

Out of a job?

That's when you can take full advantage of all the "Rites of Passage" right away.

Many of the most successful executives I've known over the years have been out of work at least once in their careers...and some, several times. The difference between these "winners," and others less successful, is in how creatively and aggressively they've handled their unemployment. Much of the helpful information in this book comes from observing them. Read on, and you'll have the benefit of their knowledge and experience.

On the other hand, by far the most misunderstood job-changing resource...at all points of an executive's career, and *especially when he's out of work*...is the executive recruiting industry. Here, there's no way you can get past the myth and misinformation, unless you can get an insider's perspective on the upper levels of the recruiting profession. And that's just what you'll have by the time you're halfway through this book.

And if you decide you'd like to take a post-graduate course in how executive recruiting operates at the highest levels of management, read Appendix III. See an assignment from start to finish through the eyes of the recruiter handling the search. Read straight through this book, and you'll know as much about how recruiters deal with executives as if you've actually been a recruiter yourself.

So now you know what we're up to.

**Let's just glance at a bit more of what's to come,
and then we'll get down to business.**

By the time you complete these "Rites of Passage," you'll clearly understand the motives and methods of every sector of the "people business." Everyone from the employment agency that got you your first couple jobs after college (which today calls itself a "management consulting," "executive recruiting," or "executive search" firm)...right through the most prestigious recruiters...to the "outplacement" and "executive marketing" segments of the industry.

As an upwardly-mobile executive, there's a good chance that sometime during your career you'll be involved with every one of the "professions" that move executives around. Therefore, it's worthwhile to take this once-and-for-all-in-a-hurry opportunity to see how you should deal with each in a way that best serves *your self-interest*, which often may not match theirs. For example, one of many practical suggestions is as simple as this:

"Watch the money change hands!"

That's a good rule in general. And especially helpful, when you're the subject of a commercial transaction.

And of course, dealing with "professionals" in the "people business" isn't the only way to advance your career by casting your eyes outside your current company. We'll polish every facet of your game...from handling your own personal contacts...to "networking" your way among helpful strangers...to telephone technique with recruiters to smoke out whether what they're calling about is in your best interest...to creating a really persuasive resume...to handling interviews with both employers and recruiters for your maximum advantage...to conducting a direct mail campaign...to negotiating an employment agreement. And lots more.

Whatever could put you a thought or a step ahead in the advancement of your career we'll try to cover. And wherever a "professional" in the "people business" might be a step ahead of you, we'll even the odds. Beyond that, everything is up to you.

Four Main Ways To Go

I can't know your situation at this moment.

Your degree of job satisfaction may range anywhere from totally delighted to utterly disgusted. You may even be unemployed and in the midst of an all-out search for your next position.

You may be so pleased with your current employer and your progress that you don't want to hear about any opportunity unless it can advance your career at least three to five years. At the other extreme, you may be delighted to hear about anything even remotely close to your latest job.

Over the years, your circumstances will vary. And you'll probably come back to this book at different stages of your career. Therefore, we'll proceed on the broadest possible assumption...that you're interested in *everything* you can possibly know about changing jobs. This is a complex and fascinating subject, but it centers on a few fundamentals.

The Four Methods

There are really only four basic routes to a job outside your current company:

1. Personal Contact...getting in touch with people you already know.

2. Networking...getting in touch with a series of people others refer you to.

3. Executive Recruiters...the various species of "headhunters."

4. Direct Mail...letting the mailman take your message more places than you've got time to visit and phone.

Before we're finished, we'll also consider one minor related possibility...answering newspaper ads. Also two extremely intriguing alternatives that don't aim for a corporate payroll but may put you there anyway...becoming an independent consultant, and attempting to buy a sizable business. And of course we'll also cover lots of other matters, such as resumes, interviews, "outplacement," and even some dress-for-success tips. But let's format our discussion around the four most basic job-changing methods.

Each of these four will get enough attention to exploit all of its possibilities and avoid its pitfalls: one chapter each, for Personal Contact and Networking; plus six for Executive Recruiters, and three for Direct Mail.

These fundamentals will take up half of our time together...11 of 20 chapters...so I've organized with them. But there's lots more to know, and we'll cover it all.

She, He, and Me

Pronoun practicality. Today outstanding executives are women, not just men. I tried doubling up with lots of "he and she" and "him or her." Awkward! And *inadequate*. In fairness, many of these twins ought to be "she and he" and "her or him." Finally I decided to use convenient wording.

If you're a woman, you'll see yourself in this book. And if, after all that's happened, you still aren't recognized and rewarded by your company, this book will help you move.

Personal Contact:
Pursuing the People You Know

Approaching and surpassing $100,000, you've got something you didn't have early in your career...*valuable personal contacts.*

Pick up the phone. Senior officers at most of your competitors will accept your call or call you back.

So will lots of other high-level people who do business in your industry...from direct customers, wholesalers, and distributors...to suppliers of raw materials, components, sub-assemblies, and packaging...to providers of services such as engineering, contract manufacturing, accounting, banking, advertising, management consulting, market research, and PR.

A few of these people have hire-and-fire power over jobs that could be excellent next steps in your career. And many more are in a position to hear about openings that might interest you, and possibly even to make an appropriate introduction.

Personal contacts are the resource you'll turn to first, when you think of changing jobs.

People you already know are your #1 asset.

If you can get your ideal job just by talking to them, why do anything more?

There's a big difference between talking to someone you've known awhile...possibly very well, and maybe for years...and talking to a stranger whose name you've just been given. In the next chapter, we'll discuss "networking" the strangers you meet at the suggestion of someone else. But let's start right now by getting in touch with people you already know.

True Personal Contact has advantages over Networking, Executive Recruiters, and Direct Mail:

> **Greater Impact.** Talking with friends and associates is easier and more effective than with strangers.

> **Better Confidentiality.** Long before you're ready to "go public," you can speak to the people you trust.

> **Less Need To Persuade and Sell.** People who already know your professional skills and like you personally don't have to be convinced.

> **Maximum Efficiency.** Why bother writing a resume? And why deal with lots of letters, phone calls, and appointments...if you don't have to?

No question about it. If you can get the career-advancing job you want through Personal Contact, it's the quickest, easiest, and most pleasant way to go.

Unfortunately, *LUCK* plays a starring role in what you accomplish through personal contacts. *Who* do you know? And does your inquiry come at the *opportune time* when someone you know happens to have, or know of, the right position. If so, great! If not, you'll have to proceed to other job-changing methods we'll discuss in subsequent chapters.

But now let's look at my all-time favorite "case history" of successful job-changing by Personal Contact. We'll see one of America's most gifted marketing-oriented general managers get into the position of needing a job change...and then actually achieving one. And he does both in what I believe to be the prevailing world-record time. These events happened. Only the identities have been changed to protect the guilty:

> Several years ago Matt Marketbuilder, a suave, marketing-oriented general manager from New York City, became President of Specializer Foods Company in a smallish city we'll call Oaktreeville. Specializer markets nationwide under a famous brand name, just like a big corporation. However, it's actually a cooperative owned by growers of the main ingredient of the company's products.
>
> Unfortunately, at the time Matt arrived, America's appetite for foods containing the key ingredient was declining, and supply was increasing...trends that threatened the financial health of the farmers who owned the company.
>
> Happily, within just a few years Matt accomplished a management miracle. He brought out hugely successful new products based on the special ingredient, and producer prices rose 300%, while costs declined slightly. The growers were delighted.
>
> Matt was assisted by his brilliant secretary, Lucy Local, wife of Larry Local, a lifetime Oaktreeville resident. Besides accompanying Matt to his frequent business meetings in the nearby town of Midday, which were usually held at the Midday Motel, Lucy also took care of his expense reports, which she documented by saving his American Express bills and vouchers from Midday Motel.

On Monday of the eventful week that interests us, Matt determined that Lucy's services were no longer required. . .strictly a management decision, and one in which Lucy did not concur.

So, resourceful to the very end, Lucy filled an envelope with expense account documentation, and mailed it to Matt's clever wife, Sylvia Fox Marketbuilder. Lucy didn't bother to include a note, figuring that Sylvia would know what to do.

Mrs. Marketbuilder indeed required no explanation, and added none herself, as she merely transferred the data to a fresh envelope, which she then forwarded to Lucy's husband, Larry Local, at his business address.

That's why, early Saturday morning, when Larry might otherwise have gone squirrel hunting, he arrived on the front lawn of the Marketbuilder residence, with his trusty rifle, and opened fire on the front windows. Matt grabbed a pistol and returned the fire, while Sylvia hurriedly summoned the sheriff.

That afternoon, with Larry safely in custody, a hastily-convened meeting of the Board of Directors of Specializer Foods accepted Matt's resignation.

Early that same Saturday evening, Matt made just one phone call which proves, more graphically than any other example I know of, the advantages of Personal Contact over all other job-changing methods.

Matt called Bernie Bigdeals, who'd been Matt's boss several years earlier. Bernie, now Chief Executive of a huge diversified corporation, picked up the phone at his home, halfway across the U.S., and received an unvarnished account of the circumstances under which Matt was now offering his services.

Result? Monday morning. . .approximately 38 hours after a single Personal Contact phone call. . .Matt reported to work as President of the Foods Division of Bernie's conglomerate.

Before Larry was even out on bail, Matt was already at his desk in a stylish office more than a thousand miles from Saturday's unpleasantness, holding meetings and making decisions as the much-more-highly-paid President of a corporate subsidiary several times the size of Specializer Foods in Oaktreeville.

How's that for an eventful weekend? As they say, "Truth is stranger than fiction."

In 17 years of executive recruiting, plus almost that long as an executive myself, I've never come across a more perfect example of job-changing by Personal Contact. Absolutely every aspect was at its optimum, including the accident of *timing*. Not only did Bernie Bigdeals have hire-and-fire *control* of an attractive job, the job happened to be *open*. And not only did he *know* Matt, he'd *directly supervised* him, and had first-hand knowledge of his ability and personality. Moreover, there was *no possibility that Matt's performance had declined since they worked together*, because his success at Specializer Foods had been widely publicized in the trade press. And of course Matt's *reason-for-leaving* couldn't have been clearer.

The moral of this story, if there is any, certainly isn't that crime pays. In the long run, it doesn't...for marketing geniuses, or anyone else. But we can all have a lucky, or an unlucky, day. And apparently it's possible to have notable amounts of both kinds of luck on the same day.

The point is that luck is fully as important...and often more so...as skill in determining what you'll achieve through your personal contacts on any given day, or in any three- or six-month period that you happen to be interested in a career change.

Fortunately, however, there are techniques that will polish your proficiency and improve your odds. Let's look at them.

Take inventory of all your personal contacts.

Arrange them in priority order, and focus on the ones who can be most helpful.

Personal contact is time-consuming.

True, just one out-of-the-blue phone call to a former boss, that lengthened into a three-hour employment interview, solved Matt Marketbuilder's problems with possibly-world-record speed. But everything just happened to work perfectly. Matt enjoyed a moratorium on Murphy's Law on that one day in his life when he needed it most. Unfortunately, Murphy keeps pretty close watch on you and me. Personal Contact, for us, involves a long series of lunch and breakfast dates, other appointments, and countless phone calls which, added together, take up lots of time.

Therefore, it's extremely important to plan your personal contact campaign carefully. Before you reach for the phone, try to think of everyone you know who might be worth contacting. Only when you've identified all the people you might call, can you determine who you should call, and in what order.

Matt Marketbuilder obviously chose to make his first call to his most likely contact. And if Bernie Bigdeals hadn't solved Matt's problem, you can bet Matt's *second* call would have gone to his second-most-likely contact, not to his thirteenth. Moreover, if a more subtle across-the-lunch-table approach would have been more likely to succeed, Matt would surely have employed it.

Determining Priority:
Who to contact earlier...and spend more time with... is a trade-off between two issues:

1. **Relevance: how likely to control, or at least know of, appropriate jobs, and**

2. **Knowledgeable Enthusiasm: how likely to react favorably to your availability.**

Obviously, if you know him well, the Chief Executive of the company in your industry you'd most like to work for should be number-one priority. He controls at least one job you'd want...maybe several. But if you merely shook hands with him at a convention four years ago, and he's unlikely to remember, then you'd better get a new introduction. Or write him a letter, as you would any other important stranger.

On the other hand, a first-class former subordinate who's always considered you a genius, and who now runs a small but respected supply, distribution, or service company in your industry, might also be a high-priority contact. There's no spot for you in his organization. But he knows what's happening in your field; he's enthusiastic about you and eager to help; and he's intelligent and discreet...not an oaf who might smudge your image while trying to polish it. His eyes and ears could be very beneficial.

Above all, beware of the perverse natural tendency we all have, to get in touch with the people we know best and are most comfortable with, rather than the ones who can do us the most good. Remember:

> You *can* make a relevant contact more enthusiastic, but you *can't* make an enthusiastic one more relevant.

Allocate your time accordingly.

Here's a hierarchy for ranking the twin trade-offs:

Relevance

1. Control of Jobs. These top-priority people have hire/fire power, or at at least influence, over a job you'd want. Think of CEOs, outside Directors, and heads of functions such as Human Resources, Finance, Marketing, Manufacturing, R&D, etc.

2. Vantage Point. Lower-priority, but still valuable, these contacts are extra eyes and ears. Consider middle managers in companies that interest you, and other people in your field...suppliers, customers, and consultants.

3. Neither Control nor Vantage Point. Lowest in relevance are the people outside your field altogether. Some may be widely connected, and you may be interested in off-the-wall suggestions. So there's no harm in an occasional try for serendipity. But give it low priority.

And now the opposite trade-off. How well and how favorably does the contact know your achievements, and how well does he like you personally?

Knowledgeable Enthusiasm

1.   Co-Workers. First-priority goes to your former supervisors, subordinates, and peers. No need to convince. Just update them on your latest exploits, and they're automatically enthusiastic. On the other hand, if you suspect their opinion from the past is negative, don't bother. Nothing you say now will overcome what they believe they saw with their own eyes.

2.   Closely Dealt-with Outsiders. Suppliers, customers, consultants, and others you've dealt with also have enthusiasm...or lack of it...based on prior direct experience. Moreover, they've probably heard about you from your superiors and subordinates. They can't be quite as sure as if they'd seen you from inside your company, but they're capable of justified enthusiasm. If it exists, take advantage.

3.   By-Reputation-Only Contacts. You've met these people and know them slightly. And, although they've never done business with you, they've surely heard others speak about you. Consider trade press editors, trade association executives, competitors you've met at industry functions, suppliers who've solicited you and customers you've solicited where no business ensued, etc. There's a little more going for you than with a stranger, but not much.

4.   Non-Business Connections. These are the very same people listed as number-3 under ''Relevance.'' You may know them very well indeed, but they're not part of your business milieu. Hence, they're ''long shots'' as job-advancement contacts.

Scoring Your Contacts

The purpose of these lists is merely to encourage you to think about all your possible contacts and emphasize the ones most likely to be helpful, rather than the ones you'd most enjoy getting in touch with.

However, you can use the lists for a combine-the-numbers game, if you temper it with judgment. The lowest combined number, 2, is obviously best, as Matt Marketmaker demonstrated. The highest, 7, is least likely to be helpful. And the numbers in-between provide roughly comparative rankings.

> ## Now the most valuable suggestion I know on how to handle personal contacts:
>
> ## Ask for a reference instead of a job.

This technique was pointed out to me fourteen years ago by the President of a New York advertising agency. And the logic behind it is so compelling that...to this day...it's still my most helpful tip on personal contacts.

Imagine the following conversation. You're not out of a job. However, you could be, and all the same logic would apply. But for our example, let's just say you're unhappy, and want to make a change. Today you've asked a former boss to lunch. You admire each other and enjoy working together, and you've both made outstanding progress since leaving the company where he supervised you. So you pop the question:

YOU: "Laggard Corporation has been a great learning experience, and they've taken good care of me financially. But I've gone about as far as I can, until my boss's boss retires in about five years. Meanwhile, the company itself is going nowhere. We're in three markets...and they're *all* declining."

"So frankly, Jim, my reason for wanting this lunch with you is to see if you might have anything for me over there at Upward Corp. I tremendously enjoyed working for you at First Corp. What do you think? Is there something I can do for you?"

JIM: "Gosh, Bill, I'd love to have you on my team again. In fact, you're one of the best people I've ever had the pleasure of working with."

(Long pause)

"But, unfortunately, no. I just don't have anything for an outstanding manufacturing-oriented general manager right now. In fact, I just went outside a couple months ago to fill a Divisional slot that would have been perfect. Got a good guy. But I'd rather have you. I wish you'd called me then. I'll definitely give you a ring next time a job like that opens up."

That's it. You asked. He answered. Matter closed. You both order coffee, split the check, and get on with the remainder of a busy day.

But now let's go back and change your script. Let's have you ask for a reference instead of a job:

> YOU: "So frankly, Jim, my reason for wanting this lunch with you is to ask a favor. I've decided to leave Laggard Corporation within the next few months to a year or so...as soon as I can line up something worth moving for. I'm already putting out feelers. And at some point I'll need some confidential references. Would you be willing to talk to a few people about what I did for you at First Corp?"

> JIM: "Yes. Absolutely! I'd be delighted. You're one of the very best people who ever worked for me. In fact, as you recall, *I* was the guy who persuaded you to get out of finance and go into manufacturing, working for me. I told you you'd get into general management faster that way. And of course you did, because a year and a half later I gave you that sick little division in North Carolina, where you not only had your own plant, but your own marketing as well. And then you turned out to be a 'natural' in marketing."

> YOU: "What was it that made you think I'd do well in manufacturing?"

> JIM: "Well, you were such a *practical* finance guy...not just a 'green eye-shade' type. You had so much curiosity and creativity. In short, you were a *problem-solver*. I was particularly impressed when you went down to Savannah and worked out that inventory-control system that we later installed in all the plants.

> "Of course the rest is history. I moved you up to Division Manager in the shortest time of anyone who ever worked for me. The skeptics fought me tooth and nail. But I said, 'What can we lose? We've been trying for years to sell that operation, and nobody will touch it. We'll probably have to shut it down anyway, so why not give the kid a chance?' "

> "Frankly, I was as surprised as everyone else with the turnaround you accomplished. And your strong financial and systems background had a lot to do with it.

"Bill, I'd be delighted to be a reference. I just wish I had a spot for you at Upward. That opening a couple of months ago would have been perfect! Damn! I'd much rather be getting you myself, than just recommending you to someone else!"

See the difference?

In both instances you told Jim you've decided to leave Laggard. And in both he told you he's sorry, but he doesn't have anything for you at Upward.

However, something very different happened when you asked for a reference than when you asked for a job.

Answer to a reference: "Yes. Absolutely!"

Answer to a job: "Unfortunately, no."

So you could say that the answers are as different as *Yes* and *No*. That's true. But, in fact, they're even more different. When you asked about a job, you got *one* answer: No. But when you asked about a reference, you got *two* answers: the job answer, No, plus a resounding Yes on serving as a reference. *The reference inquiry achieved everything the job inquiry did, and more, too.*

Moreover, the reference question served as a *springboard for further conversation about you.* Jim did what all newly-recruited references do: reviewed his background on the "referencee." If we'd listened longer, we'd have heard him probing for even more information... further recollections of what you did for him, and news of how you've "kept up the good work" since he lost track of you.

Above all, the biggest advantage of your asking for a reference, rather than a job, is the *positive and open-ended frame of mind* Jim takes away with him as he leaves this thoroughly enjoyable lunch with you.

Ordinarily, under similar circumstances, Jim is directly asked for a job. The accident of timing almost always guarantees that he won't have an opening. And it's always awkward to have to say so...especially to a colleague who, unlike you, may be out of work, and whom Jim might want to think about for several days (and possibly meet alternative candidates) before offering to rehire.

So when Jim is asked if he has an appropriate job, he normally hastens to say No...*and then piles on convincing reasons why not.* That way the asker won't suspect that Jim has any hesitancy about *him.* Your requesting a reference rather than a job was a refreshing change. It allowed Jim to reassure you by talking about your merits, rather than why he has no job. You let him say:

"Bill, you're great! *And here's how great I think you are.*"

You didn't force him to say:

"Bill, you're great! *And here's proof that I have no job for you.*"

Therefore, Jim's commitment to you is far more open-ended...both in outward promise, and psychologically as well. If you'd asked for a job, Jim would have coped with your query right on the spot by explaining that there wasn't one, and why not. The matter would be finished and disposed of. No follow-up to come.

But you asked for a reference. Request granted. Jim *accepted an assignment.* Follow-up *is* forthcoming. Far from disposing of your inquiry and closing the matter, Jim leaves the lunch table recalling what it was like working with you, and preparing to tell others.

"Too bad," Jim muses, *"that I don't have something for Bill. Everything I said was true. He really is one of the best guys who ever worked for me. So versatile! And a real problem-solver. Wish I could be hiring him, instead of just recommending him."*

A month goes by. You've almost forgotten your lunch with Jim. And then out-of-the-blue, your secretary says he's on the line:

JIM: "Bill, I've just had an idea. You wouldn't consider going back to being a Finance guy, would you?"

YOU: "It's certainly nothing I've had in mind. I love general management for the same reasons you do. And besides, it was you who took me away from finance back in 1980. Are you admitting you gave me a bum steer?"

JIM: "Well, hear me out. I've kept thinking about you off-and-on since our lunch, and frankly I couldn't quite figure out why. But then the light clicked on. It's because I'm bucking for President and Chief Operating Officer of the entire corporation over here in about four years, when Keith retires, and Ken moves up to Chairman."

"So I've got to groom a successor. My General Managers are doing okay with their own relatively small units. But they're all up from Manufacturing or Marketing. None is really strong in finance. And I have a hard time believing that any of them will ever be able to monitor and supervise *several* businesses."

"Now, what brought all this thinking to a head is that Friday our President asked me if I might consider giving up my Financial Officer to our Energy Industries Group. They've got problems, and I'd like to cooperate. You don't score points for being selfish. But up to now, he's been my ace in the hole. I've been bringing him into monitoring the businesses, and in a couple years I planned to have one or two of them report to him. . .sort of gradually building him into my successor."

"But Bill, in terms of my agenda, you've got even more to offer than he does. So here's what I propose: Come to my Group as CFO. Since you're already a proven general manager, I'll announce that the two large businesses we have 'on probation' for possible divestiture will report directly to you. . .I'll remove them from our regular divisional structure. And I'll also announce that you're our point man in looking for acquisitions for the Group. . . something we're actively interested in, especially if we can dress up and sell off something we already have."

"Clearly you'll come in with Group Officer overtones. As CFO and basically my right-hand man, you'll be in on the Management Reviews of all the operating units. Plus you'll have two good-sized businesses of your own. They're sick ones, but that's not so bad, because if they stay sick it's not your fault, and if they get better, you're a hero. So you're line, as well as staff. You'll update your credentials at a higher level as a Financial Officer. You'll get experience in acquisitions and divestitures. And you'll have one foot in the door as Group Officer and my successor, if we both play our cards right and you help me look good."

"What do you say, Bill? Can we have lunch and talk about it?"

Wow!   Sounds like a great opportunity. Aren't you glad you didn't get to Jim until after he filled that Division Manager job that "would have been perfect"?

And aren't you also glad you asked him for a reference, rather than a job? That was a good tactical move. You left Jim with a refreshed memory of your skills and achievements, and what it's like to work with you. When you and he shook hands outside that restaurant, he walked away with an open-ended assignment to think about you and to tell others about you. As it turned out, the person he convinced was himself.

What about purely social contacts?

Generally they're low-priority in advancing your career. But the rare exceptions can be wonderful!

So far, we've only concerned ourselves with your business contacts.

Indeed, our priority-list "numbers game" ranked purely social contacts at the bottom. . .3 on Relevance and 4 on Knowledgeable Enthusiasm. They don't control or influence jobs in your industry. . .or even know about them. And, not having worked with you in business, they probably haven't observed your professional abilities closely enough to be knowledgeably enthusiastic about them, even though their unbounded personal enthusiasm for you may have them convinced. . .rightly or wrongly. . .that you're outstanding in your work.

When it comes to asking you to work for them, your close friends may subscribe to the generally wise policy against hiring personal friends as business subordinates. Hence, trying to nudge them in that direction may prove both embarrassing and frustrating. Certainly it puts your friendship at risk.

And when a purely social acquaintance recommends you to someone else, the potential employer may be wise enough to realize that the recommendation isn't backed by any firsthand knowledge of your professional competence. You might be better off, if possible, coming in under more knowledgeable and less biased sponsorship.

And if you take a job-changing campaign with you into the recreational parameters of your tennis, golf, or athletic club, there's the very real danger of becoming thought of as "poor old Joe, down on his luck and bending everyone's ear"...a hapless aura that will lower your self-esteem, further depress your spirits, and probably rub off on your family members in the same social orbit.

Now, having duly pointed out the downside, I must also tell you that there are marvelous exceptions to the generally wise policy of not trying to use purely social contacts to advance your career.

Time and time again I've seen marginally appropriate...and even marginally competent...executives catapulted into prominent positions they would never even have been considered for on any objective basis. On rare occasions I've seen these appointments occur even when the employer had a slate of ideally qualified candidates, several of whom he would actually have preferred to hire. An opportune personal contact tipped the scale!

Nowhere is it written that you have to be the best obtainable candidate for a job in order to turn in an acceptable performance. Therefore, I can not report to you that less-than-optimum choices inevitably fail and are thrown out. It's just not so. Indeed, some have become my clients, and I've watched them succeed brilliantly...largely because they're very intelligent and have lots of common sense. But in part, too, because together we quickly recruited outstanding subordinates for them, who really *do* know the fundamentals of the businesses involved. And of course, within a year or two, the competent "surprise" choice will have filled in any significant gaps in background.

Moreover, serendipity knows no bounds. A widely-connected social friend just might introduce you to an employer who needs precisely what you offer. Stranger things than that happen every day.

The Bottom Line: Diminishing Returns

After you've depleted your ideal business contacts, you may indeed want to try a few of your likeliest social contacts. Only your own good judgment can tell you what you should and shouldn't ask of someone you know.

However, here's a suggestion that applies to every form of job-changing activity, including every variation of Personal Contact: *Don't do too much of it!*

There are several techniques to advance your career, and we'll look at all of them. Since the amount of time you can devote to career development is necessarily limited, it's important not to spend so much time on any one activity, that you neglect the others. Take advantage of the most obvious opportunities that all the techniques offer, and don't pursue any to the point that your time could more productively be spent on something else.

CHAPTER

4

Networking:
Pursuing the People You Don't Know

Networking is a form of Personal Contact. But much *less personal* than getting in touch with people you already know.

Networking is contacting people your *contacts* know...and people *their contacts* know...and people their contacts' *contacts* know.

Because it's done face-to-face, Networking is "personal contact" in that sense. And since someone you've *met* introduces you to...or lets you use his name with...the next person you see, it's also "personal contact" in that sense. Unfortunately, however, there's a big differ-

ence between asking people you already know for help and suggestions, and making the same requests of strangers you're sent to.

That's why we're looking at the two techniques separately, even though a lot of people prefer not to distinguish between them. And why we'll concentrate on getting only the good out of networking, and avoiding its pitfalls.

Networking is a powerful tool you should learn to use effectively. Whether you give it heavy emphasis, or just let it happen spontaneously, *some networking is inevitable in virtually every job-changing situation.*

First let's look at the advantages and disadvantages of networking, including its most famous advantage:

"Networking increases your contacts geometrically."

For people who are actually out of work, Networking may well be the most popular method of finding another job. Certainly it's the most widely-recommended way...particularly since the advent of the "out-placement" companies that employers hire to help fired employees find new jobs.

As those ardent proponents say:

"Networking increases your contacts geometrically."

The concept is that everyone you approach, while probably not personally in control of a job that would interest you, can at least refer you to several additional people. And each of those can send you to several more. If each person only passed you along to one further person, your progress would be *"linear."* But each Networking visit presumably leads to multiple further visits, so your progress is *"geometric."*

Everyone has at least a few contacts. And through Networking, those few can mushroom. Consider these advantages:

> **More people meet and know about you.** Your finite circle of acquaintances expands infinitely.
>
> **People who want to help *can* help.** Only one hard-to-find person will provide your ideal job, but everyone can suggest additional people to see.
>
> **There's high impact in a face-to-face visit.** Particularly in comparison to a printed resume in the mail, or languishing in a file.
>
> **Here's a process you can initiate.** Rather than passively wait for a recruiter's call, you can be as active as your time and energy permit.
>
> **The job you find probably won't require relocation.** Local visits lead you toward local jobs.

Appealing as its advantages are, Networking also has significant disadvantages:

> **It's time-consuming.** Making and keeping Networking appointments is slow, arduous work.
>
> **There's no confidentiality.** You can't network without making your intentions public.
>
> **You reach relatively few people.** You're doing well if you make and keep 2 or 3 Networking appointments per day...not enough to survey the overall employment marketplace very quickly.
>
> **Requesting favors from strangers isn't easy.** Asking help from friends is hard enough; pursuing other people's friends is tougher still.
>
> **Focus is random and local.** If you want to scour the nation for jobs in a particular field, a series of random local visits isn't the way to do it.

At its best, Networking is Personal Contact freed from the limits of just one person's contacts. At its worst, Networking is Personal Contact on a mass-production basis, with virtually all of the "personal" removed.

Where on the spectrum you position your own version of this highly individualistic medium is entirely up to you.

> ## Now let's look at networking in practice.
>
> ## Some of its implications are obvious,
> ## but others are not.

Let's go back to Jim, who wanted you to consider becoming his CFO and potential successor, and let's change the situation. Now let's say that he's *not* "bucking for President and Chief Operating Officer in about four years, when Keith retires, and Ken moves up to Chairman." Let's say, instead, that Jim just got to Upward Corp. nine months ago. He's still consolidating his own position, and the Keith/Ken scenario is at least 8 years away.

We'll also change the facts to make your problem immediate. Laggard Corporation has just reported a disastrous first half, following a big loss last year, and the Chairman is folding three losing Divisions into your profitable one, which will be headed by the Group Officer, his son-in-law, who's been your boss up to now. You and three other General Managers, plus a great many sales, marketing, administrative, engineering, and production people are suddenly out of work. Confidentiality is no longer a factor in your job-changing efforts.

However, Jim feels exactly as he told you he did. He's sorry that he didn't know of your availability when he had that "perfect spot a couple months ago." Unfortunately, he doesn't foresee having another opening for a General Manager in his Group for at least the next couple years, and by then you'll already be somewhere else.

But Jim *does* want to help. Let's listen as he calls his friend and favorite customer, Ned Nice, Founder/Chairman/CEO of a fast-growing multidivisional company that makes electronic controls and specialty motors:

> JIM: "Ned, last week I had lunch with one of the best young General Managers who ever worked for me, Bill Versatile. In fact, I promoted him into his first general management job several years

ago, when I was at First Corporation. Gave him a division that had been a loser for years...one we'd tried to sell and couldn't *give* away. We were almost ready to shut it down. Well, he pulled off an amazing turnaround...improved efficiency, lowered costs, modified the product line, and brought in some new customers. He got the thing very respectably into the black and kept it there for two years. In fact, he put it on a good growth trend, so that we had no trouble unloading it at a favorable price.''

"Bill's done a lot of equally fine work since then, most recently at Laggard Corp., where he turned around a loser and made it the only profit-generator in their Speciality Products Group. Well, I won't go into all the details, but they're using his Division and basically his staff as the nucleus, and merging all four Divisions of Specialty Products into a single unit, which the Chairman's son-in-law is going to head. So Bill, who's done another extraordinary job, is out of work!''

"As you know, I've filled my Division Manager opening. If I'd had any idea I could have got Bill, he'd be here right now. I'd even fire a couple guys to fit him in, but I can't make another change so soon after getting here myself. That's why I thought of you, because you're looking for a President of that motor company you just bought. Of course I say that selfishly, because with a guy like Bill in charge, that business would take off, and you'd be buying a lot more of our stuff to put into it.''

NED: "You really think he's that good?''

JIM: "Darn right. I only wish I could have him myself!''

NED: "Well, on a recommendation like that from you, Jim, I think I've got to at least meet him. But, unfortunately, I'm in about the same position you are. I finally found a candidate I like for that job, and he's agreed to take it. In fact, I sent him an offer letter last night by Federal Express. Unless they come up with a big counteroffer, my job is filled. But have Bill call me and come over. There's always the chance my deal may fall through.''

JIM: "And even if it doesn't, maybe you can refer him to some other people. He's a great guy, and I'd appreciate any help you can give him.''

NED: "I'll certainly try. Thanks for thinking of me, Jim.

There you have an ideal example of Networking. Everything is operating entirely in your best interests. You can only gain from Jim's effort to be helpful.

Jim:

1. knows you well,

2. enthusiastically recommends you, and

3. unequivocally asks help for you.

Ned:

1. knows Jim well,

2. respects his judgment, believes his recommendation, feels a friendly obligation to him, and

3. is very likely either to have a job for you, or to be able to refer you to someone else who can be helpful.

When you meet Ned, you've got almost as much going for you as when you met Jim. At least Jim has tried to set it up that way. Indeed, given Jim's top-notch credibility with Ned, and his outstanding recommendation of you, Ned may even be hoping that his deal with the other candidate does fall through.

But alas, your cookie crumbles. The signed-and-returned employment contract from Ned's new Division President is on his desk by the time you arrive for an interview tomorrow morning. Ned likes you on a personal basis, and wants to oblige Jim. So he treats you to an early lunch. And afterward, he makes several phone calls in your behalf. One is to Sam Supplier, from whom Ned buys a lot of components:

> NED: "Sam, I don't know whether you need a Division Manager over there or not, but I just had a very impressive young man in my office that you ought to take a look at. He's one of the casualties at Laggard Corp., where they've had that bloodbath. A very able guy, according to a friend of mine, who thought he'd be good for President of that motor company I bought. But it's too late. I just hired somebody else. Could you meet him and see if you can use

someone like him? And if you can't, could you maybe introduce him to some other people who might need a good executive?''

SAM: "Sure, Ned. I'd be happy to help. I really don't think I need anyone at quite that high level. But let me meet him and see what I can do to refer him to others who might.''

NED: "Thanks, Sam. I knew I could count on you.''

No question about it. Sam Supplier will cheerfully see you to oblige Ned, who's one of Sam's biggest customers. He'll also set up further appointments for you. He almost has to. But this time there's no specific job in mind. And Ned can only relay Jim's endorsement. He doesn't speak from firsthand knowledge. So Sam doesn't hear quite the same glowing words Ned did.

And by the time Sam sees you and begins passing you along to people who owe him a favor, the transaction may be on quite a different footing. There may even be a disclaimer thrown in:

SAM: "Say, Phil, would you do me a favor and see a guy who's looking for a job? He was sent to me by my biggest customer, Ned Nice at Buyathonics, and I've got to show I've tried to help. His name's Bill Versatile. I don't personally know how good he is, since I've never worked with him. But he seems like a reasonably intelligent guy. He's one of the crew they threw out over at Laggard Corp. And Phil, if you possibly can, please try to pass him along. I did almost 15% of my total volume with Buyathonics last year.''

PHIL: "Okay, I'll help...even though you've hit me at a really busy time. But, *I* did pretty good business with *you* last year. And I appreciate it. You can count on me, Sam, anytime.''

And so it may go. As you get further away from the people who know you and believe in you, there may be less interest in you as a potential employee and in helping you find employment. And as that phenomenon sets in, Networking, which is basically one of your most useful job-changing techniques, becomes less worthwhile. You spend lots of time on appointments, and yet the value of that time may be considerably less than outward appearances suggest.

> ## We've just looked at classic "please-help-him-as-a-favor-to-me" networking.
>
> ## Today there's a more modern and aggressive form: networking-as-a-contact-sport.
>
> ## You should know about it.
> ## But use good judgment in practicing it.

I call it *NFL Networking*.

Consider it Networking-as-the-ultimate-scrimmage. What used to be a rather prim and polite pastime, not too far removed from lawn bowling and croquet, has been transformed into one of the roughest contact sports in the business world today.

Unemployment is a nasty thing...especially for the $100,000+ executive. Cutting off his income is like trying to choke off his air supply. He'll fight for life just as fiercely as any other wounded and cornered animal. Motivation he's got. Give him a strategy and he'll execute.

So, long before it appeared as a major national sport, the stage was set for NFL Networking. There were plenty of players available...all of them adequately motivated, without resort to Pro Football's megabucks. The only things needed to get a good rough game going were aggressive coaching and a new set of rules.

Enter the "Outplacement Counselors." Pervasive growth of the outplacement industry, which is paid by employers to help fired executives find jobs, has provided the missing factors: an aggressive and creative coaching staff which, in turn, has provided appropriately revised rules. Networking is the number-one favorite job-changing technique among these professionals, and they have contributed greatly to the advancement of the game.

The basic problem with the classically polite lawn-bowling-and-croquet form of networking...the please-help-him-as-a-favor-to-me version...is its passivity, its lack of vigorous combat. The job seeker is put into play by someone else, who wishes to be helpful and therefore opens doors and makes appointments that the executive might otherwise have difficulty achieving on his own. Merely capitalizing on these thoughtfully-provided opportunities, the unemployed executive keeps these dates, presents himself and his achievements as pleasantly and persuasively as he can, and graciously accepts whatever is offered at the conclusion of each appointment...employment, offers of further help, or merely good wishes. Regardless of the outcome, he expresses genuine appreciation for the time he's been given, and he may attempt to kick an extra point with a "thank you" note.

How bland and wimpish! In these days when there's more mayhem in a love song on MTV than there used to be on *The Untouchables,* the game of Networking was obviously long overdue for an update. That modernization has been brilliantly accomplished in NFL Networking.

The breakthrough change has been to free the job-seeking executive from prior restrictions on his actions in the game. Indeed, he's now encouraged to seize and retain, if possible, total initiative for every aspect of play. No longer does he passively wait to capitalize on play-making opportunities created for him by others. Under professionally coached NFL rules, the job-seeker initiates every phase of play, and fiercely defends his prerogative not to surrender the initiative to any other player. Let's first scan the new rules, and then I'll interview Axel Bludgeon, reigning world champion NFL Networker.

Rules of NFL Networking

1. Never fail to get into the office of anyone whose name is mentioned to you.

2. Never depart with less than 3 new names.

3. Never leave follow-up solely in the hands of the person you just saw.

Now let's talk to Axel Bludgeon, who's emerged victorious for the past three years as the most aggressive job-seeking executive in the U.S. under NFL Networking rules.

JOHN: "Congratulations, Axel. You've won again! When you first got into NFL Networking, did you ever imagine that you'd become champion and hold the title three years in a row?"

AXEL: "Thank you, John. But before I answer your question, I also want to thank all those executives who helped me win. A big annual victory like mine is just a series of daily skirmishes. And if those guys hadn't let me beat them down to get an appointment and come in, then I couldn't have forced them to give up the three names so I would leave. So thanks, fellas. . .and ladies. . .I owe it all to you!"

"Okay, now I'll answer your question. No, when I first started Networking in NFL competition, I had no idea I could stay unemployed for three years, despite meeting close to 1,000 executives *in their offices*. Surely, I thought, somebody would want to hire me, and then I'd be out of contention. But early on, I met some of my competition. . .like in corporate reception rooms, where we were both waiting to see different executives. And when I saw what wimps they were, I was pretty confident. Did you ever meet Pete Polite, or Carl Courteous, or Cathy Considerate? I think the longest any of them lasted was four or five months!"

JOHN: "Axel, NFL Networking is really only a few years old, and some of our readers may not be familiar with it. Would you please explain how it works?"

AXEL: "Sure, gladly. First, somebody has to give you a name to get started. And then you go right ahead as if it were standard old-fashioned pre-NFL Networking. You call up the person at their office and say:

> 'Hello, I was talking to so-and-so, and he told me to call you. I'm in the process of a career change, and I'd like to come in and see you for just 15 minutes to get the benefit of your thoughts and suggestions. Now, I'm *not* going to ask you for a job. It's just that so-and-so speaks so highly of you, and he feels your advice could really be helpful. When would you like me to come in?' "

JOHN: "What if this person is too busy to see you, or maybe doesn't believe you're going to be out of there in 15 minutes? What if he'd rather just tell you what you want to know on the telephone? Then he can hang up when your 15 minutes are over."

AXEL: "*NOBODY* is too busy to see me. That's NFL Rule #1, *Never fail to get into the office of anyone whose name is mentioned to you.* I can't let him cop out on 'busy,' or I'd never get to see anyone important. And I sure can't go ahead on the phone. That's clearly against the rules, precisely because he *can* hang up on me in 15 minutes. Of course, *nobody,* even Pete Polite, would be in-and-out of an *office* in 15 minutes. Who ever heard of a 15-minute meeting on any subject? It's impossible. Once I'm in there, I'm good for a half-hour at least. And pretty often 45 minutes. How do you think I got to be National Champion? Under-promising and over-staying is an important technique."

JOHN: "Another question on your basic spiel. If so and so ically wants this guy to see you, why doesn't he call the guy himself?"

AXEL: "Good question. Look at NFL Rule #3, *Never leave follow-up solely in the hands of the person you just saw.* I never leave anybody without finding out who they have in mind for me to talk to. That's NFL Rule #2, *Never depart with less than 3 new names.* If they say they'll call a few people and try to set up some appointments, I demand to know *who* they intend to call. That way, I'm no longer at their mercy. If they don't bother to follow up, I can go right around them, call the people they mentioned, and say they wanted me to meet those people, which of course they did. That was one of the first things my coach taught me."

JOHN: "Speaking of your coach. . ."

AXEL: "Excuse me, John. But let me just go back to your other question about why not have the guy call for my appointment instead of calling myself. That question shows that you just don't grasp the fundamental change in networking

from the old sissy way to the new NFL tactics. Under the old
rules, I *could* leave it up to the person I just saw to call and
arrange my meeting with the next person. Because under the
old way, the person I just saw would know and like me enough
to really *want* the next person to see me. Or at least he'd
have a good dollars-and-cents *business* reason to pass me
along. Under those circumstances he really would follow up.
And I could walk out of his office without forcing him to tell
me the names of the people he was thinking of calling in my
behalf. Under the old style, people would be seeing me because *he wanted them to.* The fundamental motivation of the
game would be *him* saying:

> *'Help Axel as a favor to me.'*

"But today, under NFL rules, I've got to see lots more people and get lots more referrals. And many of those referrals
have got to come from stone-cold strangers, who don't know
me from a hole-in-the-wall, except that I'm in their office and
I won't leave until they give me names. If I simply walk out,
do you think they're going to call their friends and business
contacts and tell them they've got to see me? Don't be naive!
Under the new rules, it's up to *me* to keep the game going.
Since the guy I just saw isn't likely to put much pressure on, *I*
apply the pressure, and say he told me to do it. Instead of
trying to get him to say, 'Help Axel as a favor to me,' I
say...or at least I imply:

> *'Help me, or I'll see to it that you're in trouble with him.'*

"Now of course I can't *really* get the guy I'm calling in trouble with the one who told me about him. But *he* doesn't
know that! Get my drift? The guy whose name I'm using
doesn't care much one way or another whether I get my next
appointments...certainly not enough to call for them himself. In fact, he'd be too embarrassed to call and be as pushy
in getting me an appointment as I can be when I use his name
to get my own appointment. So you see the new rules put *me*

in charge of the game and don't depend nearly so much on how other people feel about me.''

JOHN: ''Very interesting, Axel. I see you've really given a lot of thought to your game.''

AXEL: ''I've had to. You see, the intimidation of NFL networking is psychological, not physical. So the entire game is mental strategy. It's not easy to get a no-agenda meeting with a really busy person. And the ones who aren't really busy aren't important enough to want meetings with. And besides, I'm not the only job-changer who's calling them. Some senior executives get several calls a week just like mine. So I've got to be the guy who gets in when the others are turned away. I've done a lot of thinking about the psychological handles I can use to manipulate these people...first to get an appointment, and then to get the names I came for, so I can leave. Do you want to hear what I've come up with?''

JOHN: ''Why yes, if you feel you want to give away such strategic information.''

AXEL: ''No problem. Just because other people know what the levers are doesn't mean they'll be able to pull them as hard as I do. Here are the psychological weaknesses I can appeal to in getting what I want, and I try to go for as many as possible in each case:

Friendship. Personal friends want to help if they can.

Altruism. The desire to help another human being in need. There's a streak of 'Good Samaritan' in everybody.

Greed. The desire to do business with the person whose name I mention...in the present and the future.

Fear. Concern that if they don't do what I want, it will prejudice business and personal relationships with the person I name.

Guilt. The feeling that if they don't do what I ask, they'll be letting down the person I mention, who probably *would* do what I want for somebody they sent to him.

Charm. The idea here is that if I'm face-to-face with people for a half hour, I can get them to do anything I want...from hiring me to spilling all the names they know. I always go in counting on charm as my main leverage, and then I wind up using anything else that works better.''

''Now, John, there are two other possibilities I've thought about but never used, because they're against the rules... even the rougher, more realistic rules of the NFL. They're *Sex* and *Bribery*. The closest I've come to those is that I've sometimes used a CEO's girlfriend as the name that referred me. Since, technically, that's just using one name to get another, it's perfectly within the rules. And it *does* get attention!''

JOHN: ''Well, Axel, you've certainly been generous in sharing your expertise with us. One final question...and I'm almost embarrassed to ask it so late in our interview...but what is the exact connection between the National Football League and the NFL Networking title you hold?''

AXEL: ''Don't be embarrassed, John. We're a relatively young sport, and just about everyone still asks that question. There's no connection. My sport is purely an individual one-on-one activity...not a team sport, and nothing to do with the National Football League. It's the *Networking by Force League.*''

JOHN: ''Thank you, Axel Bludgeon. And best wishes for another year of unemployment through obnoxious Networking by Force.''

There you have it: up-to-date, truly aggressive networking, as practiced by a master. Axel Bludgeon is managing to get into the offices of a great many executives...and to walk out with the names of plenty of additional executives, whose offices he'll also penetrate. He has virtuoso mastery of the techniques of modern high-pressure networking. It's the objective he's lost sight of. *Axel is not getting hired.*

> **There's a "catch 22" in basing a job campaign on the aggressive new style of networking.**
>
> **Using force to generate appointments offends the people you're trying to impress.**
>
> **Let's look at this problem...and ways to overcome it.**

If you're in a high-profile position...in control of attractive jobs, or likely to know about them...chances are you're up against a lot of Axel Bludgeons these days. Either you're *seeing them and resenting them.* Or you're *fighting them off and feeling guilty.* "After all," you think, "just a slight turn of the corporate-wheel-of-fortune could throw *me* into Networking. And then how would I want people to react to me?"

But your work week is more than filled with your job. And if anyone's going to get an extra half or three-quarters of an hour from you, it ought to be a family member or a friend...not some stranger, who drops a name and insists on an *appointment* for a "15-minute" matter, instead of straightforwardly handling it by phone.

On the other hand, if you're currently out-of-a-job, you're in an even worse position. What are you supposed to do...ignore today's most widely-recommended job-seeking method? Walk away from advice your former employer may have paid upwards of $15,000 for? Possibly delay restoring proper income to your household? And all because you're too prissy or sissy to do what others are doing every day?

If you're the appointment-giver, you're weighing the "clout" of the name that's dropped. How much do you revere or fear it? What's it worth in business gained or lost? Would the "name" see someone you sent him? *Would* you send him anyone? Is your caller *really* close to the "name" he's using? How busy are you? Do you *like* the caller's voice and manner? Do you *want* to help him? Does he sound willing to accept your best efforts right now on the phone, or must you flatly say "No"? Or are you willing...*or forced*...to say "Yes"? Only you can decide. And only on a call-by-call basis.

In this situation one thing is clear. If you're the appointment-seeker, you've got the more difficult decision to make. Pressure or no-pressure? And how much pressure? If you push too hard, you can alienate the person you're approaching. . .even if he feels obliged to see you and even if he gives you further names.

Moreover, you could easily lose the respect and sponsorship of the "name" you're using. Regardless of what you imply, you only have a slight and probationary acquaintance. If you wield the "name" like a warclub, there's a good chance the person you're approaching will ask the "name" about you. He'll find out your relationship is tenuous at best, and he'll feel obligated to let the "name" know about your foolhardy use of his most precious asset. Then you'll be on two you-know-what lists.

Overaggressive Networking can backfire into "mop up" calls disclaiming connection with you. I make such calls. And I always inform my friends and contacts when their name is inappropriately used with me. My loyalty is to them. . .not to the strangers they've mistakenly tried to help.

Obviously you don't want to portray yourself negatively, while seeking appointments to present yourself positively. Here are some ways to get around that dilemma:

> *Emphasize close, rather than distant, contacts.* The nearer along the networking chain you are to the people who know, respect, and genuinely want to help you, or have a business reason for doing so, the less pressure you'll have to use in getting appointments. Consider shifting to widely-connected purely social contacts, before relentlessly pursuing reluctant strangers.

> *Consider leaving appointment-solicitation in the hands of the person you've just seen.* If someone says *he'd* rather call his contacts than have you call them, back off. . .even though this violates NFL rule #3. If he does set up dates, you're way ahead. You walk in with no prior record of bullying. If he doesn't follow up, you can probably call and slip in *one* discreet reminder, plus an offer to save him bother by calling the contacts yourself. If he fails to proceed on either basis,

you've probably lost the right to use his name with those people. But you never really had it anyway. Maybe someone else will introduce you. Or you can write letters and introduce yourself.

Listen carefully during your self-introductory phone call. Tune to the "vibes," as well as the words. Whether you're being obnoxiously pushy is subjectively up to this listener, at this moment, of this call. It's not up to you, nor to any "Counselor" who has instructed you. If you've only met your sponsoring "name" during a brief networking visit, no matter how cordial, he's not *your* friend. He's the friend of the person you're calling. The only interpretation of this phone call he'll ever receive and believe will come from his long-standing contact...the person you're talking to. Don't sacrifice a successful prior networking contact through insensitive handling of a later one.

Also, reactions to your networking calls will differ with each person you phone, and even with the day and moment your call happens to come in. Be alert and flexible.

Consider accepting immediate help on the phone, rather than holding out for a visit. There's inherent weakness in your logic when you insist that you must have a face-to-face appointment, and yet you'll "only take 15 minutes" and "not ask for a job." If it's true that you only want "the benefit of your thoughts and suggestions," and only 15 minutes of them, then why not accept them right now on the phone?

Of course, what you *really* want is to *display your personality and charm,* which you expect will expand the 15 minutes into a pre-employment interview, or at least a "we-forgot-all-about-the-clock" brainstorming session. After dozens, and even hundreds, of calls like yours, and plenty of appointments like you're asking for, the person you're calling knows exactly what you want. If he's refusing it, and offering a valuable substitute, be smart. Accept and benefit. Make the most of what you can get. Otherwise, you may exhaust the time your respondent is willing to give you and wind up with neither on-the-phone help, nor an appointment.

Realize this. Calls like yours are frequent. And everyone's delivering the same high-pressure get-an-appointment script. When the person you call tries to get you to deal with him in the efficient and logical way he prefers, you have two choices: (1) Do so, and stand out from the crowd; you may so impress him with your alertness, common sense, and flexibility that he may decide to see you after all. Or (2) stick to the script and increase the pressure; prove your ability to follow instructions, while disproving your flexibility and resourcefulness.

One further point: Armed with the kind of resume you should be using (which we'll thoroughly discuss later on), you'll feel more confident than you do right now, to speak by phone and follow-up by sending your resume by mail or messenger.

Make lots of polite contacts, keep records, and use time as your ally. Rather than besiege and bully a few key contacts, deal lightly-and-politely with lots of them. And be sure to keep careful records. That way, you can graciously leave follow-up in the hands of others, if they prefer. You won't forget to inquire about loose ends. And with lots of contacting underway, you won't be tempted to push anyone too soon or too stridently.

Concentrate on your current industry, where talking to you will seem most relevant. Except for your own purely social contacts, the people likeliest to grant you appointments will be in your industry, not unrelated fields. They'll expect an interesting conversation, which may even include new competitive scuttlebutt gained in your job-searching travels. So besides helping you, they'll figure there may also be some benefit for them.

Try to have something other than just your employment interests to talk about. The most irksome aspect of a networking appointment is its one-sidedness. Unlike almost every other

business meeting, this one has nothing in it for your host...
that is, unless he might want to hire you. And 99% of the
time, he knows in advance he won't. He spends time, possibly risks valuable contacts, and maybe takes on a follow-up
assignment. Yet he personally has nothing to gain. No wonder he's unenthusiastic!

Try to think of a topic that may interest your host, and offer it
as part of the agenda:

> "I'd really appreciate your thoughts and suggestions.
> And maybe, since you're planning to build your own
> plant in Brazil, you'd be interested in some of the things
> we found out."

Who knows? Besides melting your host's resistance, you may
get scheduled for more than 15 minutes. Incidentally, Chapter 18 is devoted entirely to activities which, if they match
your career objectives, enable you to conduct a meeting of
genuine interest to your host, while still doing the same self-
selling you'd do in an ordinary networking session.

*Trust your own good instincts, good manners, and good taste,
whenever they conflict with what "experts" are telling you to
do.* You're just as able to judge what behavior will and won't
turn people off, as any "expert" urging a commando raid.
And unlike Axel Bludgeon, you want to get hired. Most people
don't hire foot-in-the-door vacuum cleaner salesmen...or subtle
extortionists...into high-level executive positions. And they're
not comfortable entrusting their valuable contacts to them
either. Through Axel's type of manipulation, someone may
have to see you. But he doesn't have to like you. And you'll
be a lot better off if he can do both.

*Use all the various job-changing techniques for what each
can do best.* Many "outplacement" advisors urge Networking almost to the exclusion of everything else. By the time
we've examined all the *Rites of Passage,* you'll see Networking in clear perspective among all the various job-

changing methods, and you'll have the skill to use each when it's most appropriate.

If you're ever out of work, Networking is one of the techniques you'll inevitably turn to. It's always available as a productive, open-ended outlet for your time and energy. After you've done about all you can with your direct Personal Contacts and Executive Recruiters, and you've even conducted an exhaustive Direct Mail Campaign, Networking will still beckon to you:

"Make another contact, and get several more to make."

That's Networking. Used sensibly, it can be richly rewarding.

Now let's network in-reverse.

**Instead of meeting whoever your contacts send you to,
let's pick someone you want to meet,
and find a contact who can introduce you.**

**I call this technique "Targeted Networking."
And you'll benefit from it, even if you never change jobs.**

Is there a Chief Executive you want to meet?

Maybe it's a CEO whose head of a division, or a corporate function, is nearing retirement age with no replacement in sight. Or possibly a CEO with a division or a function so mismanaged that he *should* be looking for a new executive, whether he is or not. Or maybe a CEO who's searching for candidates, but using a recruiting firm that can't propose you, because your company *also* gives it some business. Or perhaps a CEO with a corporate asset that's well managed, but falling far short of its potential, because nobody in his organization sees that potential as you do.

Who do you want a personal introduction to? A high-ranking business or financial executive? Or perhaps the head of a university, a scientific association, a philanthropic foundation, an art museum, a professional sports league, a labor union, a charity, or an opera/symphony/ballet company? The possibilities are endless. But the method of identifying someone you already know, who also knows the person you want to meet is the same.

If your "target" is prominent enough to be listed in a few of the many directories being published today, then a visit to the library should do the trick.

Glance at Appendix I. My Research Director has introduced you to dozens of directories you'll find in most large libraries. If you should ever conduct an all-out job search which includes a direct mail campaign, you may even want to buy some of these books. He's made that quick and easy too, by providing phone numbers (many are no-charge 800's) that will put you in touch with the publishers.

But now let's get busy and look up someone you want to meet:

ARNOLD P. ACCESSIBLE
CHAIRMAN AND CHIEF EXECUTIVE OFFICER
ADVANTAGEOUS CORPORATION

Begin by checking his listings in *The Reference Book of Corporate Managements,* published by Dun's Marketing Services, a division of Dun & Bradstreet, and *Standard & Poor's Register of Corporations, Directors, and Executives.* You'll see something like this:

> **CH BD CEO—ACCESSIBLE, ARNOLD P.,** b 1933; m; 1955—
> Univ of Michigan, BBA; 1957—Dartmouth Coll Amos Tuck Sch,
> MBA; 1957–1959 Army; 1959–1961 Entry Corp, Reg Sls Mgr;
> 1961–1967 Advancing Corp, Sls & Mktg Mgr, VP; 1967–1975
> Larger Corp, VP Mktg, Sr VP Mktg; 1975–present Advantageous
> Corp, 1975 Pr Consumer Products Gp, 1977 EVP, 1979 Pr COO,
> 1981 Ch CEO, now Ch Bd CEO Ch EC; Dir.

You may also find Mr. Accessible in Marquis *Who's Who in America:*

> **ACCESSIBLE, ARNOLD P.** corp. exec.; b Petersburg, Va., July
> 7, 1933; s. Franklin and Julia (Keys); m. Sally Slade, 1958 (div.
> 1974); children: Nancy L. (Mrs. Thomas Morse), Paul D., Stephen
> K.; m. Lacey Tracey Parker Aug. 12, 1974; Children: Ralph T.,
> Adam N. B.B.A. U. Mich., 1955; M.B.A. Amos Tuck Sch.,
> Dartmouth Coll.; LL.D. (Hon.) Pepperdine U., 1982; asst. sls. mgr.,

reg. sls. mgr., Entry Corp., 1959–61; sls. & mktg. mgr., v.p. mktg.,
Advancing Corp., 1961–67; v.p. mktg., sr. v.p. mktg. & sls., Larger
Corp., 1967–75; pres. consumer products group, 1975–77, exec.
v.p., 1977–79, pres. & chief operating officer, 1979–81, chmn.
bd. & chief exec, officer, Advantageous Corp., 1981—, also dir.;
dir., Diversified and Amalgamated Corp., Global Triumph Corp.,
Consolidated and Conglomerated Corp.; bd. dirs., Center for Enlightened Thinking; bd. dirs., Foundation for Fostering Progress;
chmn. bd. dirs., Fashionable Ballet Theatre Foundation; chmn. exec.
com., dir., Drug Rehabilitation Outreach Services; mem. Sigma
Alpha Epsilon, Phi Beta Kappa. Presbyterian. Clubs: Metropolitan,
Century, Sleepy Hollow. Home: 641 Fifth Avenue, New York,
N.Y. 10022. Office: 345 Park Avenue, New York, N.Y. 10022.

These entries are typical. You'll usually find a business history, plus
varying amounts of personal and outside-activity/interest information,
depending on how expansively the "biographee" filled out each publication's questionnaire. The books aren't supposed to copy each other,
so each may have information the others lack. Check several.

Let's see who Mr. Accessible is sure to know. Anyone you know too?
The possibilities are obvious:

Former Companies. He worked at Entry Corp., Advancing Corp.
and Larger Corp., before joining Advantageous Corp. Scan your
memory for prominent people you know, who were at those places
when he was, and might have stayed in touch. Chances are 3 or 4
possibilities come to mind.

Present Company. Look at the senior officers (8) and particularly
the outside directors (11) listed for Advantageous Corporation.
Know any?

Services to Present Company. Directories will tell you who Advantageous Corp. uses for Accounting, Investment and Commercial Banking, Advertising, and Law. From perhaps 6 to 10 such
firms, you probably know 3 or 4 people who might be working
closely with Accessible.

Fellow Corporate Board Members. Now we really hit pay dirt!
Accessible is on the boards of Diversified Amalgamated, Global
Triumph, and Consolidated & Conglomerated. These average about
15 members each, and insiders can introduce you just as well as
outsiders; so here are 42 people (14 × 3) to consider.

Fellow Non-Profit Board Members. Another treasure trove! The *Encyclopedia of Associations* (see Appendix I) will indicate chief executives, but you'll probably have to request annual reports to determine board members. Or your secretary can phone for that information. Mr. Accessible is on these boards: Center for Enlightened Thinking, Foundation for Fostering Progress, Prestige Ballet Theatre Foundation, and Drug Rehabilitation Outreach Services. A couple are very large boards. Figure an average of 17 members (not counting Accessible), so four boards yield 68 people who could introduce you to Mr. A. Know any of them?

So far, then, here are your potential ''introducers'':

People at Former Companies	3
Senior Officers at Present Company	8
Outside Directors at Present Company	11
Suppliers to Present Company	3
Fellow Corporate Board Members	42
Fellow Non-Profit Board Members	68
Total potential contacts so far:	135

Plus Purely Social Contacts. All 135 people we've identified so far are working with Mr. Accessible in a business context...or at least serving with him on the board of a non-profit organization. If none of the 135 contacts is a ''natural,'' his memberships in the Metropolitan Club, the Century Club, and the Sleepy Hollow Country Club may provide a link. Ask your closest friends in those clubs if they happen to know Mr. A well enough to make a friendly introduction. It's a long shot, but worth a try.

A Few Parting Comments About Targeted Networking

Targeted Networking is a lot of work. You won't do it, unless there's a very compelling reason...probably to meet someone who controls an ideal job for you. And that job either is open...or looks from your vantage point as if it should be.

Then an all-out effort to reach your ''target'' may be justified. But when you do, be sure you're easy to say ''Yes'' to. Use the strategy we discussed in asking for a reference, rather than a job. Don't frontally attack. Instead, do lots of listening and subtle questioning. Maybe toss in one or two of your best ideas as possible approaches you might explore if, on closer inspection, things are as they appear.

The strongest response you can hope to get at the end of your meeting is:

> "This has all been very interesting. I'll be thinking about our discussion, and we probably ought to get together again."

If the best way the person you've reached can use you is to fire whoever has the job you're aiming for, he may ultimately decide to do so. On the other hand, he may come up with a different way of using your talents that appeals to you even more. But one thing is almost certain: If you go in with guns blazing, naming names and suggesting tough action, you'll get the fast easy answer..."No"...rather than the one you want..."To be continued."

And do watch for diminishing returns.

Networking..."targeted" and otherwise...is a valuable tool. But the further networking takes you away from people who actually know you and can vouch for you, the weaker your referrals will be. And if you try too hard to get appointments with reluctant strangers, your behavior may become stridently self-defeating.

Unfortunately, only a few of the people you'll meet while networking will *at that moment* control a suitable opportunity...or know of one. Which brings us to our next topic, Executive Recruiters, who're often knee-deep in situations you'd love to find out about.

Executive Recruiters:
Two Types, Depending on How They're Paid

You couldn't be at, or reaching for, $100,000+ and not already know a lot about executive recruiters.

Probably you've been placed in one or more jobs yourself by a "headhunter." And chances are, you've also used professional help in identifying people to work for you.

So, what can you possibly find out that you don't already know?

Plenty! Because we're going to look at recruiters from an entirely new angle...*your self-interest*. And that's *not* the way they've been presented to you up to now.

There are, of course, two kinds: contingency and retainer. The difference is in how they're paid. The contingency firms get paid only if and when someone they submit is *actually hired*. And the retainer firms are paid for their professional skill and effort, *regardless of whether anyone they provide is hired*.

Even though the employer pays both types...and you never do...your self-interest is very different, depending on which type you're dealing with. And often that's not easy to determine. These days, both look the same, and call themselves by the same names. Even more confusing, both types may switch their compensation method, when it suits their self-interest...not yours...to do so.

Moreover, it's not a matter of "good guys" and "bad guys." Your self-interest very seldom lines up with *either* type. So in this and later chapters, you and I will figure out:

1.   What's best for you with both types, and

2.   How to tell them apart...in person and on the phone.

Even when a recruiter you've known for years shifts opportunistically from one mode to the other, you'll recognize that shift, and react accordingly.

But we won't stop at polishing your reactions. You're going to reach out to these people, and get them to do more for you.

When we're finished, you'll know as much about recruiters as if you'd spent a decade of your life working in their industry.

58

WARNING

You are approaching Dullsville…the only speed trap in this book. Before you exit this chapter you'll say, "Why is John slowing me down with the history and business methods of the recruiting industry? I just want to be a **candidate**; *I don't want to run a firm!"*

Bear with me. Obey the speed limit. Master every concept. In the following chapters, when we're whizzing along the beltline, you'll see why we took this tour of the downtown business district.

> **Understanding their hidden financial arrangements is the first step toward understanding all headhunters that come your way.**

On the surface, contingency and retainer recruiters are far more alike than different. Both:

Fill executive positions. Recruiting is the same function, regardless of payment method.

Are paid by the employer. You won't pay either type.

Range in size from small, intimate firms to multicity giants. You can't tell them apart by the number and size of their offices.

Have handsome quarters. Neither type has a monopoly on ambience.

Call themselves by the same names. ''Executive Recruiters,'' ''Management Consultants,'' ''Executive Search Consultants.'' Both types use all the same words. And the public calls both kinds ''headhunters.''

Keep vast files of resumes. Both will accept your mailed-in resume and keep it on file, along with the resumes of people they've interviewed.

Fill jobs from resumes on file. That's why they both maintain such extensive files.

Telephone employed executives. When your phone rings, either type may be calling.

The fundamental distinction between the two kinds of firms is in how they're paid.

Contingency Payment

Contingency recruiters are paid by employers only if and when someone they submit is actually hired. They may just go through their files and send over a few resumes. Or they may do telephone investigation and persuasion to develop candidates, and then interview them, to screen a highly appropriate group for the "client" to see. Either way, these recruiters are operating strictly "on contingency"...on the *chance* that someone they submit will be appropriate and attractive enough to actually get hired. Otherwise, there's no fee. If the employer hires his son-in-law, his next-door neighbor, somebody who mailed him a resume, someone submitted by a different contingency recruiter, or nobody at all, the contingency recruiter gets nothing for his efforts.

Retainer Payment

Retainer recruiters, on the other hand, *are paid by the employer regardless of whether anyone they submit is actually hired.* They're compensated for their professional skill and effort. Like the doctor, who's paid whether the patient lives or dies, and most lawyers, who're paid whether their case is won or lost, the retainer recruiter is paid merely to *attempt* a solution. He's not required to achieve one. Sons-in-law, neighbors, contingency-recruiter-submissions, mailed-in resumes, internal promotions, and positions left unfilled don't keep him from being paid.

> ## Does it sound like the retainer recruiter has the better deal?
>
> ## Why doesn't every recruiter operate on retainer, rather than contingency?
>
> ## Everyone always asks these logical questions.

Approximately half of the executive recruiting organizations in America today operate "on contingency," and the other half work "on retainer.'' With equal numbers on each side of the compensation issue, the answer certainly isn't that the contingency firms don't know what the retainer firms are doing. Indeed, many contingency firms also accept retainer assignments, and retainer firms sometimes slip opportunistically into the contingency mode.

Percentage fees are about equal for both types.

Clearly, which method of payment a firm chooses is not explained by the amounts involved, because fees for both are very similar. The leading retainer firms charge one-third...33.3%...of estimated first-year's compensation of the executive sought.

Most of them bill that amount in monthly thirds or fourths during the three- or four-month period the search is expected to require; searching beyond that point, if necessary, continues without further fee. If, when the search is over, the recruited executive earns more than the early estimate, a final bill brings the fee to 33.3%. A few price-competitive retainer firms charge 30% and fewer yet charge 25%, but 33.3% is typical among top-ranking firms. A very rare few charge a fixed negotiated fee for each project, which may come to even more than 33.3%. All retainer firms allow cancellation of the project, which stops the billing cycle when work is stopped. If termination comes after the three- or four-months of billing, the recruiter keeps the full fee.

On the other hand, the typical fee for a contingency firm is ''1% per thousand, up to a maximum of 35%.'' Under this formula, the contingency firm gets 35% of estimated first-year's compensation on positions over $35,000, whereas their charge on a $26,000 job is 26%. Retainer recruiters hardly ever work on positions under $35,000, whereas contingency recruiters often do.

Recruiters choose retainer or contingency status, depending on whether or not they want to be obligated.

The reason a recruiting organization chooses one payment method over the other is the *degree of commitment it's willing to undertake*. The retainer recruiter promises to search diligently...even exhaustively... for qualified candidates. The contingency recruiter does not.

A retainer recruiter accepts full payment for doing a successful search as his three- or four-month billing cycle elapses. Having taken the money, he's under a heavy obligation. He's been paid for success. So he'd better come up with it. Otherwise his reputation and the future of his business will suffer. Even if the client is capricious in rejecting candidates, or makes unrealistically low offers, or in any other way fails to recognize good candidates or drives them away, the retainer recruiter must try to deliver the desired result to someone who's already paid for it.

The contingency recruiter, on the other hand, has no such problem. His "client" pays absolutely nothing for effort, nothing for candidates...unless and until someone the recruiter submits is actually hired. If what the employer wants proves difficult to find, or hard to deliver at the intended salary, the contingency recruiter shifts his attention to an easier target.

Here's the contingency recruiter's philosophy, as summarized to me by one of the finest people in that field:

> "I don't mind if I don't get paid for every speck of work I do. I can fill three easy ones, John, in the time it takes you to do one hard one on retainer. And at the end of the year, I'll bet I count up as much or more money than you do. And everybody I collect from is somebody who actually got an employee from me. I tried retainer, and I stopped. When you accept a retainer, the client thinks he *owns* you. I value my freedom!"

Touché! His point is well taken. After 17 years as a retainer recruiter, I agree. "Three easy ones" can be done on contingency as quickly as one "hard one" on retainer. However, retainer assignments tend to be at higher salaries, so fees tend to be higher. What makes the "easy ones" less difficult is that they're usually at a lower level, where both the number of openings and the supply of good candidates are more numerous.

So who knows who's ahead on total fees at the end of the year...retainer or contingency recruiters? Both types have co-existed for 30 years, and the industry today is split about 50 / 50. Chances are, we'll have both types for many years to come.

> **Now you know the two payment methods, and why a recruiter chooses one or the other.**
>
> **As we'll see later, your self-interest is different with each type. Therefore, it would be convenient if each would stick to his chosen method.**
>
> **Unfortunately, some recruiters of both types switch back and forth.**

You can probably guess why some recruiters sometimes shift gears.

Contingency firms also accept retainers.

Many contingency firms ''also accept retainers,'' or ''also do search'' (meaning the same thing). The idea is to get the employer to pay a fee for the firm's attention, and thus nail down more time and effort than his opening would otherwise merit under the ''easiest-first'' priorities of contingency operation.

There's also another interesting wrinkle when a contingency firm accepts an optional ''retainer.'' Normally the contingency firm is one of many such firms ''working on'' the employer's ''listing,'' and must race the others to fill it. The retainer arrangement gives the firm an ''exclusive'' on the job, and a respite from the race. Nonetheless, being accustomed to focusing on openings that are easily filled, the contingency firm may still balk at giving too much time to a resistant project ''on retainer.''

The solution: accept retainer payments during several months of exclusivity, and afterward, if the job proves hard to fill, merely refund all or most of the retainer...thus pleasing the ''retainer'' client with the firm's ''honesty,'' while winding up no worse off than if the same work had been devoted to the opening on a non-exclusive contingency basis. Such a refund is *never* made by a true retainer recruiter.

Retainer recruiters sometimes "lob one in" on contingency.

Occasionally, a retainer recruiter may volunteer a candidate without being paid on retainer to look. But not often. *And only under cover of an excuse* (more about this later).

The reason for the retainer recruiter's furtiveness about his rare grab for a contingency fee is that, if it becomes known that he's willing to provide candidates without being paid to find them, then his clients will ask for more "freebee" candidates, rather than pay his customary retainer.

Since retainer payment is more stringent and prestigious than contingency, the contingency recruiter can accept retainer assignments without jeopardizing his contingency status. On the other hand, the retainer recruiter can *not* toy with contingency activity without endangering his retainer status.

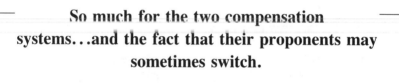

So much for the two compensation systems...and the fact that their proponents may sometimes switch.

Contingency and retainer recruiting are different businesses: brokerage, and consulting.

They have different "roots"...and methods... which you should know about.

Despite their surface similarity when you deal with them as an executive intent on forwarding your own career, contingency and retainer recruiters are really operating two different kinds of businesses. And that's true, even though each may sometimes resort to the other's payment method.

The contingency recruiter is basically a broker, and the retainer recruiter is fundamentally a consultant. This clear distinction prevails, even though the contingency recruiter often gives the employer valuable advice, and the retainer recruiter has to deliver employees; advice won't suffice.

⌐ Contingency recruiters are in the brokerage business. ¬

Contingency compensation. . .payment only if and when an introduction leads to a sale. . .is the central characteristic of all brokerage businesses.

The real estate agency is a perfect example. No matter how much work the broker puts in. . .no matter how many prospects are shown the property. . .there's no fee until there's a sale or lease. The broker is really a clearing house of "free market" information, helping interested buyers and sellers find each other. *It's a volume business.* The more properties "listed," the more chance of having what any buyer wants. And the more prospective buyers who register their interest, the more chance that one will want what any seller offers. *It's a competitive business.* Lots of other brokers are trying to make matches among the same prospective buyers and sellers. *And speed is important.* Move fast, or the seller will have sold. . .or the buyer will have bought. . .through another broker.

"Roots" of the Contingency Recruiting Business

The contingency executive recruiting firm is today's highly-evolved version of the "employment agency" and the "personnel agency" of the '50's, '60's, and '70's. Indeed, any firm with "personnel" in its name probably works on contingency, even if it also seeks retainer business. Most, but not all, such firms you'll encounter at or near $100,000+ have by now removed both "personnel" and "agency" from their names.

Up until the mid-'60's, contingency firms usually called themselves "agencies," and got all of their "applicants" to come in and "register" by running newspaper ads for highly attractive jobs that had been "listed" with them, plus prototype "jobs" designed to attract the type of people they specialized in "placing." In those days the employee paid the low fee...6% to 12% of annual compensation. As the demand for good employees heated up in the booming '60's, employers began paying agency fees as a way of competing for the best people. And with employers paying, the agencies raised their fees to the 20%-to-25% range that had been successfully pioneered by the retainer recruiters.

Changes in Terminology, Decor, and Salary Level

As contingency firms evolved toward the higher fees of the retainer firms, they also adopted their terminology. They became "management consultants" doing "executive search," and they submitted "candidates" rather than "applicants." "Personnel" and "agency" were dropped from company names. Along with upscale prices and terminology came elegant offices, and the solicitation of truly executive-level listings. Twenty years ago, contingency firms would never have been "working on" jobs at or near $100,000. Today many of them are, even though the vast majority of their work is at lower levels.

Newspaper Ads and Telephone Solicitation

Contingency firms always have...and still do...run a lot of advertising in newspapers and trade publications. It's the fastest way to bring in plenty of candidates to submit on the jobs listed with them...their "searches," under modern terminology. Most truly retainer firms never advertise any job they fill. This is true throughout the U.S., although not in Canada and the U.K. So if you see a firm advertising its jobs, it probably does most of its work on contingency. Conversely, *not* advertising strongly suggests...but doesn't prove...that a firm is primarily "retainer."

As percentage fees and salary levels both rose, the contingency firms could afford to put more effort into attempting to fill each of their higher-level openings. When newspaper ads didn't draw enough of the right candidates, they began telephoning employed executives, exactly the same way retainer firms do. Today both types of firms telephone extensively, and both send out lots of letters.

Industry Specialization

Most, but not all, contingency firms tend to specialize in a single industry, such as consumer products, publishing, retailing, health care, high-tech, banking and brokerage, etc.; and/or a particular category, such as marketing, sales, finance, EDP, engineering, law, etc. Not being guaranteed payment for their efforts, they gear up for high-volume cost-efficiency, and that generally means moving around lots of similar people in the same industry.

Today many industry-specific contingency firms have evolved to the point of requesting retainers for almost every job opening presented to them. Yet they still do not accept "searches" that require looking beyond the people their ads are bringing in, plus a not-too-burdensome number of phone calls to contacts they already know. If a firm does any contingency work, chances are it tends to do all of its work in its accustomed contingency-oriented manner.

Interviewing and Screening

Because the contingency recruiter isn't assured payment, he usually can't invest large amounts of time in interviewing and screening candidates for any particular opening. The decisive employer who lists frequently, gives clear specifications, and actually hires what he's asked for will, of course, get more attention than someone who provides less business and is vague and capricious. However, in a *brokerage* business like contingency recruiting, the more candidates any employer is shown, the more chance he might hire one. So the rule-of-thumb is:

"When in doubt, send 'em out!"

In other words, do not screen restrictively.

Non-exclusivity and the Need for Speed

An employer who uses contingency recruiters likes to list the same job simultaneously with *lots of them*. After all, he pays nothing for their efforts. And since they're not obligated, he's unsure how much, if anything, any of them will do for him.

Not having an "exclusive" on the job, the contingency recruiter must act quickly...if he decides to act at all. He's in competition with other contingency recruiters, and also with all the executives who may be sending their resumes directly to the employer...not to mention the employer himself, who may promote from within or hire his next-door neighbor.

Financial bias precludes a consulting relationship.

Since the contingency recruiter is paid only if and when one of *his* candidates is hired, he's financially biased. Therefore, he hardly ever acts as a consultant to the employer. Unless he enjoys extraordinary personal rapport with the employer, he's never asked to evaluate any candidates he doesn't supply, and he never interviews internal candidates.

Where's the price-tag?

In contingency recruiting, the price-tag is *on the head of each candidate submitted by the recruiter.* The more candidates, the more chances this broker has to make a sale.

On the other hand, if there are several obviously-appropriate candidates in the marketplace that the contingency recruiter *hasn't* contacted and tagged, then each one of them represents a definite risk that he'll lose the sale. Therefore, at levels high enough for candidates to be clearly apparent, and in industries the contingency recruiter is familiar with, he'll certainly get on the phone and attempt to affix his price-tag to the head of *everyone* who's at all likely to be hired into the job that's listed with him. Indeed, he may even try to get his tag on the heads of all the most obvious candidates, even if the opening has *not* yet been listed with him.

At or reaching for $100,000+, you're now a high-profile target for the contingency recruiters serving your industry. Sometimes it will be very much in your self-interest to go along with what they propose. Other times it will *not* be. Subtle and fascinating issues and tactics are involved, and we'll examine them in the next chapter.

But now let's look at retainer recruiters.

Retainer recruiters are in the consulting business.

Unlike the contingency recruiter, who's presumed to be biased in favor of the candidates he'll make money on, and against all others, the retainer recruiter is in an economic position that allows him to be objective. Moreover, his professional prestige and expertise are usually substantial enough to be considered part of what his client is paying for.

Therefore he's a consultant. But he'd better come up with some very impressive people. Words alone won't justify his fee.

"Roots" of the Retainer Recruiting Business

With the exception of one narrowly-specialized New York firm, retainer executive recruiting didn't exist until after World War II. But as America returned to a prosperous peacetime economy in the late '40's and the '50's, and boomed in the '60's, many corporations needed more and better managers than they were developing internally.

The solution: Hire an aggressive third-party to scout the best managers at competitive companies and persuade them to consider a career-advancing move. No more settling for the ad-answerers and the unemployed as served up by the agencies. And no need to become involved in the tacky matter of directly soliciting a competitor's key employees. This new gospel had an appealing ring, and it had charismatic missionaries, some of whom are memorialized in the names of today's giant firms: Gardner Heidrick, John Struggles, Sid Boyden, and Ward Howell, among many others.

A New Process...with No Advertising

Retainer recruiting was a radical idea in the late '40's and the '50's, when it first took hold. Employers were asked to pay an expert in the identification, evaluation, and persuasion of executives to address his time and skills to the filling of a key opening, *without any guarantee, or even a promise, that he would succeed.* And the fee was a hefty *20% to 25% of annual salary.*

Tough terms. And during the early years, a tough sale.

But 25% of annual compensation is only three months' salary for the position (even today's 33.3% is only four months). *Not* unreasonable, if it provides a truly different and superior recruiting process.

Obviously, running ads and screening applicants could never have supplied the necessary point-of-difference. Employers were already doing their own advertising and screening. And the agencies did the same thing at *no charge,* because they were billing the employee.

The retainer recruiter's answer to hesitant employers. . .from the beginning, and still today:

> "We don't just advertise and hope that somebody good will see the ad and feel like *approaching us.* We research the companies and industries of maximum interest to you, and find out who the *very best people* are. Then *we approach them.* The best people are usually well challenged and generously rewarded where they are. They're busy with their fast-rising careers, not reading and answering employment ads. They're the ones you want to meet. And they're the ones we go out and get for you."

After thirty years, the original promise of retainer recruiting still represents its highest expression. Whenever an excellent retainer recruiter is sufficiently unimpeded by entangling client relationships, he can study an entire industry and select its best people as candidates. Then his client can hire the best, and thereby shift the competitive balance of management power in the industry. And management is the number-one competitive factor. As I always tell my clients when we set out together to fill a position:

> "Somebody's got to have the best person in the industry.
>   Why not you?"

So the pioneers of retainer executive recruiting turned their backs on advertising. Instead, they reached for the *telephone,* and it became the symbol of their new profession. Advertising was out. Phoning was in. And, among the leading retainer recruiters, it's been that way ever since. Even in Canada and the U.K., where many prominent retainer recruiters *do* advertise, telephoning is their primary technique.

My fondest memory of one of the great founders of the field is the evening when Ward Howell dropped in at my office in the Olympic Tower. As we drank a toast to his retirement and watched the changing colors of the sunset on St. Patrick's Cathedral, he told me about the earliest days of his great firm in 1951. Having left McKinsey, which eliminated recruiting from its consulting practice, he operated temporarily from a *phone booth* in Grand Central Station, until he could set up an office.

Specialists in Senior Managers...Not in an Industry

The vast majority of truly retainer firms...the ones making absolutely no referrals "on contingency"...do *not* specialize in any particular industry. This may seem ironic in view of the fact that the very first retainer firm (founded before WWII) was, and still is, a specialist in the retailing and fashion industries. But it's readily understandable. Modern executive recruiting is a process that can be employed with equal effectiveness in any industry. So the early firms offered their skills to employers in every field, and the overwhelming majority of exclusively-retainer recruiters do so today.

Retainer recruiters do specialize, however, in the *higher levels of management*. Corporations willingly accept a pay-regardless-of-hiring fee-structure when looking for senior managers. And of course salaries... and hence fees...are higher at the higher echelons. So the retainer recruiters seek upper-level assignments, while shunning lesser ones.

Moreover, at the senior levels, target people in the target companies are highly visible...as visible to a non-specialist as to a specialist. Also, any significant degree of industry-specialization tends to severely restrict the number of companies the retainer recruiter can tap, because of "don't-bite-the-hand-that-feeds" considerations. Most retainer recruiters would rather serve lots of industries with minimal restriction, than just one in a handicapped manner.

Full Participation in the Hiring Process

Paid regardless of who's hired, the retainer recruiter is normally used by his clients as a *consultant*.

Unlike the contingency recruiter, who's presumed biased in favor of the candidates on whom he'll earn a fee, the retainer recruiter is often asked to interview and evaluate candidates whom the employer finds on his own, and internal candidates too.

Where's the price-tag?

The retainer recruiter's price-tag is on *his professional services,* not on your head.

Far from being a broker operating on contingency...and thus owed nothing unless a purchase is made, the retainer recruiter *has a professional relationship* with the employer. He's brought in as an outside expert...fully-paid, fully-involved, and fully-trusted.

Moreover, since he's being paid to look for exactly what his client needs, the retainer recruiter's candidates are presumed to have been *found specifically for the client who's footing the bill.* Therefore, the retainer recruiter *must never offer the same candidate to more than one client at a time,* whereas the contingency recruiter always offers the same candidate to as many potential employers as possible, as fast as possible.

The professional relationship between the retainer recruiter and *his* clients...and his *firm's* clients...creates two severely restrictive "off-limits" barriers against you:

1. He may not be able to touch you, even when you're the best person in the world for his client's position.

2. If he can show you any jobs at all, he can't show you many.

The way a retainer recruiter is paid...for his skill and effort, rather than on contingency...creates a professional relationship between his firm and the employer. And that relationship creates two barriers that prevent you from seeing all but a very few...and perhaps *all*...of the jobs you'd want, which are "searched" by any retainer firm, no matter how large.

Even if the retainer firm handles dozens...or hundreds...of jobs per year that you'd be appropriate for:

1. *You may not hear about ANY,* and

2. If you do hear about some, chances are it *won't be more than two or three within any 12-month period.*

Two different aspects of the retainer recruiter's "don't-bite-the-hand-that-feeds" relationship with his, and his firm's, clients create these severe limitations. And there's virtually no way around them, no matter how many of the firm's offices you visit, nor how many of its recruiters you know personally.

Barrier #1: The You-Work-for-a-Client "Off-Limits" Rule

Let's begin with the barrier that can keep you from seeing any jobs at all.

Because he's being paid to *strengthen* the client organization, the retainer recruiter has a corresponding duty *not to tear it down*. When the client agrees to pay the recruiter to attempt to fill an empty office, he has a right to expect that the recruiter won't simultaneously...or shortly afterward...try to empty another office.

Indeed, no employer will ever willingly contribute to the financial health of any recruiting organization that currently is...or soon will be... working against the health of the employer's organization.

As a Result: The Industry-Standard "Off-Limits-for-Two-Years" Rule

How long should a retainer recruiter have to consider a client's employees "off-limits," after being paid for a consulting assignment?

For a while, at least. But certainly not forever. Over the years, the retainer recruiting profession has almost universally acquiesced in the "Two Years Rule." Indeed, I would be hard-pressed to name a single respected firm that does not adhere to it. Here's the rule, as stated in the Code of Ethics of the AESC, an industry professional association:

> "The member will not recruit or cause to be recruited any person from within the defined client organization for a period of two years after completion of such assignment unless the member firm and client agree in writing to an exception."

Translated, the rule means that any company that pays a retainer recruiting firm to assist it is "off-limits" to that recruiting firm for the next 24 months. If, during that time, another assignment is received, the "off-limits" boundary extends *24 months from the completion of the latest assignment.*

Large retainer firms with dozens of recruiters and multiple offices handle hundreds. . .and in the largest firms way over a thousand. . .jobs per year. Therefore, at every moment they may be handling dozens, and perhaps even hundreds, of jobs that would be right for you. Unfortunately, they also have hundreds of client companies "off-limits," and there's a strong chance that your employer may be among them. If so, you'll hear of *no* opportunities from that firm.

Just one example will illustrate the dimensions of this phenomenon. In *Fortune* Magazine of October 9, 1978, Heidrick & Struggles was quoted as having 2,000 client companies off-limits. . .a disclosure that stirred up considerable comment among corporate users of large recruiting firms, who previously hadn't been aware how many companies were not being "searched" in their behalf by the largest firms.

Heidrick & Struggles had grown still further in revenues and number-of-recruiters by September 1984, when *Manhattan, Inc.* did a feature story on the leading member of that firm, the same person who six years earlier told *Fortune* that his firm had 2,000 companies "off-limits." Now, however, he stated that there were only 800 client relationships.

Whether 2,000 or 800 client companies are "off-limits" at America's third-largest recruiting firm, you can see the very substantial possibility that your employer is "off-limits"...at this or any other sizable retainer firm. And that's particularly true if you work for a major company, since big companies are the ones most likely to have used several recruiting firms within the past two years.

Regardless of how outstanding you are, you won't hear about any job *suitable for you* from any firm your employer has used in the past 24 months. You may, however, be called to suggest people for jobs that obviously *wouldn't* interest you.

Moreover, the barrier isn't removed if you contact the firm and ask to be considered.

It doesn't solve the "off-limits" problem if you approach the retainer recruiter yourself, instead of waiting for him to call you. If he were unethical, he'd approach his client's employees and, with their cooperation, merely claim that they approached him. Therefore, the recruiting firm protects itself from any seeming impropriety by not involving you at all in its projects. The ethical retainer recruiter won't empty offices in any company where he's been paid to help fill them...at least not for two years, according to standard industry practice.

Barrier #2: The You're-Allocated-to-Another-Recruiter-Within-the-Firm "Off-Limits" Rule

Under this rule, which is virtually universal among retainer recruiting firms:

> *You'll never hear about more than one-job-at-a-time*
> *...probably no more than two or three per year.*

You may simultaneously be asked to suggest candidates for several jobs that would *not* interest you. But when it comes to jobs you'd personally be interested in, virtually all retainer firms will only let you know about one-at-a-time.

The way it works is that only one-recruiter-at-a-time is given permission within the firm to contact you. And he's only allowed to tell you about one-job-at-a-time. Not until you declare yourself uninterested in job #1 do you have any chance of being told about job #2. And unless the very same person you turn down has a second job he wants to ask you about, chances are that weeks or months of inside-the-firm red tape will have to unwind, before another of the firm's recruiters can tempt you with something else.

Searchers usually take three to four months, plus a while afterward during which secretaries "close out" completed searches and return non-recruited executives to the "pool." Therefore, even if you're given maximum exposure, you probably won't see more than two or three. . . or conceivably four. . .of any retainer firm's appropriate-for-you opportunities per year.

Not allowing prospective candidates to know about more than one search at a time is based on two compelling business reasons:

1. *Clients of retainer firms pay handsomely for each candidate.* On a $100,000+ position, the recruiter bills upwards of $30,000. . .more than $6,000 each, if there are five candidates. *Client A* would be furious if any of his $6,000 candidates were simultaneously provided to *Client B*, against whom he'd then have to compete in the hiring process.*

2. *Filling jobs is the objective; accommodating executives is not.* Therefore, any executive who is shown any job. . . unless he refuses to consider it. . .must not be distracted by alternatives. Suppose an executive lives in Greenwich, Conn., has two kids in high school, a wife with a lucrative local job, and a beautiful house with a 6% mortgage. Even so, he's willing to consider an attractive position in Nome, Alaska.

---

*With contingency recruiters this consideration doesn't apply, because clients pay nothing for candidates and are billed only when someone is actually hired. Therefore, contingency firms introduce all candidates to as many employers as possible, but sometimes with sad results for the candidates, as we shall see in the next chapter.

Needless to say, he'd better not find out about an equally or more attractive situation only twelve miles from his home.

Point (2) above also has an unfortunate corollary for the *unemployed* executive. He's presumed to be "hungrier" for a new position than someone who's happily employed. Therefore, he's more likely to be shown jobs involving unattractive features...relocation, lateral responsibility, modest compensation, unstable and small companies, etc. And he won't hear about anything more attractive until the first project chosen for him has been disposed of.

How These Barriers Operate Within the Recruiting Firm

It's simple. Every recruiter in a retainer firm is forbidden to phone any executive as a prospect for a job until he checks to determine that the executive:

1. *doesn't work for a client*

    AND

2. *hasn't been allocated to a different recruiter* doing a different search.

Only if the retainer recruiter is lucky enough to hurdle both barriers, does he have permission within his firm to tell you about a career opportunity. Otherwise, it doesn't matter that you're his closest personal friend, or that he knows you're extremely unhappy with your current circumstances which, if allocation-to-another-recruiter is the problem, *may even include unemployment.*

The recruiter who wants to "use" you as a candidate simply cannot break the "off-limits" rules under which virtually all retainer firms operate. These rules are for the economic benefit of the firm *and* its individual recruiters. When one firm member helps himself by breaking the rules, he hurts his company and his colleagues. *Such behavior is not tolerated.*

Isn't there some way around the retainer firm's off-limits rules?

**Not if the firm is ethical, and looks out for
its own interests, rather than yours.**

The you-work-for-a-client barrier will always prevent you from being called as a potential candidate. However, it usually won't prevent your being called as a *"source"* of suggestions of other potential candidates. But only if the job would clearly be inappropriate for you...too junior if it's within your function (a Chief of Financial Planning, if you're a CFO), or in a different function (Marketing, rather than Finance). But even then, the recruiter will ask you only for executives *not currently working for your off-limits company.* He'll want people who've been there and left, and people at competitive companies.

If the job might appeal to you personally, you will *not* be called, *even for suggestions,* because of the obvious danger that when you express personal interest and are told you're off-limits to the recruiter because of client conflict, you'll merely go straight to the employer. After all, you don't care about the recruiter's "don't bite the hand-that-feeds" problem. It's not your problem...nor that of the recruiter's client, whom you'd like to work for, and who'd be delighted to have a chance to consider you.

If a job represents a fine career opportunity for you, and you'd be an ideal candidate, then both you and the potential employer are hurt... not helped...when the recruiter has to keep you apart. Therefore, the recruiter doesn't want you showing up on his client's doorstep and illustrating what fine candidates he's forced to withhold. And he certainly doesn't want your present employer to find out that he's emptying your office, after just being paid to fill the one down the hall. For both reasons he'll steer clear of you.

Moreover, it wouldn't be any excuse to say that you went ahead on your own after the recruiter specifically told you he couldn't make an introduction because of the You-work-for-a-client "Off-limits" Rule. After all, tempting you with the job, and then telling you that *he* couldn't introduce you is exactly the way he'd manipulate you into the hands of his latest client, if he were a sleazy operator with no ethical policy.

Looking Five Chapters Ahead

That's it. Now you know the ground rules.

All the basic facts that govern your dealings with recruiters...both contingency and retainer...were in the chapter you just finished reading. From here on, we'll look at the *implications* of those facts.

Think of dealing with recruiters as a game. You now know how the game works. But there's still a wide-open opportunity to improve your skills as a *player*.

The stakes are high. If you play expertly, and have a little luck, you may never have to do anything more to achieve career advancement outside your current company than just to handle recruiters effectively. Don't worry about what recruiters *won't* do for you. What they *will* do, if you treat them right, can still be the most favorable of all outside influences on your career.

That's why we'll pay special attention to the subject of executive recruiters. To polish this extremely important part of your career-advancement game, I'm not just going to hand you some written instructions, and walk away.

Far from it. You're going to get the nearest thing to *actual practice...* to rigorous drill and real experience...that a book can provide. Rather than just telling you how to hold the bat and how to swing, I'm also going to throw you a systematic series of all the fastballs, curves, sinkers, *and spitballs* that you're likely to encounter in big league play at or near $100,000+ .

What's more, you're going to meet the same concept more than once, and in more than one context. So, as you read on, don't feel that you must take notes or mark pages whenever you hit an intriguing new insight. Just understand it...and zip right along. Chances are, I'll throw you the same pitch again, from a slightly different angle, until it's a permanent part of your business sophistication.

In the next few chapters you're going to develop a whole new set of *reflexes.* From now on, you'll automatically reach for your maximum advantage every time you encounter a recruiter. You'll be thoroughly accustomed to major league pitching. And you'll be batting 1000...or darn close to it.

Here's how we'll proceed. First we'll check out *your self-interest* when you deal with *contingency recruiters* (Chapter 6) and *retainer recruiters* (Chapter 7). And then, knowing what's best for you with both types, we'll make sure you get it when *you call them* (Chapter 8), when *they call you* (Chapter 9), and when you *do business* with them (Chapter 10).

And finally, after you've absorbed this entire book as background, you'll get a post-graduate course in Appendix III. There you'll witness the filling of a high-level executive position through the eyes of a fine retainer recruiter at a large and prestigious firm. After you've seen the process through his eyes, it will never look quite the same to you again.

Of course, I can't absolutely guarantee that this regimen will make you a life-long whiz at dealing with recruiters. But I'll be very surprised if it doesn't.

Contingency Recruiters:
Look Out for Yourself

This chapter...and the entire book...aims relentlessly at one objective: *your self-interest.*

What's best for *YOU!* Not for contingency recruiters. Not for retainer recruiters. And possibly not for your current employer, who'd rather not lose you to a better opportunity.

Early in your career, your self-interest neatly matched the interests of contingency recruiters. Chances are, one or more of them gave you invaluable help in entering the business world, and possibly in climbing the first few levels of the corporate pyramid.

But at or reaching for $100,000 + , your interests are no longer quite the same as those of *any* recruiter...contingency, or retainer.

Sorry about that!

You're on your own now. And in this chapter we'll focus on your self-interest whenever the recruiter you're dealing with is working "on contingency"...whenever he gets paid *only if you're hired*.

> ## Chances are, your career got some of its early momentum with the help of a contingency recruiter.

Forget how special you are now.

Years ago you were a commodity in vast supply: a management trainee; a financial analyst; an assistant account executive or an AE at an advertising agency; a "member of technical staff" in an R&D lab; an engineering manager; a plant superintendent; a computer programmer or analyst; a lending officer in a bank; a field salesman or a zone manager; a copy editor; an assistant or full product manager...I could go on and on, but you get the idea.

Early in your career, you were just another face in the crowd of bright young people striving to get ahead. You needed all the exposure you could get. So you were properly grateful to find a friendly "counselor" at an agency (which today probably calls itself an executive recruiting or search firm), who saw the good qualities in you.

This "counselor" sent your resume...and extolled your personality and "potential"...to personnel departments and middle-managers all over town. Finally, you landed the job you wanted. You appreciated your "counselor's" help, and you may have kept in touch with him for years. Maybe you got a subsequent job through him. And perhaps you've used him as a source of junior- and middle-management people reporting to you, as you've moved further up.

Most of us who've climbed the corporate pyramid have warm memories of several fine contingency recruiters who touched our lives in a very positive way. Certainly I do, and I'll bet you do too.

Very helpful earlier, the contingency recruiter no longer serves your self-interest the way he used to.

Now you're at, or within striking distance of, the senior-management level. You're already earning $100,000 + , or reaching for it. You've outdistanced the crowd. You now have an impressively responsible position. You've made a track record. Your resume speaks for itself. Remember the contingency recruiter saying, ''Keep it on one page''? That was because you hadn't done enough yet to justify more. And besides, he was your spokesman in the Personnel Department.

Today you don't need an advocate trying to break down Personnel Department doors for you. And when it comes to contacting the CEO or any other senior executive who'll take the initiative in bringing you into a company, you *don't want an advocate*. You can write your own covering letter and submit your own resume. And doing so will be considered more straightforward and dignified than if you're served up on a platter by a headhunter with a financial stake in promoting an introduction.

Avoid having a price-tag on your head.

Whenever a contingency recruiter introduces you to a company, you arrive with a price-tag on your head. . .usually in excess of $30,000, if you're a $100,000 + executive.

It doesn't matter whether or not the recruiter has been specifically requested to offer candidates for an open position. The price-tag is firmly affixed. Maybe he's just taking a flyer and sending your resume with no prior request for it, and possibly no prior contact at all with the employer he sends it to.

Nevertheless, if it's the recruiter who draws the company's attention to you, you can't be hired without his being owed a fee. Standard industry practice is that such referrals are "solid" for at least six months. All incoming resumes are date-stamped and filed in the Personnel Department. And if two contingency recruiters submit the same person, the recruiter whose submission arrives first is the one who gets paid.

Racing You to Your Employment

Anyone paid on contingency has this objective: *to receive a fee when someone is hired.*

Ideally, the recruiter pursues his goal by securing a listing from an employer with a specific *job* that he and other recruiters are invited to try to fill. He then *races the other contingency recruiters to fill the job.*

But suppose a contingency recruiter. . .or a retainer recruiter who shifts opportunistically into the contingency mode. . .encounters an exceptionally desirable *employee.* Then, despite having *no listed job* that this employee fits, the recruiter may nevertheless decide to attach his price-tag, and *race to all the companies this employee is likeliest to wind up working for.* After all, new job openings occur every day There may be one the recruiter doesn't know about.

Let's assume that you're not just good, but outstanding. You're one of those exceptional executives that companies will surely hire if they have an opening. "Seen is as good as sold."

Moreover, the list of companies in your industry that might want you is just as obvious as your excellent record and personal attributes. Those companies, of course, are the ones you'll logically contact first when you're interested in changing jobs. They're also the ones where you may already have your own personal contacts. And they're where, even if you're not already personally acquainted, a letter and resume from you may spark immediate interest.

Therefore, the contingency recruiter has no time to lose. Since you're talking to him, you're probably talking to *other headhunters too.* And soon you'll be in touch with the most obvious *employers* as well.

So he may immediately submit your resume to all the companies most likely to hire you. If he's ethical, he gets your verbal okay first; if not, he doesn't bother. Either way, he moves quickly, to get your resume submitted before any other recruiter does. . .*and before you do*. After all, if your resume is dated and in-the-file before his submission arrives, he'll be out-of-luck. . .regardless of who got there first. Therefore, he ''covers'' you at all the companies you're most likely to join. A few dollars worth of typing, copying, and postage just might produce a $30,000 + fee. . .or at least insure against losing one.

Would a recruiter be so brassy as to write and phone a CEO or another key officer he didn't already know personally?

Absolutely. CEO's and other senior executives I work with on a retainer basis have shown me this kind of mail many, many times. Moreover, their secretaries say it's often followed by persistent phone calls. . .especially if an opening has been reported in the trade press. Of course the more usual and circumspect submission will be to the Personnel Department in any company the headhunter normally does business with. There, he can't afford to overreach the people who give out the contingency listings of lower- and middle-management jobs.

The Harm That's Done to You

What's wrong with the above scenario from your point of view? After all, you're not paying. You don't care who does or doesn't collect a fee. You just want to find the right job to advance your career. Isn't it a good idea to be introduced by a professional, who'll do everything possible to promote the idea that you ought to be interviewed?

No. The entree you achieve by personal contact, networking, or an impressive letter and resume you send is likely to be more, rather than less, persuasive than a headhunter's. The recruiter may have saved you some effort, but it's not likely that he's enhanced your image.

Assuming you get interviewed and hired and the headhunter gets paid, it's true that you haven't been economically hurt, since these days the employer always pays employment fees.

But the sad fact of the matter is that you're far less likely to get seen. . . much less hired. . .than if you'd arrived under your own steam, with no $30,000 + price-tag attached.

Behind-the-Scenes After an Unsolicited
Referral by a Recruiter

Notice I did *not* say "by a *contingency* recruiter." Any referral that is not specifically requested by the employer is "on contingency," even if made by a prestigious retainer firm in a convenient lapse from publicly-professed behavior.

Step One:

Letter and resume arrive; perhaps followed by phone calls from the recruiter.

Step Two:

Material is duly filed in the central Personnel Department.

Step Three:

You make contact. Through personal contact, networking or your own mailing. Or even a fortunate accident.

Maybe you meet Mr. Decisionmaker on an airplane, or on the golf course, or at a trade show, or at your daughter's swimming meet...whatever kismet the fates send, or you can contrive. Impressed, he begins to think about meeting you in his office, with an eye toward potential employment. He doesn't have anything specific right now, and your background may be a little off-beat. But he's intrigued with you and thinks, "Let's have him in here. We can shoot a few ideas around, and I can at least pick his brains. Maybe nothing will come of it; even so, no harm done."

Step Four:

Mr. Decisionmaker follows proper company procedure. He calls the personnel department first, as everyone is supposed to before scheduling a meeting that could lead to employment. Let's listen:

DECISIONMAKER: "Have we got anything on a Bill...I guess it must be William...(fill in your last name)? He's over at Stodgy Corporation. I met him last evening and he impressed me. I don't exactly have an open slot and maybe I won't be too interested after I know him better. But then again, I've been thinking of several ways I might do some reorganizing."

PERSONNEL ASSISTANT: "Oh, yes, Mr. D. I've found him in our file. William P. (you!)...the Stodgy Corporation. Yes we have his full resume here."

DECISIONMAKER: "How could we? I just met him for the first time last night."

PA: "The resume was sent in by a Mr. Ralph Quick of Quick Associates, a headhunter firm...letter dated the 14th and we got it on the 19th. Mr. Quick also phoned us, and I see he also sent a letter to Mr. Big, which Brenda sent down here for us to file."

DECISIONMAKER: "Well, what does all that mean to me? I met him at my daughter's swimming meet. Diane beat his daughter by just one second. They were both awfully nice...congratulated us as we were leaving...and he and I got to talking. No connection at all with Quick Associates, whoever they are."

PA: "They're a pretty decent headhunter firm, and we've listed with them from time to time. I think they hit with a manager for our New England Region a year or so ago. I suppose that if anything *did* develop between you and Mr. (you!), we could call them and tell them about the swim meet and all and maybe they'd..."

DECISIONMAKER: "No, never mind. It's not worth the trouble. I really don't have my thinking squared away yet. "Bye now. Have a nice day."

Sandbagged! And you never knew what hit you. The headhunter didn't know either. Maybe he's a very nice guy...perhaps a personal friend. He might even have backed off, rather than jeopardize an opportunity for you.

Too bad you had a price-tag on your head.

> ## There are three circumstances under which you might be submitted "on contingency."
>
> ## And in all three, you're better off getting to the employer on your own.

Let's take a close look at your self-interest in every possible situation where you might have the alternative of introducing yourself...or being introduced by a recruiter operating "on contingency," whether he's normally "contingency" or "retainer."

Possibility One: The employer has NOT listed the position with the recruiter.

Submitted "on contingency," you arrive with a $30,000+ price-tag on your head. Nobody asked for you. And now the company is $30,000 *less interested in seeing you than if you'd submitted yourself*

Possibility Two: The employer HAS listed an opening with a fine and highly-ethical contingency recruiter.

Now we've got a much closer case. However, I think you'll agree that you're probably better off to reach the employer on your own...having had nothing to do with the contingency recruiter, and not knowing that he had a listing for the same job you hear about and apply for on your own, or accidentally find open through personal contact, networking, or direct mail.

On the negative side, you won't have the recruiter advocating your candidacy. But is he primarily in touch with Mr. Decisionmaker or with the Personnel Department? And of course, if you're ever discussed with the recruiter (not likely, because he's biased), he may "faint-praise" you and plug his people.

But you cost *zero,* and the contingency recruiter's people have all got

$30,000+ price-tags on their heads. Even without advocacy, you can count on an objective evaluation by the employer.

The situation would have been different several years ago, when you were a recent graduate, or a junior- or middle-manager trying to get a leg up after just a few years' experience. Then you may have needed advocacy, just to be considered. Today you and all the other candidates at your level have track records that can...and will...be objectively compared.

Let's even be a little cynical. Not having to make a capital investment of $30,000+ to acquire you, Mr. Decisionmaker can feel *freer to try you out*. If you don't succeed, he can dump you, without having $30,000 worth of egg on his face. You have a political, as well as an economic, edge.

Possibility Three: The employer has assigned a search to a retainer recruiter. Now another recruiter submits you without a listing from the employer.

This happens much more often than you would think.

Sometimes a contingency recruiter may submit you without knowing that a retainer search has been assigned. You're a nifty candidate, so Mr. Contingency attaches his price-tag, and races to your likeliest employers. Or Mr. C. reads in a trade paper about an executive switching companies, thereby creating an opening at the former company. Bang! He's in touch with you, and your resume is on its way.

On the other hand, perhaps the recruiter operating "on contingency" *does* know that a retainer recruiter has been engaged...and chooses to involve himself anyway. Consider the following examples:

Perhaps a contingency recruiter regularly gets lower- and middle-management listings from a company. He "hits" well, but the company assigns its highest-level openings to retainer firms. Knowing of an ongoing retainer search, Mr. Contingency "lobs one in from the sidelines."

Or perhaps there's a "shoot-out" in which several *retainer* firms compete for a search. Here are two ways I've personally seen unethical retainer firms "go contingency" in an effort to snatch victory from the jaws of defeat:

> 1.   Write the "lost" client expressing regret at not being chosen, and enclosing resumes of "some great candidates we had lined up for you."
>
> 2.   Call the employer after three or four weeks have gone by, ask if the job has been filled (of course it's too early), and offer to do "a computer run, to see if we come up with any-one your other firm isn't showing you."

No retainer arrangement, and no charge unless someone is hired in (1). And in (2), a nominal fee of $1,000 for the "computer run," after which one of the firm's recruiters also spends two weeks on the phone trying to scrape up candidates...something a contingency firm with a non-exclusive "listing" might also do. The "computer run" was just a flimsy excuse for reversion to contingency operation after failure to achieve a retainer.

As a retainer recruiter myself, I can tell you that I and most other re-tainer firms would never even imagine such unprofessional behavior. Yet, as the "shoot-out" winner, I've personally witnessed both exam-ples (I could never have dreamed them up) as performed by two of America's most famous retainer firms. Incidentally, I'm pleased to re-port that both failed to make any headway. But they must succeed sometimes, or they wouldn't try such gambits.

Whenever there's an on-going retainer search, for which the employer is paying the full fee (in both instances above, more than $10,000 per month over a three-month period), you're at a monumental disadvan-tage, if you get "lobbed in from the sidelines" on contingency. The $30,000+ price-tag on your head is *in addition* to the $30,000+ being paid to the retainer recruiter. Hiring you will cost over $60,000! You're like a doubly-inflated basketball the headhunter is trying to slap through the hoop.

> **The only time you gain from an
> introduction by a contingency recruiter is when**

> ## 1.   there's a legitimate listing, and
> ## 2.   it's from a company you wouldn't have contacted, if the contingency recruiter hadn't persuaded you.

Obviously, you're better off without a price-tag on your head. So you really should develop direct contact with all the companies of potential interest to you. That requires some effort. But your reward is being an unencumbered prospect for employment with the companies you consider most attractive.

Indeed, why not cultivate good professional rapport with all the major competitive companies in your field? Someday you may be interested in working for one of them. Or you may ask some of their people to work for you.

A Proper Contingency Referral...Helpful to You and to the Client

But now let's suppose that "out of the blue" a contingency recruiter who has a definite listing from a company you admire calls about the position and persuades you to pursue it. You didn't know the opening existed. Or if you did, you previously chose not to follow up.

Having (1) had a true listing and (2) persuaded you to pursue it, the contingency recruiter has done both the employer and you a service, and he deserves to be paid.

You must, in good conscience, *pursue the opportunity only through him*. It's too late to contact the employer directly. Indeed, the employer wouldn't respect you if you tried to go around the contingency recruiter at this point.

Moreover, because the contingency recruiter has a bonafide listing, there's a good chance that the employer may receive several candidates from him and discuss them with him, thus generating valuable feedback that the recruiter will share with you...another benefit to both you and the employer.

A good, ethical contingency recruiter, under these circumstances, is doing what a good retainer recruiter would do. This is particularly true if the contingency recruiter has an *exclusive listing* and there are no candidates from other contingency recruiters, and no ''no-price-tag'' candidates who reached the employer directly. Under such ideal circumstances the contingency recruiter becomes a full and objective participant. He's not kept in the dark about candidates from other sources, because there aren't any. And he's not presumed to be economically biased. Every candidate came from him, and he'll be paid regardless of which one is hired.

But beware of a different fact situation
that would look the same to you as a potential candidate.

Now we'll assume that the contingency recruiter. . .or a retainer recruiter switching into the contingency mode. . .has *not* been in touch with the employer before calling you. He's merely following up on an item in this morning's edition of your industry's trade paper. Let's monitor his call to you:

CONTINGENCY RECRUITER: ''Have you heard that Bob Smith, the Marketing VP at Acme, has resigned and is going over to Zolo as President?''

YOU: ''No, that's interesting news.''

CONTINGENCY: ''Well, I don't think there's a better guy in the industry for that job than you, and I'd like you to be a candidate for it. What do you say?''

YOU: ''Absolutely! I've always admired Acme and the President over there, Hal Clay. . .brilliant, and a very nice man. Count me in. I'd love to be considered.''

CONTINGENCY: ''Great. I knew you'd see it that way. I'll get back to you.''

Sorry, Charlie! You just got a price-tag on your head. Unless Clay has set up a barrier to unsolicited referrals, using his secretary and a simple form letter I'll include later in this chapter, you and any other obvious candidates Contingency can line up are about to have your resumes mailed to Mr. Clay with a pushy letter from Contingency, who has *not* been asked for his assistance.

Unfortunately for you, Clay has assigned Richard Retainer to do a fee-paid search. Moreover, Clay doesn't yet have his secretarial defense system operating.

So Clay is handed Contingency's letter and the enclosed resumes. He calls Personnel, and Contingency is identified as "a good resource, who hits pretty well for us on sales jobs and some middle-managers too; really knows our industry and where the bodies are." Rather than offend Contingency, Clay sets up his defense system for the future and writes Contingency a note informing him that Retainer has been engaged to do a search, and that no further candidates should be proposed by Contingency, "although these will be considered."

Then, along with a list of names he's personally thought of as prospects, Clay gives a copy of Contingency's letter and its five enclosed resumes to Retainer, saying:

> "Check these out, if you wish. I'd be willing to pay the double fee if you find that one of them is the best we can do. I don't know any of these guys from Contingency except Charlie (you!). He'd have been on my list too, but you've got his full resume in this stuff here. He's young...maybe a little brash...but he appears to have lots of drive and creativity. Also some good common sense, and that's not easy to find. I talked to him at his company's booth at Product Expo last winter. I'd definitely be willing to consider him if you think we should."

Did you ever hear from Retainer?

No? You're not surprised, are you? It's inconceivable that Retainer would want his $30,000 project "completed" by a candidate from Contingency...thus making Retainer's efforts superfluous, and doubling the cost of filling the job to $60,000.

Of course, all this is happening before you and I have finished our look at "Rites of Passage." You'll be handling things a lot differently after our guided tour through the land of headhunters...especially Chapter 9 on "How to Handle a Recruiter When He Calls you."

You'll never again bend over and let any recruiter...contingency or retainer...paste a price-tag on your head, unless he passes your rigorous testing to make sure he has an appropriate client relationship.

You have no obligation to serve as a lottery ticket just because a recruiter calls you on the phone. If the company hasn't asked him to submit candidates, you and he are on the same footing. It's up to you whether he sends your resume or you send it yourself. Certainly the straightforward approach is more to your advantage, now that you're a recognizable executive at, or reaching for, $100,000+.

Here's the letter executives use to fend off unwanted contingency referrals and maintain their right to see and talk to whomever they wish, without having an uninvited outsider try to interpose fees of 25% to 35% on what would otherwise be free speech:

```
Dear _____:

I am Mr./Ms. _____'s secretary, and I
open his/her mail.

I opened your letter recommending a person (or
people) to Mr./Ms. _____.    I'm not
passing it on to him/her or to anyone else in
our organization, because* we have an execu-
tive recruiter on paid retainer to handle the
project you refer to.  We have not listed our
opening with agents and are not accepting
agent referrals.

So I'm returning your letter.  I have not
passed it or its contents to anyone else in the
organization, and have not kept a copy of it.

Thank you for your interest.

                Sincerely,



        Secretary to _____




*Omit "because" clause, if inapplicable.
```

Don't fall for the old "let me represent you" line.

There was a time when "headhunters" did represent potential employees, but they no longer do. As we discussed in the previous chapter, prior to the early '60's, the people who today are contingency recruiters, and are paid by the employer, used to label themselves "personnel agencies," and were paid (usually 6% to 12%) by the people for whom they found work, just like the Hollywood agent who, for a 10% to 15% fee, represents Paul Newman or Sophia Loren.

A person who represents someone else is called an "agent" and the person represented (called "principal" or "client") is *always the one who pays*. And the fee, of course, has to be affordable. You wouldn't even consider paying 25% to 35% of your first year's compensation to be "represented," and Paul and Sophia wouldn't either!

True representation is intended to help get a person hired, not discourage it. Only if you were paying would you be "represented." Otherwise, any "push" you get from a recruiter is more than offset by the drag of the $30,000+ price-tag he applies. Neither the dictionary and legal definition of "representation," nor common sense, allow any recruiter. . .contingency or retainer. . .to imply that he "represents" you. Don't you let him imply it either.

So, when a contingency recruiter calls, you must find out unequivocally, that he already has a firm agreement to *represent the employer,* who's promised to pay if and when one of the recruiter's candidates is hired. Notice that the agreement must apply to *the specific job being discussed;* previous deals with the same employer are irrelevant. Remember, *if the recruiter had been able to obtain a legitimate listing before contacting you, he would surely have done so.* "I didn't have time" or, even worse, "I came to you first" is no excuse.

If you learn. . .and you'll probably have to dig to get a straight answer. . .that the recruiter does *not* have a specific agreement with the employer about the specific job he calls and asks to "represent" you on, then there is only one answer:

"No, thank you, I'd prefer to represent myself!"

The recruiter you know may give you
more trouble than the one you don't.

Just as crime statistics show you're more likely to be murdered by a family member or an acquaintance than by a stranger, you're also more likely to be hurt by a recruiter you know well than by one you don't know.

Opportunistic handling of the people they know tends to become a habit pattern among some of the recruiters who specialize in a certain industry. They watch the trade press with eagle's eyes, and have the ears of a bat when it comes to the rumor mill. And in incestuous industries and job categories with lots of movement from company to company,* it's not surprising that recruiters come to regard almost every "match" as one they should have made.

It's just a short step from reading with disappointment in the trade press about job changes made without any recruiter involvement where the recruiter happened to know the new employees...and by name at least, the employers...to the point where the recruiter feels that:

1. This industry is my domain, where I know the people. They are my inventory...built up through the years.

2. Therefore, whenever people I know move, whatever companies they go to owe me a fee. I'm entitled!

3. I must act aggressively to make sure I don't lose out on any of the fees I'm entitled to.

4. Therefore, whenever an obvious opening occurs, I must line up and "submit" all of the people most likely to wind up in that spot.

---

*Exactly the types that tend to be served by contingency recruiters...the retailing, consumer product, advertising, hospitality, transportation, hi-tech, health care, and publishing industries; and the marketing, sales, financial, EDP, engineering, and legal categories, regardless of industry, are typical.

Earnestly feeling approximately as described, industry-specific contingency recruiting firms. . .or more often today hybrid contingency-and-retainer firms. . .seem almost innocently oblivious to the disadvantageous position in which they put unasked for ''candidates'' in relation to others with no price-tags on their heads.

Self-Interest: The Bottom Line on Contingency Recruiters for the Executive at, or Reaching for, $100,000+

When it comes to referrals involving yourself as the candidate, the situation is clear. You're always better off getting to the employer entirely on your own, unless the contingency recruiter has:

1. a *valid listing* from the employer (not obvious)

2. which is *exclusive* (no other recruiters. . .retainer or contingency. . .are involved; also not easy to know), and

3. the job is one which you wouldn't have pursued if it weren't for the contingency recruiter's persuasion.

On the other hand, if the contingency recruiter alerts you to a fine opportunity you wouldn't otherwise have found out about. . .or persuades you to pursue one you were aware of but otherwise would have ignored. . .then he's done you and the employer a very valuable service. You owe him your full cooperation. . .and your thanks.

Above all, don't fall for the ''let me represent you'' line. Unless *you're* paying the $30,000+, and therefore are not placed at a disadvantage relative to all the ''no-price-tag'' candidates, you're in the best possible position when you get to the employer on your own. This is usually true too, although less obvious, with respect to *retainer recruiters,* whom you and I will look at next.

Retainer Recruiters:
Look Out for Yourself

Welcome to the posh and prestigious realm of the retainer executive recruiters.

These are the headhunters whose efforts and expertise are valuable enough that they must be paid regardless of whether anyone they introduce is hired.

These are the recruiters who usually...but not always...get the assignments to find executives at $100,000 + .

And these are the executive search consultants you can almost...but not entirely...be certain will never slap a price-tag on your head, and race you to your most likely employers.

Yes, even some of the most prominent retainer recruiters may occasionally shift into the contingency mode...for their benefit, not yours. Then everything I told you in the previous chapter applies. Consider yourself forewarned.

But now let's take a look at your self-interest in dealing with a retainer recruiter who's operating strictly as a retainer recruiter should.

Getting to the employer before he engages the retainer recruiter is very much to your advantage.

With the retainer recruiter, just as with the contingency recruiter, you're way ahead if you get to the employer before he does. Consider these advantages:

The employer saves time and $30,000 + . No employer will hire you just to avoid a fee. But if you're right for the job, he's glad not to wait three months for somebody to find you. And not spending $30,000 on a retainer recruiter pleases him just as much as not spending $30,000 on a contingency recruiter.

You're a class of *one*. The retainer recruiter would present several candidates. You're good. But don't be overconfident. The employer just might hire one of the others.

There's no risk that the recruiter won't present you. We'll soon discuss six reasons a retainer recruiter may not present you. By getting to the employer before he does, you've by-passed all six roadblocks.

The employer is more open-minded and flexible. You may not have precisely the background the employer insists on getting in return for $30,000 + . But whatever you have that's not ideal may look quite attractive before firm specifications are written and lots of money is being spent to pursue them.

The job may be tailored for you. If you arrive when the employer is only beginning to analyze his business problems that require outside talent, he may include your availability in his thinking.

I can't overemphasize the benefits of reaching an employer *before* he's committed to either kind of search...retainer or contingency. By the time a search is assigned, a specific job is being filled. Detailed specifications have been written. Potential employees who show up at that late date tend to be thought of as either *relevant* or *irrelevant.* Try to arrive before you're considered a square peg, merely because the opening has been declared a round hole.

**After a retainer search is underway,
you're best off meeting the employer
as one of the retainer recruiter's "finds."**

Unfortunately, that's not easy to accomplish.

With a retainer search in progress, over $30,000 is being spent to have a consultant look for you. And with the money already spent, you're best off walking in as living proof that it was well spent. You have these advantages:

You're custom-selected for the job. Meticulous specifications have been drawn up, and you've been found in response to them.

You're expert-recommended. A professional commanding a substantial fee has identified, examined, and proposed you.

You're *not* challenged by an expert. Despite his financial impartiality, the $30,000+ expert may still tend to see more merit in candidates he finds than in ones that, being impartial, he evaluates as *"also* excellent." Talk is cheap. It's human nature...and good business...to want the client to feel he got *more* than an objective discussion for $30,000+.

You confirm the employer's wisdom. He decided to hire a consultant. *You prove he was right.*

No question about it. If you can't get to the employer before the retainer recruiter does, then your self-interest is best served if the recruiter "finds" and presents you.

But *will* he?

Not unless you meet a surprisingly restrictive set of six criteria...three of which have nothing to do with your ability to do the job.

When all six of these criteria are present, your self-interest is served by the retainer recruiter.

His introduction is the best possible way to reach the employer in situations that meet the following conditions:

1. When he's searching to fill a job *you could perform exceptionally well;*

2. When he's searching for someone with *exactly your qualifications;*

3. When he's *personally convinced* that you possess those qualifications;

4. When you're *not blocked by the You-work-for-a-client "Off-limits" Rule;*

5. When you're *not blocked by the You're-allocated-to-another-recruiter-within-the-firm "Off-limits" Rule;*

6. When the recruiter *doesn't already have plenty of other fine candidates.*

Don't you wish there were just one criterion? And of course the one you'd cling to would be #1...*a job you could perform exceptionally well.* However, even #1 can be a pain. "Exceptionally well" doesn't mean "competently." Since the retainer recruiter is being paid upwards of $30,000 to "search," what he finds had better be *something special.*

But suppose you are special. And, at least in your opinion, you're absolutely the right choice for a specific position you know is being "searched" by a retainer recruiter. Suppose, too, that you've found out his name and his firm's name. Should you call him? Or should you go directly to the employer instead?

There's a "catch 22" when you know there's a retainer search and you know who's doing it.

You don't want to be overlooked.

But if you go to the recruiter, you're playing "Russian Roulette" with up to 5 bullets in your 6-shooter.

The only one of the six criteria on which you have direct information is #1. You know that *you could perform exceptionally well.* That's the harmless chamber in your revolver. However, even then you may be wrong. . .not about your abilities, but about the job content, which may be differently defined for the new person sought than for the former one, and for people with similar-sounding jobs in other companies.

With respect to each of the other five criteria, you don't know if it's "no problem," or possibly a fatal shot.

For you to get to the employer through the retainer recruiter. . .admittedly the ideal route. . .you've got to survive all six potentially eliminating criteria. How different from regular "Russian Roulette"! With only one chamber loaded, and only having to pull the trigger once, the traditional game is as safe as badminton when compared with trying to get a retainer recruiter to "present" you on a job you know he's "searching." Then, five of the six chambers *may* be loaded, and you've got to pull the trigger on all six, hoping that *none* of them is.

We've covered #1. Forget about whether or not you can *do the job.* Let's look at the remaining five of these invisible threats to your candidacy. You should have gone directly to the employer, rather than playing with your Retainer-Recruiter-Revolver, if even one of the other five chambers has a hidden surprise for you:

2. *If your qualifications and experience aren't EXACTLY as specified.* For $30,000 +, the recruiter is expected to hit the target. If others match the specifications more closely, he'll present them, not you. On the other hand, if you get to the employer directly, and he meets and likes you, he may observe special abilities, or experience, or fine personal characteristics that outweigh your deficiencies. Even if he merely forwards your mailed-in resume to the retainer recruiter, he's implicity *expanding the specs* to include you.

3. *If the recruiter isn't personally convinced* that you've got the right stuff. You may seem more appropriate to the employer than to the recruiter. If so, let's hope you meet them in that order. Meet the employer first and you're in the running. Meet the recruiter first and you're dead.

4. *If you're blocked by the You-work-for-a-client "Off-limits" Rule.* Then you must go to the employer. The recruiter's "don't-bite-the-hand-that-feeds" problems mean nothing to the employer. He'll ship you to the recruiter...or deal with you himself, if the recruiter refuses to touch you.

5. *If you're blocked by the You're-allocated-to-another-recruiter-within-the-firm "Off limits" Rule.* The only way you'll ever hear about two appropriate-for-you jobs simultaneously within the same retainer firm is if *YOU go to employer #2.* No recruiter will ever tell Client #2 that you're his at a cost of $30,000 +, but he may have a hard time hiring you, because the firm is also providing you to Client #1.

6. *If the recruiter already has plenty of other fine candidates.* Whenever you're one of a great many people who'd be appropriate, *ordinary statistical odds* will usually kill you. The recruiter doesn't need you, because he already has a full slate.

Two facts are clear:
1. it's nice to be among the retainer recruiter's "finds,"
2. but that's not going to happen very often.

SO

There are two things to do:
1. go directly to employers, and
2. get known to lots of retainer recruiters.

How strong is your interest in changing jobs *right now?*

Would you merely like to hear occasionally about career-advancing alternatives to a job you love and would hate to leave? Or are you eager to move? Are you out of work? Your degree of interest in changing jobs will dictate how much you do.

But what to do is obvious.

Go directly to employers.

As we've just seen, you're better off if you get to the employer before the retainer recruiter is brought in. Even when you find out for sure that a retainer recruiter is working on a specific job you'd love, there's a strong likelihood that he won't "present" you for one or more of the six reasons we just looked at. And of course, 99% of the time you won't know the job exists...nor that the recruiter is working on it... nor that one of the six reasons stands in your way.

So, as a general rule, going directly to employers is your smartest move.

When you're not interested in changing jobs, of course, you won't be contacting any employers. But when you're *very* interested in a change, it's in your self-interest to contact as many employers as possible, as effectively as possible. How to do that will be one of the many "Rites of Passage" we'll cover later on.

Know as many retainer firms as possible.

Since it's clear that each retainer firm. . .no matter how large. . .is only going to show you a very few opportunities per year that would interest you, the only way you can know about more recruiter-handled opportunities is to *know more firms*. Certainly your self-interest lies in that direction, and how to achieve that goal is something else we'll look into.

Contingency firms, however, are another matter. If a firm offers *any* contingency services. . .even though it also offers retainer services. . . consider it a contingency firm and look out for the potential disadvantages we examined in the previous chapter. You're probably already acquainted with some very fine contingency firms which have agreed never to submit you without first identifying both the employer and the job, and getting your advance approval. I suggest limiting your involvement with contingency firms to the ones where you have this high level of personal rapport.

Reach out to firms you don't know only if they're *exclusively* retainer, and hence unlikely to jeopardize their "pay-me-to-look" status by circulating your resume to any company that hasn't paid.

And now a logical question everyone always asks:

Wouldn't getting in touch with lots of retainer recruiting firms make me seem too readily available?

Absolutely not.

Retainer recruiting firms do not call each other up and compare notes on who's been in touch with them. Neither do employers.

And of course no two retainer firms will ever be "searching" the same job simultaneously, since no employer would ever pay two suppliers to do the same work at the same time.

Therefore, no employer. . .and no retainer recruiter. . .will ever find out how many other recruiters and employers you've been in touch with.

Limiting the number of retainer recruiters who know about you doesn't increase your value to anyone. Such "exclusivity" merely reduces the number of attractive positions you'll know about, by reducing the number of firms that know about you.

The only potential problem you could have along these lines would be if you happened to contact both the employer and his retainer recruiter simultaneously. Then the employer might feel that the recruiter didn't have to look very hard to find you. However, the recruiter will also present several other fine candidates who *weren't* obvious, so he's in no trouble for presenting one obvious candidate. Indeed, he might have seemed remiss *not* to identify and check out the obvious one.

Notice that medium-sized and smaller retainer firms are likely to do you just as much good as the largest ones.

Don't neglect medium-sized and smaller firms. After all, no retainer firm, no matter how large, and how many of its jobs would interest you. . .is likely to show you more than one-at-a-time and two-or-three-a-year. Therefore, a firm that annually handles only thirty jobs you'd want may be just as likely to show you three-a-year as a huge company that handles three hundred you'd want.

Incidentally, from the sophisticated employer's point of view, the smaller firms can sometimes be *far more valuable as recruiters* than the largest ones, because they're far less handicapped by the "You-work-for-a-client" and the "Allocated-to-another-recruiter-within-the-firm" barriers.

Don't imagine that being well known to a retainer firm will get you exposed to the most attractive opportunity they have in terms of your self-interest.

As you know, the firm will only tell you about one-opportunity-for-you at a time. . .usually no more than two or three per year. Chances are that "Murphy's Law" will have you allocated to an opportunity in Hog

Wallow Bend, when the firm is asked to fill the job you'd love in an ideal company just twelve miles from your home.

If this happens when you're actively "looking," and you fail to reach the nearby employer, don't blame the retainer recruiter handling the Hog Wallow Bend search...nor his colleague doing the Hometown search. And don't blame me. You knew that you should have been in touch with the target employer directly. *You're* the one who failed to watch out for your self-interest.

Contact retainer firms long before you're ready to move.
Avoid the "he's-in-trouble-so-we-can-show-him-anything"
presumption.

Getting in touch with a recruiter raises an unfortunate presumption. Executives ordinarily do so only when they're out of work, or in trouble, and anxious to move. The more recent the contact, the more it looks like the difficulty is *now!*

So if your resume is a recent arrival, you'll probably be earmarked for something relatively unattractive. The firm *won't* feel you have to be lured away from a great situation. And once you're allocated to a recruiter for a search, nobody in his firm can contact you on anything else, until he's finished his project and his secretary has "returned you to the pool." You'll never know if something more attractive is co-pending, or comes along during the weeks and months before you're back in circulation.

Keep in touch as your career progresses.

For all the reasons we've just seen, it's good strategy to have your up-to-date information in the files of all the exclusively-retainer recruiting firms well *before* you actually want to move. Each time you get a major promotion, use that opportunity to send the announcement memo to the firms you've had contact with.

The implication is that you're continuing to move ahead on the fast track. You're the type of person the retainer firms want to show their clients. You're not in trouble. You're not answering the newspaper ads placed by the contingency firms. And you certainly can't be offered uninteresting, low-salaried, out-of-the-way jobs. Your announcement arrives at a time when you're obviously on a high. And the firm updates its file on you accordingly.

> **But suppose you're only belatedly contacting retainer firms, and you want to move right now.**
>
> **Should you try to visit several offices and meet several recruiters in the largest firms?**

No. Make contacts that are convenient and time-efficient. But don't waste lots of valuable time that you could devote to other aspects of a well-rounded job search.

Remember that even the largest firms will allow you to see only one position-for-you at a time...probably only two or three per year. Once any firm has a file on you and you've met even one of its members, you're about as fully involved as you can possibly be.

Moreover, if any firm is already *actively discussing* any job with you, you know that you won't hear about anything else from them until that search is completed, or you've declared yourself a non-candidate... *and* until the recruiter's secretary has returned you to the "pool."

The only sure way to get strongly involved with any retainer firm, large or small...and with any retainer recruiter, regardless of firm...is to be frank and helpful whenever you're called to solicit your personal interest and/or suggestions. Then *you're* helping the recruiter, not trying to get him to help you. If you sound impressive on the phone...and you genuinely try to help...those facts will be duly noted in your file.

Later, when other recruiters in the firm get their hands on your file, the first recruiter's comments will encourage them to call you for suggestions, even when you don't personally look like the solution to their problem. Gradually, over the months and years, you'll meet many of the firm's recruiters by phone, and...when you're appropriate to be interviewed...face-to-face as well.

Just as you can't get a baby in a month by getting nine women pregnant. . .or if you're a woman, by encouraging nine men to get you pregnant. . .you also can't become the darling of Korn/Ferry or Russell Reynolds Associates by hustling several of their recruiters simultaneously. Rather than spending lots of time trying to reach more recruiters in the same large firm, you'd be better off contacting additional firms.

Go to the employer
before you hear about his job from the recruiter
. . .not afterward.

You must reach the employer before the retainer recruiter tells you about the employer's position. Once you hear about the job from the recruiter, it's too late for the direct approach.

Of course, if the retainer recruiter is free-within-his-firm to deal with you, and he's likely to decide you're an ideal candidate, you don't want to "go direct." Then you bask in the spotlight of his recommendation. You're part of what the employer paid upwards of $30,000 for. . .a "finalist candidate."

But suppose you're interviewed by the retainer recruiter. . .in the office, or just on the phone. . .and he decides you're *not* a "finalist." Maybe you lack something the employer has clearly asked for. You feel, on the other hand, that what's missing is outweighed by special advantages which, when the client's aware of them, will cause him to widen his specifications to include you. . .and perhaps others like you.

Now, however, it's too late to do what you easily could have done earlier. Now you *can't* go straight to the employer. If you do, it will be an outrageous affront to the recruiter. And remember that the retainer recruiter, unlike the contingency recruiter, is financially-unbiased. Therefore, he usually helps the client evaluate *all candidates from all sources,* not just the ones the recruiter supplies. Someone you've slapped-in-the-face will probably be asked his opinion of you.

On the other hand, if you'd gone to the employer *before* the recruiter turned you down, the employer might have pronounced you a worthy candidate. Or asked the recruiter to check you out...indicating that your deficiency wasn't disabling. Then, the recruiter could have "adopted" you. Indeed, you'd have broadened the specifications and *made his work easier.*

Now, however, you're a pain in the neck! Now you've *defied* the recruiter. And you've *called his judgment into question.* Why didn't he at least see you as a close case? Why didn't he at least *ask* if you were worth considering?

Pursuing a recruiter's client after the recruiter rejects you is unforgivable. Your centrally-maintained file will be annotated. No other recruiter in the firm will ever risk a similar experience. *You'll never again be a candidate of that firm.* Yes, Virginia, there *is* a death penalty!

Going to the employer before...
rather than after...talking to the retainer recruiter
not only avoids his wrath; *it may delight him.*

Once you get to an employer and persuade him you're a viable candidate, hidden blockages with the retainer recruiter disappear. Either the employer meets and evaluates you without involving the recruiter; or, more likely, he passes you on to the recruiter, who's forced to follow up.

If you were held back merely because the recruiter had plenty of other fine candidates, he may keep plugging his "finds." But he'll also "adopt" you. And he'll be glad to get the job filled, regardless of who's hired.

If "You-work-for-a-client" was the barrier, the recruiter may reveal it to the employer as his excuse for not "finding" you. Secretly, of course, he'll be delighted that you've innocently helped him complete his search.

If "You're-allocated-to-another-recruiter-in-the-firm" was the problem, the recruiter will never admit it, because this handicap of larger recruiting firms is never publicly exposed. However, he'll be equally pleased to have this roadblock out of his way.

Whatever the barrier may have been, you've broken through by going straight to the employer. *And the retainer recruiter is probably just as happy as you are with the result.*

**By now you may be saying: Wait a minute!
Aren't you telling me two diametrically opposite things?**

**1. I'm better off as the recruiter's "find" than
just walking in off the street, and yet**
**2. I should go straight to the companies I want
to work for.**

Isn't this inconsistent?

No. Most of the time, your *only choice* is to contact the potential employer directly. Because most of the time you won't know:

> 1. that a suitable position is open, and
>
> 2. that a retainer recruiter is filling it, and
>
> 3. who the recruiter is.

And unless you know all three facts, you have no choice. Contacting the recruiter is impossible.

Even in the rare instance when you *do* happen to find out all three essentials, you'd better think long and hard before you go to the recruiter, instead of the employer.

Whenever you contact a retainer recruiter on a job you know he's handling, you're playing Russian Roulette with potential bangs in five barrels.

Play those odds if you want to.

I wouldn't.

One final note on retainer recruiters:

There is one terrific way to get around a retainer firm's rules and learn about the position you'd like best among all those the firm is filling.

This "end run" can only be scored if you've already established a close personal friendship with one of the firm's recruiters. . .a relationship built over a period of years. Your friend probably first called you as a potential candidate. You weren't interested, but you went out of your way to offer excellent suggestions. Several became "finalists" or valuable "sources" of further ideas. You've made money for the recruiter. You've also been trusted with secrets that never leaked out. Maybe you've even had lunch with him on several occasions.

Now you want to move. So you call your friend and ask if there's anything at his firm that might meet your objectives.

> YOU: "Jim, I'd really like to get out of this family owned business and into a big conglomerate where I can develop a track record with full P&L responsibility for a good-sized subsidiary, and I was wondering if there's any way you could possibly let me know what's going on over at your place that might fill the bill."

If your recruiter friend wants to. . .he certainly has no obligation other than friendship to "go around the rules". . .he can do the following:

> *1. Get your file.* He'll call the central record-keeping location to nab it, if no other recruiter has it. And if someone does have it, he'll get "wait-listed" to receive it next time it's free. This will pull you away from searches that don't appeal to you.

> *2. Look up the firm's assignments that could interest you.* He'll consult his computer terminal or a weekly-printout for this information.

> *3. Tell you the relevant searches, and help you select the ONE you like best.* Probably there will be 20 to 50 or more

such assignments among the various offices and recruiters of a large retainer firm doing upwards of a thousand searches per year. The computer screen or printout will tell your friend the location, name of company and subsidiary, projected salary range, and name of the firm-member doing the search, for every active project. How far out on a limb he'll go to reveal these facts to you will depend on how much he trusts you to keep the discussion *absolutely confidential*.

When you and he agree on the best opportunity for you that his firm is working on, he'll then call up the recruiter handling it:

YOUR RETAINER RECRUITER FRIEND: "By the way, Dick, I know somebody who'd be terrific for that Ideal Subsidiary project you're working on for Conglomerate Corporation. In fact, he's a personal friend of mine, and I happen to have his file right here. Not only would he be right-on in terms of his background, but I'm sure he'd be interested. Would you like me to send you his file?"

DICK: "Is he really good?"

RECRUITER FRIEND: "Outstanding! I've tried several times to get him to be a candidate on general management projects I've been handling. But he works for a family-owned mini-conglomerate and they've kept giving him more money and responsibility, so I've never had anything he was willing to spring for. In fact he's practically running the place now."

"They're about $350 million in everything from consumer products to a grey iron casting company. But he's finally decided that it's time to build his career in a big public company; he's gone about as far as he can where he is."

"Your project makes sense, because his experience is perfectly in line...and you've got a high enough salary on that job to be able to afford him. Most public companies don't pay as well as Conglomerate Corporation."

DICK: "Well, if you think he's that good, let's go ahead. I've got three fine candidates right now, and I could use a fourth to round out the slate."

RECRUITER FRIEND: "Fine, I'll put his file in tonight's pouch. You'll have it tomorrow. I'll tell him to expect your call."

But remember, your retainer recruiter friend can only do that if he's sure you're going to play square with him.

If you later contact the employers on some of the other searches your recruiter friend has told you about, *it'll be obvious that you violated his trust.* Every one of the firm's clients that you reach is likely to involve his recruiter from the firm in evaluating you. And every recruiter will check the firm's central files to get permission to deal with you. Bang! Your deceit is *automatically* exposed! If you cheat, you'll be black-listed by your friend's firm, and you'll lose one of the most valuable recruiter contacts any executive can ever have.

How To Handle Executive Recruiters
...When You Contact Them

We've come a long way together in exploring the two types of recruit-ers...contingency and retainer...and your self-interest with both. I've also shown you quite a bit about how to handle each type.

But that hasn't been our main thrust. I've raised "how-to-handle" issues only as they came up in the context of the basic "self-interest" concerns.

Now, as we continue our trek through the land of headhunters, let's cover all the remaining "how-to-handle" information. This chapter's on "when-you-call-*them*," and the next two will deal with "when-they-call-*you.*"

Soon we'll have seen headhunters from every angle, except the inside of their own offices. And that vantage point, too, is available to you in Appendix III. There you'll observe an executive search from start to finish, through the eyes of the recruiter. That account...fictionalized, of course, to protect everyone, and to make sure it covers everything you should know...is your postgraduate course. Do take it. But only after you've read the whole book as background for it.

Meanwhile, back to the matters at hand.

Sometimes you won't be content to wait for the recruiter's call.

Obviously, you'd love to have the most respected retainer firms phoning every few months to tempt you with leap-ahead opportunities.

Then, if you happen to feel stymied and frustrated when a call comes in, you can say, "Interesting...tell me more." With very little effort...perhaps not even the preparation of an up-to-date resume...you'll be swerving past the obstacles at your present company, and gaining momentum on the fast track.

But suppose that right now you're known to only a few firms...and not well known. You have no close personal friend at any major firm who'll go out on a limb for you as we saw at the end of the last chapter. You're a stranger to most of the firms. And you want them to know you...as favorably and as soon as possible.

Be careful. Don't go "cruisin' for a bruisin'."

Whenever you develop a strong determination to seek out recruiters and spark their interest, you're ripe for trouble.

You're in just the right frame of mind to be delighted when a contingency recruiter proposes to put a price-tag on your head and rush to potential employers before you do. And you're equally vulnerable to having that same price-tag applied by a retainer recruiter, who's so impressed by you that he's tempted to slip momentarily into the contingency mode.

With enough of the right bad luck, you can even wind up with a double price on your head...tagged for $30,000 + by someone lobbing you in on contingency, with respect to an opening that a retainer firm is already being paid over $30,000 to fill.

> ## The first step in handling an executive recruiter is to figure out which type you're dealing with ...contingency or retainer.

You certainly can't tell from the name on the door, since these days both contingency and retainer recruiters call themselves by exactly the same names..."executive recruiters," "management consultants," "executive search consultants," etc. And you can't tell from the office decor, since both have posh layouts.

Moreover, both types fill $100,000 + positions, although they're far more frequently handled by retainer firms than by contingency firms. Both may have the utmost polish...*and impeccable integrity*. And to make things even more confusing, both types may switch opportunistically to the opposite payment method.

A warm welcome is a hot clue.

It's only natural, when you're presenting yourself to a recruiter, to want a favorable reaction.

Ironically, it's a contingency recruiter inclined toward the broadest possible distribution of unasked-for resumes, who will be most eager to grant you a courtesy interview. After all, his business is attaching price-tags to people and scattering their resumes to the four winds. He *wants* people coming in.

So if your appointment is easy to get, and the visit itself rushes along very favorably, warning bells should go off in your head. You may be "working with" a recruiter who feels you're "highly marketable"...a lottery ticket to be played with a few dollars worth of postage.

Beware of the recruiter who tells you what you want to hear.

Imagine someone arriving for a courtesy interview. After the opening pleasantries, he hands the recruiter his resume. As the recruiter scans it quickly, the executive speaks to reinforce the major points, telling about present responsibilities and outstanding accomplishments. The recruiter looks thoughtful...smiles...and renders a verdict:

> "Well, this is a very impressive resume! And you've also impressed me on a personal basis, Bob, as we've been sitting here talking. I'm really glad you came in. You seem like just the kind of executive who'd do well in several companies I'm thinking of that I could present you to."
>
> "Just leave a copy of your resume with me. I'm going to see what I can do to get you some interviews."
>
> *(He stands up and shakes your hand.)*
>
> "I think I can help you."

An executive who didn't know as much as you already do about recruiters might make a serious error in interpreting what we just saw. He might meet his wife for lunch and say:

> "Just had a great meeting! I saw an executive recruiter who was really impressed, and he said he'd be working to help me."
>
> *(Time out for a discreet hug to express the good mood.)*
>
> "Let's put some champagne in the fridge; I've got a hunch it won't be long now before we're celebrating!"

This guy's interview was certainly no cause for rejoicing. Quite the contrary. *The recruiter just gave his guest fair warning that he intends to begin racing him to the employers most likely to want to hire him.*

It was obvious from a scan of the executive's resume and the fine personal impression he made that he was highly employable, if unemployed...or obviously ready to move up, if currently employed. So the recruiter is about to offer the executive...with price-tag attached, of course...to all the appropriate employers he can think of.

When a recruiter circulates a resume to various likely employers it's called *"floating"* the resume. I consider it absolutely reprehensible for *any* recruiter, whether contingency or retainer, to refer the name and background of any individual to any employer without the prior knowledge and consent of the individual.

And *every* recruiter will invariably tell you he would never do such a thing. In fact, however, it seems to happen fairly often...and it may be done by both contingency and retainer people. *"Floating resumes"* is a little like child abuse. Everyone is revolted by the idea. But there wouldn't be a term for it if it didn't happen.

What To Tell the Eager Recruiter

Whenever you hear a recruiter say he thinks he can "help," the best thing to do is grab your resume and head for the door. Tell him you don't want to be submitted, unless he contacts you ahead of time and gets your approval to offer you to that particular employer for that particular opening.

Indeed, it wouldn't hurt to write him a letter to the same effect. As we discussed in Chapter 6, you absolutely do not want a recruiter preempting contacts you'd be better off making on your own.

The Old "Tell Him, but Don't Let Him Know You Told Him" Technique

The conversation we've just imagined is, after all, a pretty blatant announcement of the recruiter's intention to "float" his visitor's resume. Some approaches are much more subtle. For example, some recruiters actually *obtain your permission* to send your resume to literally scores of prospective employers. The discussion goes something like this:

RECRUITER: "Well, Ted, you look like an outstanding consumer products marketing executive. I think you're ready to become overall vice president of marketing for a diversified consumer products company...or maybe it's about time for you to move up to the presidency of your own division of a very large consumer products conglomerate.''

YOU: "That all sounds good to me."

RECRUITER: "I'd like to test out some of the types of companies you'd be interested in working for. Now I could see you fitting in beautifully at Bristol-Myers, or Colgate. Or maybe American Home Products or General Foods, or Nabisco Brands, or Carnation out on the Coast."

YOU (assuming that the conversation is purely speculative): "Well, yes, I think I could fit in at any of those places...and I wouldn't mind moving to California."

RECRUITER: "Or I could see you being successful and enjoying yourself in one of the big cosmetics companies, like Revlon or Estee Lauder."

YOU: "I guess that's a possibility, too."

RECRUITER: "Or you might go all the way to the fashion field with a Kayser Roth or a Burlington Industries."

YOU: "Well, I hadn't really thought about it, but I guess if the right thing came up..."

RECRUITER: "Or I could even see you in one of the more advanced and forward-looking industrial companies...they're sometimes interested in grabbing a consumer marketing generalist with an outstanding track record. I'll see if I can come up with any companies like that. And have you ever considered getting into the marketing of financial services, or information products, or..."

The recruiter talks on and on, outlining what seem like nothing more than attractive options for the future development of your career. You think he's merely mentioning some of the types of companies for which he might consider you, if and when they come to him with an appropriate opening to fill.

But he's deliberately taking your nods and smiles as permission to send your resume to all of the companies and industries he's mentioned. If he does a good job of canvassing your interests and mentioning potential employers, you may find that he's outrun you to almost all of the companies you're likely to end up working for.

As times goes on, you may find out by accident that your resume has been submitted to the companies that the contingency recruiter mentioned to you during your courtesy interview. Perhaps you'll see Mr. Decisionmaker at another of your daughter's swim meets. Remember him from Chapter 6? This time he mentions that he happened to notice that your resume is in his company's personnel department's files, submitted by Quick Associates.

You call Ralph Quick to protest. His response:

> "Don't you remember when we met in my office? We talked about a number of companies you'd be interested in. So I submitted you to all those companies. As a matter of fact, I kept notes on our visit and jotted down that long *list* of companies we discussed; it's here in your file. I've put in a lot of effort to help you."

What to say when, during a courtesy interview, you run into a recruiter who's preparing to race you to all the employers he mentions, is this:

> "You've talked about a lot of companies. I hope you don't intend to send those companies my resume, when you don't have a specific assignment from them. I've already made contacts myself with a number of companies, including many of the ones you've just mentioned. And I'm going to be contacting others."

> "Therefore, I'm not authorizing you, or anyone else, to submit me to *any* company without letting me know first what company you've been engaged to represent, and what job that company has asked you to fill. You *must* check with me first...before you submit my name anywhere. You must get my 'go-ahead' for that particular job at that particular company."

Getting in to see an overly-aggressive recruiter is as easy as slipping on a banana peel.

Getting your foot in the door at the best retainer firms can be difficult. Some clout will help.

Getting into a prominent retainer recruiting firm usually isn't easy. After all, every retainer recruiter needs you only if he personally happens to have a search at the moment that calls for someone with exactly your qualifications.

In a recent issue of *Texas Business,* the chief of the Houston office of one of America's largest retainer firms came out with the most forthright statement I've ever seen in print on this subject.

> "People are always trying to break through to us, but our secretaries are very well trained. The only time an unsolicited call or a resume will make it through is if a recruiter is searching for someone with that background."

Nonetheless, most retainer firms will, if you persist, arrange for you to receive a courtesy interview...often with one of the most junior members of the firm, who's forced to handle PR duties that the more senior and busier recruiters try to avoid.

If you're a very high-level executive, then just your resume in the mail and a followup phone call will probably get you a courtesy interview. One reason is that you may be someone the firm can use to fill one of its current or future assignments. But a far more likely reason is that the firm wants to get acquainted with you now, so they'll be in a better position to solicit your recruiting business later, when you're building your own team in a new job. And that solicitation will occur, regardless of whether they're involved in your transition.

Even if you're not at quite such a high level, but have a fine track record, well communicated by an impressive resume, you can probably wangle an interview. But if you're just one among many high-potential middle-managers-on-the-way-up, then the *clout of a referral* is essential. And it's always helpful, regardless of how prominent you are.

But whose name should you drop? Whose referral will give you the most clout? I'm continually amazed at how naive many executives are in picking names they think will blast open a reluctant recruiter's door. Here are the people who might refer you...ranked from most to least clout:

> *1. Ideally, someone who spends lots of money with the firm you're trying to meet...*the Chief Executive, or the head of Human Resources, or another senior officer of an important

client. The recruiter will always shake a hand that has shook a hand that feeds.

*2. Next-best is someone able to provide future recruiting business...*the Chief Executive, or the head of Human Resources of a non-client company. And that's especially true if there's already been a hint that business could be forthcoming.

*3. People who've helped the recruiter in other important ways...*someone the recruiter *placed in a job,* even though that person hasn't yet spent money with the recruiter. Or a *very-well-thought-of candidate* on a past search. *Or a valuable "source,"* who's provided much-needed information. Having befriended and profited from these people, it's hard for the recruiter to deny them the favor of seeing you.

4. The least clout...even negative clout...comes from the mention of a competitive executive recruiter, proudly referred to as someone you know well and have done lots of business with. It seems bizarre to me that many executives think that invoking a competitive recruiter's name will force a courtesy interview. Why should it?

Every recruiter wants to think of every candidate as a potential future *client,* not just a possible solution to today's search. If you stress your well-established relationship with another recruiting firm, not only will you *not* obligate the unfamiliar recruiter to give you a get-acquainted interview, you'll make him leery of ever proposing you at all. Why should he jeopardize a solid client relationship by bringing in someone who's known to favor another recruiter?

The Limited Goal of a Courtesy Interview: "To Be Continued"

Of course, you *hope* to just walk in and find the retainer recruiter hard at work on a search that represents an exciting next step in your career.

Or if he isn't, you hope he'll take you right down the hall to meet another recruiter who is.

Don't you wish!

What you're hoping to gain from an interview that *you* ask for sounds far too much like what you'd be lucky to get, even if you were already well known, thoroughly checked out, and eminently respected by the recruiter you're meeting...not just an attractive "walk-in" making your own unsubstantiated assertions of background and achievement.

Moreover, the recruiter handling your courtesy interview has no authority to declare you a candidate on any search except the few he's personally handling at the moment you're in his office...probably no more than eight to ten. So even if you have him totally convinced, and even if he's with a large firm handling upwards of 1,000 searches per year, the statistical odds are infinitesimally small that what you're selling is what *he's* buying on the day you walk in.

So keep your goal realistic. Expect only to demonstrate these three points:

1. *Valuable experience*...potentially appropriate for some client someday, but probably *not* for a current search of the person across the desk from you today;

2. *Excellent track record*...consistent and impressive achievement; and

3. The *personal characteristics* that tend to indicate...but don't guarantee...a fine executive.

Once you've successfully registered these points, a warm *to-be-continued, but-later-and-probably-by-someone-else"* assumption will suffuse the conversation.

That's it. That's all for today. Take "yes" for an answer! And, like any other good salesman, leave before your "sold" customer begins to have renewed doubts.

> **Prove you're an effective business communicator, and your courtesy interview is a success.**
>
> **Prove you're *not*, and you're finished at the firm.**

The courtesy interview will be short and superficial enough that you can easily get through it without revealing that you don't do your job very well. Challenging discussion on that subject won't come until you're brought back as a potential candidate on a search.

But the get-acquainted interview *will* reveal whether or not you're potentially *an attractive candidate*. To prove you are, you'll have to demonstrate one attribute that's important for success on the job, and even more important for success as a candidate:

You must be an effective business communicator.

Prove that you have the common sense to figure out what's important for you to cover, and the poise and confidence to put it across in a limited time.

If you don't show these abilities in your courtesy interview, the recruiter will assume you won't in a client interview...or on the job. And he'll mark you as an unlikely candidate for future searches by his firm.

> **Do unto the retainer recruiter as he'd like to be done unto:**
>
> **Thoughtfulness and efficiency will win him over.**

When you arrive for a courtesy interview with a retainer recruiter, you're getting...free...his most precious resource, the only inventory he has to sell: *his time.*

Format your visit so you don't waste it:

    1. *Express appreciation* for seeing you.

2. *Exchange pleasantries.* Maybe admire something in his office. Probably mention the contact who brought you together. Whatever. A few unhurried but brief pleasantries will make sure that you don't just barge in and take over.

3. But then, *get right down to business.* You'll get plus-points, not demerits, for being organized and efficient. You've asked for this meeting. So it's okay for you to subtly assume some early initiative. Chances are the recruiter aches to say, "Let's get this over with, so I can get back to my search work." By moving along, you give him what he wants, without forcing him to be impolite enough to ask for it.

"How much time do we have?"

As attention turns toward your "sales pitch," try to get a sense of timing:

> "How long do we have? I realize you can't afford to give me the same amount of time you would if this were an interview on one of your searches. So I'll fit my background into the time you have for it."

It won't seem pushy to ask for time parameters, if you do it out of sensitivity to the recruiter's needs. And it'll certainly help you pace yourself. Not overstaying will dazzle and delight the recruiter, because hardly anyone else is ever so considerate and efficient.

The average recruiter spends about one-hour to an-hour-and-a-half interviewing a candidate he's referring on a search. Therefore, you can't expect to get more than one-third as much time...about *thirty minutes maximum.* And, if you can get in and out in 15 or 20 minutes, the recruiter will breathe a sigh of relief, admiration, and gratitude...thinking to himself:

> "Wow! That guy was really on the ball. He knew what he came for, and he got his message across. He was very efficient, yet thoroughly pleasant, attractive, and likable. What an effective executive he must be!"

Bring your resume...and hand it over.

Good business communication is two-fold: written and oral. And the written is indispensable to an effective courtesy interview with a retainer recruiter.

You'd never attempt an important presentation at your company without visual aids, and a persuasive document. If you were presenting a budget review, or requesting money for an acquisition, or proposing a new product introduction, you'd use charts or slides, and a good "leave-behind"...the tools that help a business audience "track" your message, and refer to it later.

Similarly, at the courtesy interview, you must have your resume. You asked for this meeting. So you're obviously selling. This is no time to play coy and say, "Oh, I don't have a resume." Or "It's not in finished form yet." *Of course* you have a resume. And it wasn't difficult...or vastly time-consuming...for you to prepare it. After all, you *are* a highly competent and well-organized person.

Believe it or not, quite a few executives deliberately employ the irksome tactic of showing up for a courtesy interview without a resume... perhaps because there are several how-to-get-a-job books that recommend it. Don't fall for that advice. The premise is that you'll appear "less eager" by not having a resume. Or that you'll get a second shot of the recruiter's time and attention when your resume and follow-up letter arrive in the mail.

Face it. Your eagerness was out of the bag when you asked for the courtesy interview. And the recruiter's lasting impression will be formed while meeting you face-to-face. It won't be something he reads later. Indeed, he may not bother to read anything you send later. Don't be tempted to play the "withhold your resume" game. It's obvious and obnoxious to every experienced recruiter.

Bring in a polished resume and leave it behind. Then immediately after meeting you, the recruiter can conveniently set up a file that states your experience and track record...to which he'll add his fresh-in-mind favorable comments about what an effective communicator you are.

The recruiter's comments will be far less favorable if you have to "wing" your presentation without a visual aid, and if afterward you tell him to wait for the mailman to deliver a clear impression of you.

Four Loathesome Lines...and One Bad Attitude: Retainer-Recruiter "Pet Peeves" About Courtesy Interviews

Retainer recruiters consider courtesy interviews a "necessary evil"... whereas contingency recruiters run newspaper ads to encourage them.

So you're "swimming upstream" to even get a courtesy interview with a retainer recruiter. He's busy looking for people who fit several narrowly-specific searches and...no matter how polite and cordial he may be...he's more likely to think of you as an interruption, than an opportunity. Therefore, you'll want to avoid several amazingly prevalent mistakes that executives make in seeking and handling courtesy interviews:

> *1. "Let me buy you lunch."* Here's the #1 loathesome line, that makes every retainer recruiter cringe. Lunch is too much time, when you're not part of a current search. With only five lunch dates per week, the recruiter can't allocate them to people who...for now at least...aren't the ones he's looking for.
>
> The only situation where you probably *will* have lunch with a retainer recruiter is when you're suggested by somebody who spends lots of money with him. Then *he'll* take *you,* as a display of respect for the person who referred you. Bear in mind, too, that lunch isn't an ideal setting. You may be overheard. Also, it's hard to read and handle papers. They're forbidden at most private clubs, and awkward anywhere, until you're down to the last few minutes over coffee.
>
> *"Let me buy you lunch"* also has an insulting twang. Is the retainer recruiter so hard up socially and financially that he can be manipulated with a free lunch? Indirectly, of course,

the offer also says that the person making it is petty and cheap...vigilantly conscious of who pays at the lunch table.

A truly seductive offer, on the other hand, could be made by changing just one word in the hated "Let me buy you lunch." The retainer recruiter would be thrilled if you could truthfully offer: "Let me buy you *time.*" And of course you can, by being considerately well-organized and brief when...at your request...you visit him.

2. *"What do you think of my resume?"* This question wouldn't be so bad if it were asked right up front to indicate that the executive wants to use the session for free counseling, instead of pushing himself as a potential candidate. But it usually comes after having answered all the recruiter's questions, and used up all the interviewing time. Then it demolishes the visitor's image as a secure, decisive executive. It's a loser's question...a departing plea for further attention, from someone obviously frustrated and frightened because he isn't getting much response to his job-changing efforts.

Polish your resume to your satisfaction. Ask help from anyone who's knowledgeable. *But don't spoil your courtesy interview!* Winding up with a question about your resume is like winding up a chart presentation to your CEO with: "What do you think of my *charts?*"

3. *Don't ask for career counseling.* Just as bad...and usually delivered at the same wrong time...is a request for career advice. Don't say, "With my background, what do you think I ought to be doing next?" Or, "What level do you think I'm ready for?" Surely, if you know anything, you know that. If you need counseling and psychological testing to figure out what kind of job you're suited for, get it *before* you reach the retainer recruiter. Don't ask for it at the end of a courtesy interview when your time is up.

4. *"How's the job market?"* This question should *never* be asked. The market is always elusive to almost every executive at the moment he wants to change. But ultimately it turns

out to be excellent for the outstanding executive. The other types, of course, have difficulty regardless of the economy. So here's another downer that implies you're a fearful, frustrated loser.

5. Don't demonstrate a "God's gift" attitude. Don't be the person who comes in rather pompously, feeling that the retainer recruiter obviously needs grist for his mill, and ought to grovel in gratitude for grist like him. If you take this attitude, you're dead. The underlying assumption, of course, isn't true. There's a *glut* of grist. And plenty of the finest executives have a pleasant, straightforward, cooperative attitude. You'd better, too, or you'll be cancelled out.

Don't be misled by what's said at the end of a courtesy interview: the "pseudo review" of searches in progress.

At the end of your courtesy interview with a retainer recruiter, he'll probably look at a book or a computer screen to check a list of current assignments...information visible from where he's sitting, but *not* from where you are.

If the firm is a large one, it may handle well over 1,000 searches per year. You know darn well that there probably are several...perhaps dozens...that would represent excellent next steps in your career.

Since reading this book you also know, of course, that you'll never hear about more than one at a time. But now that you've been through an exploratory interview, you surely expect to hear about *at least one* that looks like a potential fit.

In fact, however, unless you come very highly recommended, have made an incredibly fine impression, and your interviewer is personally looking for someone exactly like you, that's not what will happen.

Instead, referring to his notebook or terminal, the retainer recruiter will give you a *pseudo-review of current assignments.* He'll summarize several of the firm's searches, in a performance that will seem confusingly like the ''ideal relationship'' review I showed you at the end of the last chapter. But it will be different in three important ways:

*1. There will be something unacceptable to you about every job that's mentioned...*industry, function, compensation, title and reporting relationship, size of business, or calibre of company, etc. And each ''fatal flaw'' will be one that would be obvious to anyone knowing what you just told the recruiter.

*2. The identity of the company will not be revealed...*unless the position has already been filled. ''Too bad you weren't here a few weeks ago when we recruited the...''

3. You won't walk away knowing for sure that you'll be a candidate on the job you like best among all those the firm is actually working on.

Suppose you sense that, in his interview-ending review of current assignments, the retainer recruiter is deliberately overlooking the searches on his list that would be highly attractive to you. Or, if he *does* read off pertinent searches, you suspect he's adlibbing into the description of each job a factor that he knows will make it unacceptable to you.

You're probably right!

But don't feel bad. You just received the standard *''pseudo-review of current searches,''* which most retainer recruiters almost always use to close a courtesy interview.

Why do they do this?

Because turning to a reference, and appearing to check what the firm has underway in your field and at your level implies that:

1. you passed the recruiter's screening, and

2. you'll be called when the firm receives more-appropriate assignments.

The recruiter doesn't have to declare you a non-candidate; *you do that yourself.* Meanwhile, you're quickly on the way out of his office... happy in the knowledge that there are obviously no prejudices against you and no failure to understand and admire your qualifications.

Chances are the retainer recruiter will close your courtesy interview like this:

> "Well, it's always an accident of timing, whether we have anything that fits or not. I'm sorry these jobs today are either in the wrong place or too low paying. Of course, there's that one job that *would* interest you. Unfortunately, I'm not handling that one, and I think I heard that it was filled last week. But I'll check, and if there's still a chance on it, I'll call you. Meanwhile, I'll put your information into our system and we'll wait to see what new assignments we get. Thanks for coming in. We'll keep in touch."

That's what he *says.* Here's a smorgasbord of possible meanings; take your pick:

> "You look right for a search one of our other recruiters is handling. But he may already have all the candidates he wants for now. I'll tell him about you. But I'll save him the bother of dealing with you if he doesn't want to, by not telling *you* about him."

> OR

> "There's a search here that looks perfect for you. I'll pass your material along to the recruiter handling it. He can check out your story with someone else he may know in your company before deciding whether or not to talk to you."

> OR

> "I see that my colleague down the hall is doing a search you'd be perfect for, and it's exactly what you want. But *I'm* likely to get a similar search within the next month or two. I may as well save you for myself."

OR

"Too bad you're such a vague communicator, and so unattractive to boot. You'll *never* be a candidate on one of our searches."

OR

"Mister, I *had* to be nice to you, because you were referred by a client who spent $250,000 with this firm last year. But I don't buy your act. No way."

Don't place a lot of significance on it...one way or the other...if you get the usual "pseudo-review" of current assignments at the conclusion of your courtesy interview with a retainer recruiter. How favorably and how soon you'll hear from his firm...if at all...may have very little to do with what was said as you walked out.

How To Handle the Recruiter Who Calls You

You're happily employed...doing an outstanding job for a fine company that recognizes and appreciates your contribution, pays you well, and has you on its fast track toward bigger and better things. You're not dissatisfied. You're not thinking about leaving.

Then the phone rings.

Your caller says he's an executive recruiter filling a major position in your industry at a level you realize you'd have to wait at least two, and maybe five to seven, years...or longer...to achieve in your present company. Are you interested?

Perhaps you should be.

But only if the opportunity stands up to some important questions you can raise over the phone, and only if the recruiter himself passes your savvy scrutiny.

Your caller *may* be working on a retainer basis...or on a legitimate contingency listing...to fill a job that could advance your career. On the other hand, he may be "trolling" for resumes by describing an extremely attractive but nonexistent opening...or an actual and widely-publicized opening which he has *not* been requested to fill.

He may be calling because he's heard great things about you through one of his dependable contacts who knows you. But it's equally possible that he's calling you "cold," just because you're at the right level in a company he's "targeted" to explore, in which case he has no idea whether you're terrific...or just two weeks away from being fired for gross incompetence.

He may even be soliciting you and your company as a possible executive search client under the guise of approaching you personally with some non-existent "opportunity."

> **How you react to a recruiter's call depends entirely on his relationship with the employer.**
>
> **There are only three possibilities:**
> 1. a retainer search assignment,
> 2. a valid contingency listing,
> 3. no relationship at all.
>
> **Figure out what he's up to, and you'll know how to handle him.**

By now you know where your self-interest lies with respect to all three relationships a recruiter may have with an employer.

And, despite a dizzying dose of doubletalk that may be administered when you try to figure out what the relationship is, there are only three possibilities. Let's review them, and then let's take some phone calls.

1. A Retainer Search

This is the ideal relationship from your point of view. You're too late to reach the employer ahead of the recruiter, and maybe get the job without competition from recruiter-supplied candidates. Now a recruiter is being paid $30,000+ to look. Therefore, you're best off as one of his "finds."

If the caller is on a true retainer assignment, you'll want to cooperate.

2. A Valid Contingency Listing

This is a good, but somewhat less-desirable, relationship, as far as you're concerned.

If the caller has a contingency listing directly from the employer on the job he's describing to you, then you may wish to cooperate. Generally speaking, however, you're not obligated to do so.

There is only one narrow set of circumstances in which you're morally obligated to go ahead with a contingency recruiter...or forego the opportunity. We'll cover this subject later.

3. No Relationship at All

This is a lousy situation from your point of view. The recruiter couldn't get either type of relationship with the employer...retainer or contingency...so now he wants to tie *you* up!

If the caller...whether normally a retainer or a contingency recruiter...has no direct arrangement with the employer on the job he's calling you about, you do not want to cooperate.

So much for the ground rules. Now "Let's go to the phones," as they say on TV.   First, an easy one.

YOUR CALLER: "Hello, I'm Joan Chase from the executive recruiting firm of Randall Radley Associates, and I'm calling because I have a situation that might be of interest to you or perhaps to someone you might wish to recommend."

YOU: "Oh, I know your organization. It's one of the fine retainer firms. I've met a man named Stevens in your company; do you work with him?"

CALLER: "No, Bill's in our Atlanta office, and I'm calling you from Cleveland. But of course we know each other."

Enough already!

You know the firm and its fine reputation as a retainer recruiting organization. This woman is obviously with them, because she knew Stevens and volunteered his correct location. So let her go on, and listen open-mindedly. She appears to be entirely on the up-and-up, and doing exactly what she says she's doing.

"But," you say, "couldn't she be who she is and still be calling about a job on which she hasn't been in touch with the client, intending to 'float' my resume?"

Not likely. She seems to be a rank-and-file recruiter in a well-known retainer firm, just grinding out one of their regular assignments in the regular way. Remember that retainer-only firms hardly ever jeopardize their "pay-me-to-look" status by offering resumes they haven't been paid to find. Let's put your conversation with Ms. Chase "on hold" for a while, so you can answer a more challenging call.

This time we'll listen as you smoke out the intentions of someone who really *is* planning to "float" your resume. Ironically, this caller is someone you've known and been friends with for years...a contingency recruiter specializing in your industry, who helped you find one of your early jobs, and whom you've used occasionally to recruit subordinates during your rise to $100,000 + .

CARL CONTINGENCY: "I suppose you saw in the trade papers that Ken Williams left Universal to become President of Amalgamated. That means they'll be needing a new President over at Universal, and I don't think there's anyone inside who's up to the job. As you know, Blake Stevens, their new VP - Marketing, was just promoted to that level from head of the field sales force a few months ago. He's certainly not ready for the presidency. And they surely won't give it to some Finance or Manufacturing guy in such a marketing-driven company. What do you say, Bill? Would you like me to put you in the running for the Presidency over there?''

What an easy example!

You're immediately skeptical. You're surprised that Carl would be seeking a President. As far as you know, his mostly-contingency practice...while widely and justifiably respected...hasn't been filling positions at quite that high level.

Moreover, Carl is being perfectly straightforward. He isn't saying he's been *requested* to seek candidates for the Presidency of Universal. Indeed, he makes it clear that he's merely reacting to what he's read in the trade papers and drawing his own conclusion. No search has been assigned. Or if one has been, it's obvious that Carl doesn't have it. He hasn't been briefed by the CEO of Universal. If he had been, he'd have told you so.

Since Carl is referring to an opening publicized in the trade papers, it's a situation that everyone in your industry knows about. Indeed, you've probably already been thinking about writing or calling the Chairman of Universal. You know him slightly, because you were on a panel he chaired at your industry's trade convention two years ago.

Have you missed your chance to go ahead on your own, just because Carl's phone call reached you before you made your move?

Absolutely not.

Let's see you take it from here:

> YOU: ''Thanks for the call, Carl. In fact, I've been thinking along those same lines. I've intended to call up Crandall Reese, the Chairman over there, or send him a letter and a resume...I haven't decided which. I was on a panel he ran at the trade convention in

Las Vegas a couple years ago. *Now, Carl, I gather that Mr. Reese hasn't put you on retainer to find him a President, has he?''*

CARL: "Well, no he hasn't talked to me specifically about this situation. But I've filled quite a few jobs over there during the past several years. I'm perfectly sure I can present you."

YOU: "Thanks for offering, Carl, but I'd rather not. I'd prefer to be in touch with him on my own. I'd rather handle it myself."

Simple as that! You figured out that Carl has no mandate. So you turned down his offer to interpose himself between you and the employer. He offered. You politely refused. The only explanation you needed to give was:

> "I'd rather handle it myself."

Now, you're just as free to get in touch with the Chairman directly as you were before Carl called. If Mr. Reese hasn't yet engaged a recruiter, he may decide to meet you and perhaps one or two other obvious prospects. Indeed, he may make his choice without ever feeling the need to hire a retainer recruiter, or to put out contingency listings. On the other hand, perhaps he already *has* hired a retainer recruiter. If so, you're still free to be part of that person's project, without the handicap of an extra price-tag applied by your friend Carl.

However, don't become overconfident. Carl wasn't really trying very hard. He helped me help you, by delivering a classic pitch designed to demonstrate the basics.

Now let's take a much more challenging call. This one's from a prominent *retainer* recruiter whom you know and trust. You'll have to be more alert and probing, because Randy's not going to send you the obvious signals Carl and I contrived for you in the previous example. Randy's going to give you the full treatment:

RANDY RETAINER: "I'm not sure if you're aware of it, but I've done several recruiting projects over the years for Pete Pinnacle, the Chairman over at Acme Consolidated. He's got an opening at the top of his Industrial Products Division, what with Jason Evans leaving to become Chief Executive of Trombley Consolidated.

You'd be absolutely perfect for that spot, now that you've got a few years' experience under your belt as number-two in an operation that's almost their size and, if anything, is doing even better than they are. What do you say? Would you like to be a candidate on it?''

YOU: "Maybe, Randy. I've been thinking it's time for me to take over my own show, and I've been wondering what they'll do to fill Jason's job. I thought maybe they might promote somebody from one of their own divisions. If they stay inside the Industrial Division, I'm afraid I have to agree with you...nobody there would be as good for the top job as I would be. Matter of fact, I was thinking of maybe dropping the Chairman a hint that I might be interested...possibly through one of his outside Directors I know pretty well, or through another friend of mine, who's one of their biggest distributors.''

"Tell me, Randy, has the Chairman definitely made up his mind to go outside to fill that job, and has he put *you* on retainer to do the search?''

RANDY: "Oh yes; he's got to go outside. It doesn't make any sense at all to take somebody like Charlie Adams...who's doing a great job, by the way...out of their Maritime Division and put him into Industrial Products. And the same goes for Clem Smith, who's Executive Vice President of their Defense Systems Division. He's a great guy and certainly ready to run his own operation. But it ought to be something closer to his field. He's never sold to any customer but the Pentagon. Really they don't have anybody over there who'd be as appropriate as you would, to take charge of Industrial Products.''

"Why do you think I called you? Not just because we haven't talked for awhile. Today we're doing business. I want you to be a candidate. In fact, I think you'll be the strongest of all the candidates I'll be presenting. What do you say?''

YOU: "As I said before, I might be interested. But I didn't quite get your answer to the other part of my question. Have you personally got a retainer search assignment to fill this position? Because, if you do, then I'd like you to tell me a lot more about what the Chairman has told you he's looking for. Has he put you on retainer to solve this thing?''

RANDY: "Well, not exactly. Not quite yet. But I'm sure that if I let him see someone as ideally appropriate for his Industrial Division presidency as you are, that'll make it obvious to him that he *shouldn't* stay inside. What do you say? Would you like to go for it?"

This time you had to work a lot harder. And you were up against a tough adversary...a well-known retainer recruiter, whom you certainly wouldn't have suspected of "floating resumes." Randy knew plenty of detailed information. Moreover, you were well aware that he had previously done high level recruiting within that company.

But even this retainer recruiter you've known and trusted for years failed to pass your savvy scrutiny, now that you're challenging *every* headhunter who calls you, to find out whether he has a client assignment and what the exact nature of that arrangement is.

Now you're faced with a choice.

Randy has previously worked for the Chairman on retainer. Maybe he'll be asked to do so in this instance, too. If so, he may not be enthusiastic about your candidacy...on this or any future job...if you're uncooperative now. On the other hand, the Chairman doesn't *always* use a recruiter when he hires a high-profile person from outside. And even if he does assign a retainer search, he may not choose Randy this time.

Indeed, if Randy were confident of getting a retainer search to fill this opening, he'd have waited to get his mandate before contacting you or anyone else. Maybe he suspects the Chairman will promote from within...or "go it alone"...or choose another recruiter. Maybe the Chairman already *has* chosen another recruiter.

(Time out while you decide what to do.)

Congratulations!

You've decided to remain your own person. I thought you would. You didn't get where you are now by allowing people to manipulate you.

Now let's see how gracefully and inoffensively...yet firmly...you handle this situation:

> YOU: "Thanks for offering, Randy. But I'd rather not have you bring me up with the Chairman until you've got a firm search assignment from him. Why don't you take the next few days to get in touch with him and see if he wants you to take charge of finding someone on the outside for the presidency of that division." (You know this won't be easy for Randy...if it were, he'd have done so before calling you; but he can't say that.)
>
> "Please don't tell him that I might be a candidate. I want to keep my options open. If the Chairman *does* assign a search, there's nobody I'd rather see get that project than you. But if you don't, I want to still be in a position to go after him through informal connections, or to be contacted by the recruiter he does select, or maybe just to drop the whole thing. I'm going to be away on Wednesday and Thursday. Why don't you call me on Friday and let me know how you made out? I won't do anything until I hear from you."

See...it wasn't all that difficult. You caught Randy proceeding when he didn't have the proper basis to do so. But you didn't make a fuss. You didn't back him into a corner. And you also didn't allow him to corner you, which was the purpose of his call.

Congratulations again. You matched wits with a master...and you came out ahead.

Always qualify the recruiter.

Even if you know him well, you still don't know his connection with the employer.

By now it's easy to see the central truth that you should always keep in mind when answering every headhunter's call: You don't know for sure whether your caller has a definite arrangement with an employer, and you don't know what the exact nature of that arrangement is. Since both points are important, you'd better clear them up before agreeing to anything the recruiter proposes.

And you're *able* to find out…as you've just proved. You caught a prominent retainer recruiter, whom you personally know and respect. He was about to put a price-tag on your head in one of his exceedingly rare departures from his professed way of doing business. Firmly, but gracefully, you stopped him. If you can do that, surely you can figure out what just about everyone else who calls you is up to…and *react strictly according to your own self-interest.*

But before we leave Randy Retainer, let's speculate on his motives. He may have a strong relationship with Pete Pinnacle, the Chairman of Acme Consolidated. Maybe Randy's altruistically concerned that the Chairman will make a less-than-optimum appointment from the inside, if not confronted with unasked-for resumes from outstanding outsiders. It's far more likely, however, that Randy has a weakening, marginal, or defunct connection with Mr. Pinnacle, and suspects or knows that another retainer recruiter will be the one officially looking for the next President of Acme's Industrial Division.

No retainer recruiter will ever attempt to submit you on contingency if he can readily get himself hired on retainer to look for you. And the likeliest reason *he* can't get hired is that somebody else already has been. If so, you'd better be the other recruiter's "find"…or the employer's. Otherwise, you probably won't be hired.

**Ironically, when you're a high-level executive,
your resume is much more likely to be "floated"
by a recruiter you know well, than by a stranger.**

It's no accident that the two people you've caught intending to forward your resume without a proper employer-mandate have both been people who know you well…not strangers. If you're a senior executive, that will usually be so.

And *when a true retainer recruiter is involved,* that will *virtually always* be so. The reason, once again, harks back to his normal fee arrangement…to get paid *for the act of looking,* regardless of whether anyone is hired. Therefore he normally never offers resumes without first being paid to find them. If he did, the employer would think, "Why pay him just to look, when he'll submit candidates without being paid, just like a contingency recruiter does?''

Therefore, a true retainer recruiter breaks his operating pattern...if at all...only on very rare occasions when he has no shot at a fee unless he does something drastic. And even then he won't, unless he knows the potential "candidate" on a personal basis well enough to hide behind this excuse:

> "He's *someone I've known very well for a long time,*
>   and he'd be perfect!''

The retainer recruiter can never admit he *actually looked for new people* that he's sending over on a contingency basis, because to do so would destroy his claim to be strictly a retainer recruiter.

The *contingency* recruiter, on the other hand, has a different problem. He isn't usually asked to fill extremely high-level positions. Therefore, he lacks credibility when he claims to have a high-level executive tied up, and accessible only through him. He almost *has* to say:

> "This is *someone I know very, very well.''*

**If you're a middle- or lower-level executive, my tip
that the headhunter likeliest to float your resume
is probably someone you know well does not apply.**

The further down you are from President, General Manager, or head of function such as Finance, Manufacturing, Marketing, R&D, etc., the more numerous are the positions in which every organization can use your talents, and the more frequently...perhaps even continuously... the organization has an opening at your level that urgently needs to be filled.

Under such circumstances, suggestions of potential candidates tend to be much more welcome, regardless of source. Contingency listings may be handed out to virtually any headhunter who asks. And resumes may be cheerfully accepted and kept on file, even though the headhunters submitting them haven't bothered to secure a listing in advance.

Indeed, as I pointed out in Chapter 6, when you're seeking a foothold at the bottom- and middle-levels of the corporate pyramid, being pushed by an aggressive contingency recruiter may be very helpful. It may get you noticed, when you wouldn't be otherwise. And the contingent price-tag on your head may not matter much, because it's a low fee at your low salary level; and paying agency fees is pretty much standard practice when lots of openings have to be filled and a busy personnel department doesn't have time to pick over hoards of applicants.

Don't fall for the "you should be represented" comeback.

Whenever you respectfully, but firmly, refuse to be introduced by any headhunter who lacks an employer mandate...or by a contingency recruiter who has one...you'll invariably be socked with the usual high-pressure pitch:

> "Surely you don't want to be *unrepresented!*"

Just say:

> "Yes, thank you, in this particular instance that's
> what I prefer."

Only if you're a glutton for futility will you try to get the recruiter to admit that being your "representative"...your agent...would require that *you* be the one paying him and not the employer, as you and I discussed in Chapter 6.

Unfinished business with caller #1...

Once you established that Joan Chase was from a well-known retainer recruiting firm, you gave her the benefit of the doubt and let her complete her pitch. Chances are...999 out of 1,000...that she's working on a regular retainer assignment. Since she's a rank-and-file member of the firm, and since she didn't previously know you and have a cordial relationship with you...nothing outside the ordinary character of the firm appears to be involved in her routine call to you.

Nonetheless, it won't hurt to ask:

YOU: "Who's your contact on this assignment? Are you working directly with the Chairman?"

CALLER: "Yes, I had a meeting with him and with their Vice President of Personnel last Wednesday."

Stop beating a dead horse. Clearly, she's doing a retainer assignment. You're just as well off to deal with her as with the client himself.

But now let's take another call.

YOUR CALLER: "Hello, this is Mae Findham from Seekim Associates. We're management consultants specializing in the field of executive search, and I'm calling you about a very attractive position that might be of interest to you...or if not to you, to someone you might wish to recommend."

YOU: "I'm sorry, I didn't quite get the name of your firm. Did you say, Seekim Associates? How is that spelled?" (She tells you.) "And you're located here in Chicago? Or where are you calling from?" (She tells you.) "Let me have your phone number, in case we get interrupted, so I'll be able to call you back. I'd like to hear what you have to say, but I may not be able to stay on the phone any longer than just a very few minutes right now. But go ahead."

CALLER: "Well, of course I can't be specific as to the actual identity of the company, because this is a highly confidential assignment, but there's a..."

YOU (Here's your opening; jump on it.): "Oh, why is that? Are they firing the person who has the job now, and he doesn't yet know about it?"

CALLER (slipping away): "Well, you might say it's something like that, although not exactly. All I can tell you for right now is simply that I'm not at liberty to disclose the identity of the client."

YOU (interjecting again): "Well, I certainly don't want to press too hard for the client's name, if you're not in a position to give it. Are you working on retainer? Or is this a contingency assignment?...in which case I can perfectly understand why you aren't comfortable in being specific about the client."

CALLER: "Rather than concern ourselves any further at this point about who the client is and why I can't give you that information, let me just tell you this...it's a client we have served many times over the years, and one I personally know very well. But right now let me tell you a little more about the job so we can see whether it's an attractive one for you to consider, or whether you would prefer to recommend someone else."

You now let the recruiter drone on, and you pursue the full line of questioning we'll look at in the next chapter for screening any "opportunity" that's pitched to you over the phone. However, the tone of this conversation so far has been sufficiently mysterious and evasive to let you know that you may well be dealing with a headhunter who, at best, has a non-exclusive job listing, and indeed may not have any direct commitment from any employer. *You will proceed with caution.*

If Ms. Findham had been a retainer recruiter with an assignment conferred directly by the employer, she would have immediately told you so, explaining that her secrecy was not because of a tentative mandate, but rather because of specific reasons why it would hurt the employer if his search became known.

Does a headhunter's calling you about a job force you...legally or morally...to pursue the job only through him?

Have you lost your right to contact the employer directly?

Usually not.

Of course, if he's a retainer recruiter being paid to look for you, you want to be one of his "finds." You hope he will introduce you. If he refuses, you can ignore his "wet blanket" and go directly to the employer. He'll resent your action, and "blackball" you for all future searches by his firm. But he can't stop you.

With the contingency recruiter, the shoe is on the other foot. He'll seldom say no to you. He *wants* to submit you...with his price-tag attached, of course. But you may prefer to go directly to the employer without his tag. Can you?

Usually you can.

If the contingency recruiter *hasn't* identified the specific employer and job to you, you have no obligation whatever to let him apply his tag and send you onward to an undisclosed recipient. You're just as free after his call as you were before it, to canvass any and all employers you wish and offer your services.

Even if he *did* tell you precisely the employer and the job on which he wants you to be his candidate, and even if he has a valid listing, you're still at liberty to contact the employer directly if some other source of information...apart from his phone call...has also made you aware that the job is open and likely to be filled from the outside.

But be forthright; otherwise the recruiter will think you took advantage of his call and sneaked around behind his back. Just tell him that you're already aware of the opening through other sources, and that you may or may not wish to follow up on your own. The contingency recruiter won't be pleased with your decision, but there's nothing he can do about it. You have every right to refuse his offer to make an introduction that you prefer to make yourself.

Suppose the contingency recruiter just happens to be someone you don't like or respect. You don't want him to know whether you're willing to be a candidate or not, and you don't *ever* want to be submitted to any employer by him. Just say:

> "George, I'm not sure whether I want to be a candidate over there, or that I want to go there through you. Please do not submit me. I think I'll wait a while and read about the situation in the trade papers. Then, if I decide afterward that I want to go ahead on my own, I won't feel I've taken unfair advantage of this phone call from you."

Needless to say, you must *really* dislike the contingency recruiter to take this approach. But it's your prerogative. Any recruiter...contingency or retainer...merely *offers* to introduce you. He doesn't own you.

The only situation in which you're morally obligated ...and possibly legally too...to go ahead with the contingency recruiter, or not at all, is when he:

1. **has a valid listing from the employer and**

2. **has revealed a situation that you wouldn't have known about, or wouldn't have pursued, if he hadn't caused you to do so.**

You know what's fair and what's not. Let your conscience be your guide. When the opening is not public knowledge, and you learn about it only from the recruiter, then you *are* morally obligated...and perhaps legally, too...to pursue the opportunity only through an introduction made by him.

Similarly, if the existence of the job was known to you through other channels, but the recruiter told you about attractive hidden features which caused you to go ahead when you wouldn't have otherwise, then too, fairness demands that you pursue the position only through the recruiter.

When a contingency recruiter has a valid listing, the employer has agreed to pay the recruiter if he hires someone the recruiter places before him. So, if the reason you know enough to contact the employer is because the recruiter has contacted you, then the recruiter has done his job and has earned his fee.

Moreover, in my opinion, that's true even if the recruiter doesn't specifically identify the employer, but drops clues enabling you to *guess* the employer, or presents the job so tantalizingly that you canvass *all* the employers in your industry attempting to hit the job the recruiter has told you about.

It would be highly improper for you to "go around" the contingency recruiter under any of those circumstances, in an attempt to make yourself less expensive for the employer to hire. If you were to do so, any ethical employer would consider your behavior sleazy in the extreme. He should forego hiring you on the basis of low moral character. And if, by chance, the employer were to be sufficiently devious himself to applaud your actions, his own moral character would be such that you'd be better off not working for him. Or, perhaps, you'd deserve each other.

Here's a question a lot of people ask:

"Is there any sure and easy way to tell whether a headhunter who calls is from a contingency or a retainer firm?"

There's no simple "litmus test."

But the calls you've taken throughout this chapter have all helped sensitize you to "contingency vibes" and "retainer vibes."

An aura of secrecy is one of the strongest clues that your caller may be approaching you from the contingency direction. Often a contingency recruiter will be highly vigilant that you not figure out who his employer/client is unless and until you agree to be a candidate...and maybe, even then, not until just before you go to see the employer.

That's because your knowing creates several hazards to his earning a fee: *You* may go directly to the employer. You may start grapevine rumors that send *other candidates* to the employer. And those same rumors may send *competing contingency recruiters* to the employer. Your call from Mae Findham was a classic example of "contingency vibes," telegraphed by a secretive manner.

So, as early as possible in any phone call from a headhunter, you may as well ask the ultimate question:

> "Are you *on retainer* to submit candidates for this job, or are you working *on contingency?*

The recruiter on the other end of the line may be a bit shaken by your highly aware and direct question. If so, his momentary discomfort may be your answer.

On the other hand, if he's glib and experienced, chances are he'll give you a side-stepping answer:

> "Oh, I *regularly* send this client outstanding people."

OR

> "We have a long-term relationship with them, going back to 1980, when we recruited the person who's now General Manager of their Catalog Marketing Division."

OR

> "We have a *standing order* to send them people we feel would be right for the businesses they have."

The variations are endless. But the theme is consistent. *Previous* contact is invoked to suggest a definite arrangement to fill the job the recruiter is phoning about. Unfortunately, in the words of the immortal Gershwin tune: "It Ain't Necessarily So."

If in doubt, call "time out."

Another thing you can do to "qualify" the recruiter on the other end of the line is to interrupt your conversation, offering to call back later. Meanwhile you have time to do a little investigating.

One indication that a U.S. recruiting firm *doesn't* operate on contingency is membership in the Association of Executive Search Consultants (AESC), a professional association founded and supported by retainer firms. You can call them at (203) 661–6606.

Unfortunately, however, the AESC has only about 70 members, out of an estimated 1,000 or more qualified retainer recruiting firms now operating in the U.S. Moreover, in recent years some of the largest and best-known firms have dropped out of the association. Hence, not being in AESC says nothing negative about the firm you're trying to check on. It may be among the hundreds of qualified firms who haven't joined, or among the major ones who've left.

Another expedient technique you can use to determine whether a recruiting firm operates on contingency...or more often contingency *and* retainer. . .is simply to call the firm's switchboard and ask what kind of arrangements it offers an employer interested in using that firm to find an employee. Ask the receptionist or secretary who answers:

> "With your firm, is it necessary to pay even if nobody you supply is hired? I know some firms operate that way. . .'on retainer,' they call it. . .but that's *not* the kind of arrangement I have in mind."

The telephone-answerer may conceivably give you a more straightforward response than you'll get from an executive of the firm, who'll be trying to size you up and will speak much more cautiously. The receptionist may say:

> "Well, I know we *prefer* to work on retainer, but sometimes we also work the way you have in mind. Let me put you through to someone who can tell you more."

Doing Business with the Recruiter...
on the Phone, and in His Office

Okay. When a recruiter calls, your first reaction is to find out exactly who he is and...even if you know him well...the exact nature of his mandate, if any. How appropriately he's tied to the employer and the job may be far more important than how attractive the job is.

From here on, we'll assume that you've examined the recruiter and his client relationship, both of which are fine indeed.

You've accepted him. Now let's do business with him.

Interestingly, whereas your first few minutes of the recruiter's call were somewhat adversarial...you brought up something *not* on his agenda...now that you're getting down to business, your interests and his are almost identical.

Of course, he's still trying to sell you something which you may be wise not to buy. That will be true up to the moment you accept the employer's job and resign your present one. But during this initial phone call, you and the recruiter *both want to know the same things...* although in opposite order of priority:

His Priorities	Your Priorities
1. *Are you qualified?*	1. *Are you interested?*
2. *Are you interested?*	2. *Are you qualified?*

You want to find out whether the *job* is right for you...and whether the recruiter knows enough about it to actually have a proper assignment to fill it. The recruiter, on the other hand, wants to know whether *you're* right for the job. And if not, he doesn't care how interested you are.

Let's do it *your* way.

Let's indulge your priorities. First, are you "interested"? And only secondly, are you "qualified"?

If you've got a job and the recruiter's trying to get you to consider a different one, then *you're the buyer* and *he's the seller*. He'll have to follow your agenda, if you just assert it:

> YOUR CALLER: "I'm in the process of filling an exceptionally attractive position for a management information executive in your industry, and I've heard some very good things about you. But I'm not entirely sure that your background is a 'fit.' Tell me, first of all, are you in charge of systems-development throughout the corporation, in addition to supervising all the data centers?"
>
> YOU: "Yes, I am. But I'm in very good shape here at Outstanding Corporation. Before we go into my background, why don't we

just see if the situation you have is something that I ought to think about. And if it's not for me, I'll try to suggest some other people who'd be more appropriate.''

Right at the outset you've got things rolling in the direction that's best for you. You've conveyed a pleasant, receptive, helpful attitude. But you haven't given up your superior bargaining position. You've politely asserted your obvious advantage.

Already the recruiter is sizing you up. On a subliminal level...and probably on a conscious level, too...he's now alert to the fact that, on this call, he's dealing with a highly aware and competent person. Maybe you're the one he's looking for.

Of course, if you were out of work and the recruiter were calling in response to your letter and resume, your buyer/seller roles would be reversed. You'd be willing to answer all his questions about your background and track record prior to hearing the specifics of the job he's filling. He'd be the buyer.

Ask probing questions about the opportunity.

They will:
1.   further qualify the recruiter;
2.   rule out a no-benefit opportunity;
3.   at the same time, demonstrate you're the calibre of person the recruiter wants.

If there's some reason for you not to deal with the recruiter, or not to be interested in the job, you want to find out right away. Then you don't waste your time or his.

Ask probing questions. Simultaneously you'll find out whether the position is worth considering, and whether the recruiter is well-informed enough to really be on retainer to fill it. Sometimes, *although far less often than most people think,* even a retainer recruiter may not be at liberty to identify the employer. But if he's tied in, he can describe the *job* in detail.

So ask everything that will help you see whether you should spend any time beyond the initial phone call to explore the opportunity:

What are the specific responsibilities?

What's the title?

What position would you report to?

How many subordinates? With what functions?

Is it chief executive, reporting to an outside board? If it's president or general manager of a subsidiary, does it report to the CEO, or to the COO, of the parent? Or is there a group officer in between?

If it's a top marketing job, does the sales force report to it? How large is the sales force? How many product managers? Are manufacturers' reps and distributors used? Which ad agencies? Budget? Media mix?

If it's chief financial officer, does the position have responsibility for administration, management information services, internal auditing, subsidiary controllerships (straight or dotted line), etc.?

If it's a top manufacturing job, does manufacturing engineering report to it? Quality control? Purchasing? Physical distribution? How about off-shore operations and plants? Plants within the subsidiaries?

If it's a top engineering job, does it just include new product engineering? What about quality control and manufacturing engineering?

Don't trust the title to describe the job. Whatever your specialty, ask, ask, ask! And then go further:

What's the boss like? What characteristics does he value most in his employees? What's his preferred working style...lots of documentation or very little paperwork...lots of autonomy or close supervision?

What's the location? Would you have to move?

What about compensation? Will it include an incentive program? Stock options?

What's the structure, momentum, and atmosphere of the company and/or division? Highly centralized, or decentralized? Growing...plateaued...in trouble? What are the short-term, intermediate, and long-range goals of the business? What's its share-of-market, and its reputation for quality and customer satisfaction?

Why is the job open? What specific business problem is supposed to be solved...or opportunity exploited...by going outside to fill this position? What happened to the person who's had it up to now? And the person before?

I could go on and on. And you have every right to do so too. Find out whether it's worthwhile for you and the recruiter to go to the trouble of a face-to-face interview.

Fortunately, the same questions that will convince you to proceed will simultaneously show the recruiter that you're the calibre of person he seeks...an alert, analytical executive, who can quickly ferret out key issues and come to an informed decision.

Indeed, the more your questions show an awareness of the problems and opportunities facing your industry and specific companies in it, the more he'll be sure that you're someone his client wants to meet.

**If the opportunity is wrong for you,
it will probably be for one of three reasons:
1. wrong responsibility,
2. wrong location,
3. wrong money.**

Save your time...and the recruiter's.
Dispose of all three in the initial phone call.

Chances are you can't be certain, just from the recruiter's call, that the job definitely is for you. That will take in-person, in-depth meetings with the client, not just the recruiter. But you can quickly find out why the situation is not for you.

All of the top-three turnoffs can be smoked out in the initial phone call. And they'll eliminate 90% of the "wild goose chases" you might otherwise be subjected to:

1. *Wrong Responsibility.* Question the recruiter. The job had better be considerably more attractive than the one you have now. A same-echelon job in a much larger and finer company can be an excellent reason to move. So can a higher job in a same-level company. But money alone usually isn't enough. And if you're on the brink of a breakthrough where you are, say so. There's no reason to withhold information at the outset which, in the end, will cause you to say "no thanks."

2. *Wrong Location.* If the job isn't commutable from your home, you can certainly decide

   a. whether you're willing to relocate at all, and
   b. if so, whether the proposed location is acceptable.

If either answer is *no,* or if you have to poll and persuade your family, say so. If your wife's or husband's career isn't portable, or if your children are in special schools, or if you want your daughter to keep that swim coach who has her almost ready for Olympic tryouts, or if you can't desert an ailing parent, then you can immediately...or after an evening or a weekend to think it over...rule out a job that requires relocation.

Don't waste your time, the recruiter's, and possibly even the employer's, on an interview, when your personal life prevents your taking the job. If you do, you'll prove you're a lousy decision-maker. And then the recruiter won't call when he gets another fine opportunity that *doesn't* require relocation.

3.   Wrong Money. The recruiter almost certainly will not tell you upfront exactly how much his client prefers to pay. And of course, until the job is filled, nobody knows what will be negotiated.

However, the recruiter has a very good idea what the *upper limits* are. He's undoubtedly found out what peer-level jobs in the client company pay. And a smart recruiter always asks the compensation of the position directly above the one he's filling. So even if he doesn't want to "go public" by telling you, the recruiter does know "how much is too much."

So how do you uncover too-low money?

Simple. Just give the recruiter a clear idea of what you're making now, and what improvement you expect within the next year. If the recruiter is someone you already know and trust, or appears to be a first-class professional from a respected firm, you may decide to be forthright:

> "The responsibility is very attractive. I'd certainly like to be running my own show. But I'm not sure this situation would make sense for me *financially*. My base is going up to $150,000 on August 1, and I'll earn about a 20% bonus on top of that. So we've got to be talking significantly over $200,000 for me to come out with any improvement in money."

If you're less confident about the recruiter's integrity and confidentiality, just give him the bottom line without saying anything specific he can repeat to others about your compensation:

> "I like it here and I'm very well compensated. However, I *would* be willing to listen if you're talking well over $200,000. Otherwise, I'm really not interested in changing."

Knowing where you stand on money, and knowing he almost certainly can't go over $175,000 in base-plus-bonus, the recruiter will immediately pull back and ask you for suggestions of other able people in your field. Best of all, he'll regard you as smart and decisive. You haven't wasted his time. Expect to hear from him again, when he has a higher-paying job.

"Sounds like a lateral move."

Quite a few executives. . .almost routinely. . .react to every new situation they're phoned about with an irritatingly common cliché:

"Sounds to me like a *lateral move.*"

Using these precise words is a bad idea, because they're a formula response. Hardly ever will any new situation be exactly on a par with what you have.

So skip the cliché. But use the same approach. Latch on to the specifics the recruiter mentions, and point out all the ways the proposed job doesn't appear to be an advancement:

> "Of course I already *have* my own profit center, and we've been doing well since I took over three years ago. We're already larger in sales. . .and I'll bet a lot stronger in profits. . .than the company you're proposing, even though they've been around longer and lots of people probably still think they're bigger than we are."

OR

> "Of course I'd love to have a 150-person sales force, because so far we've had to use manufacturers' representatives, and I'm only just now getting a few of our own people into the field. But here I have total responsibility for all Marketing, reporting to the President. And if I understand you right, in the situation you're describing I'd be reporting to a Vice President of Marketing, who also has a Product Management group that I wouldn't be involved with. I think I'm better off to stay here and keep building this business. . .and wait for you to call me again in a couple years when we've made even more progress. Then you may have a job like his for me to consider."

OR

"They're a big outfit, and I believe you when you say that I can probably make a nice improvement in salary by going with them. But money isn't everything, by any means. Increased responsibility and long-term career progress are what really interest me. Tell me what this opportunity might do for me in those terms."

See what you've done? You've virtually forced the recruiter to give you more information right there on the telephone.

If you're going to say "No," do so as soon as possible.

Move the conversation quickly to your key decision points. These are issues that only you know about, since they have to do with your current situation and your career objectives.

And as soon as you know you'll ultimately say "no," by all means do so. Then offer to suggest more appropriate candidates. You'll not only save time; you'll enhance your image in the eyes of the recruiter. Seeing how efficiently you handle his inquiry, he'll figure you're equally adept at your job. Expect to be called again!

If you don't find any disqualifying negatives, let the recruiter "sell" you by phone ...and then ask for more information by mail.

If your caller does have an attractive opportunity, hear him out. Let him sell you.

Then ask for a little homework. Have the recruiter send you an annual report, a 10K, a proxy statement, a product catalog and price list, a description of the position...whatever will supplement your telephone impressions. If the recruiter doesn't have such materials, chances are he's not on retainer.

Suggest a time when you'll call the recruiter...or he'll call you...to continue the discussion, after you've studied those items. A retainer recruiter. . .highly paid to serve his clients' interests. . .will gladly call you in the evening or on the weekend, if that's what you prefer.

Never pretend to be interested if you're really not.

Some executives, unaware of the behind-the-scenes workings of a recruiting firm, will pretend to be interested in a job, just to get to know the recruiter. . .in the hope of discovering more-appropriate openings than the one being described.

As you can see, this strategy is way off base. If you express interest in the search you're called about, the recruiter's firm *won't show you any other job* until that project is finished and all the files are returned to the central talent pool. . .which may take several months. It's a guaranteed method for staying *out* of the action at that firm for a substantial time.

If you say "No," try to offer helpful suggestions ...even hook the recruiter into your network.

If you're not interested, always try to suggest people who'd be more appropriate. Also suggest people the recruiter should talk to as "sources." They wouldn't want the job, but probably can suggest potential candidates.

Indeed, if you're highly impressed with the recruiter, offer to *let him use your name*. Help him get through to the people who know you, but don't know him. He'll be grateful. . .and will chalk up another reason why you should be one of the first people called when he or someone else in his firm undertakes a search that could interest you.

In closing the phone conversation, also be sure to let the recruiter know what sort of an opportunity *would* excite your interest. Might as well plant a seed for the future. If you've been competent, warm, and helpful, the climate is right.

Beware of the recruiter who wants to meet you after you've said "No."

If you've clearly pointed out mismatches between the recruiter's proposal and your situation, and he still urges you to come in for an interview, you should suspect him of wanting. . .above all. . .to apply his tag to your head and see that your resume is widely circulated. Chances are, he won't merely be wanting, as he'll say, ''to know you better for the future when the right thing *does* come across my desk.''

Generally speaking, true retainer recruiters are extremely busy finding the people clients are paying them to look for today, this week, this month. The successful ones have very little time or inclination to interrupt their on-going searches to meet anyone. . .no matter how able and attractive. . .who doesn't fit a current search.

The odds are overwhelmingly against any retainer recruiter. . .no matter how large the firm he works for. . .ever personally getting the exact project that's right for you at the exact future time when it's appropriate for you to move. Expect him to behave accordingly. *And be wary if he doesn't.*

How much manipulation are you willing to put up with?

Lots of recruiters. . .sometimes encouraged by employers who'd like them to operate that way. . .will try to get you to come in for an interview without telling you the identity of the employer you're being considered to work for.

After you've expressed potential interest in their proposition, they go on to say something like this:

> YOUR CALLER: ''Naturally, of course, I can't give you the identity of the employer *on the telephone*. We can talk much more frankly in my office, if you'd like to come in and explore this situation further. And do bring your resume. We can look it over as we talk, and we'll have it in case we decide to go ahead.''

What baloney!

Is the recruiter's phone bugged. . .or yours? Conceivably, a switchboard operator might overhear *yours* if you're at work. But his shouldn't be a problem. And he raised the point. . .you didn't. Any legitimate concern...and only you will have it...can be eliminated by continuing this call via your home phone tonight, or on the weekend. And all first-class recruiters...retainer and contingency...will gladly do so.

Re-read what the recruiter said. Did he promise you he'd identify the employer, even if you *do* go to all the trouble of visiting his office, *and* you hand him your resume, *and* you submit to an interview? No, he didn't! And don't expect him to, if you meekly go ahead as he suggests.

Obviously the recruiter wants the option of knowing everything about you and conveying nothing specific to you about the identity of the employer...if indeed he's actually been engaged by one.

Plenty of recruiters would like to proceed that way. But no employed executive has to accept such ground rules. Indeed, the unemployed executive who objects to them will be considered a lot more formidable than the one who doesn't. Let's hear how you pick up the conversation:

> YOU: "Oh, I have no problem with the phone; we're perfectly free to go ahead."
>
> "Also, I can't tell you whether I'm interested in interviewing for a job unless I know what the job is, and of course *that includes knowing what company I'd be working for*. I'm doing very well here, and haven't been thinking at all about making a change. On the other hand, what you're suggesting does sound interesting...at least on the surface. Is there something more you'd like to know about me, in order to see whether you think we should go any further?"

The ball's back in his court. If he wants you for a candidate, he'll just have to be more forthcoming now, while he has you on the phone. You're warmly open and cooperative...offering to address any potential shortcomings.

If the recruiter doesn't come forward now and ask his key questions which might disqualify *you*...and let you ask your key questions that might disqualify the *job*...he knows he'll lose you. Then he'll have to go to the trouble of finding someone else with your qualifications...and with your interest in the opportunity. Someone who, unlike you, is willing to submit to a highly one-sided procedure. That means someone more insecure in his job...or as a person...than you are. And unfortunately, the employer probably won't be as interested in that person as he would be in you.

So even if you're sitting at the other end of the wire absolutely quivering with delight at the prospect of having a shot at the position the recruiter has described, *you have clout.* Use it.

What will the recruiter do now? One thing's absolutely certain. He won't think less of you just because you're not a pushover. His next move will depend on the actual motives behind his call to you:

1.   If he's trying to tag your head prior to nailing down a proper client assignment, he'll forget that idea...meanwhile telling you, "Too bad; you're missing out on a great opportunity!"

2.   If he was going to befriend you, and later pitch for your executive recruiting business, after this non-existent "search" is...alas..."cancelled," he'll forget that idea.

3.   If he has a retainer search, and is merely proceeding with approach #1 of his standard "M.O.," he'll shift smoothly into approach #2 and, in return for your telling him what he needs to know, he'll tell you what you need to know...including employer identity, which he'll request you to "keep confidential." *Expect this result 80% of the time.*

4.   If he has a retainer search and also a legitimate mandate for secrecy *from the employer,* he'll come out with a specific and plausible reason for not being able to name the employer:

YOUR CALLER: "I'm sorry, but I really *can't* identify the company. The person in the job is going to be fired, and we're lining up a slate of candidates who'll be all set to go when that happens."

> YOU: "Well, I guess I won't be standing there all inter-
> viewed and waiting, when the other guy gets the axe.
> But do call me when you're in a position to be more
> specific. I definitely might be interested, depending on
> who the company is. Meanwhile, I appreciate your
> thinking of me. Thanks for the call."

Only in possibility #4 was there any legitimate employer-dictated need
for confidentiality. And I'm being very generous in estimating that
such a need may actually exist in as many as 10% to 20% of the instances when a recruiter calls you. Then, of course, he can't back down.

But what will he do? By holding out, have you lost your shot at the job
he called you about?

Probably not. Chances are, you've made yourself more desirable.

In all likelihood, when the recruiter briefs the employer on the executives who were willing to be interviewed without knowing who they'd
be presented to, he'll also describe the two or three *even more impressive ones*...like you...who wouldn't go along with that procedure. He'll
explain that he can re contact thooo, ao ooon ao the employer litts the
secrecy. Chances are ten-to-one that the employer will immediately
say:

> "Don't wait. Open up to them right away, so that we can
> meet any of those who are willing to talk to us, right along
> with the candidates you've already interviewed."

So, even in this rare instance where there was an employer-imposed
mandate to interview without disclosing company identity, you came
out just as well by standing firm as you would have by caving in. In
fact, you probably look stronger and will be more sought after than the
people who jumped at the chance for a "blind" interview.

Of course, if you'd been out of work when the recruiter called, your reaction might have been different.

If your caller had been from a *retainer* firm where you'd been trying for
weeks to get a courtesy interview, you'd instantly have accepted the

invitation. However, you'd have known that interviewing on this job would have assigned you to this search, even if you weren't told the employer's identity. Therefore, you probably wouldn't have been returned to the firm's talent pool for consideration on anything else, until after the "mystery" search was completed.

Of course, you'd *never* have submitted to interviewing by a *contingency* recruiter without being told to whom you were being offered, unless you were sure that the firm is totally ethical. Otherwise, they might have taken your willingness to be offered to one undisclosed employer as permission to covertly submit you to any company that might hire you.

The furthest I'd be willing to compromise, if I were you…

If I were happily employed, I'd never agree to be interviewed for any "opportunity," no matter how attractively described, unless I knew in advance the employer's identity. However, if I were eager to move, I might propose the following:

> YOU: "I'd be pleased to meet you and discuss my background, which seems to be exactly what you're looking for. The only thing I ask is that you not submit me to any employer without telling me who I'm being offered to."
>
> "You can tell me who it is after the interview, if you decide to present me. Or tell me that you have other candidates that you prefer, and therefore you *won't* submit me. Or tell me *you don't know yet* whether I'll be submitted, and you'll get back to me later if I *am* to be submitted."
>
> "I just don't want my name and information submitted to anyone without knowing who it is. Is that OK with you?"

Even employment agencies for clericals accept the proposition that "applicants" have the right to say in advance what companies they are and are not willing to be presented to. When you state your position in this way, *no legitimate executive recruiter can refuse.* But do so on the phone prior to your interview…when you'll have more clout, and you'll get a clearer answer.

You can push the recruiter toward frankness by being frank yourself.

To encourage a "let's get down to it" telephone discussion, volunteer a thumbnail review of the points...pro and con...that should spell "go" or "no go" to the recruiter:

> YOU: "Look, I'm in charge of all marketing and sales over here, reporting to the President. I moved up to this job three years ago from head of product management. Since then we've been making very strong gains in market share, volume, and profitability. Here are a few things you should also know, however: I'm 54 years old and I don't have an MBA. In fact, I don't quite have my BS. My only college has been at night at NYU, and I've let that program slide since my promotion to this job. I'm about 15 credits shy of a BS in Marketing. Also, you've got to be talking *over $150,000* or you can't reach me on money.

It's all there!

That took you less than a minute to say. Yet it summarizes the key points the recruiter would have tried to draw out in a face-to-face meeting.

If the recruiter knows his client will never accept a noncollege-graduate (and in my opinion, that's very shortsighted), or won't want somebody in his 50's when the search has already turned up several outstanding candidates in their late 30's, then both you and the recruiter will be spared a useless interview.

On the other hand, if the prejudicial factors you raise are not disabling, then you've undoubtedly "sold" yourself to the recruiter with your 60-second summary...a virtuoso display of cutting through to the heart of a matter. The employer will be identified, and you'll be invited to meet the recruiter.

If the recruiter is uncertain about the employer's attitude toward the factors you've laid on the table, he'll:

1.   say that his client is a wonderfully broad-minded person who'd never break the "equal-opportunity" laws, and

2. promise to get back to you with "further information,"
    once he's "ready to go ahead."

Meanwhile he'll find out what his client really does feel about the points you've raised. If and when the recruiter calls back, you'll know you're not wasting your time by exploring a job you'll never, in the end, be hired for.

Special Note for Employers Using Executive Recruiters

Your first impulse...particularly if you haven't been served and coached by top professionals in the recruiting field...will be to request your recruiter to keep your project "highly confidential," and perhaps not to reveal your identity until after he's interviewed the executive and "confirmed that he's really a strong candidate."

The less competent your recruiter is...and the less honest, as he competes for your business by telling you what you want to hear...the more likely he'll imply that he can provide such "confidentiality" and still get you the strongest possible candidates. Don't imagine for one minute that this is true.

The executives most willing to go along with such treatment are out of work (which doesn't necessarily mean they're not good)...or in difficulty...or so marginally qualified for your job that they're thrilled to pursue it, regardless of the overbearing procedure.

Executives who are already at the right level for your job, and are currently employed by companies that think they're excellent and reward them accordingly, will not be clogging their calendars with interviews by recruiters who won't tell them who they're being solicited to work for.

Face-to-Face with the Recruiter: Your Interview for the Job He Called About

You and the recruiter have accomplished about as much as you can over the telephone. You tried to disqualify the opportunity, and you couldn't. You're not "sold." But you *are* interested. So you're going to go see the recruiter...or possibly he's coming to see you. Now what?

Now you prepare for the meeting!

That's right. Even though the recruiter called you; you didn't call him. Even though you agreed to the meeting only after he drowned you in charming persuasion. Still you *prepare*. This meeting is far more important to you than to him. It's just part of one day's work to the recruiter. But it could change...for better or worse...your entire career.

So take some time to figure out what you want to accomplish. What questions do you want answered? And what do you want to communicate, so that the recruiter will rank you among his finalists, and will accurately convey your best features to his client?

Your Two-Fold Agenda: Selling and Inquiring

...with Emphasis on Selling

One objective must be virtually in-the-bag by the end of the meeting. The other can be pursued later by phone, if necessary.

If time runs out on your interview and you haven't asked quite all of your questions...or if new ones occur to you afterward...you can always phone for answers. Is there anything wrong with this?

> YOU: "A few important questions occur to me that we didn't get a chance to cover when we were together..."

No, nothing at all out of line. But imagine this call:

> NOT YOU: "Unfortunately, Paul, I was so busy asking questions during my interview, that I got home and realized I hadn't told you some additional...and very impressive...things you should know about me. Make yourself comfortable, and I'll begin reciting my further virtues to you now..."

You get the point. You had plenty of chance to challenge the job during one or more phone calls before your interview. And you can phone with more questions later. The interview is your chance to let the recruiter find out how ideal you'd be for the position. Don't wind up with you convinced that the job's right for you, and the recruiter not convinced that you're right for the job.

Of course you can try to fill in omitted selling points with a followup letter. Indeed, that's your only shot. But the recruiter's impression will be overwhelmingly based on your face-to-face interview. It's almost impossible to raise your ranking by anything you mail in afterward.

So ask *and* sell. *But don't fail to sell.*

At the outset:
1.   **determine how much time you have, and**
2.   **reconfirm the ground rules, if necessary.**

As in the courtesy interview, you'll be wise to ask:

"How much time do we have?"

And if you've got to leave within a limited time, let the recruiter know right away:

"I hope I've scheduled enough time for this, and I'll be glad to come back if you want me to...But I couldn't avoid setting up another meeting at four o'clock. So I'll have to leave here by three-thirty."

Forewarned, both you and the recruiter can modify your agendas to fit the pre-acknowledged time slot. Such a statement isn't discourteous; it's the mark of a thoughtful and efficient executive.

Candidate interviews by recruiters usually range from an hour to an hour-and-a-half. I personally devote far more time to them, but I also pre-screen more restrictively and invite only a few exceptional people to interview. Each recruiter has his own personal style. Achieve your objectives by adapting to his game plan.

Another point. If you agreed to this meeting without knowing in advance the identity of the employer, you should also re-confirm, right upfront, the ground rules that were negotiated earlier:

"You know, Boyd, you still haven't told me who the employer is. Your feeling was that at the end of this meeting, you'd know whether or not you'll be presenting me. Then you can tell me *who it is*...if we're going ahead...or that I'm *not a finalist* if we won't be going further. That's just fine with me. What I really want to be sure of is that we're agreed that I won't be presented anywhere, unless I know in advance where that will be."

Beginning with a recapitulation of points agreed on earlier over the phone is merely appropriate businesslike procedure. But if you delay them to the end of the interview, the same points will seem nagging and distrustful.

Set up an informal agenda.

Once timing is established, it's not offensive...and can be helpful...to send up another trial balloon:

YOU: "I don't know where you want to start. I do have some potential reservations about the job...especially since reading the 10K and proxy statement you sent me. Or do you want to start by talking about me? I just know that before I can agree to be a candidate, I'll have to have answers to a few key questions."

Your concerns aren't such "show-stoppers" that you should have phoned and possibly cancelled your interview. But they do have to be addressed. The recruiter can now decide whether to tackle them right away, or to go ahead and talk about your qualifications, with the understanding that he can't sign-off until your questions are answered. Indeed, your down-to-business approach may encourage him to proceed just as frankly:

"Let's take a look at *our main questions* first, and cover whatever else we have time for at the end. My two basic questions about you are: How much experience have you had in acquisitions and divestitures? And what happened at Yesterday Corporation?"

Or the recruiter may even say:

"Look, I'm already convinced that you're one of the best candidates in America for this position; let's get your questions out of the way first, and then let me tell you some further things I've learned about the job.''

The better you and the recruiter know how much time you both have, and the issues of greatest interest to the opposite party, the more useful...and persuasive...the meeting will be.

Do you have a resume?...and do you hand it over?

Yes! You never come to a recruiter interview without a resume. And once you're satisfied that you're dealing with a professional you respect, you don't hesitate to hand it to him.

As a successful executive at $100,000 + , you know about visual aids and leave-behinds. A resume is both. Even if you're more concerned about getting information than communicating it, the resume will still be helpful. It will speed the recruiter's inquiry...and make more time available for *your* questions.

If you're being courted by the recruiter, and the job seems only marginally attractive, just bring in the last resume you made...even if it's ten years old. Update your home address and phone number. Also jot down on a sheet of yellow pad the dates and titles of your more recent jobs. Your early career will be thoroughly covered, and you can talk your way forward from there. First-class recruiters always type up their own version of candidate information. So informality won't count against you, even if you wind up meeting the employer.

On the other hand, if the position could be a major career breakthrough, it's certainly worth the time and effort to prepare a highly-persuasive resume, stressing your most recent...and presumably your greatest...accomplishments. Not only will it help the recruiter understand and communicate what you've done, the very act of creating it will prepare you to meet the recruiter *and* the employer. You'll be in command of facts-and-figures...not only on what you're doing now, but on what you've done in the past.

If you just bring an old resume, be sure to *read it over*. I'm amazed how many people hand out papers they seem totally unfamiliar with. Time is wasted as the recruiter, who's freshly read your information, seems to know more about your early career than you do. You're a dud as a business communicator, when that happens.

Also, be prepared to *talk* your way through your work history. Some recruiters will read your resume carefully, asking questions and making notes. Others will set it aside and ask you what happened. You won't score points with a "tell-me" recruiter if you clam up and say, "It's all there in the resume."

Bring along any supplementary information you may need.

If you don't have an encyclopedic memory, bring a few sheets of statistics, so that you can refer to them when a performance question arises.

A recruiter's interview has two purposes:

1.   to obtain information, and

2.   to see how well you handle yourself and how thoroughly you seem to understand what you're in charge of.

Short answers are better than long ones. And specifics are far better than vague generalizations. You may not want to hand over confidential charts. But have them handy, to remind you of the numbers you've achieved. Vague, nonspecific communication will count against you.

Be honest about negatives.

Be frank upfront about major negatives that referencing will highlight. Expect the recruiter to check you out before he passes you along to his client. If you've been fired, or if profits have evaporated under your management, he's probably going to find out. And it will be a strike against you that you tried to conceal the information. No one has a record of perfect achievement. And many very able people have been fired. Offer a brief explanation that establishes your version of the matter, but don't highlight it, and don't be defensive.

Don't view the recruiter as your "advocate."

Bear in mind that the retainer recruiter is paid to represent the corporation's best interests, not yours. Don't expect him to conspire with you about the best way to present your qualifications. It would be a breach of professional ethics to try to convince his client that you're a strong candidate when you're really not.

Are there any special considerations associated with your candidacy?

If so, bring them up.

Anything that could make you more costly or inconvenient to hire than other candidates should be brought out during...or prior to...your interview. Then the recruiter can forewarn the employer, and you'll be considered from the beginning with your "disadvantages" in full view.

If you're the best person, then simultaneously with his growing interest in you, the employer can think of ways to deal with your special needs. Above all, there won't be "unpleasant surprises" later, to throw cold water on your candidacy and raise doubts about your candor.

For example:

> You have a low-interest mortgage, and without a "mortgage-differential" from your new employer, you'll lose $60,000 to $80,000 in after-tax out-of-pocket costs.

> You'll lose $40,000 in profits on stock options which won't vest for another ten months.

> You have a child with a costly medical problem, and you can't afford to move unless the illness won't be excluded as a "pre-existing condition" under the new company's insurance.

> You're in the midst of renovating your house, which could be tough to sell right now at its proper value. You'll have to stay where you are, unless you can have the services of a home relocation company that will price it fairly and take it off your hands.

> You have a pension that vests, all-or-nothing, in seven months,

and you'll move prior to that only if you can negotiate a settlement with your present employer or receive special treatment from your new one.

Tell the recruiter about any problem that may require modification of the way his client normally handles a new hire.

Prepare yourself for a later client interview.

If it looks like the recruiter is "sold," and you're going to be a "finalist," ask questions that will get you ready to meet the employer. Take advantage of the recruiter's knowledge of his client's situation. . .either at the end of the interview if there's time left, or in a later phone call. Find out exactly what the employer is looking for, and get a sense of what to expect at the interview.

The Ideal Result: "To Be Continued"

Just as with the courtesy interview, a positive ending to this session is the sense that exploration of your candidacy is "to be continued." If and when it becomes clear that you're a "finalist," accept "yes" for an answer, and leave. And if there are questions in your mind about whether you should be a candidate, resolve them with the recruiter and either decide to go ahead or withdraw.

Executive recruiters can be frustrating.
Grin and bear it.

From the job-changing executive's point of view, retainer recruiting firms seem dismayingly inefficient. When you deal with a large and respected firm, you know that, at that very moment, they're handling hundreds of searches. . .many of them almost certainly an ideal "next step" for your career. Yet you only hear about one at a time. And which one is largely accidental, depending on which recruiter in the firm happens to be in a position to deal with you, what jobs he's trying to fill, and what success he's had with each of them.

For example, he may show you something in Distant Falls, a place that doesn't particularly appeal to you, because that's his most urgent search at the moment. Meanwhile, he says nothing about the job that's even more attractive, and located only twenty minutes from your front door... simply because he already has more candidates than he needs on that one.

There's very little you can do about the haphazard way your involvement with a retainer search firm unfolds. It's simply the way those recruiters work...a method that's not designed to favor *your* interests as a job-changing executive.

Still, a good, ethical retainer recruiter does know of jobs that can advance your career. Under the right conditions, he and others in his firm may show you at least one opportunity...possibly even two or three... within the year or so that you may be seriously thinking about a move. And you can know more opportunities handled by retainer firms, if more firms know you.

Consider the highly-professional retainer recruiters as *one conduit* to career opportunity...and the highly-ethical contingency firms as another.

But now that you know how executive recruiters really work, you can clearly see why they shouldn't be the only way you seek to advance your career. At least not when you want to move fairly quickly. And not when you want the widest possible knowledge of what's available in the marketplace.

11

Being Where You Can't Be
. . .and Selling When You're Not There

Isn't it too bad that you can't be everywhere at once, and find out about every major career opportunity that might interest you?

Wouldn't it be great to have your own equivalent of a spy-in-the-sky satellite that could survey a forty-mile radius of your house. . .or the entire USA. . .or the world. . .to identify all the situations you'd like to know about, whether current openings, soon-to-be-openings, or searches underway at recruiting firms?

Then you'd be sure not to miss any situation that could foster your career.

Of course there's always the chance that you'll learn of career-enhancing job possibilities through personal contacts and networking. . . talking to old business friends and associates, meeting lots of new people, and picking the brains of everyone you reach.

Unfortunately, although face-to-face communication is the most powerful form of contact, your time is limited. No matter how diligent you are, you simply can't be everywhere at once. You'll make your networking contacts one at a time, maybe two or three a day, a dozen or so a week...not exactly a speed-of-light satellite reconnaissance... and likely to miss *most* of the jobs available "out there somewhere," which your contacts don't happen to know about.

You've also clearly seen that retainer executive recruiting firms aren't going to show you everything they know of...only one job at a time, perhaps two or three per year.

In fact, there's only *one way* in which you can even attempt to find out about *all* the available or soon-to-be available jobs that may be the right "next step" for you. And that's through a well-conceived, thoroughly-executed direct mail campaign. Every person you write to at the right level...and we'll discuss later what that level is...gives you a shot at knowing about another job that might advance your career.

But isn't direct mail a weak method?

Many people think direct mail is a weak technique, particularly for a job search. I've had lots of senior executives ...even top marketing executives (who should know better)...say to me:

> "John, I don't believe in direct mail. It's not effective. Nearly all the letters you send are either thrown away or relegated to the Personnel Department for a polite 'no-thank-you.' Therefore, you just don't get anywhere with a direct mail campaign. It doesn't have the punch that personal contact does."

Mostly true. But whenever I meet people who criticize direct mail as weak and ineffective, I remind them of their own reactions when they've needed to hire someone they were having a tough time finding:

> "When you had a really difficult hiring problem, and you urgently needed someone with a particular background to fill an important spot, didn't you *then* follow up by contacting *everyone* whose resume came to your attention and seemed to show exactly what you were looking for?"

Invariably they reply:

> "Well, of course *then* I did. *Anyone* would."

So I press the point:

> "What if, instead of the mailman bringing that resume, it just blew in through the window...all tattered and dirty, along with a bunch of autumn leaves? Wouldn't you still call up the person if he or she looked like the possible solution to your problem?"

You know their answer. It would be yours too.

My first-hand experience as a retainer executive recruiter doing searches at the $100,000 + level for the past seventeen years has proven beyond doubt that mailed-in employment inquiries do get attention.

In about one out of every two searches I conduct, the ultimate decision-maker who hires me hands over at least one...and more often several...resumes he's collected before calling me in. Approximately a third of those have been forwarded by outside directors, employees, customers, suppliers, lawyers, accountants, etc. (the product of personal contact and networking). The majority, however, were merely delivered by the mailman. And of course I'm not called...and never see the resume...when anyone is so tempting that there's an interview, offer, and acceptance without any need for me.

It's all a matter of timing.

The key advantage of direct mail is not how strong a medium it is, but the fact that it's strong enough, if it reaches a decision-maker *at exactly his moment of need.*

Moreover, it doesn't matter what method you use, if you reach the decision-maker when he has *no* need. Even you-in-person...with all your persuasive logic, charm, wit, elegant grooming, and both your new shiny shoes...won't achieve a sale, if your host isn't seeking what you're selling. That's always the problem...with most networking calls, and with most mailed-in resumes, too.

On the other hand, your resume, dog-eared and folded, that a CEO happens to find protruding from the pocket on the seat ahead of him when he flies the Concorde to Paris could net you an exciting phone call. The same lucky break might also occur if you happen to sit next to him on the flight...assuming of course that he talks to seat-mates.

The value of direct mail is not in how it's delivered, but rather in the great number of potential buyers it can reach simultaneously, in order to stimulate one or two of the rare few who happen to have the right need at the right moment.

**Use direct mail to reach the whole
universe of potential buyers.**

**That way, you'll be sure to hit the very few
who are actually ready to buy.**

Consider what corporations do. The President and the Chief Marketing or Sales Officer may personally contact key accounts that provide enormous volumes of business. Customers who buy fairly often will be handled by the direct sales force...perhaps 150 to 300 people spread across the country. And finally, to reach customers in out-of-the-way places or who order only once-in-a-while...customers it isn't feasible to serve with salesmen...companies rely on direct mail, or telephone marketing, or a combination of both.

But even telephone calls have serious limitations. You can only call so many people per day. Your listener will seldom stay on the wire long enough to hear a comprehensive sales pitch for a complex product. And afterward there's nothing left behind on paper to refresh his memory and encourage follow-up.

So the method companies turn to when they want to cover the whole market at once. . .to get where they can't send a salesman, and yet deliver their entire selling message and have it remain afterward in writing. . .is a wide-ranging direct mail campaign.

Indeed, direct mail *is* effective, or it wouldn't be so widely used. The proof is in your mailbox every day. If direct mail weren't effective, the companies who send it would soon be out of business, having thrown their money away on something that doesn't work.

You're surprisingly similar to the other products direct mail sells very effectively.

What kinds of products are sold through direct mail? Not the inexpensive, uncomplicated things that everyone needs every day. Soap, corn flakes, diet cola, floor wax, and nationwide "fast food" chains are best advertised in TV commercials aimed at the entire population. Such products are easily-understood. Just about everybody is a potential purchaser. And the whole story can be boiled down to 30 seconds or a minute. Forget the "cents-off" coupons. The long letters in your mailbox are not about cake mix and laundry detergent.

What *are* those long letters about? Seldom-purchased products and services that:

1. only a few people out of the vast population are likely to need and be able to afford at the moment they get the advertisement, and

2. require more explanation and persuasion than can be crammed into a 30-second or one-minute TV spot, or even into a one-page magazine ad.

Examples: professional-development seminars; building lots and timeshare condominia; insurance plans; encyclopedias; expensive "limited-edition" books, porcelains, and store-of-value collectibles; tax planning and investment services; special-interest magazines; economic newsletters. . .those sorts of things.

You see the analogy. An executive is a seldom-acquired item. . .very costly, unique, and relatively complicated to understand and evaluate. The best way that the marketing geniuses of the twentieth century have figured out to spread the news about such an item is by direct mail advertising. And the amount you receive is dollars-and-cents proof that it's effective.

The Three-Fold Marketing Science of Direct Mail

Compared to the stardust world of covergirls, cowboys, sunsets, laundry-room drama, and bar-room humor of the TV commercials and magazine ads for consumer products, the fact-packed mailings that promote business publications and economic newsletters look pretty prosaic and predictable.

And they are. Direct mail…of all the marketing arts…has been the most quantifiably studied and refined over the past 50 years. Today it's about as close to a *science* as anything that's also highly creative can possibly be.

Every time an advertiser sends out a multi-million-letter mailing, he first prepares several different "test" versions and tries each one on thousands of potential customers. He finds out which will bring in the most orders per $1,000 spent on paper, printing, and postage.

Therefore, each national mailing you receive represents a new high-water mark in the advertiser's knowledge of what does and doesn't work in delivering a complicated sales pitch by letter.

There are a lot of intricacies to selling by direct mail. I won't bore you with more information than we really need for our purposes, except to say that knowledge on the subject breaks down into three categories:

1.   Copywriting effectiveness,

2.   Prospect identification (list selection), and

3.   Statistical assessment.

You and I won't bother with point 2, which has to do with figuring out how to select, combine, and refine commercially-available lists of names in order to come up with the recipients for a particular mailing. That's because you'll be assembling your own list, based on your personal objectives, interests, and geographic preferences.

But we *will* take advantage of the most fundamental principles direct mail experts have learned with respect to points 1 and 3. In the next chapter we'll apply the key principles of direct mail *copywriting* to the creation of a compelling resume. And in the following chapter. . .along with lots of other essential information. . .we'll look at the *statistical* aspects of a direct mail campaign to advance your career.

But before we go one step further, let's see whether direct mail is something *you* should seriously consider.

The Networking vs. Direct Mail Trade-Off

If you reach someone when he has no need and knows of nobody else who has a need, there's no sale. And it doesn't matter whether you get there in person or in writing.

The advantage of a personal visit. . .networking. . .is its human interaction. Your host may not have or know of a job that could advance your career. But seeing and befriending you. . .and wanting to do a favor for the person who referred you. . .he can usually be persuaded to pass you along to several others. Your contacts will, indeed, *"increase geometrically."* But "geometrically" *only* until you have more people to see than you have hours to go see them. After that, you've got strictly a linear progression of appointments to make, two or three a day. . . probably ten to fifteen a week.

The advantage of direct mail, on the other hand, is that you can reach an unlimited number of people simultaneously. Therefore, *you can inflate that number to the point of very high probability* that you'll reach some of the rare few who actually do need what you're selling at the very moment you happen to make your contact. And when you finally *do* reach someone with an immediate need for what you're offering, that person is likely to be interested. . .even though no mutual acquaintance made the introduction.

Is there a downside to direct mail?
Will reaching the potential decision-makers in
lots of companies make you seem:
     a.   too available?
     b.   too eager?
     c.   unwanted and unloved?
     d.   desperate?
     e.   none of the above?

The answer, of course, is E, "none of the above." And the reasons why, when you think about them, are pretty obvious.

No chief executive nor anyone else in control of a job that might represent a valuable career advancement for you is sitting breathlessly by his "IN box," waiting for your letter and resume to arrive...that is, unless he's one of the infinitesimally rare few who right then happens to have that job wide open, urgently needing someone like you to fill it.

The person who doesn't need what you're offering will merely throw away your mailing, or pass it along for filing and a courteous "no thank you." He's *not* going to pick up the phone and ask his peers in other companies and his contacts in the leading executive recruiting firms if they also got your mailing, and what did they think of it, and what are they going to do about it, and weren't you stupid not to have known in advance that he and they didn't need anyone like you right now.

The fact is, either he'll do you *some good,* or he'll do you *no harm.* And in the "some good" department, you may be pleasantly surprised. If a colleague in his own organization, or a friend, or an executive recruiter calling him for suggestions happens to mention a need for someone like you, the person who's just received your resume and doesn't need you himself will probably pass your resume along, just as one of your networking contacts would.

And if your mailing is so impressive that the recipient or his personnel department saves a copy for a few weeks or months, he might wind up referring several inquirers to you. When extremely well done, direct mail can, with luck, take on a bit of the same "geometric" dimension networking has.

"But," you ask, "will I diminish my lustre and usefulness to the prestigious retainer recruiting firms if I conduct a direct mail campaign?"

No. A lot of people worry needlessly about this possibility, so let's examine it.

First of all, every retainer recruiter will automatically *assume* you've sent your mailing to all the other *retainer* firms and to a wide range of companies, because it's in your best interest to do so. No two retainer firms are ever working simultaneously on the same project; therefore, you have to reach all those firms to reach all their projects.

Of course, it's unthinkable that you would simultaneously be presented..."sold" at the rate of $5,000 to $10,000 and more per candidate...to more than one client of the *same* retainer recruiting firm for the reasons we looked at earlier. But there's no client PR damage to either firm when two different retainer firms present you to two different companies. If either or both of these companies should find out, they can't blame their *own* retainer firm for what a different one has done. And of course, the companies normally *won't* find out, because they're competing for the same talent at the same time. Therefore, they're certainly not exchanging information on candidates.

Moreover, the idea that you may also have written to his client company won't scare away the one-and-only recruiter in a sizable retainer firm who, for the moment, has the right to deal with you. He always expects you to have taken that perfectly logical step. And he has no reason...or method...to reward you if you haven't. Indeed, going directly to companies is the only way you can possibly break through the barrier that confines you to this recruiter and his client company, while putting you "off-limits" to all the other recruiters in his firm and to all their client companies.

Believe it or not, if you're really a good candidate, the retainer recruiter is less worried that his client won't be amazed when he identifies you, than he is that the client will think he's a dope for not finding you when you've already made yourself obvious to the client company.

The bottom line on trying to be more attractive by being less known:

It doesn't work!

Known is like pregnant; you're known or you're not known...by each person individually. The way the relationships we're interested in work, each player in the game either knows of you or he doesn't; they're never going to gang up on you and take a poll to see *how many* know about you.

What will *make you less attractive is being unemployed a long time, and the fewer people who know about your fine background and your availability, the more likely that might happen.*

The only circumstance where being widely known *is* dangerous to your economic health is when a recruiter *operating on contingency* submits you...price-tag attached...to companies who never specifically engaged him to do so. Getting around on your own is altogether different. It's great. Circulate!

Enough about the "why" of direct mail; let's take a look at the "how." And in the process, we'll add the persuasiveness of direct mail copywriting to your resume.

You may never need to conduct a direct mail campaign to advance your career, although it *is* one of the "Rites of Passage" you should be aware of.

But you and every other executive should always have a persuasive sales-representative-on-paper standing by, ready to go anywhere...by hand or by mail...to do the best possible job of communicating your abilities and achievements to people who haven't witnessed them first-hand. That's a resume. And its purpose is *to be where you can't be and sell when you're not there.* Direct mail marketing is the *science* of doing just that...the most thoroughly understood and quantifiably proven of all the marketing techniques.

In Chapter 13, I'll tell you how to conduct an effective direct mail campaign for purposes of your own career development.

First, however, I want to show you in Chapter 12 exactly how to use proven direct mail copywriting techniques to make your "sales representative"...your resume...as compelling as it can possibly be, regardless of how it's delivered.

Your Personal Sales Representative

As an upwardly-mobile executive, you need a really good personal sales representative...one that can be where you can't be, and sell when you're not there.

You need a resume.

And it should be as persuasive as you can possibly make it. Indeed, it should be compelling enough to take on the hardest selling challenge of all: to make "cold calls" on complete strangers...and get results.

That's what a resume has to do as the core of a direct mail campaign. It arrives uninvited and unexpected. And usually it's assisted by nothing more than a brief covering letter. If it can convince someone who's never before met or heard about you to call you up or to write you a letter, then surely it can do everything else you could ask a resume to do.

You can trust such a resume to be your spokesman whenever you can't be present. Whether you leave it behind after a successful interview, or send it ahead hoping to get an appointment, it will give every recipient the same persuasive, ungarbled message you'd convey in person. Effective all by itself, your resume will also be an indispensable aid to anybody who wants to "sell" you to someone else...from the recruiter telling his client about you, to your potential boss telling *his* boss, to the CEO telling his Board.

Before we start creating your optimum "Sales Representative" resume, let's discuss why it's worth the effort, and dispose of your excuses for not making it.

It'$ your most valuable credential.

How long did you spend in undergraduate college...four years? And maybe in grad school after that...two to five years? And besides the time...the money? And for what?

Alphabet soup. Credentials! Stuff on paper that you hoped...and to some extent you've found...could enhance your earning power and career achievement, in addition to culturally enriching your life.

Suppose it takes you a month, at the outside, working every spare moment nights and weekends, to compile a succinct but compellingly information-packed recounting of what you've learned and achieved since college...the only things a potential employer really cares about and pays you $100,000+ for. The resume you wind up with is the most valuable credential you can have today. Again it's symbols on paper. But this time far more negotiable at the bank!

"I don't need a resume right now, since I'm not considering a change."

Great! Now's the ideal time to examine your career and demonstrate its value. Now...when you have the leisure and the objectivity to do a really thoughtful, comprehensive job.

Tomorrow's paper may bring news of an unexpected opening at a leading company in your industry...one that's likely to be filled from outside, and one where you could easily reach the decision-maker through networking, or maybe just by picking up the phone. He'll probably ask for your resume. Is it ready?

And shouldn't you also have your most persuasive possible resume on file at some of the top retainer recruiting firms? Why not prepare them to call you occasionally and tempt you with potentially breakthrough alternatives to the fine job you have now?

The "total immersion" study of your career and its accomplishments that's necessary to produce the ultimate "sales representative" resume will help...indeed force...you to size up (1) where you stand now relative to your long-range goals, and (2) how special you really are...or aren't...relative to your peers. Maybe you're already gaining momentum in the passing lane on the fast track. But maybe you're just cruising along an access road. There's no speed limit on your career, so why not step on the gas?

"I don't need a resume because it's classier not to have one."

Well, at least it's less work.

"I don't need a resume because I'm not looking. And when the prestigious retainer recruiter comes after me, he'll create my resume."

That's true; at least so it will seem to his client. Even if you hand him an excellent resume, his secretary will re-type it, so that it will appear consistent with the papers he presents on his other candidates.

But suppose he's got a really terrific opportunity for you...*and five other people.* Do you want to rest your case on what he'll write from memory after an hour or so of conversation? If you hand him a highly persuasive resume, he won't make it worse to match the rest. And if he has to write it, chances are he can't make it good enough to match the best.

"Fortunately, I don't have to bother writing my own resume; the people who fired me have paid for outplacement services."

Some things are more important to you and to your future than they are to anyone else. The document that positions you in the employment world is one of them.

Incidentally, three chapters from now (Chapter 15) we'll look at out-placement...another of the "Rites of Passage."

Okay, we've got the "why's" and "why not's" out of the way. Now let's talk about your ultimate credential, the true "Sales Representative" resume... strong enough for use in direct mail, and therefore best for every other use, too.

Direct mail selling is the hardest test persuasive writing can be put to. By mailing to large numbers of potential purchasers, it's possible to blanket so many that you'll surely hit a few who have a need at the exact moment your envelope arrives. But grabbing attention, engaging interest, and convincing strongly enough to stimulate action...that's still a lot to ask of mere words on paper. You'd better send something powerful. And the core of your package is your resume.

The only reason that a resume blown in through the window...or abandoned on an airliner...or delivered by the postman...prods any recipient into action is that it's an effective salesman. It's *a persuasive piece of writing* that communicates enticingly and fully enough to convince the reader that the person behind the resume might be the solution to the reader's problem.

That's what your resume is: your "Sales Representative" on paper, who'll speak for you when you can't be there. And that's true regardless of whether your resume:

1. *arrives "cold"* in the mail, or by accident, or

2. *is hand delivered*. . .by you yourself, or by someone who's met you, and wants another person to know you as fully and favorably as he does.

Indeed, as we shall see, a resume effective enough to perform in these situations will also be effective when:

3. *You offer it as an orientation aid at an interview.*

. . .And now for the shocker.
What's the number-one principle of direct mail copywriting?

In almost every industry, there's a bedrock principle discovered years ago. . .and reconfirmed again and again through the experience of everyone in the field. . .until it becomes the rule that all know and follow. In real estate, for example, it's:

"Location is everything."

Or, stated another way. . .

"The three principles of real estate are:
(1) location, (2) location, and (3) location."

In direct mail copywriting, as in real estate, success or failure is proven in dollars and cents. Before any company sends a mailing to 5 million or 15 million households, several different versions are tested, ranging from short to long copy, and trying new gimmicks, such as envelopes that look like bank statements, bills, and telegrams, etc. Objective: to see which variation pulls in the most orders per thousand dollars of cost.

Some of the new gimmicks test well and are used. Others are forgotten. But, like real estate, direct mail copywriting has one bedrock principle that everyone respects...proven during fifty years of testing and re-confirmed by test after test today:

"Long copy sells."

Proof of this honored axiom is delivered to your home every day. If shortness worked, brevity would be in your mailbox. And all the companies now using long-copy direct mail could achieve multi-million dollar savings in paper, printing, and postage...everything that makes a fat letter more expensive than a thin one. Those companies aren't stupid. They test. They don't spend more money unless the results *more* than justify the extra cost.

Incidentally, the experts tell me that the only exceptions to the "long copy sells" rule occur with simple products that every recipient is already thoroughly familiar with before the mailing arrives. In such cases, explanation of the *product* is unnecessary, because only the briefly-stated *offer* is new.

For example, you can sell someone a half-price subscription to *Time* or *Fortune* with a postcard or a little self-mailer envelope, whereas it will take several pages of facts and pictures to persuade the same person to sign up for a "four-months-free, cancel-and-pay-nothing" offer on a *new* publication.

When you get in touch with a prospective employer, you're always an unknown new publication. You're not *BusinessWeek, Forbes,* or *The Wall Street Journal,* and don't you forget it!

There are, of course, a few executives who might get by with brevity instead of a convincing dose of long copy. At the top of the next page is a note that one of those prominent people might use very effectively. Unfortunately, it probably wouldn't work for you or me.

```
Hello...

I've pretty much finished what I set out
to do here.

If you think I could be helpful to your
company, please give me a call.

                    Sincerely,



                    Lee Iacocca
```

John's Fire-in-the-Forest Analogy

I had a very successful career as a consumer products marketing executive before I got into executive recruiting 17 years ago, and I've thought many times about the question of *why* long copy invariably sells complicated, expensive items by direct mail much better than short copy does.

The experts either say:

"People need a certain amount of *convincing* to break down their barriers";

or they say:

"Who *cares* why? Experience proves that long copy works!"

Well, over the years I've come up with a little analogy which has helped satisfy my need for a "why," and it may strike a responsive chord with you, too.

Hitting people "cold" with a written sales pitch and taking them all the way from no-such-thought-anywhere-in-their-heads to the point of picking up a phone or a pen and taking action requires quite a process of change to take place step-by-step in their minds.

Think of the process as a chain reaction analogous to building a fire in the forest when you just have one match. Before you strike that match, you must have the entire makings of your fire all laid out. First you find some tinder...maybe an old Kleenex,® or some dry leaves. Then you add dry twigs and small dry sticks. Then some bigger sticks and branches...as dry as you can find. And on top of everything else some big branches and logs...dry, if possible, but if not, the other stuff burning under them will get them ready to burn. What you've assembled will keep the fire going all night, or at least long enough for you to round up more fuel.

You wouldn't dream of wasting your match by starting the chain reaction with only part of your fuel in place. You'd have everything ready. Otherwise, your fire might get off to a promising start...and then go out.

Something similar, I submit, must happen when a mailing convinces its reader to buy a complicated, expensive, seldom-purchased item. The letter must take him from complete unawareness and indifference...to first spark of interest...to casual but somewhat more interested reading...to avid devouring of all the information provided...to phoning or writing the sender. Since we know for a fact that short, sketchy copy doesn't perform as well as longer, more informative copy, I submit that the reason may be too little fuel.

The reader may have a first flicker of interest...which may grow into casual, and even attentive, reading. He's not yet convinced to make a phone call or write a letter. But he *is* willing to read further.

Suddenly the fuel runs out. The reader would have considered more information...*but it wasn't there!* And not deeply involved, he doesn't bother to send out for more facts.

You've got just one match. Don't waste it!

You have your reader's attention when he first glances at your resume...whether it blows in through the window or the mailman brings it. Your match is lit and burning. It ignites the dried leaves. But if you haven't laid out enough persuasive facts to fuel the chain reaction, your match is wasted. You've sparked attention. But there's no bonfire. And your phone doesn't ring.

> ### Q: What happens when you apply direct mail copywriting to your resume?
>
> ### A: It goes from 2 pages to 4, 5, or 6 pages... and it contains 4, 6, or 8 times as much of the persuasive information employers are interested in.

"Look, John," I'll bet you're saying, "forgetting for the moment the fact that everyone has always told me resumes should be brief, not long...and maybe conceding that the direct mail people do know about stimulating action through a written sales presentation...still I can't let you get away with saying that *doubling* the pages from two to four will *quadruple* the persuasive information."

I knew I'd grab you with that idea.

But think about it for a minute. On two pages you're barely able to list your name, address, office and home phone numbers, college degrees, a couple personal facts, and lay out a reverse-chronological listing of all the companies you've worked for and the progression of titles and responsibilities from college to now...all requisites of a good resume. Certainly that's true if you create a nice clean layout with lots of white space separating all the elements, so that where you've been and what you've done is easy to scan...a point we'll get back to later.

So in two pages, you *are* able to list all the job titles you've held and give a skimpy description of responsibilities for the more recent and important ones. Unfortunately, you haven't got room to say much, if anything, about what you *achieved* when you held those responsibilities. And achievements proving you're special are what a prospective employer is looking for.

Everyone has been given responsibility. Only a special few...you among them, I hope...have given back anything really substantial in the way of achievement.

Let's say that in a nice, open, quick-to-scan layout, with your chronological units floating in a decent amount of white space, you get 400 to 500 words on a page, 800 to 1,000 on two pages...and 75% of them are devoted to covering the mandatory data. That leaves about 200 to 250 words for accomplishments that could make you stand out as interesting...and hopefully special...in the eyes of a potential employer.

Now go from two pages to four. You've got room for 1,600 to 2,000 words...800 to 1,000 more than before. And *every additional word* can be devoted to achievements, because the basics were already covered in the two-page version. Add your original 200 to 250 words on achievements, and the box score looks like this:

	TOTAL WORDS	BASIC DATA (WORDS)	ACHIEVEMENTS (WORDS)	% INCREASE IN ACHIEVEMENT WORDS
2 Pages	800–1000	600–750	200–250	—
4 Pages	1600–2000	600–750	1000–1250	400%
5 Pages	2000–2500	600–750	1400–1750	600%
6 Pages	2400–3000	600–750	1800–2250	800%

> **But now let's go back to the point about everyone telling you to keep your resume brief. Who told you? And when? And why?**

Who and When?

Was it your "Counselor" at the contingency firm that helped you get your first job out of college or graduate school? Was it someone who "worked with" you or "headhunted" you as you moved into middle management with your second or third job?

Face it: in those days you hadn't done anything really significant yet. At that stage no one has. Or if they have, nobody is prepared to believe they have.

From entry level up through middle management you're somewhere from a "GI Joe" to a first lieutenant in the army of industry. What an employer wants to know is where you've been. . .how fast you're moving up. . .and how closely your experience matches what he wants done. That information fits neatly on one page. . .certainly no more than two. Indeed, if you're bright, attractive, and ambitious, it won't matter if your entire early career has been spent working on a string of corporate *flops!* You won't be blamed. You didn't commit the corporation to those misadventures. And you weren't so centrally responsible for implementation that anyone will figure you made a good idea fail.

Today, however, you're in an altogether different situation. You're at or reaching for $100,000 +. Now you're at least a "field commander." You legitimately *can* claim some victories. And you can be held responsible for some defeats. *Your resume must deliver more factual information.*

Also consider the "why" behind the advice you're given.

If you're now at $100,000 +, and *"when"* you were told to "keep it brief" was yesterday, and *"who"* told you was a prestigious retainer recruiter. . .then maybe we should consider *"why"* he said that.

The most obvious reason is that you only have a fleeting moment of your reader's time and attention before he'll give up on your resume as too tedious to figure out, and toss it aside. *This reason I totally agree with.* However, I don't agree that the solution to the problem is to strip away your persuasive factual information.

The other reason could be that the retainer recruiter has orally "presold" you to his client, so your resume doesn't have to be persuasive.

My reaction to this reason from your standpoint is "OK...*but.*" The recruiter is introducing several other candidates besides you, and if you have some impressive achievements, you want them clearly known to the employer as he chooses between you and the others.

Your resume must perform two functions. Brevity suits one...and defeats the other.

Your resume absolutely must do two things. Unfortunately, while brevity achieves one, it defeats the other. Therefore, unless you're Lee Iacocca, brevity isn't your answer.

1.   Quick Orientation

Your reader will allow your resume only about thirty seconds...no more than a minute...to orient him to who you are, and whether you might be relevant to his needs right now. Certainly that's true if it arrives "cold" in the mail or is blown in through the window; he'll spend *more* time with it, not less, if he's paid a retainer recruiter over $30,000 to look for it.

Most of the time your resume will reach the reader when he doesn't need you. Your "one match" will burn less than a minute. By then, if you've done a poor orientation job, he'll have dumped you for being too tedious and confusing. And even if you've done a good job, he'll almost always have dumped you for not being needed right now.

2.   Thorough Convincing

But in the rare, rare instance when you do happen to hit a reader at the moment he has a need you might fill, and you quickly orient him to that fact, then he's willing to extend his attention span a bit further.

He didn't find you irrelevant. Now he's looking to find you ordinary. But, wait a minute; you've been involved in several things that were impressively successful...another "turn off" bypassed. Okay, but probably those programs were conceived, planned, and strategically implemented by others, and you were merely a supporting player. No, wait another minute; your clear, succinct explanation of the reasons underlying the actions that were taken certainly sounds like you were the strategist, not just the "gofer." Your reader decides:

> "This guy is *interesting*. I'll read to the end. And then I'll go back over this whole thing again. If he still looks okay, maybe I'll even call him up."

As you see, a very brief resume could have performed the quick orientation and helped your reader turn off. Unfortunately, it probably couldn't have turned him on...and on...and on...to the point of picking up the phone and calling you.

> **Fortunately, a resume written according to the "long copy sells" principle of direct mail copywriting is capable of walking and chewing gum at the same time.**

Right away you're probably saying, "I can see, John, where long copy will be great at 'Thorough Convincing,' but won't it interfere with 'Quick Orientation'?"

No. Not if you're careful to make your resume *visually accessible*. Format and layout become extremely important. Just make your resume:

Scannable!

Your reader will glance at 3, 4, 5, or 6 pages if it's instantly evident with just one glance what's on each of those pages. If you arrange your resume right, the recipient will probably glance through *all* of the pages before reading *any* of them. That's everyone's normal impulse as a reader anyway. You probably flipped through this book before you began reading it page-by-page. Fortunately, with resumes in particular, it's easy to help that normal human tendency along.

Don't you just hate topically-oriented resumes?
Don't you wish everyone did?

I have never yet met anyone who likes to receive a topically-oriented resume.

You know the kind...where practically the whole thing is a list of claimed accomplishments, presented entirely out of context of when they happened...who the executive was working for...what his title, responsibilities, reporting relationships, and staff were...and what the size and nature of the businesses were. Finally, if you're lucky...and it's not always there...you find a deliberately sketchy little "Chronology of Employment" buried at the end, from which...if you're not already too turned off...you try to guess when and for whom and from what position of how much authority those previously-claimed management miracles were achieved.

You and I are in the overwhelming majority in disliking topically-oriented resumes (also sometimes euphemistically referred to as "achievement-oriented"). When on the receiving end, virtually everybody prefers the good, honest, comfortable, easy-to-read old-fashioned kind, where name, address, and business and home phone numbers are at the top, and work history proceeds backwards from current job on the first page to earliest on the last page.

Everyone's recognition of...and preference for...
the standard-format resume solves your "scannability"
problem, without getting you into the brevity trap.

If you don't go out of your way to confuse your reader, you've got the scannability problem solved...no matter how long you choose to make your resume.

Everyone in a position to read the resume of anyone at or reaching for $100,000+ has read hundreds of resumes before. If yours is in standard reverse-chronology format, and each employer/time/position copy-block floats in enough white space to make it clear where one segment ends and the earlier one begins, *your reader will go on automatic pilot. . .* scanning through any number of pages in just a very few seconds.

One page or five, he quickly sees that you're *not* somebody he can use right now. But if by stroke of lightning you happen to have dropped into his hands at precisely the time he *does* need someone with a background even remotely like yours, he'll read on. . .and on. Having your entire "fire" laid out, you've got an excellent chance that your reader will proceed all the way from flicker-of-interest to action. Expect a phone call or a letter!

Not only does the standard reverse-chronology resume solve the scannability problem; it's also more convincing, because it's more straightforward.

Forget about "long copy sells." Assume that two resumes, one reverse-chronological and the other topical, are *the same length. . .any length.*

The one that deliberately strips away the employment context from the claimed accomplishments not only frustrates the reader's comprehension, *it also raises the presumption that there must have been some very good reason for doing so.* "This guy obviously has something to hide," thinks the reader. "I wonder what it is."

Usually it's too-brief tenure at the latest or two latest jobs. . .and maybe at lots of jobs along the way. That's what the reader immediately suspects. And readily confirms, if a truthful "chronology" is included anywhere in the resume. And assumes if it's not.

Wanting to de-emphasize their latest job and not put it at the top of a reverse-chronological list is overwhelmingly the reason executives turn to a topically-oriented resume. . .even though when they're personally hiring, they hate to receive one. That's a mistake. It's better to deal with the problem straightforwardly.

Turn the page for a successful lead-off entry for a reverse-chronological resume:

1988 (9 months)

FLY-BY-NIGHT SCHLOCK ELECTRONICS CORP.

Vice President - Engineering

> After seven years of increasing responsibility at Bell Laboratories Division of AT&T, I was recruited as Chief Engineering Officer of this fast-growing four-year-old maker of video games and electronic gambling devices ('87 sales, $22.5 million), by the Founder/CEO, who'd been his own chief engineer.
>
> Six months later, I still hadn't received the equity stake which was a primary incentive to join, and still hadn't been allowed to install any of the operating changes I felt could benefit the company. So I proposed and the Chairman agreed that I should re-distribute my duties to subordinates and seek a situation where I can assume a more assertive role.

1979 - 1988

BELL LABORATORIES DIVISION, AT&T

Group Director - Laser Engineering Department

By the third paragraph on the top page of his resume, the writer is back to talking about the AT&T chronology and the accomplishments he *loves* to discuss. Above all, he hasn't been forced into a topical resume...a cure far worse than his mild disease.

If you're right, John, that almost everyone prefers to read standard-format resumes, why do people write the other kind? And do the executives who *write* them *also* dislike receiving them?

Questions I've always been curious about, too. So I've checked into them with the people who've handed me topical resumes over the past 17 years.

Invariably, once we got down to talking frankly, these people pointed out problems similar to the one I just dealt with, which made them feel they were forced to give up the standard reverse-chronological format. I can't recall a single person maintaining that he went to the topical format because that's the type he preferred to receive.

> **And now, maestro...an appropriate drum roll
> and cymbal crash as we unveil a sample resume
> written according to the "long copy sells" principle
> of direct mail copywriting.**

It's from Sam Sage, one of the many executives you'll meet when you view an executive search through the eyes of a retainer recruiter in Appendix III.

As you look at Sam's resume...begin by doing what everyone always does with a resume. *Scan* it for a few seconds.

What function does Sam perform?

Who's he done it for?

How long has he been at it?

See if Sam's someone you might need right now. Chances are he's not. And you'll see that at a glance.

Next...before you actually read the resume...do me a favor. Ask yourself:

Could a shorter resume have turned you off any faster?

Would Sam be any further ahead if it had?

Having scanned the resume, do me another favor. Change the fact situation. Pretend that you now have even the slightest...the weakest possible...glimmer of interest in someone even remotely like Sam. For that reason, you're inclined to begin *reading* the resume.

Are you interested enough to continue from page 1 to page 2?

From page 2 to 3? All the way to the end?

Face it. If you're not interested enough to spend the two or three extra minutes it'll take you to finish reading about Sam, you're certainly not interested enough to call him up and kill an hour or two meeting him face-to-face.

Finally, after you *have* read all the way to the end, ask yourself:

Could Sam have "sold" you better with a shorter resume?

Would knowing less about Sam have made you like him more?

What information could he have withheld in order to *really* turn you on?

And is that information anything that even the briefest one-page resume *could* conceal?

SAMUEL P. SAGE
219 Warringer Drive
Denton, New Jersey 07299

Home: 201) 719-0932
Office: (212) 121-3000

1983 – Present

FARRINGTON LABORATORIES
(Merged into Pan Global Pharmaceuticals Ltd. in November '88)
New York, New York

<u>Vice President – Chief Marketing Officer</u>

Recruited to this privately-owned $500 million maker of prescription drugs as Vice President – Chief Marketing Officer by Blair Farrington, Founder/Owner/CEO in 1983, when sales were $224 million.

Mr. Farrington doubled what I'd been making in the same position at the much larger (then $590 million) Swiss-owned Medica Suisse USA Ltd. But the primary incentive was this 72 year old gentleman's plan to take the business public with me as his successor, after we worked a few years together to increase volume and improve profitability. Instead, the company has been purchased by...and merged into...Pan Global Pharmaceuticals (November '88). With their acquiescence, I'm seeking a new challenge... hopefully a Presidency; otherwise Chief Marketing Officer with early transition to general management.

Following (with Mr. Farrington's permission) is a summary of the company's performance since I joined in '83 and 3 years prior:

	Sales ($millions)	% Change	Pre-Tax Net ($millions)	% Change	% ROI
'88	507.2	+31.5	84.6	+62.4	28.1
'87	385.7	+24.9	52.1	+52.3	24.6
'86	308.8	+36.1	34.2	+43.1	17.2
'85	226.9	+23.2	23.9	+39.8	12.7
'84	184.2	-17.7	17.1	+81.9	9.4
'83	223.8	-2.4	9.4	-16.8	3.6
'82	229.4	+4.5	11.3	+6.6	4.9
'81	219.6	+7.2	10.6	+8.2	5.7
'80	204.9	+6.1	9.8	-1.1	9.1

The product line was reduced from 618 SKU's in '83 to 309 profitable items in '86 (expanded with new products to 384 by '88). 109-person sales force was reorganized into 11 regions in '84 and expanded to 225 people by '88.

Nine profitable new drugs were introduced via cross-licensing agreements with other manufacturers ('88 sales, $129 million; $31 million pre-tax net), and $11.7 million pre-tax was generated by granting licenses to other companies.

SAMUEL P. SAGE - 2

Physicians' top-of-mind brand-name awareness of our three largest-selling drugs was raised from 18% in '83 to 62% in '88 by a massive sampling, detailing, and professional advertising campaign (budget tripled from $9.4 million in '83 to $29.1 million in '88).

As a result of Farrington Labs' excellent growth trend and high profitability, Pan Global paid 30 times estimated '89 earnings in a 50%-cash/50%-stock transaction.

1980 - 1983

MEDICA SUISSE USA LTD.
Marshall Plains, New Jersey

Vice President - Pharmaceutical Marketing

Rejoined this $1.8 billion Zurich-based maker of prescription drugs, veterinary biologicals, and fine chemicals as Director of Pharmaceutical Marketing, reporting to the Managing Director - USA, and heading all marketing and sales for all North American pharmaceutical lines (total '80 sales, $315 million) after a two-year hiatus to aid my family's automobile business in Ohio.

By 1983 sales were nearly double ($550 million) 1980 volume, and ROI had increased from 17% ('80) to 24% ('83). Market share of U.S. prescription tranquilizer market rose from 11.6% in '80 to 19.2% in '83, and veterinary products gained 1.3 share points to 7.2% in '83.

My earlier recommendation (in '78) that the company's consumer pet-health lines be sold to generate cash for acquisition of young growth companies in the higher-margined ethical drug field was implemented while I was away ('79), and I helped identify and purchase in '80 and '81 three small companies...BioTRITON, Radio-Tra-Chem, and Synestial Laboratories...which have all grown and prospered under Medica Suisse ownership. One of these, BioTRITON, was publicly reported as having worldwide sales of $280 million in '87, with the highest ROI of any Medica Suisse business anywhere in the world.

'81   Vice President – Pharmaceutical Marketing.   Promotion in title, no change in duties.

'80   Director – Pharmaceutical Marketing.   Rejoined Medica Suisse in charge of corporate Marketing, Market Research, Telemarketing, and Sales Promotion departments (totalling 41 people); plus two sales forces...Ethical Drug (135-person) and Veterinary (32-person).

1978 – 1980

SAGE CHRYSLER/TOYOTA, INC.
Kensington, Ohio

Upon my father's sudden death (2/78), I took charge of the family business ($1.4

SAMUEL P. SAGE - 3

million sales in '78; $2.2 million '80), holding it together until my younger brother could finish his MBA at Wharton ('79) and join my mother in running the company.

Increased TV advertising, and diversified by building two Wendy's hamburger franchises (since expanded to seven). Profits nearly doubled in two years.

1976 - 1978

<u>MEDICA SUISSE USA LTD.</u>
Marshall Plains, New Jersey

<u>Group Product Director</u>

Invited to join my client from New World Advertising Agency as Group Product Director (with 4 Product Managers and 5 Assistant PM's), in charge of:

(1) Marketing existing U.S. lines...$34 million consumer (Krueger's flea-and-tick collars and home remedies for pets) and $48 million professional ($21 million veterinary and $27 million human prescription drugs); and

(2) Introducing new family of prescription tranquilizers (Dopatreem) for Rx sales in the U.S.

Since introduction of a major new Rx drug is impossible without a large field force (and Medica Suisse had only 22 salesmen carrying both Rx and veterinary lines), I cut off advertising on all lines for 10 months; used the cash flow to build a 100-person field force calling only on MD's; and launched a $10 million sampling and ad campaign for the Dopatreem line.

Result: 14 months after introduction, Dopatreem and Dopatreem X were #2 and #5 tranquilizers in the U.S., with $220 million combined annualized rate of sales. Profit from Rx lines was then temporarily diverted to help rebuild other lines to all-time high share levels.

1972 – 1976

NEW WORLD ADVERTISING AGENCY
New York, New York

Vice President – Account Group Supervisor

Joined as Account Executive on $19 million Whiskers cat food account when the AE on my P&G business moved to New World as Account Supervisor and asked me to join him. Through growth of Whiskers and acquiring new accounts, became VP – Account Group Supervisor in charge of $51 million in billings (4 AE's and 3 Assistant AE's) from Megopolitan Foods ($38 million on Whiskers and Arf! brands) and Medica Suisse ($7 million on consumer items and $6 million on veterinary and Rx human drugs).

SAMUEL P. SAGE - 4

As AE in '72, led the task force that "re-staged" Whiskers brand with CLIO-winning "Caesar-the-Cat" TV commercials and portion-control packaging that doubled Whiskers' market share from 5% ('72) to 11.2% ('76). Factory sales rose from $53 million ('72) to $149 million ('76) and advertising rose from $9 million to $26 million. Led successful solicitation of $7 million Arf! dog food account ('73), which billed $12 million in '76 (sales rose from $32 million to $79 million). Personally brought in Krueger's flea-and-tick collars ($4 million in '74) from Medica Suisse, which consolidated all their North American business with us in '75.

'75   Vice President - Account Group Supervisor.   26% 12-month sales increase in Krueger's flea collars, etc. from Medica Suisse enabled us to win their veterinary and prescription drug accounts..the first medical advertising handled by New World. Promoted for building of Megopolitan and Medica Suisse accounts.

'74   Account Supervisor.   Turnaround on Whiskers enabled us to land $7 million Arf! dog food billings ('73) and Krueger's consumer pet items ('74).

'72   Account Executive.   Entered on the Whiskers account with assignment to stem share decline (averaging 0.9 point per year since '67).

1969 – 1972

PROMOTE & GAMBOL COMPANY
Cincinnati, Ohio

'71 Assistant Brand Manager. Handled $16 million TV & print media and $4 million sales promotion budget on GLOSS-X floor cleaner. Promoted to head successful test marketing and regional expansion of new GLOSS-O floor wax.

'69 Brand Assistant. Traditional P&G home office and field sales training assignments; handled TV copy testing for Soft-Ah! paper products.

EDUCATION: BA, University of Michigan, 1966
MBA, Harvard Business School, 1969

PERSONAL: Born June 1, 1944.
Married, 3 children.
6' 1", 185 lbs.

Could Sam have made you like him better by omitting something you just read?

And if so, could even the shortest one-page resume have concealed that *particular* "something"?

You scanned Sam's resume in seconds.

You saw at a glance that he's a *marketing* executive. And a very *high-level* one.

Is there any kind of resume, no matter how brief. . .or any kind of letter, no matter how vague and misleading. . .that could have hidden Sam's basic information from you? And could he have benefitted from the concealment, even if it were possible?

I don't think so.

If you didn't need what Sam was selling, merely limiting your knowledge couldn't have increased your need.

But if you'd had even the slightest interest in anyone even remotely like Sam, then seeing how very special he is would have made you more. . . not less. . .interested.

Indeed, Sam even managed to tell you that he believes he's ready to be a president; to imply that he's recently been functioning almost like one; and to demonstrate over and over that he certainly thinks like one.

You saw, too, that Sam's been transplanted several times and has succeeded in each new context. . .even running the family car dealership. He's versatile. And his sense of loyalty. . .as extended to his mother and brother. . .is also admirable.

About the only thing you could imagine Sam wanting to hide is the fact that he's spent the most-recent and highest-level part of his career marketing *drugs*. . .a fact which, if known, might turn off a CEO looking for someone to market anti-aircraft missiles or panty hose.

But Sam can't even *name* his employers without letting his "drug experience" out of the bag. And no CEO. . .indeed, no reader. . .is going to be turned on by self-praise in mere "percentage" terms by someone who refuses to reveal who he's worked for until *after* he's been granted an interview. Straight to the wastebasket with a letter or resume like that!

After reading Sam's resume, you and I suspect that he could market just about anything...missiles and stockings included. Nonetheless, no retainer recruiter being paid $30,000+ to find a "defense" or a "soft goods" person can get by with just offering Sam plus a "he-could-do-it" pitch...even though Sam might make a good "wild card," tucked in among several "on-target" candidates.

On the other hand, if Sam can somehow get the resume we've just read into the hands of the CEO of an armaments or a hosiery company *before* he's paying somebody $30,000+ to find exactly what he wants, the CEO may think:

> "What the hell? It won't cost anything just to meet this Sam Sage. He's done some very impressive things. And frankly, most of the marketing people in our industry don't impress me at all. Marketing is *marketing!* A smart outsider like Sage might just show us a few tricks we never thought of."

Face it. Despite any kooky advice to the contrary, there's no way Sam can "package" himself differently for different employers. So he's being straightforward. And he's right! Just like you and me, others will also admire Sam's achievements...their diversity...and *the thinking behind them.* They too will envision him doing an outstanding job, no matter where he ends up.

No question about it. Sam's taken the best possible approach with his resume. He's told the *truth* openly, voluntarily, and impressively.

David Ogilvy knew what he was talking about when he said:

> "The more you tell, the more you sell!"

Notice that Sam used narrative paragraphs, rather than "bullets" to tell his story.

There are two common approaches to presenting a work history. One is to use paragraphs, with each job written up as a mini-essay. The other is to use "bullets"...sentence fragments preceded by a raised dot. Pioneered by advertising copywriters, the "bullet" format attempts to make every single point seem like a highlight.

Either style is acceptable. But, for several reasons, I strongly prefer paragraphs...very tightly and specifically written. Sentences in paragraphs are easier for the reader to comprehend and believe, because they closely resemble what he sees in newspapers, magazines, books, and other informational writing. Bullets, on the other hand, resemble advertising copy...subliminally *not* an aid to believability.

Also, sentences in paragraphs enable you to use transition phrases and conjunctions that *connect* the various statements in ways that serve your purposes better than a series of unrelated exclamations. It helps to be able to say: "In recognition, I was promoted to..." "When my report was accepted by the Board, I was asked to assemble a team..." "After consolidating these three acquisitions..." You get the idea.

Sam also made his resume factual and concrete...something many people have trouble doing. Here are a few tips:

Orient your reader with specifics.

For each management-level job, orient your reader to the size, nature, and trend of (1) the larger unit in which you participated and (2) the part of it you were responsible for. What was the size of your operation in people, sales, and profit? What was its mandate? The general business climate around it? The problems and opportunities you identified? The strategies you came up with? And the results you achieved?

Use numbers wherever possible.

Focus on quantifiable data. Give dollar figures for sales, profits, ROI, costs, inventories, etc. before and after your programs were implemented. When you use percentages, you'll usually want to give the *base*...plus any comparative figures on the rest of the industry or another part of your company that will show your numbers are special.

Avoid empty words and statements.

Omit the self-praising adjectives that losers wallow in...''major,'' ''significant,'' ''substantial,'' and ''outstanding.'' Wherever such a word is justified, a number will be far more persuasive. And never make meaningless over-generalized statements like this:

> ''Responsible for managing the strategic technical issues impacting the company's on-going core businesses.''

What does this person do all day? What's his budget? Who does he report to and who reports to him? Has his employer gained anything from having him around?

Create a mosaic.

You've seen those pictures made out of lots of little colored stones. Imagine that each promotion to a new job, each numerical improvement, each specific point of analysis and strategy is a stone. When put together in the right order, these fragments will be connected by your reader into an image of you. Don't assert what the shape of it is. Just lay out enough specific facts...stone by stone...so he'll see for himself the favorable patterns they imply. Let him create his own picture in his own mind.

If you'd like to change industries or career fields, consider making a second version of your resume... but even then, don't switch to topical organization.

Maybe you're in a declining field and you'd like to move into a growth industry. Or you're re-entering the commercial sector after a sojourn in the military, government, or academia. If so, make a special version of your resume that drains off industry-specific buzz-words and explains your exploits in terms everyone can appreciate. But resist the temptation to ''go topical'' and try to hide ''where'' while emphasizing ''what.''

Your reader will never quite be able to believe your claimed achievements unless he has a mental picture of you located at some specific place and time in the real world actually doing them. Withdraw orientation, and he drops belief. . .and probably attention, too.

Rather than resort to a topical resume, you should:

1.   Write a covering letter that says what *specific need* your reader may have that you from another field can fill for him in his field. Don't say, "Here I am; guess what I can do for you."

2.   Send your resume and covering letter to *three times as many* prospective employers as I recommend when you're changing jobs in your own field. You not only have to find the statistically rare few who need you *right now;* you have to find the even rarer subset who are also creative and open-minded enough to take a chance on someone from outside their industry.

Should you include a "career objective"?

Many resumes begin with a statement of what-kind-of-job-I-want labeled *"Career Objective,"* or simply *"Objective."*

This is a good idea when you're fresh out of college or grad school and you want to orient the "Counselor" at an employment agency, or the personnel department of a corporation, to what you're looking for. But it's seldom necessary after your career is well underway. By then, what you're prepared to do next should be pretty evident from what you've already done.

If you're retiring from the military or the diplomatic corps, or leaving academia or the priesthood, then maybe your resume should begin with a statement of what you seek in the business world. Otherwise, let your resume be a clear and self-confident statement of where you've been and what you've achieved. Say what you're looking for in your covering letter and through personal contact.

Creative Use of Avocational Interests in Your Resume

In general, *never mention* your hobbies and other outside interests.

If you had time to be a vestryman of your church, chair the United Fund drive, coach a Little League team, build an extension on your home, train for and run a marathon, and groom and show poodles in the U.S. and three foreign countries last year, when did you have time to work?

But if you're 58 years old, it might be good to mention your marathon running, and the fact that you're an avid scuba diver and an instructor for Outward Bound. Your stamp collection, of course, will remain in the closet.

And if you're a paraplegic, your competitive sports car driving and skeet shooting might just be a worthwhile inclusion. So might building that wing on your house, if you're missing only one arm or one leg.

If you just have a high school diploma, the fact that you're an amateur writer who's published stories in *Harper's* and *The New Yorker*...or even a trade journal or the business section of your daily newspaper... could help show that you have a mature, cultivated mind others respect. So might your membership on the Mayor's Commission for the Arts, writing computer programs as a hobby, creating mathematical puzzles, and playing duplicate bridge.

And if you're in a racial or ethnic minority and have the stomach for such a gambit, you may feel like listing your memberships in exclusive social and athletic clubs that, until recently, didn't seem to have people with names or faces like yours. Everyone else should maintain a discrete silence on all clubs.

**Now, as we wind up on resumes,
let's look at several other items of
purely personal information and how to handle them.**

Age

Don't fall into the trendy trap of leaving age off your resume and omitting years from college degrees so it can't be calculated. True, employers can't ask. But voluntarily listing year, month, and day of birth subliminally shouts "forthright and cooperative," whereas concealing age just because the law permits you to do so sends out the opposite "vibes". . .and raises a presumption that *you* think you may be over the hill.

Incidentally, employers who, in the late '60's and early '70's, considered 30 to 35 the ideal age now seem to feel that way regarding mid-to-late-40's, and they have virtually no qualms about dynamic people in their 50's. They still find a young hotshot attractive. But they no longer insist on one. I absolutely refuse to discriminate on the basis of age, and have recently had candidates in their late 50's win out over excellent candidates ten and twenty years younger.

Education

List college degrees, *with years*. . .highest and latest degree first. Forget about Cum Laude, Class President, and Varsity Letters. You've moved on to more recent and bigger achievements.

If you have several years but no sheepskin, say: "Completed three years toward B.A. at Syracuse University." And if you flunked out of several fine schools, say: "Two years of college, intermittently at Carleton, Dartmouth, and the University of Virginia." With no college, you may want to say, "Self-educated during an uninterrupted career," and then bail yourself out under the heading "Other Interests," with some suitably cerebral and cultural avocations.

Marital Status

Say "Married," "Divorced," or "Single," whichever applies and, if you wish, number of children (not names, ages, or with how many and which mates).

Gender

If you're a woman with a name like Lindsay or Leslie, or a man with a name like Carroll or Kelley, use a middle name to be more specific... or just let your reader be surprised when he meets you.

Height and Weight

Nice to put in if it's favorable; although women often omit weight because it seems sexist to raise the subject. Overweight men and women might consider listing an optimistic weight toward which they're dieting, as a way of cushioning the inevitable visual shock with some advance notice.

Religion, Politics, and National Origin

Silence!   If the reader has a prejudice, you may stimulate it.

Race

Probably silence. For all minorities but Black, surnames dispell any impending visual surprise...hardly a major consideration anyway. For the Black who wants to dispel surprise, mentioning support of any obviously Black institution...possibly along with similar non-racially-defined institutions...will do the trick.

Health

Don't mention. It's fine, or you should be writing a will instead of a resume.

Picture

Never, *NEVER, NEVER!* Nobody could possibly be attractive enough to justify the narcissism implied by attaching a picture.

13

Orbiting Your Spy-in-the-Sky Satellite

Now that your resume has been strengthened by the "long-copy-sells" principle of direct mail copywriting, let's use it to launch a direct mail campaign...the nearest thing to scanning the globe via spy-in-the-sky satellite to find the opportunities you should know about.

Delivered by mail, a powerful resume can truly "be where you can't be and sell when you're not there."

And unlike every other method, direct mail can almost limitlessly be increased in power, when you're eager to change jobs. It can also be targeted toward exactly what you want, in terms of industry, size of company, location, or any other set of criteria.

Moreover, a direct mail campaign can be modified to perform its unique functions *secretly*. **Believe it or not, you can use this powerful medium without letting your current employer discover you're "looking."**

This chapter will tell you everything you need to know to make sophisticated use of direct mail: how many letters to send, who to send them to, what to say in your covering note...and how to keep your current employer from finding out, if you want to look for a better job without risking the one you have.

The Accident of Timing

Timing is the problem.

Don't you wish we could simultaneously crack open every job that might advance your career...and do so at precisely the time you're considering a move? We'd schedule all the appropriate retirements, firings, and additions-to-staff just when they'd create ideal options for you. Then, with just a few calls to your personal contacts, and a few networking visits, and just a handful of letters, you'd be invited to explore plenty of exciting opportunities.

Regrettably, Murphy's law of career opportunity works the opposite way. Virtually all the jobs you'd be most interested in will be *filled* at the moment you decide to make a change.

Every company needs you at least once in ten years.

Unfortunately, the overwhelming odds are that they won't need you within the ten days to ten weeks that your inquiry will be considered current.

Face it. No matter how appropriate you are for a particular company, and no matter how much you'd like to work for them, and no matter who you're able to talk to inside that company...when they don't need you, they won't hire you. Appropriateness and desire don't count, if timing is off.

On the other hand, in the rare instance when the right need does exist, a compelling resume and a good covering letter will usually get you considered.

But notice of your interest must arrive at *exactly* the right time. For perhaps ten days to ten weeks, your inquiry will be considered current. Later than that, you'll be presumed to have found what you were looking for, if you're really good. And if you haven't, you'll be presumed *not* to be as good as you seemed. And if you *have* relocated, but are still willing to entertain something more attractive so soon after moving, you'll be presumed to be unstable, unethical, or both.

Harsh and unfair presumptions! But they're almost universal. Might as well face them...and work around them.

Now for the bad...and good...news:

"Playing the numbers game" with direct mail is lots of work.

However, if you're willing to do it right, you're almost certain to succeed.

The beauty of direct mail is that, depending on how hard you're willing to work, you can infinitely increase the number of contacts you make until you reach enough employers to be virtually certain that at least a few will actually need someone like you at the time you write in.

Everyone's odds are different, of course. But on average, they're about *9 to 1 in favor* of an aggressive direct mail campaign being successful for virtually everyone who makes an unrelenting effort.

On the other hand, the odds are about *199 to 1 against* the possibility that any one *letter* will arrive at the moment someone like the sender is actually needed. And the way the laws of probability work, you can't be sure that by sending only 200 letters you will actually hit one recipient who has a need. To have a statistical shot at hitting on 1 out of 200 letters, *you must send at least 1,000 letters*. From those, you can probably expect to receive about 5 or 6 interested replies...an average of approximately 1 for each 200 letters sent out.

So here's the formula for your direct mail campaign:

Send 1,000 letters...not less.

Expect to receive 5 or 6 affirmative replies...not more.

**But if you do it right, those 5 or 6 meaningful replies
should lead to 3 or 4 interviews
and 2 or 3 offers of almost exactly what you want.**

When I lay out these numbers, most people say:

"But, John, can't I get by with *less* than 1,000 letters?"

And my answer is always the same:

"Absolutely! You only need six letters. The problem is: *which six?*"

You could be very lucky and have your first six letters bring encouragement. On the other hand, the last six might be the ones that pay off. And if you get less than six interested responses, you might get the two or three that lead to offers...or you might get the two or three where you interview but *don't* receive an offer.

Success is very likely, if you're willing to operate within the realm of *statistics*. But if you insist on merely *gambling*, then just send one letter. Or six, or 600, or 900. The closer you get to 1,000, the better you ought to do. But don't complain to me that your results are disappointing if you send out less than 1,000 letters. You need at least that many to bypass mere chance and latch onto statistical probability.

And of course the odds I'm quoting assume that you're seeking a position for which you'll seem obviously relevant. If you're attempting a drastic switch of career fields, or if you're trying to overcome an apparent deficiency in your background or a glaring failure in your track record, you should probably double or triple the threshold number of 1,000 letters, in order to be realistic about the response you're likely to get.

"John, I hate the idea of 1,000 letters just to ante into the game."

"On the other hand, I love the idea of 3 or 4 interviews and 2 or 3 offers out of just 6 affirmative replies."

"Why such good odds after such poor ones?"

The reason you do so well after having done so poorly is that, although only a very few employers need what you're offering at the time you write, those few who *respond* will be the ones who *do* have a need. The only reason they get in touch with you is because they feel they might want to hire you.

And if you've done a good job on your mailing, the openings you'll be called about will be ones you prefer and are qualified for. And, of course, those are precisely the jobs you're likely to interview successfully for and wind up getting.

Also, since you're taking the initiative, rather than waiting for a recruiter to contact you, there's a good chance that your mailing may arrive before the employer hires a recruiter. If so, you won't face the usual stiff competition from five or six additional recruiter-supplied candidates. Not only do you find out about the job; you're early enough to have a better-than-usual shot at getting it.

Whether by phone or letter, your positive reply will say, "Let's meet." Anything else is a negative reply.

Typical "positives":

> "I'm going to Europe for two weeks. Call me after the 15th so we can arrange to get together."

OR

> "I'm turning your material over to Jane Cole, President of
> our Keystone Division. You should be hearing from her within
> the next couple weeks. If not, give me a call."

Typical "negative":

> "You sound absolutely wonderful! We'll remember you for-
> ever, and call you just as soon as anything arises here that
> might be of interest to you."

Unless there's an appropriate opening within just ten or so weeks after
your mailing is received, you won't hear anything further. You'll be
sandbagged by the twin presumptions that (1) if you're very good you'll
have been hired by then and (2) if you're not hired by then, you probably weren't very good. Moreover, there'll be little reason to dig deeper
than ten weeks into the files, because similarly attractive and more current mailings will have arrived since yours came in.

"But how can I possibly find 1,000 companies I might want to work for?"

Don't worry, you can...there are plenty of reference books to help you.

Perhaps only a dozen companies in your industry...or less...pop to
mind as obvious places to pursue your upwardly-mobile career. If so...
and if you're in no hurry...then maybe you should map out a program
of "targeted networking" to reach the CEO or another officer you should
be in touch with in those companies.

When you're not committed to a near-term move, about the only use
you'll make of direct mail is to send your "sales representative" resume to the leading retainer recruiting firms, so that they'll know about
you and perhaps call when they undertake projects in your field. A list
of firms is included as Appendix II of this book.

But when you're eager to move, it's time to launch your "spy satellite," and you've got to send out at least 1,000 letters to lift it into orbit.

Then the procedure...although arduous...is simple.

Make friends with the reference librarian at your nearest large public, university, or corporate library and ask to see all the directories listing companies you might want to work for. Appendix I of this book will familiarize you with the available references beforehand, and will alert you to pertinent books your library may not have. Narrow your choice to the two or three volumes that interest you most, and settle down with the one you consider first-priority.

Every book, or its sub-sections, will be organized alphabetically. Pore over the pages one-by-one. Glance at each entry from "A" to "Z," noting size of company, location, product line, number of employees, etc., and decide whether or not it's one you might enjoy and make a rewarding contribution to. If so, copy the information you need, and move on through that book...and others...until you've got 1,000 or more companies to write to.

You'll use some of the same books we saw earlier as aids in "targeted" networking. For general information, look at *Standard & Poor's Register* from McGraw-Hill; *Million Dollar Directory* from Dun & Bradstreet; and *Directory of Corporate Affiliations* and *Standard Directory of Advertisers* from National Register Publishing. Also check the industry-specific references listed in Appendix I. And contact the trade association of your industry, which probably publishes a directory.

If you can afford it...and in view of the time you'll save, you probably *can* afford it...consider buying the one or two books that interest you most. Appendix I lists the price of the book, plus the publisher's address and phone number, so you can telephone to have your own copy delivered by Federal Express or United Parcel. Billing on your credit card, most publishers can have their book on your desk within 24 hours. Then you can thumb through it at home, scribble on it, or otherwise abuse it in any way that speeds your work. However, you really should visit the library before you purchase, since some of these books cost upwards of $300 and $400, and the highest-priced ones all cover pretty similar information.

**Start with the most obvious companies you should contact
...and keep broadening until you have 1,000 or more
that really interest you. Once you get rolling,
they're not hard to find.**

Most people begin their mailing list with companies in their current industry. You undoubtedly know the top ten or twenty in your field. But you may be surprised to discover 100 or 200 smaller firms...many of which might get a real boost from the right person added to their management team. And these smaller companies, although probably offering less prestige and perhaps a lower salary, may also offer advantages, such as less bureaucratic red tape, and even a significant equity stake...things you can't possibly get from the giants.

Also bear in mind that you'll undoubtedly want to send *several* letters to each of the largest corporations. Those near the top of *Fortune*'s 1,000 list have many subsidiaries that are larger than entire corporations lower on the list. And each has its own CEO, chief financial officer, head of manufacturing, head of R&D, and head of marketing and sales, etc. Look up the parent in National Register's *Directory of Corporate Affiliations,* and you'll probably wind up sending letters to five or ten separate operating units in each of *Fortune*'s top 100 corporations.

And don't, by any means, feel that you must arrive at your minimum of 1,000 letters by staying within your current field. If you're a financial or an MIS manager, your skills can be used in almost any industry. Might as well write to every one of the *Fortune* 1,000 and most of their subsidiaries. As head of manufacturing you're more specialized, but the processes you know are used for many other products than the ones you're making right now. If you're in marketing and sales, look for industries selling to the same customers, or through the same channels of distribution. Whatever your job, you have relevance to many industries including those from which your current company buys its components, raw materials, and supplies...and to which it sells its goods and services.

Don't worry, you'll soon have your list of 1,000 companies...and, if you're really aggressive, 2,000 or more.

And while you're at it, you may as well send letters to all of the prominent retainer recruiters in Appendix II. Indeed, if you're in the midst of an all-out job campaign, you should purchase a directory (see Appendix I) and mail to every one of the more than 1,000 U.S. retainer firms. If you ignore even one obscure retainer firm, you turn your back on opportunities that no other firm will show you.

One of the great advantages of direct mail is that it can be concentrated on a very specific target, in order to achieve objectives you might not accomplish any other way.

Remember, as you look through the directories, that one of the main advantages of direct mail is that it can be *targeted*.

If, for example, you want to move to a different location...for later retirement in a warmer climate, or for putting your children through college, or for aiding your aging parents...you can make geography a key criterion (and there may be a "Metro" directory from Commerce Register to help). If you want to move from a technologically obsoles cent industry into one that you feel will be on the leading edge of technical and market growth for the next decade, you can look up the companies in your favorite fields and mail only to them.

If you're sick of dealing with products you find boring and of little real value to society, you can write only to companies which provide products or services you find interesting and intrinsically beneficial. And if it's big-company bureaucracy and politics you'd like to leave behind, you can mail only to companies with no more than 500 employees...or 100, for that matter, because directories list companies that small and smaller.

You get the idea. The beauty of direct mail is that the choice of each corporate mailbox is entirely up to you. The industries, companies, and locations that recruiters present to you will be chosen at random, *except for a strong bias toward offering you more of exactly what you have right now.* On the other hand, the companies...and non-profit organizations...you decide to mail to will be the ones you really want to explore.

"Making a list of 1,000 companies seems like so much work! Can't I have someone else do it?"

It's true that selecting a mailing list of 1,000 potential employers is a time-consuming project. So you may be tempted to delegate it to someone else...a secretary, a professional researcher, or an outplacement firm which, to save itself effort, may try to discourage you from conducting a tailored-for-you 1,000-letter direct mail campaign. *Resist the temptation!*

There's no substitute for your own decision-making. Only *you* can decide how you feel about various companies: products that interest you vs. ones that don't; large vs. small company; high vs. low prestige; preferred vs. unattractive location; entrepreneurial and fast-growing vs. stable and well-established organization; regional vs. national or global operation; risk-taking vs. conservative environment; etc.

Would you be willing to work for a casket company if it were in your preferred location...or if you could be its president? Would you work for a struggling company in real danger of going under if you could have the number-one or number-two spot? Would you leave your industry in order to stay in your present location? Which seemingly unlikely companies might actually appeal to you? No one else can answer these questions. This research...tedious though it may seem...must be done by you.

Moreover, the process of considering and deciding these potential trade-offs is a valid, creative exercise which will help you come to grips with your own talents, desires, and goals. No two people going through the same directory, even if they have the same background, will come up with the same list. Each person makes his own subjective judgments...and gains new self-knowledge.

One thing I can assure you. I have never seen a dynamic, creative executive set out to develop a mailing list of 1,000...or even 2,000 or 3,000...companies and fail to do so. And never has such a person failed to comment enthusiastically afterward about what a valuable self-assessment process compiling his list turned out to be.

Write to the CEO
...or a person two levels above your target job.

At the same time you're scanning directories and deciding what companies you'll write to, you must also decide *what position* on their organization chart is your ideal point of contact. When you're writing about a top-level executive position, you certainly can't send out letters addressed "Dear Sir/Madam" or "To Whom It May Concern."

Who should you write to?

One thing's for sure: never settle for simply sending your letter to the head of personnel. Although every chief executive should take full advantage of the very great help his or her chief of human resources can provide, regrettably few do.

If you're expecting to be president and chief operating officer of an entire company, of course you'll direct your letter to the chairman/CEO; or if it's a subsidiary of a conglomerate, you'll address the conglomerate's group officer responsible for that subsidiary or, better yet, the chief operating officer of the overall conglomerate.

My general suggestion is to address your letter *two levels above the job you want*...to the person who supervises the boss of the job you're aiming at. Since titles can be misleading and lines of responsibility aren't always clear, it's much better to aim too high than too low.

There are several advantages of aiming high:

> First, the person just one level above your target job...your potential boss...may be in trouble. If so, he's certainly not going to invite you in and show you around...only to become his future competition. If you'd written to his boss or his boss's boss, you might even have been considered for *his* job, a level higher than you'd have guessed.

> Moreover, your letter gains "clout" by being passed downward. If your potential boss gets your letter from the mailman, he can dispose of it casually. If it comes from a superior, he's far more likely to follow up.

And the higher the person who receives your letter, the more positions he may know of in subsidiaries or affiliates at an appropriate level for you.

Indeed, your letter may even spur a CEO or division-leader into taking action to replace a shaky manager. . .and you may be a candidate to fill the new opening. Or the senior executive may want to talk to you because he knows that a whole department is going to be restaffed after he gets rid of the head of it.

Therefore, write to a real, living person. . .addressed by name and title. . .who has the function you think appropriate to control the boss of the job you've got your eye on.

Directories are approximately 35% out-of-date when they arrive . . .and go downhill from there.

Someone must phone to check each name, title, and address. Fortunately, this is a job you can delegate.

The main reason a directory is marked "1989" is to get everyone to buy it, even though they already have one with "1988" on it.

Publishers do make an effort to update, by sending out questionnaires and clipping published announcements. But an incomplete effort at best. Worse yet, the revision process ends when the book goes to the printer several months prior to the date on the cover. And chances are, you won't use the book until several months after it's published. Meanwhile, corporations are continually reorganizing, and the average senior executive remains in any position only about three years (a few more if he's CEO). So, you can see why more than a third of all directory information is inaccurate.

Sending your mailing to the wrong person in the organization. . .or to someone no longer there. . .won't achieve your purpose. Therefore, someone must *always* check by phone to see that each person a directory has indicated for your mailing actually has the title, function, and name-spelling listed. Unless you phone to confirm, about 350 of your 1,000 directory-generated mailings will be wrongly addressed and probably worthless. In effect, you'll only be sending 650...not enough to escape chance and launch into statistical orbit.

Enlist any competent help you can get...secretary, temp, college student, wife, mother, teenage daughter or son. Whoever calls should ask for the person's secretary...bypassing the operator/receptionist...and follow approximately this script:

> "I'm sending him a letter and want to be sure I have the right information. He's chief executive?" (or some other title you seek). "And the exact spelling of his name...and the address is?"

Then probe for reassurance on other key points:

> "Executive Vice President...is that for the entire corporation, or for a specific subsidiary or division?"

> "Vice President of Operations...does that include responsibility for the Management Information Systems function?"

> "You say he's gone? Who took over his duties?"

> "Oh, *he's* not? Then who *would* be in charge?"

Unfortunately, the automatic activities of the outplacement industry have altered forever what you must do, and how effective you can be.

Recognize today's facts of life ...and work around them.

Fifteen years ago, you could have written to the chief executive of a *"Fortune* 500" company, and his secretary might have handed him your letter and resume along with the rest of the mail. And that might have happened even if your letterhead, resume, and envelope were obviously mass-produced...automatically typeset on the same equipment and printed on identical pale-ivory paper.

But today that same CEO routinely receives dozens of such letters per week. Indeed some high-profile CEO's get that many per *day*. Not surprising, when you realize that these CEO's are programmed into the word-processing equipment of scores of outplacement firms "counseling" thousands of executives. Here's what the secretary to one of those CEO's has to say:

> "We get a big pile of outplacement letters every day. Usually they're the assembly-line kind, where everything matches. But sometimes they're disguised as personal letters with no resume enclosed. Those are easy to spot too, because a real personal letter doesn't begin 'Dear Mr.,' and the applicant wouldn't *dare* write 'Dear Harry.' "

> "So on every employment letter, my assistant who opens the mail runs off a form response and sends the letter to Personnel for filing. Mr. _____ can't spend his time reading that stuff or he'd never get any work done. However, sometimes, if an extremely impressive letter comes along, and I know he might be looking for that kind of person, I put it into a folder he does glance at. 'Cream-of-the-crop,' we call it."

You see the problem.

Automatic mailings by the outplacement firms have virtually destroyed the receptivity of all their standard targets...the CEO's of America's leading companies. We'll design a letter for you that will stand out from the crowd. Even so, it may not escape the standardized handling of such letters in the offices that get bushels of them.

The only solution is to write at least 1,000 of your letters to senior executives who are *not* likely to be on the outplacement "hit lists." Send to Presidents of the appropriate *subsidiaries* of the largest companies. Send to heads of functional departments. Send to the CEO's of companies that, although interesting to you, are not at the top of everyone else's list. And in *"Fortune* 500" companies, be especially careful to restrict yourself to the person only two or three levels above the job you want...probably not the CEO.

Don't feel you must ignore the most obvious targets. Do let your outplacement firm send your mailing to them. . .or send to them on your own. But supplement any mailing to these high-profile executives with at least 1,000 letters to others who *aren't* being deluged. That way you won't be counting on a normal reaction to your mailing among people whose circumstances are no longer normal.

> ## Now let's design a covering letter that will do the best possible job of making whoever receives it want to look at your resume.

To get any attention at all for your resume, your covering letter absolutely must convey two essential messages regarding you as a human being, and you as the potential solution to an immediate business problem:

1. This is a *fine person,* obviously desirable as an employee.

2. He might be *for me,* possibly the executive I need right now.

If what your reader sees on his desk doesn't shout *"fine person,"* then he'll never bother to check your background to see if you're *"for him"* right now.

> ### So first of all we'll make sure your covering letter conveys the right personal impression.
> ### Then we'll perfect the story it tells.

Right away and above all, your covering note must. . .at a glance. . . label you as a first-class individual, regardless of background.

You must instantly be perceived as an intelligent, well-educated, socially poised, tasteful person. . .dynamic not passive, self-confident and cordial but not obnoxiously pushy, oriented toward delivering what others are interested in, an effective communicator, basically competent and commonsensical, and maybe even *interesting!*

Now I'm not saying that you, I, or anyone else can instantly prove for sure that we have all those fine characteristics in 300 words or less. But we'd better not give off even the slightest subliminal hint that we *don't* have them. Your reader won't even consider the contribution you could make to his organization, if you don't seem like the sort of person he wants to bring into it.

There's a double standard. Employers will tolerate employees with less than ideal human characteristics if they're outstanding performers on the job. But they won't go out of their way to bring in anyone who doesn't "feel" right to begin with. And face it...perusing your resume is going out of the way. The easiest reaction is just to throw it in the wastebasket. *Your covering note must not give off any negative "vibes."* And in that regard I submit the following:

Don't seem insensitive, bumbling, and not customer-oriented.

You've already avoided the biggest pitfall in this direction by phoning ahead to make sure you've got your reader's name-spelling, function, and title right. Your letter has come to the right person, and has approached him with impeccable courtesy.

Avoid looking tasteless and cheap.

Recent college graduates can get by with plain typing paper for their covering letter. You can't. Good quality stationery with your name, home address, and phone number, steel-engraved at the top, is ideal. Monarch size (7¼" x 10½") looks especially nice clipped to a standard-size (8½" x 11") resume, and if you boil your message down to attention-grabbing brevity, it'll fit on a Monarch page. Paper should be crisp, with rag/cotton fiber, in classic white or a *very* pale tint of grey or ivory. Ink should be black (or conceivably grey if you use grey paper).

Get both Monarch and standard-size stationery...mostly Monarch, because you'll use it for the "cover letter" that accompanies your resume (also for "thank you's," etc.). Envelopes, on the other hand, should be mostly #10 (business-size), because they will hold your resume, in addition to your Monarch letter. Put your return address on the envelope-flap, rather than the front (on both sizes), because that looks more like truly "personal" stationery. And before you buy, check the Yellow Pages for "Engravers"...*not* "Stationery, Retail." Buy proper quantities for a direct mail campaign, and you'll get the same low prices accountants, lawyers, and businesses enjoy.

Unfortunately, about eight weeks' lead time is required for true steel engraving. If you're rushed, substitute "thermography," and in just two weeks get cheaper but noticeably less elegant raised-lettering, which is produced with ordinary printing and plastic resin. Keep the design understated...three or four lines, each no more than 2¼ inches long... with your phone number smaller but legible on the bottom line.

Unless your covering letter describes unusual circumstances that make it appropriate, never use your current employer's stationery.

Don't appear pretentious.

Veer toward modesty and matter-of-factness in name, address...and stationery. Imagine a letterhead from "Cottsworth O.M. Kensington-Smithers IV," who says he lives at "Nine Chimneys," followed by street number, etc. What fun it would be to throw *his* resume into the wastebasket! Moreover, since you're sending a business letter, avoid all gimmicks on the stationery...family crest, house-picture, yachting flags, crossed polo mallets, colored or shaggy borders, etc.

Avoid looking like the passively-packaged product of an outplacement firm.

Today so many fired executives are being processed by outplacement firms, that every retainer recruiter and almost every senior executive knows the #1 tell-tale sign: perfectly matching paper and electronic typesetting used for covering-letter stationery, resume, and envelope.

Following the theory that "colored papers stand out on an executive's desk," most of these firms eschew classic white and turn instead to a shade I call *"Outplacement Ivory"* (their second-favorite is light grey). And of course everything matches, because it's all produced at the same time on the same paper by the same equipment.

"What's wrong," someone might say, "if my mailing openly proclaims that the people who let me go nonetheless cared enough to buy me outplacement services?

Only this, in my opinion: Your reader will be more interested in what you have to say if he feels it's been written and sent to him solely by you, rather than by someone else who's been paid to get you out of one office and into another. There's nothing wrong with accepting outplacement help. But you'll seem more confident and creative...less hapless and passive...if you appear to be preparing and sending your own correspondence.

Therefore, make sure your covering letter and resume *don't* precisely match. Use engraved or thermographed personal letterhead for a covering note typed by a polyethylene-ribboned word-processing unit, and use a *different* crisp white paper for your offset-printed resume, the original of which can be neatly typed on the same machine (typesetting is not necessary). Use two different textures in classic white (my favorite), or "mix-'n-match" tinted stationery with a matter-of-factly-white resume. But don't look mass-produced. If an outplacement firm is doing your production...unlikely if you're sending upwards of 1,000 letters...then specify or supply your own non-matching papers.

So much for appearances.
Now let's get to the content of your covering letter.

This is your "free sample."
It demonstrates that you're a "fine person"
in terms of thinking and communication skills.

Only after evaluating "how you say it"
will your reader weigh "what you say."

To succeed, your covering letter must be pleasantly businesslike in tone, and conjure up the image of a competent, self-confident executive who's letting a colleague know that he's available to help, if there's a need. Somehow, a letter from such a person is never a jarring intrusion, whereas a letter from the typical "job applicant" always is.

The difference is dramatic. So few people are able to write a really good covering letter that, when one arrives, it stands out like a beacon. Its author is immediately given "plus points" for outstanding executive communication skills, and his resume is always scanned, in the hope he's offering something the recipient...corporate officer or recruiter...can take advantage of.

Fortunately, creating such an impressive covering letter isn't difficult, if you incorporate the four central attributes that outstanding ones have and poor ones don't. Be sure your covering letter:

1. **is not too long.** Brevity is essential! Get right to the point, and leave out all the useless and obnoxious things that "job applicants" put in their letters.

2. **has a central theme.** Your message must be arrestingly clear...not diffuse and blurred.

3. **offers benefit to the reader,** rather than merely harping on what *you* want.

4. **deals with compensation.**

Later on I'll cover point 1 by giving you a list of stuff to get rid of, so your letter won't be cluttered with the unproductive statements "job applicants" put in theirs. And after that, I'll show you in detail how to handle compensation to your advantage. But first let me cover points 2 and 3 by showing you a covering letter that has a clear central theme (point 2) of benefit to the reader (point 3).

This letter is from Sam Sage, whose resume we've already reviewed. Sam's an exceptionally competent executive. And from the minute we first glance at his covering letter, we begin to see how very special he is. No nonsense. No wasted words. And no claims that aren't fully backed up by his accompanying resume.

Samuel P. Sage
219 Warringer Drive
Denton, New Jersey 07299
(201) 719-0932

Mr. Sherman J. Summit
Chairman and Chief Executive
Integrated Standard Corporation
4225 Scenic Parkway
Lovelytown, New York   10591

Dear Mr. Summit:

Could I help you as a divisional president...or corporate chief marketing officer?

The $500 million company I've helped build over the past five years as Chief Marketing Officer has more than doubled sales, increased profits nine-fold, and raised ROI from 3.6% in '83 to over 28% in '88.

We've done so well, in fact, that we've just been bought out at 30 times our estimated '89 earnings by a company that's absorbing us into their own operations.

Although I'm far more interested in a fine company and an intriguing challenge than merely in money, you should know that in recent years my total compensation has been in the range of $175,000 to $250,000.

May we talk?

Sincerely,

Samuel P. Sage

Samuel P. Sage

SPS:mj

Sam rang all the bells!

Sam's central theme is sure to dilate the pupils and speed the pulse of any red-blooded CEO. . .impressive advances, in sales, profit, and ROI.

For many letter-writers those claims would be too bold. They'd be mom-pie-'n-flag *clichés* that the accompanying resume couldn't possibly live up to. But Sam's got the stuff. So he flaunts it.

Notice too, that Sam didn't waste words on anything that's obvious. His resume *is* enclosed. . .no need to say so. And *of course* Sam would like Mr. Summit to get in touch with him. . .or Sam may call Mr. S. No need to talk about that either.

Moreover, Sam didn't invoke self-praising adjectives and adverbs. Rather, by making numerical claims, he directed attention to his resume, which is packed with specific facts and figures that *demonstrate* what he can do. Sam also treated compensation in an advantageous way that we'll discuss later.

Above all, the sparseness and directness of Sam's letter tell us a lot about him. He's an exceptionally dynamic, clear-thinking person. On the rare occasions when a letter from someone like Sam comes in, the reader will always glance at the attached resume.

Indeed Sam's reader, Mr. Summit, became quite interested. As you'll see, when you enjoy what's set aside for you in Appendix III.

But now back to the work at hand. . .a couple more covering letters:

Matt Ginyus
146 College Point Drive
Skilton, Massachusetts 01128
(413) 112-2465

Mr. Gerrard Global, Chairman
International Interchemicals, Inc.
1202 Industrial Beltline
Wilmington, Delaware   19808

Dear Mr. Global:

Could any of your laboratories...corporate or divisional...be more innovative?

If so, perhaps I can help.

Within the spending limits of a young fast-growing $23 million company, and with only a 26-person laboratory, my staff and I during the past five years have produced 14 commercially exploitable new compounds...6 of which are already on the market, providing 72% of current revenue. During that time I've personally received 8 patents, and my staff have received 46.

Having proven what I can produce for a small company, I'd like to do a lot more for a much larger organization.

An exciting challenge will be the main reason, if and when I move. But you should know that in recent years my total compensation has been in the range of $95,000 to $130,000.

Please keep my inquiry confidential, Mr. Global. The published rumors that we may be acquired have prompted me to think about the world outside DrexelChem. Nevertheless, I don't want to disturb either my staff or the rest of the company just by considering alternatives.

Thank you.

Sincerely,

Matt Ginyus

Matt Ginyus

Karen S. Kash
12 Countinghouse Road
Pittsburgh, Pennsylvania 15213
(412) 999-1814

Mr. Peter R. Pinnacle
Chairman
Acme Consolidated Corporation
6902 Postal Turnpike
Pittsburgh, Pennsylvania 15224

Dear Mr. Pinnacle:

Could Acme Consolidated...or one of your largest divisions...
benefit from a strong chief financial officer?

Having been continually challenged and rapidly promoted at
U.S. Heavy Industries, last year I became our youngest CFO
since USHI was founded in 1869...I've never before thought
about joining any other employer.

But now we're shutting down our steel mills and home office
here in Pittsburgh, and headquartering at our insurance company in Hartford. Relocation would be a hardship for my
family. So I'm contacting a few outstanding Pittsburgh area
companies before committing to a move.

If you have a need, I could do an excellent job for you.

Sincerely,

Karen Kash

Karen Kash

P.S. Money is <u>not</u> my main consideration, but in recent years
my total compensation has been in the range of $130,000 to
$190,000.

Different Pokes from Different Folks!

Different as they were, all three of the letters you just read would have stimulated the interest of any reader who needed what they offered.

Why?

Because each:

1. was **not too long,** and

2. had a **central theme**

3. of **benefit to the reader.**

Sam Sage presented his outstanding track record as a marketing-virtuoso-cum-general-manager. Matt Ginyus amply demonstrated his ability to get results in the laboratory. And Karen Kash showed that she was an outstanding employee, who'd never have been available, if not for exceptional circumstances. Her letter said, "Help yourself to someone else's superstar."

Of course, the very best thing about each of these letters is that only one person in all the world could have written it. Each person came to life through mere words on paper, because those words were clear and specific, and *applied only to him or her.* There were none of the vague generalities that give most such letters a boring fill-in-any-job applicant similarity.

So before we move on to point **4. dealing with compensation,** let's list some things you'll make sure to *leave out,* which litter the letters of "job applicants."

OMIT...OMIT...OMIT!

Everything obvious, and all clichés. Letters from "job applicants" always state the obvious, and lean heavily on clichés: "Enclosed please find..." "I would like to take this opportunity to..." "This letter will serve to..." "Here is a copy of my resume for your review and consideration." "If my background and accomplishments are of interest, I would appreciate hearing from you." "Thank you in advance for your interest."

Self-evaluations. Don't bother describing your personality or your performance. You're biased, so we can't take your word for it. And if you enclose or quote something from a psychologist, we'll *know* you're on the defensive. Don't say, "I'm a results-oriented executive with a proven track record," or that you're "intelligent," "analytical," "profit-minded," "honest," "hardworking," "loyal," "reliable," or any of that stuff. "Job applicants" use those words.

Willingness to relocate. "Ho hum," if you're willing to move for a great opportunity. So is everyone else. Don't bring up relocation unless the fact that you *won't* relocate is the reason a lucky local employer has your letter on his desk. If your employer...or your specific job... is leaving town and you don't want to, you've got a good believable reason for writing your letter. Exploit it. Otherwise say nothing about relocation. And don't give personal hardship details. Just say, "My family and I prefer to stay in Indianapolis." The fact that your wife's real estate practice brings in twice what you do, or that your mother has a health problem doesn't make you any more attractive as a potential employee.

"Further information and references." Every "job applicant" is "pleased to supply further information and a list of references." But you're smart enough not to say so, and thus you further differentiate your letter from theirs. Besides, your "sales representative" resume...unlike theirs...has "further information" built right in. The next thing *your* reader will need or want is to see you.

The Mafia approach. Don't end your letter with a warning that you intend to make a followup telephone call. "Job applicants," salesmen, and Cosa Nostra do that. If your reader is a prospective "buyer," he'll take the next step. If he has nothing for you, the "foot-in-the-door" approach will just be a waste of your time and his. In fact, your warning may allow him to prepare his secretary to "deal" with you when you do call.

> ## And now "point 4"...current compensation.
> ## Rightly or wrongly, it's the #1 screening criterion.
>
> ## Every employer wants to know that "money is right"
> ## before "wasting time" on any candidate.
>
> ## The ideal covering letter gives that assurance
> ## ...and rushes the reader right into your resume.

One of the most important factors in establishing the "he-might-be-*for-me*" reaction on the part of your reader...and indeed any employer... is your level of compensation.

Yet most executives omit any mention of money...either current or desired. They worry that some employers may be frightened off because the figure is too high, and others may lose interest because it's too low. And any employer who winds up making an offer, they fear, may propose less than he otherwise would, if he knows what they're accustomed to.

What these wary executives don't realize is that by not mentioning salary, they've created a situation that's even *more* limiting. Compensation is the *single most important factor* in categorizing people as appropriate or inappropriate for a particular job. For employers...and executive recruiters as well...it provides a quick and easy way to figure out whether a candidate is "the right size." Titles can be misleading, and the importance of a given position can vary considerably from one organization to the next. Salary remains the most reliable index, since it's determined by the marketplace.

So the challenge is to mention compensation in a way that *encourages* consideration. You want every potential employer to look at your money and think:

> "Well, that's in the ballpark. He might be *for me*."

Obviously, if your money is above what his position pays, he'll figure he can't attract or hold you. And if you're earning far less, that's a pretty good indication that you're not yet ready for the responsibility his position entails.

So how do you handle compensation?

Here's a magic sentence that will do the best possible job of getting you considered:

> "Although other factors such as (fill in your own non-financial 'turn-ons') are of primary importance to me, you should know that in recent years, my total compensation has been in the range of _____ to _____ ."

To appreciate what that disclosure accomplishes, you must first:

Meet the weasels.

In consumer-products marketing, there's a term for wordings that state the truth precisely enough to wiggle through the narrow openings defined by company attorneys and government regulators. They're called *"weasels,"* after the squirmy little animals that are almost impossible to catch.

The three key phrases....*"weasels"*....in your compensation statement are: *"in recent years," "total compensation,"* and *"in the range of."* Used together, they open the way for you to state, *perfectly truthfully,* a broad range that will make you seem "right *for me*" in the mind of every reader who controls a position you could possibly be interested in and qualified for.

The *"low-end"* figure will be the least take-home pay you'd consider, assuming the job offers major advantages beyond immediate compensation. After all, the preface to your "three-weasel" sentence said, in effect, "money isn't everything to me." For this bottom figure, use a round number that approximates your tax-return "income-from-employment" for a recent lean year.

For the *"high-end"* figure, start with your top base salary within the past few years. Then add everything else you're getting:

performance bonuses (use the figures that...combined with base...represent your best year);

the amount of your employer's contribution to FICA;

the value of medical, dental, and life insurance provided by your employer;

money paid by the firm into pension and profit-sharing accounts in your name (whether or not fully vested);

any other tax-deferred compensation, such as annualized incremental value of your stock options, and your employer's matching contribution to thrift and stock-purchase plans;

and the pre-tax value of miscellaneous perks, such as a company car (less your pay-back for personal use), city and country club memberships, the right to use the company condo in Nassau for two weeks vacation per year, and the college scholarship your child receives under a competitive company-wide program.

You can even estimate this year's raise, and include that in the base of your "high-end" figure.

Thus, using the three "weasels," you can truthfully state a wide range. You'll probably end up with numbers that are $20,000 to $40,000 or $50,000 apart...maybe even more. *It's perfectly reasonable for the second figure to be 50% larger than the first:* $80,000 to $120,000 for example, or $100,000 to $150,000.

Let's imagine that you've specified a range of $90,000 to $130,000.

First we'll picture your letter reaching the CEO of a young growth company with great prospects, but with venture capitalists on its Board who don't want Management draining its life blood with high salaries. This CEO looks at your low number, $90,000, and figures he can realistically reach *up* to you. He can't offer more than $75,000 in cash compensation. But you'll have the opportunity to purchase at 50 cents per share 25,000 shares of treasury stock the company expects to take public at about $20 per share within 18 to 24 months; and as an officer, you'll have a company car. He's pretty sure he can grab your attention. So he calls to suggest a get-acquainted lunch.

Now picture the CEO of a large multi-national corporation who must fill a job he thinks is worth about $150,000. He sees your top figure of $130,000...assumes it represents your most recent year...and reaches *down* to you. After all, you're probably expecting an increase of at least 10% or 20% for making a move. Obviously, your next job should be in the neighborhood of $150,000...just what he expects to pay. So he asks his secretary to give you a call.

As you see, your "three-weasel" range of $90,000 to $130,000 has actually triggered a *"for me"* response in the minds of two very differently-situated employers. You're being considered for jobs paying anywhere from $75,000 to $150,000 a year. Cash compensation on one job is 100% more than on the other.

Moreover, you haven't given up any negotiating flexibility. You've got a shot at a job that pays even more than the top figure you mentioned. And of course you can always settle for less, depending on the job's advantages that extend beyond immediate in-pocket cash.

Mentioning money...and having it "right" for your reader...encourages him to consider your resume. And using a "three-weaseled" range lets you be "right" for every reader whose job could possibly be right for you.

And now a word of warning...

Don't fritter away the #1 advantage of direct mail. Avoid the hill-beyond-the-hill-beyond-the-hill dilemma.

Just about everybody refuses to believe they can be as good as they are, send out lots of letters describing how good that is, and not be swamped with phone calls, appointments, and interviews. Worrying that they can't cope with too many responses, they hold back on their mailing, sending only a portion of their ultimate total per day or per week.

Don't make their mistake!

Don't drop your spy-in-the-sky satellite back to earth. Don't forego the instant reconnaissance that only direct mail can give you. Instead, send your letters everywhere at once, so you'll look everywhere at once. Do an *aerial scan of the entire desert*. Survey every oasis. See all three, four, or five of them...simultaneously. Then you'll be able to pick the greenest.

Sending only a few letters, when you could have sent them all, puts you back on the ground, where you can only see as far as the horizon.

You're still looking for water in the desert. But now you're riding a camel. Suddenly you spot a brackish little watering hole in the valley below. Should you head for it? Or should you keep to the high ground and peer into the valley beyond the next hill? Maybe that's where you'll find the main outflow of the underground stream this little trickle merely foretells. If so, the water will be cool, sweet, and abundant. There'll be plants, fruit trees, and maybe even a comfortable bed for the night. And if not beyond the next hill...then surely beyond the one after that. But what if there's only sand? Then you'll fervently wish you hadn't passed up the meager security of this little spot.

You see my point.

Believe me when I say that 1,000 letters won't bring more than 5 or 6 interested responses...3 or 4 interviews...and 2 or 3 offers. *And that's **not** too much "action" to handle all at once.*

No matter how good you are, *timing* will be wrong at almost every company you contact. So send all your letters at once and get all your offers simultaneously. Then you can choose the best the market has for you at any moment in time. What's more, you'll *know* it's the best, and not a compromise you feel forced into, because you can't risk waiting to see what's behind the hill behind the hill.

Another mistake is to neglect direct mail until very late in an all-out job-changing campaign.

Ideally, it comes right up front.

For some reason many people think direct mail should only come *after* personal contact, networking, and reaching out to executive recruiters, in an aggressive job search.

There's only one logical reason I can think of to justify this view, and it's because direct mail is a lot of work. So most people don't bother with it, until after the other methods have been tried and seem to be failing.

That's really shortsighted. The *first* thing needed is an ideal resume... one written so persuasively that it could be effective when merely delivered by mail. This document is your best possible "leave-behind" in personal contact, networking, and dealing with recruiters. And when it's prepared, you've already done about half the work of your direct mail campaign.

Moreover, just as preparing your "sales representative" resume forces you to study your achievements and determine what you'll say about them, preparing your mailing list forces you to survey prospective employers and determine where you're most likely to do well and gain satisfaction. Shouldn't this strategic analysis come at the beginning, rather than the end, of your job-changing efforts?

Bear in mind that:

1. Your personal and networking contacts will only know a very few of the possibilities that exist for you in the world of work, and

2. The retainer recruiters will only show you a very few of the opportunities they know about.

So hurry up and get the five or six leads your 1,000-letter direct mail campaign can generate.

Also take advantage of the 200 or 300 rejection letters you'll get. Sift them carefully to find the unusually cordial ones...perhaps 10 or 20... from people who were so impressed by your mailing that they really *did* wish they had a place for you. Since they're at high levels in industries and companies that appeal to you, they're ideal early contacts for your networking campaign, which would otherwise be narrowly based on the people you already know.

Begin your "search" by skimming your best personal contacts and alerting the retainer recruiters you're already acquainted with. If that doesn't solve your problem within the first few days you're "looking," then chances are you're in for a full-scale effort. If so, you may save many months in the long run, by devoting two or three weeks to direct mail right at the outset.

> ## So much for the basics.
> ## Now let's take direct mail to its ultimate extreme.
>
> ### Let's mount a wide-ranging campaign
> ### right under your current employer's nose,
> ### and never let him suspect you're "looking."

First of all, you'll need an anonymous version of your "sales representative" resume. And secondly you'll need a "sponsor" to send it out for you...and to receive the five or six interested responses you're likely to get from a 1,000-letter mailing.

Your Anonymous Resume

It's easy to omit your name, address, and phone number from your "sales representative" resume. And it's not hard to describe your current and recent employers "generically," rather than identify them by name. Employers that are "ancient history" can be left "as is."

Assume, for example, that your "regular" resume has headings like the ones shown on the next page.

As you see, it's possible to substitute information about the corporation and what it does, for the name of the company. In effect, you're merely moving facts you'd otherwise provide in the first sentence of the following paragraph up into the line that normally identifies your employer.

1983 - Present

DIAMOND/ACME COMPANY
(Subsidiary of MultiContinent Industries)
Bucolic, Vermont

Vice President & General Manager

1978 - 1983

NEW-MOTION CONTROLS LTD.
Sunbelt, Arizona

Vice President - Marketing

Restate your headings like this:

1983 - Present

$90 Million Manufacturer of Flow-Control Devices
(Subsidiary of Conglomerate)

Vice President & General Manager

1978 - 1983

$250 Million Manufacturer of OEM Control Assemblies
(Privately owned)

Vice President - Marketing

Try to give concrete orientation to your reader, even though you can't "name names." Leave out specific trademarks. But state all the same numerical comparisons you'd include in an "open" version of your resume. Also give your actual college degrees (with dates), and your marital status. After all, you're not the only married person who graduated from Stanford in 1968.

Your Sponsor

You're doing something difficult. And this time you can't do it without help. You must have a "sponsor" who's willing to "front" for you... distributing the anonymous version of your resume and accepting replies from employers who are interested in meeting you.

Of course, you might instead try to be a "Lone Ranger." You *could* send out your own identity-concealed resume. And you could ask that responses be addressed to a post office box, explaining your need for secrecy, and hoping that mystery and novelty might make up for your lack of straightforwardness.

Unfortunately, this approach has already been tried many times. And as far as I know, it has always failed. Considering candidates for management positions is no joke. And people in a position to do so are too busy to fool around. Your resume won't be taken seriously unless it comes from an obviously credible source.

Therefore, since *you* can't send the resume...and you certainly don't want it circulated by some headhunter who's attached a price-tag...you need someone else who can submit it almost as straightforwardly as if it came directly from you.

You need a *"sponsor"*...a real live respectable person who'll openly send your name-omitted resume, say why he's doing so, and forward to you any interested responses he receives. Moreover, it will be a big help, if the person is rather prominent in the business world...someone obviously capable of knowing a fine executive when he sees one. Then his mailing out your resume will more than make up for your anonymity. Indeed, *it will enhance your image.*

"Sounds great, John," you say, "but who am I going to get to do that for me?"

Well, it can't be Pope John Paul II, Bill Cosby, F. Lee Bailey, or Brooke Shields. Prominent they are. But experts on who would make an ideal chief manufacturing officer for a large metal-bending business they're not. Better for your purposes...and easier to enlist...would be someone who could begin his letter knowledgeably:

"As president of a $350 million division of Innovative Steel Products Corporation, I know the importance of having a Vice President of Manufacturing who can really be depended on."

Here's a guy you and I never heard of. But he's a perfect "sponsor." Lining up someone like him probably isn't beyond your reach.

Since your spokesman should claim to have first-hand knowledge of your outstanding on-the-job performance, chances are he's a former boss or subordinate. He's probably *not* just a prominent businessman you know socially or as a fellow board-member of a non-profit institution...although "any port in a storm," as they say.

However, you don't want a sponsor who's *too* high on the corporate totem pole relative to the position you should occupy, because one essential element of his letter must be a believable statement of why... despite your being so special...he can't use you himself. If your sponsor is Chief Executive of ITT, it's hard to believe he can't fit you in somewhere. Therefore, the reader will suspect he doesn't want to.

Here are the essential elements of a "sponsor's" letter sending out your identity-concealed resume:

1. His *credentials* that make him a valid judge of executives like you;

2. His *vantage point* that enables him to endorse your on-the-job effectiveness;

3. His *recommendation*;

4. His *reason for not employing you himself*;

5. His *explanation of your need for secrecy*; and

6. His *offer* to put the interested reader in touch with you.

Now let's look at a "sponsoring" letter that meets all these criteria.

TRILOVANCE ELECTRONICS CORPORATION
1010 Solder Circle
Verdant Valley, California 95014

Michael Micreaux
President

Mr. Donald Drive
President
Peripheron Corporation
18 Silver Saddle Road
Diva Del Sol, California   95038

Dear Mr. Drive:

As Founder/CEO of a publicly-held young high-tech growth company...we started four years ago and will hit $30 million this year...I know the importance of a Chief Financial Officer who can provide absolutely reliable information without needlessly cumbersome procedures that stifle momentum.

Those people are rare, and difficult to identify. Which is why I'm writing to you.

Last week I learned that the financial executive I respect most after 21 years with IBM and NorthAmerican Dauntless Corporation...and tried hardest to recruit as CFO when I founded this company...is now willing to explore outside opportunities.

However, since he's very solidly employed, he can't afford to "go public" with his intentions. And, since I can't capitalize on his availability without doing an injustice to the person who took the plunge with me four years ago, I'm sending his identity-omitted resume to you and several other CEO's of high-tech growth companies.

If there's any chance that you may have a need, just let me know, and I'll put you in touch with one of the very best financial executives you could possibly consider.

Sincerely,

Michael Micreaux

Michael Micreaux

MM:gr
Enclosure

P.S.: Although growth environment and equity opportunity will be primary concerns, you should know that his total compensation in recent years has been in the $85,000 to $120,000 range.

What an endorsement!

**The "sponsored" mailing not only provides "cover,"
it also heightens impact.**

Someone introducing a colleague can say things about him that conventional modesty prevents the individual from saying about himself.

And such a plug is far more believable coming from a senior executive with no economic axe to grind than from a headhunter filing for $30,000 + . Moreover, a "no-price-tag" introduction is much more likely to be followed-up.

"Sponsored" direct mail is often "the only alternative" in a ticklishly sensitive situation. Fortunately, when handled well, it also becomes a highly persuasive marketing campaign.

The Dual Standard on Stationery

Notice that the "sponsor" uses his corporate stationery when recommending someone else, whereas he normally would *not* do so when proposing himself.

The reason for this dual standard is purely psychological. Corporate stationery is virtually essential to prove that the sponsor is indeed a substantial, knowledgeable person in the business world. And fortunately, the reader has no negative reaction to the use of office paper to help a colleague.

But the "vibes" are totally different when the writer offers himself. Then using his employer's paper triggers a negative reaction. His reader says, "Wow, at the same time he's trying to get me to hire him, he's ripping off his current company's stationery and postage meter."

**"I know a couple people, John, who'd be ideal
to send out a mailing like that,
and they respect me enough to do it."**

"But they're extremely busy.
I could never ask them to take on so much work."

Absolutely right! You couldn't. And you *won't*.

You're requesting a huge favor, just to have them lend you their name, mailing address, and phone number. So you've got to get virtually all the work done without burdening either your sponsor or his secretary.

Here's what *you* do:

1. Get your sponsor's general agreement to help.

2. Show him a letter you've drafted (to save him work), stressing that he may change it as he sees fit, since it's *his* letter.

3. Establish agreed-upon wording for the letter, and walk away with at least two reams of his office stationery (enough for 1,000 letters).

4. Create your mailing list, check it by phone, and have "his" letter word-processed. But first, show him a sample to make doubly sure he's satisfied. Also offer to let him see your mailing list, in case he wants to make sure you haven't accidentally hit anyone he'd rather not be "writing" to.

5. Sign, stuff, stamp, and mail the letters yourself. That's right, I said sign them...with *his* signature. Unless he feels like signing 1,000 letters, he'll be glad to leave this chore up to you. But ask before you barge ahead; this point is inconsequential to some people, and a deep emotional issue with others.

Here's what your sponsor and his secretary do:

1. Almost nothing else. After he approves your letter and list, he's just about finished. *Remember, a 1,000-letter mailing will produce only 5 or 6 interested replies...*hardly enough to create a traffic problem.

2.   Letter replies will be opened by your sponsor's secretary with the rest of his mail, and merely forwarded to you every couple days in a large envelope. These could be a slight nuisance for a week or two, because 200 to 300 recipients will send polite "no thank you's."

3.   The 5 or 6 phone callers who inquire about you will be cordially dealt with by your sponsor. He'll say he doesn't know the exact status of your explorations at the moment, but will gladly forward their name and number to you. Then, if you're not already in your new job, you'll call their office, giving your sponsor's name as well as your own, so they'll know you're the person they inquired about.

That's it. Nothing more.

But look what you've accomplished. While keeping yourself completely hidden, you've probed 1,000 companies to find the *rare* 5 or 6 who right now are interested in what you have to offer. And you've done so without tipping-off your current employer!

True, you've put a lot of work into the project. But, except for checking a few times with your sponsor, *no more work than sending the same mailing under your own name.* Your sponsor has also contributed some time. But not much. You've done everything, except sit in his office and be him when five or six people called to ask about you.

"Sponsored" direct mail can do more than keep a secret.

It's also a problem-solver.

Jim's in a tough spot.

He needn't be secretive. But he does face a high hurdle. Someone almost has to "speak the unspeakable," and it's a matter Jim can't very well bring up for himself.

See how a "sponsored" mailing can come to the rescue.

MONOLITHIC FOODS CORPORATION
White Plains, New York 11618

MAURICE MARKETIER
Vice President—Marketing

Mr. Cabot Carson
President
Family-Owned Candies, Inc.
10 Ginger Road
Scottsdale, Arizona 09099

Dear Mr. Carson:

As Vice President - Marketing of Monolithic Foods, I've seen hundreds of fine marketing executives over the years, and one of the very best is my former boss at MegaFoods, Jim McKee, who taught me most of what I know.

Recently the company where he's been Vice President - Marketing, Yumm Foods, was acquired through an unfriendly tender offer. And now at an amazingly youthful age 59...Jim ran the New York Marathon again this year...he's available for another assignment.

Although company and opportunity will be Jim's main concerns, you should know that in recent years his total compensation has been in the range of $80,000 to $120,000.

Jim's the calibre of person there's hardly ever a shot at hiring, and nothing would please me more than to bring him in here. Unfortunately, I can't do that without dealing an undeserved blow to one of the two executives who head my Marketing Department...or by giving up my own job.

So on the chance that you may have need for an exceptionally dynamic, creative, and versatile marketing executive, I thought I'd bring Jim to your attention.

Sincerely,

Maurice Marketier

Maurice Marketier

MM/jc
Enclosure

P.S.: With Jim's exceptional knack for training and recruiting, you can count on his building a strong department, with excellent people to take over whenever it's time for Jim to retire.

**Think of "sponsored" direct mail
as your "swat team," to be called in
when the going gets really tough!**

You catch the concept. The more tendency to discriminate against an executive, the more helpful "sponsored" direct mail becomes.

With direct mail, the number of employers contacted can be infinitely expanded. Maybe 2,000 or 3,000 will have to be reached in order to find 15 to 18 with an immediate need, because only one-in-three or one-in-five will consider a disadvantaged candidate. Fortunately, a "sponsor's" letter can deal with the prejudicial factor far more frankly and successfully than one from the candidate himself. . .or from a head-hunter or an outplacement firm with a fee on the line.

Whenever there's a severe problem, consider sponsored direct mail. A successful business executive who's a retired military officer can make a strong case for a former subordinate just mustering out. A former top-echelon businessman who's now an ambassador or a college president can knowledgeably extoll a current subordinate who wants to enter business from the diplomatic corps or academia. And any high-level executive can sponsor a former subordinate or boss with an attribute most employers will shun. . .lawfully or not. . .such as age, physical handicap, obesity. . .even, perhaps, return to work after a jail sentence for "white-collar-crime."

Direct mail, with or without a "boost" from a sponsor, may turn out to be the only viable "Rite of Passage" when you're looking for the exceptionally rare employer who must have. . .in addition to need, which is always rare anyway. . .broadmindedness, compassion, or firsthand knowledge that an apparent disadvantage isn't disabling.

Try it. For yourself. . .or for a friend.

**And there you have direct mail
. . .the ultimate career-development weapon.**

Results are limited only by how hard you're willing to work.

Direct mail *is* hard work.

When you're fully challenged and well rewarded where you are...and you're also being tempted by retainer recruiters...you won't bother reaching for the unlimited power of direct mail.

Indeed, direct mail as a job-changing method is rather like the police, the fire department, and the hospital. Drastic! But great to have around when needed.

Whenever more casual methods aren't enough, you know what to do.

References, Newspaper Ads, Busy Signals,
Trick-or-Treat Letters,
Buffing-to-a-Rich-Lustre, and
''Search'' & ''The Hidden Job Market''

This chapter picks up loose ends.

We've got six remaining topics that require separate chapters. But now let's take a break, and cover some matters that also merit discussion...but not a lot of it.

References

For most people most of the time, references are no problem.

Indeed, bosses, subordinates, and peers are your greatest source of career opportunity. Your current boss may promote you. Co-workers' comments may help move you ahead. And former associates may lead you to outside opportunities.

It's nice to be well spoken of. And I'll bet you are . . .almost all of the time, by almost everyone. But when you're being "referenced," you want to make doubly sure the right impression is given. Here are some suggestions:

Your first step in job-changing is to get in touch with your references.

Begin any job campaign by reaching out to your work-related personal contacts, past and present. Ask for a reference rather than a job, and achieve all the advantages we discussed in Chapter 3.

With a little effort you'll soon have plenty of pertinent people whose enthusiasm you've tested. . .and re-stimulated. . .either face-to-face, or by long-distance phone. Interviewing potential references advertises your availability. And it lets you know who's enthusiastic, and who's lukewarm.

Don't "wear out" your references.

Even though you know from the start precisely who you want potential employers to talk to, do *not* accompany your resume with a list of references. Neither recruiters nor employers expect such information until you're about to get a job offer. And you're better off not providing it.

Your references feel most enthusiastic and least imposed upon the first time they're asked about you. If they have to respond several times, fatigue and boredom set in. Their answers become perfunctory. And after a while they begin to wonder why lots of people have investigated you, and nobody has hired you.

Whose names do you give?

Since you're being considered for employment, almost all of your references must be *work-related*. Moreover, your potential employer wants to know how good you are today...not how special you were a long time ago.

So if you're employed, you must open a window on your current reputation in your present company. And if you're "between jobs," you've got to show how you were regarded in the job you've just left. The number-one person your potential employer wants to talk to is your current boss, if you're employed. Or your most recent boss if you're not.

Normally, of course, you can't deliver your present boss as a reference on an outside job. And no one will expect you to. But do try to come up with two or three people whose confidentiality you can rely on, and who know first-hand how well you're doing *now*. Perhaps a trusted subordinate. Maybe a peer. Possibly the head of a department or function who works closely with you...and ideally, with your superiors and subordinates too.

Anyone discreet who's recently left your company is a good bet to maintain confidentiality. He doesn't care whether you leave or stay, and chances are he won't be in touch with the people who do. An outside supplier or customer who works closely with your organization is another possibility. He too observes your situation. He isn't quite as knowledgeable, but can be helpful nonetheless.

If you're employed you can, of course, refuse to allow contacting of anyone in your current company. But "stonewalling" will raise doubts. Every competent and commendable human being makes at least a few friends among the people he works with. If there's *nobody* you can trust, your potential employer will surely wonder why.

On the other hand, when you're out of work, there's no logical reason why your would-be employer can't talk to your most recent boss. So even if you parted on the worst of terms, you'd better prepare for the inevitable. Much as you'd like to, you probably can't substitute your favorite boss for your most recent one.

There's safety in numbers.

The more open and helpful you are in allowing yourself to be checked out, the stronger you look right from the start...even before a single person is contacted.

So when you're about to be hired, and the time for serious referencing has finally arrived, either hand over, or volunteer to prepare, a comprehensive list. Say something like this:

> "When I'm hiring, I like to learn as much as possible about the person I'm considering. I'll put together a list of names and phone numbers, and you can call anyone you want to."

Then, taking the confident "my-life's-an-open-book" approach, supply a list that covers all of your recent jobs and includes a generous sampling of bosses, subordinates, peers, and maybe even customers and suppliers, if appropriate. Provide home as well as office phone numbers, if your references are willing to receive calls at home.

Since your list is fairly extensive, you can *edit*. You must include the person for whom you've done most of your most recent work, even if the parting was unfriendly and the evaluation is likely to be negative. Omitting him would sound a warning. But you can make sure that person's opinion is in context of others who will be objective.

Maybe, if you're lucky, the person you're worried about won't be called. Or won't be available when he is called. And even if the worst occurs...he's called *and* treats you unfairly...your potential employer has right at his fingertips the names and numbers of additional people who will balance what he's just heard with a far more fair and favorable account.

Consistency is the key.

When an employer or a recruiter talks to a reference, he wants to hear the same story he heard from you. Suppose you say:

> "I've always got along well with all my bosses, and David was no exception."

But when David's called about you, he says:

> "Frankly, the chemistry wasn't good, and the constant bickering got to be a drag after awhile."

Now you've got a problem. Much better to have provided a safety-in-numbers list of references and *forewarned:*

> "I've always got along well with all my bosses, and all my co-workers too. David was the only exception."

Don't go overboard anticipating problems and raising negatives that may not come up. Most people like to be gracious and upbeat when called as references. Even the boss who just fired you will probably feel guilty and want you to find a new job quickly and to think and speak well of him in the future.

But don't fail to lay a little groundwork, if there's a negative you're *absolutely sure* is coming. Above all, referencing probes the consistency of your story. Are things really the way you presented them?

Control possible damage by using the "reference statement."

If you've been fired and the pertinent people are likely to take a dim view of you, then the outplacement firms urge you to move in quickly with a *reference statement.*

Within the first day or two after you're fired, they say you should draft a concise statement...no more than one page...stating your tenure and performance in terms as favorable as possible to your future employment. Present it to your former boss. Will he go along with it? If not, negotiate with him until you have a written statement you can both live with. Then line up two or three additional references who are pertinent and hopefully more favorable to you. Negotiate written statements they too can live with. And make sure a consistent theme links all versions.

These statements become the "party line" when anyone inquires about your departure...former co-workers, customers, suppliers, *and potential employers.* The actual written statement is never handed to anyone; it merely becomes the agreed-on script for conversations about you. Here's an example:

> "Dale Jones was with us eleven years, and rose from Plant Superintendent, to head of Quality Control, to chief of Plant Engineering, to Vice President of Manufacturing, his job for the past three years. As Vice President, he was responsible for three plants employing 1,800 people, and he reported directly to me as President. He left because he saw the company pursuing one course and we saw a different one, and he felt his career would be better fulfilled elsewhere."

That's not a terrific reference. But you can survive it and find another job. The main thing is to have a consistent and not too damaging story told by all three or four of your current-company references. If what we've just seen is what the person who fired you will say, and you've managed to line up some other observers who will be more expansive and generous, you'll probably do fine.

According to the outplacement people who recommend "reference statements," the important tactic is to move quickly and take personal charge of the story that will be told about you. Don't wait passively until weeks later, when a prospective employer is about to phone your references. By then the situation will be out of control. The rumor mill will have filled the vacuum. And the word on you may *not* be the consistent and only-slightly-negative story you could have negotiated earlier.

Frankly, as an experienced recruiter, I'd smell fish immediately, if I called even a couple references and got nothing but strategically brief, consistent remarks. But this *is* the outplacement-advocated method for damage control, and there's an appealing logic to it. Certainly the idea of acting fast to put out the best possible story makes sense. Let's hope you never need such a strategy. But if you ever do, at least you know what the experts recommend.

What about purely personal references?

If some of your most admiring friends are also friends of your prospective employer, you may want to drop their names into your interviewing conversations. But don't list non-business acquaintances as business references.

And don't suggest your pastor, priest, or rabbi. He doesn't observe you in the office. Moreover, people who are truly moral or religious feel no compulsion to prove their virtue. And experience teaches us to suspect anyone who does.

Also, don't bring up that college or military buddy you've kept in touch with for 25 years. He's not an on-the-job observer. And friendship has destroyed his objectivity.

Who else should I talk to?

Before we drop the subject of references, here's my best tip for checking someone *else's* references. After you finish talking to each person whose name you've been given, ask if there's anyone else who would also know about the person you're checking. Who would have an even closer vantage point?

Unless you're on the phone with the reference's direct boss for the past several years, you'll surely get additional names that are even more pertinent. If the candidate has already provided those same names, you know that he's open and self confident. The unflinching relevance of his list is, in itself, an excellent reference.

If, on the other hand, the names you've been given are rather off-target, call them anyway, to compile a list of bulls-eyes. Don't phone the more-relevant people you've identified...especially if you've agreed not to go beyond a specific list. Instead, merely go back to the candidate and ask permission to contact the people you've identified. Now the whole story will spill out:

"As a matter of fact, I *purposely* didn't list Herb and Paula because there was a situation I felt they might not be completely objective about."

There's your thread. Pull on it!

Should you reply to newspaper ads?

This is a more interesting question than it might seem at first glance. And the answer is:

It depends on who placed the ad.

If it's *signed by a corporate employer* attempting to fill its own opening, go right ahead. Employer-signed ads are always authentic. And the attractiveness of the opportunity often stems from the prestige of the company that's asking you to consider working for it.

But be careful if the ad is *signed by a recruiting firm*. Retainer firms almost never advertise. On the other hand, contingency firms always do. Indeed, advertising attractive jobs that may or may not exist is the main way they get new people for their files. If you're an entry-level or middle manager seeking a toehold, the contingency firms are very helpful. And these days, they may have surprisingly high-level listings. You will, however, be self-interestedly vigilant.

The recruiter-signed ad to really steer clear of is the one with *only a newspaper or post office box number* for replies. . .no address and no phone number. A relatively new and disturbing tendency has developed among, let's hope, just a few corporate personnel departments to place ads under phony names designed to look like executive recruiter partnerships. The purpose is "to find out what's available in the marketplace," without revealing that the company has openings. Answer one of these little beauties, and you may be writing to your own employer. They're just one more reason why, if you're anywhere near $100,000, you should approach newspaper ads with extreme caution, *unless they're straight-forwardly signed by corporate employers, or by reputable recruiting firms that include their address and/or phone number.*

What to send, if you're sending anything, is easy. Send the same thing you'd send for a direct mail campaign.

And now the most obvious suggestion in this book:

People responding to your resume must never call your home...and get a busy signal!

This suggestion, of course, applies only to those rare times when you're conducting an all-out job campaign. Then you're knocking yourself out on personal contact, recruiter liaison, networking, and direct mail. You're doing everything possible to get a few people to dial that number at the top of your resume.

And when someone does call, what happens? Your line is busy!

He calls back 15 minutes later...still busy. Then 20 minutes later he calls again...and no answer.

Frustrated, he may try again tomorrow. Or you may never hear from him. The impulse to call after reading a resume is fragile and fleeting. If your reader has an urgent need and if yours is the only plausible resume he's seen in weeks, he'll surely keep trying. But if you've merely reminded him to think about a potential replacement for someone who'll retire three years from now, your reader probably won't attempt another three calls tomorrow.

What almost all unemployed executives fail to appreciate is that the calls they want to receive at their homes will be placed by executives who are 100% accustomed to calling employed people in *offices*. Every single call to such a person is answered...if not by the person himself, by his secretary or a receptionist who takes a message.

One call always works for your reader...*until he tries to reach you.* If he can't at least leave word on a machine, your image takes a nose dive. He starts out trying to phone an impressively-credentialed executive. After just one or two aborted calls, he gives up trying to reach a hapless out-of-work fellow, who obviously has to compete with the wife and kids for the family phone, and who isn't even organized enough to connect himself with the outside world.

In fact, however, *you're* the one causing most of the congestion, by making outgoing calls. But somehow that's not how the situation is interpreted. When we call a home, we envision what's on the other end of the wire in terms of our own homes. . .not an office.

So here's an appropriate telephone policy for a typical family when Dad's. . .or Mom's. . .all-out job campaign is in progress:

1. Have your current home phone number printed on your stationery and resume. Using that number as your "business line" eliminates waiting while the phone company assigns and installs a second line. Your family will have to use the new number "for the duration," informing their callers to use it too.

2. If your "business line" doesn't have "Call Waiting," the system that warns you another caller is trying to get you while the line is busy, immediately request to have that feature added. If it's unobtainable in your area, have a third line added, so you can place outgoing calls while leaving the number on your resume open to receive incoming calls.

3. Put a first-class answering machine on your "business line". . .one that takes messages of any length and can be called for playback when you're away from home.

4. Make sure every family member knows *who should answer* your "business line". . .you, your wife, and poised, responsible teenagers. . .no one else under penalty of early bed and no supper! And make sure your "business line" answers incoming calls *24 hours per day.* The call you're hoping for may be placed by an executive in another time zone, or stuck some night in an airport or a hotel room, or at home some evening or on a weekend.

Trick-or Treat Letters...
the Direct Mail You Can Do Without

I wouldn't use our limited time together to discuss these odd concepts, if it weren't for the fact that successful books have been written about them, and today they're handicapping a considerable number of people. Hence, this digression.

The "Tease-'Em-and-Spoof-'Em" Method
...a Short Letter, and No Resume Until Later

This direct mail technique was the subject of a very successful book about executive job hunting that flourished in the '60's and early '70's, went out of print for several years, and was successfully reintroduced by its publisher in the early '80's.

What it says, basically, is:

1. Send out a very brief letter that makes one or two *exciting claims*, which will surely get you an interview. *Do not enclose a resume.*

2. Go to your interview. *Do not bring a resume.* Find out what sort of person and what background the employer wants.

3. Go home and *write a special resume* proving you have exactly the right stuff. Mail it with your "thank you" note.

4. Enjoy your new job, for which only you...among all the people the employer has seen and talked to...seem pre-eminently qualified.

This method has a nice clear logic to it. If you accept *three* very doubtful premises, then the scenario will unfold exactly as promised. Otherwise, maybe you should forget this ploy. Let's consider each assumption separately.

Premise #1:

That anyone. . .short of Lee Iacocca, who included *no claim whatsoever* in his hypothetical note that we saw earlier. . .can create a short letter with *one or two claims so compelling that he'll be granted an interview* on the strength of it.

You've undoubtedly received one- or two-claim "teaser" letters from people trying this method. And, like me, you probably questioned their sanity or at least their business sophistication. This will refresh your memory:

Dear _____:

As Director of Marketing, I increased sales 30% per year during each of the past three years.

If that's the kind of performance you'd like to see in one of your divisions, perhaps we should meet.

Sincerely,

Sidney Surface

Maybe this guy did a terrific job. . .and maybe he did a rotten one. . .we can't tell. However, since he's obviously looking for work, we suspect it was the latter and not the former. How fast were sales of *competitive* products in his market rising...50% or 200% per year? What happened to profits? Did they plummet as he hyped sales with too-rich deals; filled the pipeline with unsuccessful new products now being returned for credit; and failed to weed unprofitable low-volume items from the line which, streamlined by his successor, is now highly profitable and poised for solid growth?

The fact that this guy obviously thought we'd be jumping up and down to meet him after reading his "teaser" letter confirms that either *he* thinks in a very unsophisticated manner, or he figures *we* do. Too bad. Heads he loses...tails he loses.

Premise #2:

> That anyone can go through an interview with either you or me and not have us make him say what he's done in his career so far...even if he does claim not to have a resume, or to have left it home.

Maybe he can keep us talking and answering his questions during most of his interview, and thereby keep us from figuring him out while he's in our office...although I doubt it.

But afterward, will our impression be so favorable that we'll eagerly await his mailed-in resume proving he's exactly what we're looking for? Of course, maybe he'll have been so wonderfully glib that we're left with an oral preview of his "perfect-for-us" resume. If so, and we don't hire him, he'll probably land a starring role in the Second City improvisational theatre group.

Premise #3:

> That it's fundamentally possible, even after hearing what we want, for anyone to write a "custom" resume proving they have what we seek, when a more straightforward version would have revealed they don't.

Here we have the fatal flaw of every "withhold-your-resume-so-you-can-doctor-it" scheme. This concept doesn't have to be tied to a "teaser" letter mailing, just because a widely read book links these two ideas. If it worked, the same thing could be done in every interview, regardless of how the interview is obtained. Unfortunately, it doesn't work.

Frankly, my advice is to check out a great many potential employers until you find one...or hopefully a choice among several...where you're right for the job and the job is right for you. Then your straightforward "sales representative" resume will be your ideal aid in getting the job.

You'll be a lot better off trying to *find a fit* than, through distortion and misrepresentation, trying to *fit a find*.

The "Spoof-'Em-Only Method" ...a Long Letter and Never a Resume

Here's another deviant form of direct mail, which you've undoubtedly received and may even have considered sending. This one omits the "tease-'em" lead-in and skips all the way to the "spoof-em" ending. The trick here is to avoid having a resume altogether, by writing a long letter, which will say just what you want to about your career...*and no more*.

Like the topically-organized resume, this long letter lets you escape from the revealing contours of a chronological work history, so you can spotlight whatever you wish, and leave out whatever you want to conceal. Indeed, because it isn't labeled "Resume" at all, you're not even obliged to make a bow in the direction of chronology somewhere near the end, as most people feel they must in a topically-organized resume.

If you're really desperate to bury your work history...which includes short jobs, bad references, and maybe a jail sentence...this is undoubtedly the best way to do it. Your reader will surely hanker for a revealing straightforward resume, and will presume that there must be a good reason why you've gone out of your way not to provide one. Nonetheless, you may get a long way into your "sale" before the demand for a specific chronology of prior employment comes up...especially if you send the long letter before your interview and handle yourself very smoothly during your visit.

An astute employer should very pointedly ask for your resume during the interview and...failing to get it...should ask you to take home and fill out one of those "Application for Employment" forms normally required only from lower-echelon people, which will smoke out your chronology. But if he doesn't, "Caveat emptor," as they say. "Let the buyer beware."

But now let's assume you have nothing to hide. Let's look at the long letter as a communication device, in comparison to a brief covering note and a "sales representative" resume. There's no contest. The two-, three-, or four-page-long letter lacks the crisp introduction a brief covering letter provides, and is *not* scannable the way a traditionally blocked-out resume would be. Because the long letter lacks visual organization and isn't broken up into familiar segments, it's more bothersome to the reader. It's less inviting to enter, harder to plow through, and raises naggingly negative presumptions as well. If you don't need it, don't use it.

Buffing-to-a-Rich-Lustre:
The $100,000+ Corporate Executive Image

Right now you're reading my "loose-ends" chapter. This is the spot for material that, while potentially very helpful to the person who needs it...and not everyone will...is, nevertheless, not one of the dominant themes of the book.

Certainly that's how I regard the following suggestions for polishing the $100,000+ executive exterior. Not to a high gloss, mind you, which would sparkle in the limelight at Monaco or Vegas. But rather to the rich, subdued lustre that glows in the walnut-paneled corridors of corporate power.

This list mainly polishes men. But it winds up, women, with some comments just for you.

Try for trim.

> Corporations like nice bodies as much as the Greeks did. Do what you can to oblige.

Look as if you don't work too hard.

The company may demand all your time, but it doesn't like you to look as if it's getting it. Men should stay tan all year, cheating with the latest electronic technology, if necessary. Also, men, no cosmetic is undetectable. Don't experiment.

Suit the situation.

Corporate uniforms for men, in declining order of "power-look": Navy pinstripe, plain navy, grey pinstripe, and plain grey. Very little else is acceptable, except other "classics," such as a grey herringbone or a discreet grey glen plaid and, in summer, a putty gabardine. Variety is *not* the spice of male business attire, so why bother with anything but the two best options: pinstripes...navy, and dark grey? Summer weight in those colors is acceptable and ideally comfortable indoors all year, but winter weight is elegant when climate permits. Buy all or mostly wool to avoid polyester "glitter." Either two- or three-button style. Double-breasted is okay too, but only if you keep the coat buttoned.

Don't bother with a vest unless you personally prefer it for comfort or style. However, if you buy ready-made suits, you might consider having a tailor convert merely "sewed-on" sleeve buttons to through-the-sleeve, with real button-holes. That's a detail some senior executives notice.

And please no short pants! Dry cleaners *do* shrink wool pants, which is why, without realizing it, many executives are walking around in ankle-length trousers.

For an important job interview, men, grey pinstripe is your safest choice. It's powerful enough to impress, but leaves the most powerful option, navy pinstripe, to your potential boss. Why come on with the ultimate visual powerplay in your get-acquainted meeting? After you're hired, wear whatever corporate uniform you prefer.

Forego wash-'n-wear.

Limp-collared home-laundered shirts are an economy no Corporate-man can afford. Crisp starch on collar and cuffs is essential; it even does wonders for button-down oxfords. White is best, pale blue next. For an interview with a "conservative" employer, forget fancy patterns and colors, contrasting collars, and french cuffs in the daytime. And *never* wear short sleeves beyond the laboratory and the factory, unless you know in advance that's what the CEO wears.

Silk or wool ties only.

Polyester ties are another unaffordable economy. Choose classic striped reps, and classic small repetitious patterns.

Long black or navy socks.

To-the-knee socks are mandatory, men, to make sure no shin *ever* shows. And since socks are no fun anyway, why not just stock up on a few dozen pairs of identical black ones, so you can throw away any with holes and still have plenty that match?

Shoes are no fun either.

Black (or dark brown) lace-up oxfords are a man's safest bet, but black slip-ons (preferably with no metal gimmick at the instep) are also acceptable. Shiny he-man boots are okay too, in the Southwest. But don't go anywhere, men, wearing boots or shoes with a zipper up the side.

None is enough jewelry for a man.

A plain gold wedding band is fine, and you might get by with a plain gold signet ring. But never wear college rings, bracelets, or any jewelry with a sparkly stone, even it it's your World Series ring. And please, nothing glittery gripping, or oozing out of, your tie. Also no gaudy belt buckle with a designer's initial.

And don't wear a watch that stops traffic.

Something in plain gold with a plain black leather strap is Corporate-man's ideal timepiece. Avoid elaborate watches with many dials and bezels, built-in computers, diamonds visible, metal "expansion bracelets," and anything that looks like it's intended for active sports rather than office wear.

Classic overcoats only.

If it's not what the newsman wears ''on camera'' standing in front of the White House, don't wear it, men. A trenchcoat in tan, navy or black (in order of preference) or a classic navy, grey, camel, or conservative-tweed overcoat. Avoid fur, even as a liner or trim. A hat is no longer socially necessary, so wear a classic felt only for comfort or fashion, and feel free to wear a warm cap you can hide in your pocket when you come inside.

But indulge yourselves, women. If you can afford it, an opulent dark mink is your ultimate ''power'' coat, followed closely by a conservatively-styled cloth coat in a rich fabric. A classic man-styled trenchcoat comes in third. Unless you're in a very ''creative'' industry, sporty furs and jazzy ''threads'' may do more for your spirits than for your $100,000+ executive image.

Invest in a good umbrella

Have it for interviews and important appointments. Otherwise use the same disposable ''cheapie'' we all pick up from the street vendors.

And make a capital investment in a truly fine conservatively-styled leather briefcase.

I bought a staggeringly expensive one eight years ago at my wife's wise insistence, and will probably still be using it for important occasions ten years from now.

Don't pen yourself down.

Man or woman, you can't afford the false economy of a corporate-issue plastic pen on an important occasion like a job interview. Get a classic, slender gold one, men, that won't bulge your shirt pocket. And never display more than one writing instrument at a time; there's an inverse relationship between the number of pens in your pocket and the numbers on your bank statement.

Keep glasses as simple and classic as possible.

Plain plastic frames with no glittering metal corners. . .or the plain metal aviator-style. Above all, never let the optometrist talk you into tinted lenses...either permanent, or the ones that supposedly, *but never entirely,* clear when you come inside. No one can look like anything but a mobster wearing tinted glasses indoors. Worse yet, they veil your eyes, make you seem furtive, and impede communication.

Hair heading south?

That's a man's problem you and I share. And so far all of the solutions are worse than the problem. One of the strongest prejudices in the business world today is against the man who wears a hair-piece...whether glued on or woven on. His staying employed and moving up is a great tribute to his other fine atttributes, because nothing shouts "insecure self-image" as loudly as trying to hide those several square inches of skin on top. Burt Reynolds only wears his "piece" in the movies and on TV, because it takes flattering lights and a team of hairdressers to get by with it. Any executive who attempts such a feat without comparable assistance merely displays poor judgment, in addition to personal insecurity.

And don't think that lowering the part and spray-thatching the top with hair from the sides is any better.

It's too bad that God didn't give you...and me...more hair. But he did give us a lot of other advantages, or you wouldn't be reading this book and I wouldn't be writing it. Go to a good hair stylist for the optimum "natural" cut. It's the best you can do.

And be careful; don't smell too nice.

During office hours, men, forget all the fragrance advertising you've seen. And don't overdose on deodorant, mouthwash, or hair stuff, either. Women, you're permitted a very *slight* nice smell, but not the same potion in the same portion that you'd use to "knock 'em dead" in the evening.

Finally, a "Now Hear This!" for women executives:

Avoid all clothes that make you look like an imitation man. Menswear suits with silk bow ties are strictly for the scared MBA, who'd rather look like a stewardess than a secretary, during her first six months out of Wharton. Wear a beautiful, conservative suit in a fabric and a jacket-cut that a man *wouldn't* wear...and with it, a gorgeous silk blouse that says "I make lots more money than a secretary." Also wear real gold jewelry that says the same thing. Avoid flashy diamonds and fussy patterns for daytime. But otherwise, if the jewelry is tailored and tasteful and you've got it, *flaunt it!*

Don't wear anything low-cut, slit, or peek-a-boo. But lacquer your nails, and feel free to be as naturally feminine as we men are masculine. Indeed, your quiet self-confidence in your gender will eliminate that "striving-to-catch-up" aura that too many women executives have. Use taste, quality, and affluence...not gender-denial...as the basis of your "power" look. That way, you'll assume your proper equality with the men in your organization. Moreover, even though you're not particularly trying to, you'll also be visually positioned above all the women in your company who continue to dress like ersatz men.

"Search" and "The Hidden Job Market"

This is a book of plain talk.

So I've purposely avoided using two terms that are often misused and misleading...*"search"* and *"the hidden job market."* But you'll confront them almost every day. Hence, these explanations:

"Search"

"Search" shouldn't be a problem. It has a plain meaning everybody understands...*looking for something, when you don't know where it is.*

If people in the recruiting business would use "search" to mean what you and I assume it means, there'd be no confusion. Unfortunately they don't. Even worse, they treat the word as if it has a *special* meaning. And, worse yet, that special meaning is *different,* depending on who you talk to.

So far, you and I have avoided confusion by using only one word, which has only one obvious meaning, for bringing people into an employer's organization: *"recruiting."* And when it comes to different ways of performing that function, and of *getting paid for it,* we've been specific about the distinctions. Therefore, you now know everything necessary to unravel the meaning of "search," no matter who uses the term and what they mean by it.

At one end of the market, you have the *contingency* recruiter who tells you:

"We also do search."

He means that, besides submitting resumes and getting paid only if and when one of those people is hired, he's also willing to accept a retainer and be paid for his efforts while he attempts to fill the job. And since he's assured of payment, he's presumably going to look harder and longer...hopefully right up to the point of finding the person you want.

However, it's nothing new or remarkable for a contingency firm to "do search." For over 20 years, the agencies have stopped calling themselves agencies and have stopped waiting for people to come in and "register." They still advertise attractive "come-on" jobs in the newspapers. But they also call up employed executives the very same way the retainer firms do.

So in the sense of looking-for-something-when-you-don't-know-where-it-is, the contingency recruiter has long been "doing search," and today he does it on both his contingency and his "search" assignments. Of course the *first* place he "looks," regardless of payment method, is his files. And if the answer is there, it's not necessary to look further.

On the other side of the market, you have the *retainer* firms. They pioneered the idea of looking for happily-employed executives rather than waiting for the unhappy and unemployed ones to "register." They too have massive files of resumes...mailed-in, and from people they've interviewed. Sizable retainer firms boast of having anywhere from 50,000 to 150,000 resumes. And the first place they "look" is their files. They too may find it unnecessary to look further.

The ultimate irony occurred in 1982, when the professional association of retainer recruiters changed its name from Association of Executive

Recruiting Consultants, Inc. (AERC), to Association of Executive *Search* Consultants, Inc. (AESC)...thus abandoning the "recruiter" terminology which originally differentiated them from the employment agencies. The idea was to separate the Association by name from the contingency firms. Impossible! There are about an equal number of contingency and retainer firms. And almost twice as many contingency firms are using "search" in their names as are retainer firms. Moreover, among the contingency firms using either word, "search" leads "recruiting" by a 2-to-1 margin.

So what does the word *"search"* mean, when applied to the people business? Your guess is as good as mine. Contingency recruiters use it when they want to be *paid* on retainer. But they also use it...justifiably...to describe what they *do* when working on contingency. Both contingency and retainer recruiters *may* do it when they look for executives. But then again neither may do it if, by "search," you mean looking for new people they don't already have on file.

And of course individuals, and outplacement and executive marketing companies, also use "search" to mean the seeking of *employment,* rather than the seeking of employees.

So if you tell me you want to go "search" for gold, or oil, or buried treasure, I'll say that's a good idea...and I may even come along. But if it's "search" that involves employment, "Thanks, but no thanks." It's too much bother to figure out what you mean.

"The Hidden Job Market"

This intriguing phrase...obviously invented by a copywriter, rather than merely plucked from the dictionary like "search"...is likewise used by people to mean different things.

The most prevalent and legitimate meaning is the shadowy world of job openings not yet referred to recruiters or advertised in the newspaper. However, some users expand the expression to include jobs-that-aren't-jobs-yet...situations where there's nagging dissatisfaction with the incumbent, but not yet a firm decision to fire. Also, where a need to add a new position is felt, but not yet formalized as an empty box on the organization chart.

Obviously, it's a good idea to discover such situations before others have beaten a path to them. And as long as "The Hidden Job Market" is merely a sexy way of saying "go-straight-to-the-employer-and-quickly" through direct mail and networking, it's certainly a valid concept, even if overly hyped.

The problem comes when executive-marketing and outplacement companies try to extract big money from you or your employer because they propose to *"Introduce You to the Hidden Job Market."* The clear implication is that there's an undisclosed supply of real jobs which they know about and you don't. And you'll never find those jobs unless they tell you. And they won't tell you unless they're paid a stiff fee.

After all that build-up, "The Hidden Job Market," being such a little idea with such a big bold name, becomes deceptive...or at least very disappointing. You feel "ripped off," when your "introduction" inevitably turns out to be nothing more than a description of networking and direct mail techniques.

Outplacement. . .
Adding Some Push to Your Shove

The newest and fastest-growing way to make a living from the relationship between a corporate employer and his management-level employees is outplacement.

Since about 1950, retainer recruiters have prospered handsomely from bringing executives IN. And since approximately 1970, they've been accompanied in the corporate vestibule by outplacement counselors ushering executives OUT.

Because it's become a burgeoning field, outplacement today has practitioners that range all the way from abysmal to excellent. Survival-of-the-finest is yet to come.

Take a look at this chapter even if the grim reaper is nowhere near your office. And come back here again, whenever you suspect that your job may be in jeopardy.

> **With outplacement counselors, just as with recruiters, the best way to determine your self-interest is to watch the money change hands.**

Why were there no outplacement counselors until about fifteen years ago?

Because up until then nobody had got the brilliantly creative idea that employers would pay large fees...typically 15% of the individual's annual compensation...to facilitate the discarding of executives.

The advantage of filling empty chairs in the executive suite had been seen and exploited. But nobody had guessed that corporations would pay handsomely to have executives removed swiftly, compassionately, and without a traumatic trace left behind to disturb former peers, subordinates, and superiors. The corporate undertaker/chaplain/resurrectionist had not yet offered his services.

Today when a senior executive who might "take it badly" is about to be fired, there's probably an "outplacement counselor" waiting in the next room to take charge of this understandably shocked and disturbed individual...to talk consolingly and optimistically with him...to remind and help him to remove his most valuable and personal items from his office during those last few minutes in it...to reassure him that the rest of his things will be packed up and delivered to his home tomorrow...and to introduce him to the job-hunting services and the office-until-he-gets-another-office that his former employer has graciously seen fit to provide.

Day after tomorrow...perhaps even by tomorrow afternoon...there'll be a different attache and other family pictures on the credenza. A successor will already be busying the former executive's subordinates with new assignments, and business will be "back to normal."

And everyone associated with the departed will have been made aware that he's been "very well taken care of." He has received a generous severance. And far from being cast adrift on the seas of fate, he's been provided "outplacement services at company expense." Instead of mourning another victim of the corporation they're still at the mercy of, the survivors will be thinking, "Even if the worst happens and you get fired, at least this is a company that tries to take care of you."

Does the corporation get its money's worth from outplacement?

Compare the instantaneous postpartum we've just witnessed with what used to happen, and I think you'll agree that the answer is *yes,* the corporation does get a valid service from its outplacement firm.

Prior to outplacement, the person firing our outplacee might have been in for a much rougher time. Instead of a brief five to ten minute encounter ending with, "Come, Roy, there's someone next door I want you to meet," there could have been a more protracted and difficult session with no stranger to turn Roy over to, who'd stick with him all the way out of the building.

And before outplacement, assuming the corporation wanted to appear at all humane, Roy might have been given the rest of the week as a "lame duck" in his own office, and then exiled to a small office with a shared secretary elsewhere in the building...possibly on an infamous "death row," along with other previously prominent players. In both places he might have held court, receiving farewells and furtively exchanging "don't-let-the-bastards-get-you-down" sentiments.

Just the intangibles we've touched on so far may justify what the employer pays for outplacement. If Roy is helped to find another job more quickly than he otherwise would have, so much the better. Indeed, the company may even save some money on a shorter period of "continuation pay" and sustained medical insurance, if that system, rather than lump-sum severance, is used.

And of course, even despite his swift surgical removal, at least a few of Roy's colleagues back at the office will track his progress. They'll get further "good vibes" if he feels his outplacement service has helped him find work sooner and more easily than he would have without it.

The idea of charging to help executives look for jobs had been around for many years.

The breakthrough that created the outplacement industry was getting corporations to pay.

You'll do better with today's outplacement firms, if you know the history of the "people business" over the past 35 years.

Until after World War II, when the idea of retainer executive recruiting first emerged, the only companies making money from the employer/employee relationship were the personnel agencies. *They sought work for individuals,* and were the only game in town. "Applicants" "listed" themselves, and were matched up with the jobs "listed" by employers. When employment resulted, the individual paid a fee.

The retainer executive recruiting firms began to sprout up in the late '40's and the '50's and mushroomed in the '60's and '70's. They operated from the opposite direction. They persuaded *employers* to pay them for their professional efforts to fill jobs, and their fees weren't contingent on anyone actually being hired.

Meanwhile, as the U.S. economy boomed in the mid-'60's, employers found they could compete more effectively for the best talent the employment agencies had to offer if they paid the agency's bill, rather than leaving the employee stuck with it. And by the end of the '60's, virtually all agency fees were employer-paid, just as they are today.

Simultaneously, the agencies raised their fees from the 6% to 12% they'd been charging employees in the early '60's, into the 20% to 25% bracket pioneered by the retainer executive recruiters (since risen to 33%). And as they began to be paid similar sums from the same source as their retainer recruiter rivals, employment agencies also adopted identical terminology...calling themselves "executive recruiters," "executive search consultants," "management consultants," etc., and calling potential employees "candidates," rather than "applicants."

While the two employee-seeking services...contingency recruiters and retainer recruiters...were evolving into their present forms and setting half of the stage for the "outplacement" phenomenon, there were two additional developments in the "people business" that would also fuel the explosive growth of "outplacement" today.

During the '50's and '60's, "industrial" or "organizational" psychologists were building their own specialized firms offering a wide variety of services to employers, including psychological evaluation of candidates, and counseling of employees requiring helpful intervention to avoid being fired.

The fourth and final precursor of "outplacement" was the emergence in the early '60's of companies who advertised themselves to the frustrated executive job-seeker as capable of helping him achieve for himself what the retainer recruiters and employment agencies (contingency recruiters) were not accomplishing for him. They advertised that *they could help him get a job.* Their carefully-worded contracts never said... and still don't say...that a job *will* be obtained. Only that, after parting with lots of cash, the individual will become a more effective job *seeker.*

These companies rely heavily on newspaper advertising to bring in customers; and they use a wide variety of terms to describe their services, such as "career development," "career planning," "career management," "executive marketing," "job search," and even "executive search."

The *"executive search"* misnomer is particularly flagrant. And they love to use it as a "come-on" in the names of their firms and the headlines of their ads, because it implies that they seek executives for employers...which of course is not at all what they do.

To identify these diversely-named companies for purposes of our discussion, I'll use the most accurate term, *"executive marketers,"* even though their own favorite terminology runs more along the lines of "career counselors."

> **Thus, by 1970, all four segments existed:**
> 1. **contingency recruiters**
> 2. **retainer recruiters**
> 3. **organizational psychologists**
> 4. **executive marketers.**
>
> **And one of the four was making exactly the same promise that outplacement firms now make.**
>
> **Unfortunately, it was the only segment with a bad reputation.**

The "executive marketers"/"career counselors" were promising to help unemployed executives find jobs, and to help dissatisfied executives find better jobs...a very appealing concept to sell, but a difficult one to deliver.

Therefore, these outfits were frequently in hot water with their Better Business Bureaus, District Attorneys, State Attorneys General and... when these came along later...Consumer Affairs Departments and investigative TV shows including "60 Minutes" on CBS. Their advertising and high-pressure sales pitches often implied that they represented employers looking for executives...a channel which would be opened after job-seekers signed fine-print contracts and paid hefty fees. Or there was an implication that these firms would actually *achieve* employment for those who signed and paid.

Indeed, even the remarkably large sums these firms requested were implicit promises of great things to come. "How could I have known they intended to do so little, when they were charging so much?" complained the executives who went to the authorities and to the media. In the early '60's some of these firms were charging executives in excess of $1,000. Today their fees often run upwards of $5,000...sometimes *far* upwards of that amount.

What usually got these firms off the hook was the very limited commitment in their carefully-worded contracts as to what they were actually going to do. Invariably, with all the hype and lawyer-language stripped away, it boiled down to this:

"Only you can find a job for you. We'll help with your resume, and show you how to look for a position, but you'll have to find it on your own."

As far as the job-seeking executive is concerned, that remains precisely the promise of "executive marketers". . .*and outplacement counselors*. . .today.

When only executives were paying for it, executive marketing wasn't an attractive line of business to get into.

Until "outplacement" was conceived, only a handful of firms in the entire county were able to exist by "marketing" or "career-counseling" executives. It wasn't a very lucrative or appealing line of work:

Low fees. Individuals can't spend freely. . .especially when they're unemployed.

High marketing costs. Lots of newspaper advertising was needed to bring in the executives as one-time-only, low-ticket customers. There were no multiple sales, and no repeat customers.

Low customer satisfaction. Customers seldom referred their friends. Indeed, they often consulted their lawyers and public officials. . .adding further to the high costs of this line of business.

When corporations began paying for "outplacement," everything changed.

The least viable of the four segments of the people business suddenly became the fastest-growing.

New "outplacement" firms are being formed every day, and established firms are growing rapidly. Truly, "outplacement" is "what's hot" in the "people business" today. Now that corporations, rather than individual executives, are paying, the three main disadvantages of "executive marketing" have become the primary advantages of outplacement...and there's one important further advantage as well:

High fees. Averaging 15% of the terminated executive's annual salary, outplacement fees far exceed what executives will pay for "marketing." And even where percentage-of-salary fees are identical, employers tend to buy outplacement for their highest-paid executives, whereas lower- and middle-managers tend to be the ones purchasing "executive marketing" for themselves.

Low marketing costs. With employers as customers, there are lots of multiple sales and repeat purchases. Whole departments and divisions are being shut down, with outplacement granted to everyone. Expensive newspaper advertising to locate employee customers is *eliminated*.

High customer satisfaction. Now that the executive no longer pays, there are no complaints about low-value-relative-to-cost even though cost is far higher than it ever was before.

That's because there's *no* cost as far as the employee is concerned. And even if the firing employer is overcharged, the employee doesn't care or complain. Meanwhile, the employer who pays the bill... and therefore is the real customer...tends to be well satisfied, regardless of whether the employee quickly finds a new job. After all, hastened re-employment is only one of the benefits he's purchasing...and not necessarily the main one. Indeed, in some cases, if it takes a long time for the individual to find a job *even with help*, that merely confirms the wisdom of the firing decision.

The momentum of a trend. Employment is a competitive marketplace. Each corporation tends to match the benefits other employers provide. And once a benefit is given to a few employees, the company tends to extend it on a non-discriminatory basis. Employees reinforce both tendencies...asking for outplacement because other companies give it, and because their own employer has granted it to other employees.

Moreover, the increasing tendency of employees to litigate when fired encourages corporations to purchase outplacement as a pacifier of feelings that might otherwise stimulate legal action.

> **Outplacement has two central benefits...
> one solely for the employer, and
> one shared by the employer and the employee.**
>
> **Recognizing and selling these *employer* advantages is
> the breakthrough that got companies to pay fees
> when they fire, not just when they hire.**

The benefits are:

1. Removal

I began this chapter by illustrating the advantages to the employer of getting the terminated employee off-premises immediately. "Out of sight, out of mind" makes for much better morale among the workers who remain on the job. And if *you* fired the guy, it's nicer for you too, not to meet him every day in the elevator or the parking lot.

Since the advent of outplacement, demoralizing "death rows" of fired executives who are humanely given "at least an office and a secretary" while they look for work have all but disappeared from the corporate scene. The main exceptions occur during massive layoffs, when the outplacement "counselors" may work on the employer's premises, leaving the executives right where they were, until they find other jobs.

2. Re-employment

This second benefit could be more accurately stated, "A demonstration of *concern* for re-employment." Again employee morale is the operative factor. The employer buys visible *proof that he cares*. And that proof is delivered instantaneously...just by hiring the outplacement firm, regardless of how soon or how late re-employment actually occurs.

Naturally, the corporate personnel department should be checking employee satisfaction, and steering its outplacement business toward the

firms that employees seem to like best. But beyond that, whatever results are achieved are strictly a matter between the employee and his
outplacement counselor.

**Some observers suggest that a third reason corporations
purchase outplacement is expiation of guilt. I doubt it.**

The idea is that the person who decides to grant outplacement is often
the same one who decided to fire the individual...or who so mismanaged his part of the corporation that a whole cadre of managers had to
be swept away. He feels guilty. And by granting some of the corporation's money for outplacement, he achieves some kind of atonement
and feels less guilty.

Maybe in rare instances such self-indulgent feeling is the basis for
spending large sums on outplacement. But try to picture the president
of a corporation speaking to someone who's just spent thousands...
even hundreds of thousands...of dollars on outplacement:

> "Good going, Paul! I'm glad you spent all that money so you
> could feel better. Try to spend some more tomorrow. Maybe you'll
> feel even better."

Perhaps guilt does figure in the outplacement decision. But I see sim-
pler, more publicly-supportable motives such as convenience, employee PR, fear of litigation, and peer pressure to keep up with the
humanity and modernity of other corporations.

**Now that you have a comprehensive background
on outplacement, let's pursue your self-interest.**

**If there's still time, you may be able to interview several
firms and pick the one that will do the most for you.**

I say "if there's still time," because when you're taken next door by
the person who just fired you and introduced to "someone who can
help," it's too late to have any say in selecting your outplacement firm.

The company has chosen. Now all you can do is try to get a worth-while effort from the firm they've picked.

Merely having read this book will help, because you'll have a good knowledge of all the techniques for changing jobs, and you can press for aid with the specific program you feel will do the most good. You won't just blithely go along with whatever is offered.

But suppose you're fired, and then told you'll be getting such-and-such a severance arrangement. . .which will include outplacement. As you discuss the details in the personnel department, say something like this:

> "Oh, I've heard quite a bit about outplacement. . .some of it very good, and some of it not so good. I guess it makes a lot of differ-ence what *firm* you get, and even which *counselor* within the firm. Would it be okay with you if I interviewed more than one firm and chose the one I'd feel most comfortable with?"

> "Of course I'll give first preference to the firms you recommend. And I'll stay within the right price range, if you'll just tell me what that is. But I'd also like to check out a couple firms where I've heard of people getting really good help. I don't know the names off-hand, but I can find out. . .maybe they'll be the same ones you have in mind. Would it be okay for me to shop around a bit?"

One of the main purposes outplacement serves, as far as the corpora-tion is concerned, is employee PR. Therefore, your request, when pre-sented in this rational, dispassionate fashion, will probably be cheer-fully granted.

Now let's go shopping.

You'll hear differing philosophies and recommendations.

To put them in perspective, find out the history of the firm and its principals before they got into outplacement.

Chances are that prior to entering the outplacement business, the firm's founders were involved in one of the other four categories of the "people business." Perhaps they still are. Make it a point to find out where they're "coming from," because it may tie in with how they attempt to serve you:

1.   Contingency Recruiters

One of the very best outplacement services I'm aware of was founded by two extremely smart and aggressive veterans of the contingency recruiting field. Accustomed to getting their resumes to every potential employer before their competitors did, they now run a fast-paced operation, heavy on direct mail, with pleasant suburban offices for their outplacees to sit in, and lots of appealing "extras," including videotaped group sessions to polish interviewing skills. These guys are *competitive* and everything they do is designed to "beat" what anyone else is offering. Moreover, *they've given up contingency recruiting to concentrate on their new and far more lucrative specialty.*

On the other hand, some of the most reprehensible of all outplacement operations are run by contingency recruiters who *haven't* given up their prior businesses. These folks also believe in direct mail. And they love to talk about "representation" by an "executive recruiter." Indeed, they specifically promise that their separate "recruiting division" will mail your resume to every company they and you identify as appropriate.

Their "division" will, of course, hang an implicit "price tag" on your head. But it's payable by your potential employer, so "it's no problem for you," they say. With these people, everything you should be wary of will be done to you. What's more, you'll help do it...and your former employer will pay to have it done. The "price-tagged" mailing certainly won't do as well as one that comes straight from you without the tag. But just in case it succeeds, these people are making sure they get two fees...not just one...from your employment.

2.   Retainer Recruiters

Of all four segments, this is the only one that finds it virtually impossible to operate an outplacement division, while maintaining their original line of work...although quite a few retainer recruiters have left that field to establish outplacement firms.

The reason is a "Catch 22." If a retainer firm tries to do both, their recruiting clients will question their objectivity and worry about being offered another company's "discards." Conversely, their "outplacees" will be resentful if they're refused a shot at openings being filled by the firm that's supposed to be helping them. Indeed, because of this obvious conflict-of-interest the AESC, a professional association serving the retainer recruiting industry, denies membership to any firm that also runs or owns an outplacement operation.

If you encounter an outplacement firm that also does *any* kind of recruiting, be on your guard. And if you find one that claims affiliation with a retainer-only recruiting firm, ask how they deal with a conflict-of-interest that many retainer firms consider intolerable.

3. Organizational Psychologists

Some of the top organizational psychologist firms were among the first to get into outplacement when the new specialty developed. And by now almost all such firms offer outplacement...either in addition to what they offered before, or totally replacing their original less-lucrative practice.

One of today's leading outplacement firms was originally one of America's top firms of organizational psychologists. Not surprisingly, they do excellent counseling on interpersonal skills in exploiting personal and networking contacts...which they say account for 70% of the jobs their counselees find...and in handling interviews effectively. They think of direct mail in terms of 100 letters per counselee, and they say it leads to 10% of the jobs their counselees get. (I wonder what 1,000 or 2,000 letters would do?) Here we have a classic case of a fine outplacement firm reflecting its "roots."

4. Executive Marketers

Despite the litigation and bad publicity, a few of the better executive marketing/career counseling firms survived the lean years when only individuals paid for their services, and have become quite successful now that they're tapping employers for fees. Some have given up selling to individuals. Others accept money from both directions.

When an employer pays the bill, these firms get no more squawks from their counselees than any of the other outplacement firms do. In fact their years of experience in trying to deliver some kind of results, when individuals paid far less than employers now pay, have tended to make them shrewd and practical. In particular, they tend to understand direct mail better than some of the firms that have entered the field only after "outplacement" was invented.

> ## At a typical 15%-of-salary fee, the outplacement firm is grossing upwards of $15,000 on you...and you might assume that's enough for you to take full advantage of everything they provide.
>
> ### Be careful! Test for the "Health Club M.O."

As you're probably aware, the only reason today's sparklingly-appointed health clubs can prosper is that not everyone who pays for a one-, two-, or three-year membership actually uses the club. Many lose their enthusiasm after a few visits or a few weeks, and don't come at all. And fortunately almost *nobody* uses *all* the "facilities." Some only come to aerobics classes...or just swim...or just use the machines...or play squash or basketball on rare occasions. If all the "members" came three times a week for just a couple activities, the club would be swamped and would have to shut down. Indeed, it's not unknown in the health club business to subtly discourage some members...usually the unattractive, self-conscious ones... from coming in and overcrowding an oversold facility.

Expect a bit of the same "modus operandi" at some of the outplacement establishments you'll visit. Be on the lookout for a long list of facilities and services which they "supply," but would hate to see you use to any meaningful extent.

As each service is pointed out, express your favorable impression...
and pin down a promise as to how much you'll be allowed to *use* it:

Desk Space:

"Nice, efficient layout! I'd probably be coming in just about every
day. Is there any limit on that? Would I have to book ahead by the
week...or by the day? Do newcomers have priority over people
who've been around a few months?"

Secretarial Service/Word Processing:

"Great! I'll need that, because I'm planning to send out a comprehensive direct mail campaign. I've heard you need at least 1,000
letters to get 5 or 6 leads. Any problem with that? Also, I'm a
stickler about accuracy and neatness. I assume you'll be entering
my list of names, titles, and addresses into your machine and then
playing out the whole typed letter...you won't just be filling in a
printed letter, or using a 'canned' mailing list, will you? And I
suppose everyone dictates a few personalized letters. No limit on
that, is there?"

Mailing:

"Everything goes through your postage meter, I suppose. Any
limit or extra cost on that? And if Federal Express is needed once-
in-a-while when there's special urgency, how is that handled?"

Telephone:

"Oh, I'm glad that's included. Any limit on calls? I presume you
have WATS lines, so there's no limit on long distance either? If I
wind up mailing more than 1,000 letters, and want to verify names
and titles, etc., that'll mean a lot of brief calls. That's OK, too?"

Reference Materials:

"Nice efficient-looking library. I presume you have several copies
of the main directories like Standard & Poor's and D & B, so that a
person can settle down with a book and really go through it a page
at a time for an afternoon, or two or three days in a row. I wouldn't
want to feel I was monopolizing something other people also needed
to use. How does the courtesy on that work here?"

Stationery/Resume Printing:

> "What nice printing. And what nice rich ivory paper. But I may
> prefer to use my own engraved letterhead, and maybe have white
> paper for the resume. Could I make that change at no extra cost?
> Well if not, will you use other paper if I supply it?" (Avoiding the
> "outplacement ivory" combo...or any other combo...is worth
> whatever it costs.)

You get the idea. By the time you've demonstrated your intention to
fully use even a few of the firm's facilities, you'll have a good idea of
their personality and helpfulness...and how much beyond exhortation,
coffee, and sympathy they normally contribute to a job campaign.

Be cynical!

Look for a connection between what an outplacement firm recommends ...and what their involvement in it costs them.

Neither you nor I can ever be certain why an outplacement firm emphasizes certain techniques and discourages others. The presumption I always start with is that they recommend what they earnestly believe will
be most helpful, and discourage what they believe will be counterproductive. However, you sometimes wonder.

For example, I recently had a phone conversation with a counselee,
who explained he was operating out of his outplacement firm's location
and could show up in my office within two or three minutes. Surprised
and intrigued, because that meant he couldn't be more than a block
away in absolutely the highest-rent neighborhood in Manhattan, I asked
about the facilities he was getting:

> JOHN: "They're obviously not stinting on the rent. What do they
> give you, sort of a salesman's phone-calling booth with a work
> surface?"

COUNSELEE: "Oh, no. I've got a separate room with a door and a window...and a nice wood desk, a swivel chair, and an extra chair."

JOHN: "And they let you use it as much as you want?"

COUNSELEE: "Yes. I come in almost every day. In fact, the reason I chose this place was because I liked where I'd be sitting, and the very high overall tone of the place."

JOHN: "Great! What about services?

COUNSELEE: "That's another thing I like. They've got two or three really fine secretaries here...very attractive, well-groomed, good skills. This place is a real class act...that's why I chose it."

JOHN: "Terrific! Are you putting out a direct-mail campaign?"

COUNSELEE: "Oh, absolutely not! They don't believe in direct mail here. In fact, they don't believe in any kind of letter writing. They don't even believe in answering newspaper ads."

Finally I understood. *Ambience was the competitive edge.* "This place is a real class act...that's why I chose it." Nice office, and apparently you *could* sit there. Great secretaries, too. *But don't use them to put out letters.*

This guy's outplacement firm is probably paying annual rent of $50 per square foot on the approximately 100 square feet they let him occupy...$5,000 per year (although let's hope he finds work in less than a year). In his mind, they're obviously more of a "class act" than all of the other outplacement firms in Midtown Manhattan who propose to stuff him into an open-ended work/phone unit that occupies only one-fourth as much space. His outfit has more impressive secretaries, too. However, that firm's *advice* is such that he'll be making absolutely minimal use of those classy secretaries.

It's conceivable that a more utilitarian-appearing establishment might have had some word-processing harridans in the back room who'd have implemented a much more comprehensive campaign on his behalf than the glamorous geishas currently answering his phone and serving his coffee.

Before you choose or reject any outplacement firm, be sure to find out *what kind of a campaign they recommend for you.* Are they really listening to your concerns and objectives? Do they seem to be tailoring a program to meet *your* needs? Or are they applying a standard formula?

And when you find out what their prescription will be, figure out what it will cost them to provide it. Maybe the cheapest methods for them are clearly the only ones that fit your specific needs. But make them explain why other methods, carried on simultaneously, shouldn't also be part of your program.

**Networking is the least-cost recommendation
for an outplacement firm.**

But will there be a backlash?

Networking is a valuable technique, with all the advantages and disadvantages we discussed in Chapter 4. However, in addition to what it offers you, networking also has some major advantages...and no disadvantages...for an outplacement firm.

Networking is largely a local activity. You won't be traveling around the country just for brief visits with strangers who don't have a job for you, but might provide "advice" and the names of additional people to contact. Therefore, *you won't be using the outplacement firm's long-distance phone lines and its word-processing services* to set up your appointments. Indeed, since only local calls will be involved, you'll probably stay home and make them from your den, in which case *you won't even be using desk space and local phone lines* at the outplacement service. To the extent that you occupy yourself with nothing but networking, you're virtually no burden whatever.

Unfortunately, the wild-fire growth of outplacement companies and their almost universal tendency to recommend high-pressure pleas for "just-a-few-minutes-of-your-time-so-I-can-get-the-benefit-of-your-knowledge-and-suggestions" is about to generate a backlash, if it hasn't already.

Senior executives tell me they're getting monumentally fed up with these increasingly frequent requests. The shrewder ones no longer resignedly reach for their calendars when a name with "clout" is said to have ''suggested I call you.'' They say they'll have their secretary look over their schedule and call back with a date. Meanwhile, they check the person whose name was used; find out how urgently or casually he desires cooperation; negotiate an ''I-won't-do-this-to-you-if-you'll-stop-doing-it-to-me'' truce; and have their secretary call with deepest regrets.

Beware of cheap, standardized direct mail.

Rather than appear to neglect direct mail, many outplacement firms now routinely send an impressive number of letters to standard lists.

For example, a Midwestern firm that processes about 50 executives per year routinely sends out 1,000 letters for each high-level outplacee. They hit:

> ''CEO's of 500 Major Companies'' (*Fortune*'s list)
>
> ''CEO's of America's 200 Fastest-Growing Companies'' (from *Inc.* or *Venture* magazines' lists)
>
> ''300 Leading Executive Recruiting Firms''

And, of course, the mailing is a standard ''outplacement-ivory''-combo of cover letter and two-page resume. It does not resemble a personal communication from an executive using his own stationery. And the executive is not encouraged to target his own mailing list.

Clearly, this outfit is doing more for its outplacees than the firm with the impressive secretaries that discourages sending any letters at all.

But not much. And certainly not enough to add significantly to the firm's operating costs, since they mail to standardized lists. A thousand letters woosh out the door, without ever having to keyboard a list designed for the outplacee.

Sadly, avalanches of these mass-produced mailings have virtually anesthetized the high-profile CEO's they're supposed to influence. They've become the ''junk mail'' of the executive suite, just as high pressure networking appointments have become the most-disliked cal-endar-cloggers.

Don't judge a firm on how many letters they'll send. Instead, find out who they're willing to send them to. Can it be a list of 1,000 or more people that *you* select? And are you encouraged to think creatively and expansively in framing your list? If so, your outplacement firm is ob-viously interested in your re-employment, not just their P & L.

You're lucky. Now you can go through the directories, and use the phone. You can pick the most appropriate recipients...hopefully about two echelons above the job you want, in the corporations (and subsidi-aries) you're most interested in and most likely to be hired by.

Fortunately, many of the people on your list *won't* be the obvious ones who receive a daily deluge from the outplacement firms. And of course you'll send a personal letter on personal stationery, plus a "sales repre-sentative" resume, so your mailing won't scream, "Junk mail's here!"

There's one canned list your outplacement firm *should* send your resume to.

When it comes to corporate executives, you'll want to pick your own personal list of 1,000 or more employers, choosing *your* most appro-priate recipients at the companies that are most intriguing to you. The more personalized your list is, the more likely you are to reach off-the-beaten-path executives who haven't yet been bombarded into indiffer-ence.

Retainer recruiting firms, however, are another matter. They expect to receive resumes and, of course, are interested in any that happen to fit their current searches.

There are more than 1,000 retainer firms in the U.S. And no two of them will ever be working to fill the same job at the same time. So make sure your outplacement firm hits them all. Omitting any firm omits your exposure to the jobs they're handling.

Incidentally, your engraved personal stationery and non-matching re-sume aren't as important in contacting recruiters as in dealing with cor-porations. If you only have 1,000 sheets and envelopes of "the good stuff,'' use them on your personal letters to companies. Divert your standard outplacement mailing to the retainer recruiters.

It would be nice if you agreed
on style of resume with your outplacement firm.

But that's not essential.

One of the services you're certain to get from your outplacement firm is help in preparing your resume. So one factor to check out is whether you and they agree on questions of format. *But don't get too hung up on this point.*

Chances are that, like most able executives, you're an experienced writer of concise and persuasive business prose. In fact, you've probably evaluated more resumes *for purposes of employment* than your outplacement counselor has. You know what you'd like to receive. Insist on the same attributes in what you send. *Choose your outplacement firm on the basis of what they'll do beyond helping write your resume,* which you're probably best off writing largely on your own anyway.

Only if you're one of those rare executives who's a rotten writer, and has reached $100,000 + in spite of it, will you be tempted to ''roll-over-and-play-dead'' while your outplacement counselor prepares your resume. And even then, be sure to show a draft to other executives whose judgment you trust. Let your outplacement counselor have a helpful say in preparing your resume. But not the only one. And certainly not the final one.

Find out how the outplacement firm handles phone calls.

Outsiders can't see where you're sitting,
but they can easily tell what your situation is.

These days it's a dead giveaway when you return someone's call and the phone is answered:

>''Four-six-six-two.''

Or alternatively:

>''Executive offices.''

No one with a private office and a secretary has his phone answered that way. Obviously he's been fired and is calling from an outplacement firm.

At best, the outplacement firm will have several separate phone lines for outplacees...each with "Call Waiting." One of these will be permanently assigned to you for the duration of your unemployment, and it will always be answered:

"Mr. (your name's) office."

Otherwise, the firm merely instructs you and all other outplacees to use the same number, which is answered by merely repeating the last four digits, or saying something vague like "executive suite." This is a better no-cost alternative than answering with the name of the outplacement firm...but not much better.

Extras to help get your act together: aptitude and psychological testing, individual and group therapy, and interview coaching (probably with video playback).

Perhaps the circumstances of your termination...or fortunate personal circumstances...assure you of solid office-support systems, regardless of what the outplacement company offers. Then you'll be much more interested in "extras" than in the "fundamentals."

If psychological counseling and therapy are promised, insist on meeting the person who'll deal with you...and on knowing his credentials. What you *don't* need at a traumatic time of career upheaval, with its associated pain and self-doubt, is to have your "head" dealt with by an opportunistic amateur.

Televised interview-coaching can be very helpful in "seeing ourselves as others see us." And role-playing rehearsal with a skilled counselor, who asks tough questions and makes sure you have confident reactions, can also be very valuable. What you get out of any technique depends more on the skill, good will, and time-commitment of the person administering it, than on what the brochure says.

Which brings me to your best...and most elusive...safeguard:

Referencing an Outplacement Firm:

**Don't be content with the names the firm gives you.
And don't just find out whether the counselee
liked the firm or happened to get work quickly.**

What did the firm actually *do?*

Outplacement companies are in the business of being friendly, sympathetic, and concerned. Hence, their counselees almost invariably like them.

However, if the firm has mainly been dispensing coffee, sympathy, and dubious advice, it may not have been really helpful...even though its counselees may have a favorable impression. Find out about specific recommendations and concrete help.

When outplacement firms are volunteered by your personnel department, ask for a list of the people they've sent to each firm, and call *several* from each. And when you visit a firm where you don't have access to an independent list of outplacees, try to shake hands with people who are using the facilities on the day of your visit. Remember their names and telephone later to ask your questions, when the privacy of a phone call will encourage them to speak more frankly than they would in front of the counselor who's showing you around.

Investigate as carefully as if you were about to commit upwards of $15,000 of your own money. Because in a very real sense you are.

Ask each major outplacement firm about the book they've written.

It will tell you their strategies, and help you decide whether to engage them.

Several of the largest outplacement firms have put out books on their "system" for finding another job, and most of these are available in the "Business" or "Careers" section of any sizable book store.

These books gain publicity for their outplacement "authors," and produce a second income from information already written as a handout for outplacees. Ranging from $4.95 to $19.95, these volumes are a fantastic bargain when compared to the thousands of dollars spent to get the same information through an outplacement program.

On second thought, perhaps you should check the bookstore first, and only secondarily ask the firm itself. I say that facetiously...but also on the basis of a disturbing anecdote, which I'll share with you.

An executive I've known for years called me one day, because he was considering spending $4,995 of his own money with an outplacement firm that sells its services to individuals, as well as corporations. Did I think such an investment would be worthwhile? He didn't name the company, and I didn't ask. Instead, I said:

> "Why don't you look at some of the books those firms have put
> out? Read what they'll be suggesting you do. And ask how much
> of it they'll do *for* you."

I then began to suggest several such books, naming the companies behind them. The first firm whose $19.95 book I mentioned turned out to be the one he'd been talking to:

> "Do you mean, John, that I can just walk in and buy that little..."
> (here he described and I confirmed the distinctive colors of the
> book jacket) "...book for $19.95? They waved that book in front
> of me when I was in their office. But they wouldn't let me get my
> hands on it until I paid them $1,995 for the first phase of their
> program!"

Talk about bargains. The bookstore is delivering a 99% discount!

| **Frankly, whether outplacement services are worth what they cost tends to depend more on who's paying than on the nature of the services.** |

If the former employer is paying, then by shopping around, the employee can certainly find services he considers a helpful "freebee."

But if the employee's own money is involved, it's a different story. Then he's deciding to part with lots of hard-earned cash. And he's deciding at a time when he's emotionally vulnerable, and should be conserving rather than splurging. At that moment, a high-pressure pitch to purchase "professional help" and to "invest in yourself" is analogous to an unscrupulous undertaker telling a distraught widow:

> "Surely you don't want to put your husband in this foam plastic box covered with cloth, when he could be hermetically sealed for the ages in this stainless steel casket that costs twenty times as much."

In both instances, individuals are hit by slick salesmen when their judgment is impaired. And both decisions are apt to be regretted later when value-received is compared with price-paid.

The difference between the unemployed executive and the tearful widow is that he can readily do for himself what's being discussed, and she can't. Moreover, when he reads his fine-print contract, he'll see he's actually committed to doing most of the work himself. Chances are that, later on, he'll feel like more of a dope than she will, if he signs on the dotted-line.

Outplacement firms that only take money from employers look disdainfully at the ones that also sell to individuals.

Interesting...but not very significant.

Given a choice, any supplier would rather cultivate long-lasting relationships with large corporate customers, than have to sell lots of small deals to individuals...a tacky and tedious process of squeezing blood out of near-stones.

The most prestigious outplacement firms take their fees only from employers, no longer soliciting...or greatly de-emphasizing...fees from individuals. They refer disdainfully to the firms that accept fees from job-seekers as *"retail outfits"*...a curiously-chosen epithet, because the companies invoking it charge much *higher* fees to corporations and can hardly be regarded as "wholesale."

You'll probably approach either type only when you have your former employer's money in hand, and your eyes wide open. Then you'll make your decision on the basis of what these firms actually agree to do for you...not on what they call each other.

After you've diligently surveyed the outplacement firms, you may decide to ask your former employer for money in lieu of outplacement.

Knowing that every outplacement firm's contract will make you responsible for finding your own job...and having "shopped" the firms and read their books...you may conclude that you can proceed without their help. Indeed, the aggressive campaign you have in mind may cost a lot less than the $15,000-or-more that your former company proposes to pay for outplacement.

If so, perhaps you should try to get the money instead.

Don't bring up the subject until after all the other financial aspects of your termination package have been solidly nailed down. You want your $15,000 | of outplacement money to be *in addition* to everything else...not in place of something.

And don't discuss foregoing outplacement until you've done your shopping and can give other reasons than just greed for feeling you don't need it. Otherwise you may be passing up valuable help that you really do need, in return for cash that...while substantial...won't put you ahead in the long run.

If you do try to get the money, bear in mind that *removal* is one of the main benefits of outplacement. If there's the slightest inkling that you may drift back to use the copying machines, to sponge a little secretarial service, or even to use the toilet when you're in the neighborhood, you'll never get away with cash in lieu of outplacement. Take this approach with your former employer's V.P. of Personnel:

> "You know, Susan, it seems that one of the main benefits all of the outplacement firms are stressing is the office facilities they provide, which are something *I really don't need.* I've got a complete home office that's a lot more comfortable than the little cubicles

they'd have me sitting in. And my place at home is really efficient. I'm already running off letters on my IBM-PC, which has a letter-quality printer. In fact, they look just as professional as anything a first-class secretary would put out. I even have one of those little copiers that Jack Klugman advertises on TV. So there's no way in the world that I'm going to be driving into the city to sit in an outplacement firm, when I've got everything I need right at home..."

I can't guarantee that you'll be successful with this approach. But it *is* the way to proceed.

In about half the instances I've heard of, when cash-in-lieu-of-outplacement was proposed by an employee, who was calm, cooperative, and behaved in a manner indicating that...even without professional handholding...he wouldn't be a problem to the firing employer, the individual was able to get the money.

> ## Don't underestimate the intangible values of outplacement.
>
> ## And don't overlook the chance to get outplacement *in addition* to maximum cash.

One exceptionally able executive I know has been unemployed twice in the past six years. This time he has outplacement, whereas previously he didn't. Consider what he has to say:

"First I negotiated for every penny of severance I could possibly get. I didn't even mention outplacement until after I had my money locked up. So my outplacement is an 'extra.' It doesn't sacrifice any cash."

Unfortunately, even though I did get outplacement, I wasn't allowed to choose the firm. And frankly, I don't think I've got a very good one. They've told me about networking and printed my resume and sent it around. And that's about it. I'm sure some other companies would do more."

"Even so, I feel I'm getting something very worthwhile."

"Instead of staying home, I go to the outplacement firm every day at exactly the same time I'd go to work. That keeps me from wasting extra hours in the kitchen with coffee and the morning paper, feeling sorry for myself, and playing with the kids."

"And when I get to the office, I have my own desk in one corner of a room with three other people who are also looking for work. The support we give each other is very helpful. One of my roommates is a lawyer, who got very depressed after not having an interview in over a month. When she finally lined one up, she was afraid she'd blow it. So all three of the rest of us questioned her for a whole day to get her ready and raise her confidence. We really do care about each other."

There you see a side of outplacement you could easily overlook. Just being with others who are facing and solving the problem of unemployment can be a big help.

Moreover, the executive we just heard from may be getting far more from his outplacement firm than he realizes. I know the people who own it, and they began as a fine group of organizational psychologists. I'll bet it's no accident that he's in a room with three other outplacees...actively helping them, and being helped by them.

The Bottom Line on Outplacement

Like so many other things in life, outplacement is pretty much what *you* make it. A sizable sum of your money is being invested. So if you get a chance to "shop," choose wisely.

And even if your employer chooses, you still have wide latitude in what you ask from your outplacement firm. It's your own fault if you fail to conduct a pragmatic and comprehensive campaign.

The Interview...
Making a Sales Call, and
Demonstrating the Product

Face it. When you go to an interview, a purchase decision is being made. The employer is seeing you and others to determine who he'll acquire and who he won't.

Chances are he's read your resume, which you or a recruiter sent him. Now a salesman is coming over with the actual product. Get ready. He won't just look at the paint job and kick the tires. He'll take a test drive!

You're the salesman. And you're also the *product*.

Moreover, because it's an interview...not just a social call...your host has permission to probe deeply. He can ask tougher and more personal questions than he'd ask at any other time. And he can examine

your analysis and strategy in solving business problems...yours and his...far more frankly than he would under any other circumstances.

You've got to be prepared for a really penetrating inquiry, if your interviewer takes that approach. If he doesn't, you've got to reveal yourself to him. And if the interview fails to display your merits, that's your problem, not his.

Ideally, your potential employer will wind up wanting to *buy* the car... or at least to drive it again, after he's seen and tried some others. If so, you'll be offered the job...or at least invited back for another round of interviews.

In the end, you may decide that this employer and his opportunity are not for you. But what you and I will work on in this chapter is *making sure that he doesn't conclude you're not for him.*

> ## Bear in mind that you're proving yourself on two levels:
>
> 1.   as a fine person, and
> 2.   as someone obviously able to do the job.

Your behavior and appearance will be scrutinized far more critically when you show up for an interview, than on any ordinary work day in the next ten years.

The person who's thinking of hiring you wants to be sure that you're someone he'll enjoy working with. And also someone who can walk around inside and outside the organization as a favorable reflection on the company and on him. Only if he's satisfied on these *"fine person"* points, will he concern himself with whether he thinks you can handle the job, as indicated by your experience and track record. He's hoping to find you:

Intelligent, and also "street smart," with abundant common sense;

Analytical, logical, goal-oriented, and a planner;

A skilled communicator...good at listening, speaking and writing;

Unmistakably a leader...but also a "team player," cooperative, and congenial;

Healthful, attractive, and well groomed;

Tasteful in dress and decorum;

Poised, courteous, and cultured;

Sensitive to the feelings of others...not pushy, pig-headed, or obnoxious;

Honest, loyal, and straightforward;

Politically aware, but not a political operator;

Committed, responsible, and diligent;

Cheerful and optimistic, with a "can do" attitude;

And overall, an *interesting person,* with curiosity, enthusiasm...and maybe even a sense of humor!

Virtually all of the attributes listed above will help you to do the job, once you land it. And in interviewing to get the job, don't underestimate the seemingly superficial aspects that are more "image" than "essence." Appearance and behavior are first to be noticed. And if they're deficient, you may flunk the "*fine person*" test, even though you score plenty of "but-he-could-probably-do-the-job" points.

That's why I included those tips on "buffing-to-a-rich-lustre" at the end of Chapter 14. You probably didn't need them. But some readers did. And interviewing is the time of maximum scrutiny, and therefore greatest need. For that reason, this chapter is just as concerned with interviewing behavior as with answering questions. At the end I've even included a "flight plan" for your interview.

But for now, let's forget "image," and go straight to "essence." This is a sales call. And, like any other salesman, you've got to deliver *enough persuasive information to convince the prospect that your product can **do the job***.

Interviewing is a difficult form of selling for two reasons:

1. **It's a "package deal," where the salesman comes with the product; and**

2. **The customer, not the salesman, controls the unfolding of the sales presentation.**

Ordinarily a customer can take the product, and leave the salesman. Unfortunately, you're a "package deal." Therefore you must sell with great finesse. Much as you'd like to, you can't just make a well-organized presentation, and afterward deal with questions and objections.

The interview is a unique ritual drama, in which a sales call is played as if it's a social call.

Which it's not. One of the two parties is totally in command. He's the buyer. He's the decision-maker at the end. And he's in charge all along the way. By controlling the use of time and the choice of topic in a Q-and-A format, he determines which features are brought up, and in what order, and how thoroughly or superficially each one is discussed.

And the fact that *your* sociability is part of what's being sold prevents you from saying what a regular salesman would say:

"That's a very good question. But *let's hold it* until I've finished explaining how the machine works."

"No, that's really not a problem with this machine. *Ours is the only one* which doesn't have that disadvantage."

Politeness, modesty, loyalty, confidentiality. You must display these and many other attributes, because you're "the product." Unfortunately, having to do so handicaps your sales presentation.

The first principle of interview salesmanship:
forego the monologue
…at the outset, and all the way to the end.

Because the format of the interview is ritualistically conversational, you can't give a too-long answer to any question. You can't sell yourself as socially-polished, if you monopolize the conversation.

So don't use any question…no matter how broad…as a springboard for a monologue. Instead, give a concise answer that hits the highlights in clear and specific terms, including numbers ("a little under $5 million in sales and about 150 employees") and approximate dates ("as I recall, that was in late '78").

Don't ever talk longer than one or two minutes. Finished or not, wind up your sentence, shut your mouth, and look at your interviewer to see if he wants more on the same topic…or would rather switch to something else. If he wants elaboration, he'll say so. What's more, he'll point you in the right direction:

"Interesting, and I certainly agree with your strategy. But when we tried something along those lines, we ran into trouble with the unions. How'd you make out on that score?"

Now you've got him eating out of your hand! How much better than if you'd bored him with a full explanation before "coming up for air."

Learn "newspaper style."
Written and oral, it will make you an outstanding communicator.

...And it's a lifesaver in the interview format.

Do me a favor. Next time you pick up a newspaper, notice the way every item is written:

1. The headline sums up the article.

2. The first paragraph lays out the entire story.

3. The first sentence of every paragraph tells what the whole paragraph is about.

4. And the major facts of every story always come earliest. Lesser, more detailed points come later, and the most trivial are at the end.

There's good reason for this "big-picture"-first format. It allows you, the reader, to get what you want out of the paper very quickly and efficiently. You can stop reading any article after a paragraph or two and still know the gist of the story. And when an article really interests you, you can dig deeper and deeper into the details, by reading further.

See the analogy to what you're trying to achieve in an interview? Just like you reading the paper, your interviewer always has the prerogative to dig deeper, or switch to a different topic. You can drop any article after just a headline or a paragraph. And he can divert you to a different subject, just by asking another question.

Therefore, all of your answers must be organized in "newspaper style." You've got to state your main point in the first sentence or two of each answer. You can't wallow in detail, "setting the stage" for your main point. Because if you do, a new question may cut you off before you *get* to your main point. Then you'll appear petty, illogical, and detail-oriented...even if you're not.

Surprisingly few people…even senior executives…have learned what their newspapers show them every day. Study and master newspaper style. Use it orally and in writing. Every bit of your business communication will improve…not just interviews, but memos and presentations, too.

**Just because you can't deliver a salesman's monologue
is no reason not to prepare one.**

**Analyze your product and your customer's needs,
and develop the sales message you *wish* you could
deliver in a 15-minute monologue.**

**Then divide it into brief topical capsules.
Believe it or not, almost every interviewer…
no matter how inept…will ask questions that allow you
to present everything you have clearly in mind.**

That's right. The questions you receive *will* relate to what you want to say, if you *know* what you want to say. That's because your interviewer really does want to find out how your background and achievements fit his needs, and how they guarantee you'll perform as well for him as you have for others.

Fundamentally, he wants to hear what you want to communicate. Not necessarily, however, in the order you'd like to present it. And, of course, with more attention devoted to your failures and gaps in background than you'd prefer.

So prepare as if you could deliver a salesman's monologue. If you've figured out what you should present, then you'll hear it asked for. And when each ''appropriate'' query comes along, you can drop in the right one- or two-minute capsule. Unprepared, you'd have found those same questions ''irrelevant,'' and ''not leading anywhere.'' But knowing where the conversation *should* be going, you'll more readily see the interviewer's questions as a path to get there.

How often have you been asked a question in an important meeting and given a ''so-so'' answer, only to realize afterward that you had a perfect opening to say something really favorable? That's an experience we all have almost every day. Prepare yourself. Don't let it happen in a potentially career-making job interview.

What about questions specifically designed to give you trouble?

The possibilities are endless...too many to discuss. But almost all such zingers aim for a relatively few slips and wrong answers. Those I can identify for you.

As I said before, your interviewer is on your side. He wants to find out that you are the person he's looking for. If so, his staffing problem is solved. But if you're not as good as you appear to be, hiring you could cause far more difficulty than it resolves.

Therefore, he'll ask lots of questions aimed at revealing your flaws. Even your answers to the most bland and casual queries will be scrutinized for damaging admissions. And chances are, those revelations won't have much to do with your resume-stated background. Instead, they'll relate to your personality and your management techniques... the kinds of shortcomings behavioral psychologists probe. So here are some wrong answers to watch out for...both with the employer, and with the company's psychologist, if you consent to meet him:

WRONG ANSWER: There's more bad than good.

Of all the "wrong answers," this one fits more questions than any other. So many, in fact, that I can't even begin to think up enough examples to suggest its vast possibilities. However, the minute you're about to list attributes of anyone, anything, or any situation, be sure to ask yourself:

> "How many good ones should I mention and how many bad ones?"

Decide shrewdly. Sometimes there should be lots of bad ones and hardly any good ones, as in the list of probable results you mention when your interviewer gets your reaction to an operating policy that verges on the unethical and illegal.

But suppose he asks how you feel about your current job. Obviously, it fails to utilize your prodigious talents and energy level. But don't slip! There's more good than bad; otherwise, the interviewer will expect you to be malcontent in his job, too. And in describing your current boss, there's probably a lot that's admirable, not just shortcomings; otherwise your interviewer envisions you talking negatively about *him*. Same with your reaction to the overall management of your current company. Some policies and approaches (which you will list) make lots of sense. However, certain *key* ones have serious disadvantages (obvious to any thinking person, including your interviewer).

Needless to say, you also see far more advantages relative to disadvantages when asked how the job you're interviewing for fits your talents and aspirations, and how you fit the job. Same, too, when it comes to balancing the opportunities in contrast to the obvious problems facing the industry and company you're being interviewed for. Same goes for the U.S. and its industrial and other institutions, and on and on.

You're no Pollyanna. You can see defects and problems, analyze them accurately, and conceive and execute realistic and creative strategies for dealing with them. However, you're absolutely not one of those "nattering nabobs of negativism" Spiro T. Agnew warned us about.

WRONG ANSWER: You'd live your life differently if you could.

This is the wrong answer to all those "if" questions. If you could be anyone other than yourself, who would you be? If you could go back and change an earlier career decision, what would you be doing today? Don't accept any offer to re-write your personal history. You're basically a happy and highly functional person, who has high self-esteem and is busy producing and enjoying. . .not fretting and regretting.

Also bear this "wrong answer" in mind when faced with "if" questions about the future. If you can be anything you wish five years from now, it will be something that represents fine progress along the path you're on right now.

With respect to your current and past marriages, outstanding or difficult children, and other highly personal facets of your life, probably the less said the better. . .at least until you're sure that your values and circumstances clearly correspond to those of your interviewer. You can't possibly gain anything by being either ahead of, or behind, him on these points.

And of course if you're asked whether you "consider yourself successful," the answer is "Yes" and briefly why. . .not, "Well, sort of, and I'd have been more so, if it weren't for. . ."

WRONG ANSWERS: Illustrations of your greatest talents and achievements that:
                                                    1. don't relate to the job you're interviewing for, and/or
                                                    2. happened long ago.

Not surprisingly, your strongest attributes and the achievements you're proudest of are work-related and correlate amazingly well with the requirements of the job you're interviewing for. The fact that, after eighteen years of avid competition, you recently bred, trained, and groomed a Dalmation that won Best-In-Show at the Grand National Competition of the American Kennel Club is hardly worth mentioning. Especially when compared with the fact that last month your Division's hemorrhoid remedy scored the highest market share in the 64-year history of the brand.

Don't be confused. When asked for your *"best"* achievements, always give your *latest* ones. Only when specifically asked about early phases of your career will you trot out the corresponding long-ago achievements. . .thus demonstrating that you've always been an overachiever. The greatest days of your career are now and in the future, not in the past.

A variation on this theme has to do with what you *like* most and least in your current job or the one under discussion. Your preferences will match the job you're interviewing for just as neatly as your talents do.

WRONG ANSWERS: **You've failed to develop non-business interests.**
AND
You spend time on non-business interests.

These wrong answers are bookends; they come as a matched pair. You're apt to be asked what your avocational interests are. Better have some ready to mention. Active sports are always good. Intellectual and artistic interests begin to look respectable when you get comfortably over $100,000...and they take on great lustre when you get way over $100,000. Charitable and ''cause'' interests also gain respectability and ultimately cache, as you soar into the corporate stratosphere.

However, until you're being considered for a position high enough to be corporately ornamental as well as useful, don't let on that your wide-ranging interests take any significant amount of time away from work. Chances are your potential boss wants you ''hungrier'' for corporate performance bonuses than for intellectual and humanitarian nourishment.

By the way, there's a chance you may be asked what interesting books you've read lately. Anyone who asks won't worry about your time, since reading is usually done when and where you can't work. Don't bring up the subject. But do prepare. If you seldom read, you should pick up a critically-praised *non*-business volume...perhaps a biography or a spy novel...from the current bestseller list. Comment knowledgeably. And if pressed further, mention a couple other books you'd like to read but haven't had time for. That's enough. You're joining a business, not a literary society.

WRONG ANSWERS: **Your aspirations for the future don't springboard from the job you're discussing.**

''What-would-you-like-to-be-when-you-grow-up?'' questions are just a variation of the ''if'' questions we discussed earlier. Make sure your stated objectives are consistent with getting the job you're interviewing for and pursuing it as whole-heartedly as the company could wish.

WRONG ANSWER: Anything but the frank truth about when and why you're leaving.

If you were FIRED, say so. Reference checking will surely reveal the fact, even if you still have an office and phone message service at your former company. Any attempt at cover-up will seem dishonest, unintelligent, and emotionally immature. Give a short, simple explanation, objectively avoiding bitterness and complaint. Show you can rise above temporary setbacks. Your forthrightness and maturity in comparison with most people, who fidget, fiddle, and fume, will come off favorably. More about this later.

WRONG ANSWER: The too-vague answer.

For every job you've held, know and be able to state without hesitation your title, who you reported to, what size and type unit you commanded (in people, facilities, budgets, sales, profit, market share, etc). Know too in approximate numbers the size and situation of the overall organization of which your unit was a part. You absolutely must know what you're doing now...and you should also know what you've done in the past.

Remember JFK? Most of the nation became convinced he could cope with our problems...in large part because he could speak about them so succinctly, and yet so specifically in facts and figures. It takes no more time to say "a $55 million division in Akron" than it does to say "a medium-sized division located in the Midwest." Yet the former avoids raising several unnecessary questions in the interviewer's mind:

> "I wonder what he means by 'medium-sized.' "

> "*Where* in the Midwest?"

> "Why didn't he just give me the specifics? Maybe he's afraid I'll know somebody who was there when he was."

WRONG ANSWER: "Confidentiality prevents me..."

Use common sense when it comes to confidentiality. Don't be a blabbermouth. But if the competitor who's interviewing you frankly discusses his business with you, then reciprocate. Knowing the other guy's figures won't make them your figures, and vice versa. If you've been responsible for something very brilliant and very recent, which must be screened from your competitor, just give a definite but non-specific comparison he's undoubtedly already guessed:

> "With the new line included, sales for the first quarter are more than double what they were in the same period last year. *Much more than double.*"

The sparkle in your eyes and your smile of pride and achievement will communicate your accomplishment just as well as if you'd stated the exact figure for the new line standing alone.

Remember: A lot of people who've done a poor job use confidentiality as a cover-up, which is what you'll be suspected of if you "take the Fifth Amendment." People who've done a great job are eager to tell about it.

WRONG ANSWER: More than was asked for.

One rather tricky question is to ask for your "four greatest achievements"...or your "three strongest talents"...or some other number of something favorable. Give exactly the number asked for, *and no more.* The test is to see if you'll plunge right past the requested number, piling on achievement after achievement, in a binge of self-praise. If so, you'll be revealed as a braggart, psychologically suffering from low self-esteem. At the very minimum, you'll seem to be someone who doesn't listen and follow instructions alertly.

WRONG ANSWER: A too-long answer.

This wrong answer is asked for by every agonizingly open-ended question...one of the commonest headaches of the interviewing process. Here the remedy is one of those *capsules* that I suggested you create out of the fifteen-minute salesman's monologue you're not being allowed to deliver. That highly refined quarter-hour of mandatory product description and product advantages nicely fills anywhere from seven to ten 1-1/2- to 2-minute capsules, which can be administered as requested throughout the interview.

Suppose you're zapped with this frequently-thrown open-ender:

"Tell me about yourself."

Don't be wimpy and grasp for help:

"Well, what particular aspect would you like to know about?"

Instead, just plunge in and *cope!* Take no more than one to two minutes and hit the highlights, covering everything from childhood to now. Include a few words about where you grew up, because this question is usually asked to evoke a broad-brush personal portrait. To prove it can be done, I'll give you my own:

"I was born and grew up in Reedsburg, Wisconsin, a small town of 5,000 people, where my father was a partner in the Ford car and tractor business. Worked my way through the University of Wisconsin and the University of Wisconsin Law School as a radio announcer and taught Legal Writing at the Law School for a year. Came to New York City in 1960 as Radio-TV Contract Administrator at J. Walter Thompson Advertising Agency and later became an Account Executive on various consumer products. Joined Bristol-Myers Products in '65 as a Product Manager and ultimately became Director of New Product Marketing. Next I was Director of Marketing for the Sheaffer Pen Company, and then General Manager of the Tetley Tea Division of Squibb-BeechNut. In '71 I got into executive recruiting with Heidrick & Struggles, where I became a Vice President and one of the firm's top producers of fee income. And in 1977 I started The John Lucht Consultancy Inc., specializing in the selection of high-level executives for major corporations...the same firm I operate today.

That's way under two minutes, and yet it certainly covers "Tell me about yourself." If this were an interview, anything else of interest could be asked about.

Capsules: The Interview Pain-Reliever

Gapingly *open-ended questions* are one of the worst headaches of the interviewing process. They're painful as you grope for an answer that's appropriate, clear, and succinct. And if not handled well, they can lead to the serious complication of bogged-down monologuing, which can demonstrate that you're innately a poor communicator, disorganized, less-than-candid...and more. Indeed, open-ended questions are asked, in part, because they *are* troublesome to insecure, fuzzy-thinking people, who don't communicate well under pressure...people the interviewer wants to weed out.

I just administered a capsule for "Tell me about yourself." You may not need yours, but be sure you take it with you to your interview. Indeed, take along plenty of capsules. Like the Lomotil®, Dramamine®, Tetracycline®, Accromycin®, Alka-Seltzer®, and Pepto-Bismol® you take on your foreign travels, you'll feel better knowing they're on hand, whether you wind up using them or not.

Your interview pharmacopoeia should include:

A "Tell-Me-About-Yourself" Orientation   (CAPSULE)

Already prescribed.

Key Segments of Experience and Achievement   (CAPSULE)

These are the topically-organized segments of the fifteen-minute "salesman's monologue" you'd love to deliver but can't in the conversational format of an interview. Have your selling points of experience and achievement clearly in mind, with specific figures stapled into your memory. Nothing minimizes an achievement more than failing to remember precisely what it was.

Achievements in Rank Order   (CAPSULE)

This one prepares you for any "Top Three" or "Top Five" question. Since your greatest achievements should also tend to be your most recent, you'll ponder the importance/time tradeoffs in preparing this list. If there's nothing major to report from your most recent briefly-held job, don't feel you have to make something up, just to "represent" the ill-fated career move.

Maybe you have one monumentally large achievement sure to command awe and respect...and clearly attributable to your being there as the instigator and not merely one soldier in the platoon; but it happened too long ago to be one of your "latest-and-greatest." Prepare it succintly, and deliver it *last*...third out of three, or fifth out of five, depending on how many you're asked for.

Strengths and Weaknesses   (CAPSULE)

Give this one some real thought. Your strengths are at the heart of your sales pitch, and they ought to be the right ones for this job...or you'll be better off not getting it. Be ready to name and...if asked... illustrate several. Include your high energy level.

Come up with a proper "more-good-ones-than-bad-ones" answer; the ratio should be overwhelming...maybe 4 to 1. But, within the boundaries of enlightened self-interest, also try to be honest. The standard formula for an interview-confessed "weakness" is *"A strength carried to a fault."*

Examples:

> "Sometimes I may drive my people a little *too* hard. Since I'm a bit of a workaholic, I tend to expect others are, too."

> "Sometimes I can be *too* supportive of my people...hanging on to them, still trying to train and coach, when perhaps I should just pull the plug a few months sooner."

And how's this for a reverse-spin on a weakness?

"I'm the broad overall conceptualist...the strategist, the planner, the schemer...and also the enthusiastic motivator of the team. But I'm not the down-to-the-nitty-gritty implementer. I always make sure to have an operations officer I can absolutely depend on to see that things don't slip between the cracks...and also a meticulous controller, to make sure that there are no financial surprises. Without both of those guys doing their jobs, I couldn't do mine."

Obviously, this approach will work only if you're discussing a big job in a big company. But you get the idea and can adapt it to many situations.

Reason For Leaving   (CAPSULE)

It's not enough just to avoid the "wrong answer" of saying you quit...or worse yet that you're still doing your job...when everyone who's likely to be asked knows you've been fired. Prepare an accurate capsule on what happened and what your current status is. And *keep it brief and simple!*

If the new CEO brought along his own person for your job, no harm in saying so. Add, if true, that you too might have brought along someone you knew and trusted if you were in the CEO's shoes and had such a limited time to effect such a major turnaround. Indeed, you went out of your way to cooperate with the man who's now your successor, during those first awkward weeks when you were both on the payroll and he hadn't yet been named to your job. As you see it, what he has to do to be successful is to finish installing this-and-this program which you were putting into place when the upheaval occurred, and he seems to be taking basically that approach (if true).

There wouldn't be room in this entire book for the enormous smorgasbord of familiar firing scenarios...one of which may one day happen to you. A great many, like the one above and all sorts of consolidation and staff-cutting measures, can be frankly stated and endorsed. "Personality clash" with your boss, however, normally should *not* be the diagnosis. Say instead, "Fundamental policy differences," and cite some concrete examples. You simply can't afford to be categorized as someone who can't get along with people.

The trick in discussing firing is to take an open-minded dispassionate, managerial stance. Observe, comment, and react as an informed, objective observer, who's also a very skilled manager...not as someone subjectively involved, wronged, and wounded. You're willing to stand and be judged on the wisdom of your programs and the next administration may have to continue them. On the other hand, if you tried something that failed and you were in the process of changing course, say so. You'll be judged far more on the calibre and comprehension you demonstrate, than on the fact that you were fired. Chances are, your interviewer has also been fired at least once in his career.

Your Management Style   (CAPSULE)

For your answer to ring the bells on this issue, you'd better know what style the company feels *it* has. Check in advance and also watch for clues dropped by your interviewer. The "participative" style is currently in vogue, whereby your door is open to your subordinates and their ideas, and you get results through motivation and delegation.

But for some companies you should hedge your bet...."On the other hand, nobody wonders who the boss is or where the buck stops." Other possibilities include: "Problem solving"..."I enjoy analyzing what's wrong, figuring out a solution, and implementing it." And "results-oriented"..."My decisions are highly concerned with how the result will impact the bottom line." You might add, "On the other hand, I also care a lot about my people; training and developing them and seeing they're fairly treated is extremely important." A pragmatic pastiche, plus taking the pulse of your interviewer, will you get you safely past this issue.

What Appeals to You About Our Job and Our Company?   (CAPSULE)

Capsule or no capsule, you absolutely must study the company prior to your interview, if the career opportunity is of more than casual interest to you. Read the last couple annual reports, and the latest 10-K and proxy statement. If these aren't available in a library you have access to, phone the PR Department of the corporation and pick up copies by messenger or have them sent Federal Express. Also check the latest summaries of news on the company as indexed by Standard & Poor's and available at your stock broker's office...and of course what the business periodicals have been saying, as indexed by the *Reader's Guide & Index to Periodical Literature* and the *Dow Jones Information Service,* among others.

Knowing what's going on at the company not only helps you prepare an answer to the cliché question of what you like about the company; it also gets you thinking on your interviewer's wave length long before you're in his office and on the spot.

Current Status and Long-Range Trends of Your Speciality and the Overall Industry (CAPSULE)

If you know anything at all about your present field, you certainly have some good ideas on where the action is now and where the future may lead. Marshal them. Don't just pull them together on the way *home* from an interview where the CEO of a conglomerate had more thought-provoking insights into your specialty than you did.

What Would You Like To Know About Us? (CAPSULE)

The easiest or the hardest of questions. Ironically, the more you want the job, the tougher the question is. If you're skeptical about whether the job will advance your career, you're loaded with questions that have to be resolved to your satisfaction.

But suppose you're thrilled to be considered for the job. It's with an impeccable company, and represents a career breakthrough in responsibility. Then what do you ask? Certainly not about benefits and retirement. Maybe about what they see as the key problems and opportunities to be addressed by the person who gets the job, willingness to invest in the business, and whether it's central to the company's future growth or a candidate for "harvest" and possible divestment. But be careful. Shouldn't you *know* what the problems and opportunities are?

Check for a *common view* of such issues; but don't imply you can't see, without being told, what some of the key ones probably are.

The invitation to ask questions is inevitable. Be prepared for it.

Reading...and Writing...Between the Lines

You know darn well that your interviewer will be trying to "read between the lines" of your answers...looking for accidental unspoken nuances that may be even more revealing than your statements.

So, since he's *reading*, you may as well make sure you're *writing*.

For example, when you're asked about your creativity, give some instances where you thought up a great idea that worked out well. But also give some samples of outstanding creativity within the unit you're responsible for, but which you personally did *not* think up. Give credit to the lower-echelon research subordinate whose "far-out" idea you backed with some money from your "Venture Fund," and to your CEO whose unpopular idea worked out sensationally well after you and your subordinates removed the kinks from it, and to the advertising agency that came up with the winning campaign after you asked them to give it "just one last try."

Incidentally, that until-recently junior scientist now has his own sizable section of the laboratory to run. And, far from being fired, you were able to help that ad agency win a client relationship with another division of the conglomerate you work for.

We see, of course, that you're creative. But we also read what you've written between the lines. You care about, and listen to, what others around you are thinking...*even your boss!* With you in charge, the company isn't limited to your own personal creativity. You recognize anyone's good idea when you see it. Moreover, you probably get along well with others, commanding their respect and loyalty, because you reward them for a job well done.

You get the idea. When answering questions about talents and triumphs, you have a perfect opportunity to write between-the-lines messages about your other fine characteristics and management techniques.

The "Pregnant Pause"...and How To Deal With It

The "pregnant pause" is a gimmick some interviewers use to unnerve candidates, and to force them to reveal personal insecurity, and hopefully to voice unguarded statements.

Here's how it works. After you've finished answering his question, the interviewer says absolutely nothing to move his side of the conversation forward. Dead silence. No question, no comment. He just looks you in the eye, waiting for you to panic and rush in to fill the awkward pause.

This startling stoppage may come at random...or possibly when the interviewer suspects, or wants you to *worry* that he suspects, that you're not telling the truth, or at least not the whole story. One recruiter I know loves this gimmick so much, he tries to use it on his co-workers at lunch.

The only way to deal with this behavior is to nip it in the bud. The first time your interviewer breaks the rhythm of the conversation this way, pause with him long enough to make absolutely sure he's "pregnant pausing" and to make sure he knows that *you* know that's what he's doing...maybe 20 seconds or more. Then say, kindly and helpfully, as if perhaps he seems to have lost track of the rather complex discussion you've been having:

> "Is there anything else you'd like to know about...(the question you just finished answering)?"

Treating the pregnant pause as a case of Alzheimer's Disease is the *only* way to deal with it. If you knuckle under to even one "cross-examination by silence," you'll signify that you're the insecure sort of person who submits to interrogation in this arch, smug fashion. If so, you're in for a tense, defensive interview. On the other hand, by kindly and inoffensively calling the interviewer's bluff, you create unspoken recogition and respect. If, by chance, your interviewer decides to try again, repeat the treatment.

Coping with the "Stress Interview"

Let's hope you never run into it, but there was a fad 20 years ago, which still hasn't completely died out, of giving a "stress interview." Pioneered by an executive recruiter who'd been a prisoner in one of the Nazi death camps, the idea was to discover what he called the "counterfeit executive"...the one who can't take pressure...by applying great pressure and tension during the interview. Seat the candidate with the sun in his eyes, hide the ashtrays (a lot more people smoked in those days), quickly interrupt his answers, telling him he obviously didn't understand the question, "pregnant pause," imply knowledge of information contrary to his statements. The possibilities for rude, challenging, inhospitable behavior are endless.

You'll almost certainly never get the full treatment. Even the guy who invented the process doesn't operate quite that way anymore. But you may run into someone who kicks off the interview by throwing down the gauntlet:

"I can't see how you're qualified for this job!"

He goes on from there with argumentative, demeaning, and perhaps embarrassingly personal questions. Maybe he deliberately misinterprets your answers. And probably he avoids looking at you...gazing over your head, thumbing through his calendar, and shuffling papers. You're getting an up-dated version of the stress interview.

What to do? You have to call his bluff. That may be all he wants. Say:

"I'd appreciate it if you'd look at me when I'm talking to you. If we can get this conversation on a more cordial basis, we'll communicate much better."

Maybe just saying something like that will pass his "test." If not, I suggest you get up to leave, turning back as you get to the door:

"I'd still be willing to have a good conversation with you, but this session doesn't really seem worthwhile."

Chances are, he'll call you back, say you passed his "test," and continue the interview on a new and more cordial footing. By then, however, you wonder whether you should even consider working for this guy or the company he represents. So do I.

Who's in charge of the interview
. . .you or the interviewer?

No question who's responsible for the outcome of the interview. You are. You've got to get your message across. If your appropriateness, your ability, and what a fine person you are fail to register, it's your loss. And it's your fault, not the interviewer's.

But who's *in charge?* Now that's a different question. Believe it or not, some people think that you should take charge. Go in, say "Hello," and see if the interviewer asks the questions that draw out the information you want to convey. If not, begin answering different questions from the ones he asks, and twist and lengthen your answers to make sure you cover all the important points that support your candidacy. Be poised and pleasant, but don't be afraid to demonstrate aggressiveness and leadership. . .crucial qualities in an executive.

If you're interviewing for Vice President - Marketing of a company that sells vacuum cleaners door-to-door, that's probably good advice. Barge in and take over. But for any other job, in my opinion, a much more polite and sensitive approach is absolutely mandatory.

First of all, you're selling yourself as a *"fine person"*. . .polite, socially poised, and someone who, if hired, will wear well as a co-worker over the years. Somehow, the pushy vacuum cleaner salesman doesn't fit that description.

Secondly, and equally important, if you try to take charge and control what information is covered, you may not convey what your interviewer wants to know. You may bore him with a persuasive pitch on points he was willing to concede. . .meanwhile, failing to address the doubts and concerns you would have discovered if you'd sensitively followed his lead.

Moreover, since the interview is a *demonstration* of how you think and operate, there's a good chance your interviewer may conclude that you're a "hip-shooter"...a superficial thinker, who plunges ahead before gathering information, and checking pre-conceived assumptions. After all, that's the way you behaved in your interview.

Therefore, all things considered, *don't try to grab control.* In terms of personal image, you can't afford to dominate the interview. And in terms of accomplishing your objectives, you don't really want to.

Steering the Interview with Questions and "Red-Flagged" Answers

Only your own good judgment during the actual interview can determine to what extent you can and should try to influence the direction it takes.

If you're willing to become overtly pushy and aggressive, you can cover whatever you wish. But if you want to stay within the ritual boundaries of a social conversation in which the employer has the prerogative of asking most of the questions, there are really only two techniques by which you can gently guide him toward matters you'd like covered.

Questions

You can always ask a question to see if he's interested in a subject you want to talk about:

> "Is the development and marketing of internally-generated new products a major factor in your growth plans? That's an area where I've had a lot of successful experience."

Nothing impolite or too pushy about that approach.

He may say:

> "Absolutely! Tell me about it."

Or he may say:

> "We're not entirely opposed to internally-generated new products. But over the years we've become skeptical. We

find we get a lot more for our money by acquiring underdeveloped products someone else has pioneered. Have you ever tried that approach?''

Well, now you know where he stands. Maybe you've also got success stories of the type he's more interested in. In any event, you didn't waste time and suggest future philosophical differences by giving a long recitation of exploits he's not looking for.

Red-Flagged Answers

Sometimes you can wave a red flag at the bull and he'll run for it. . . sometimes not. Even professional TV interviewers are often unbelievably nearsighted. The famous actress winds up her answer:

"Of course, that was back when I was still stealing cars for a living. . .''

And the oblivious interviewer moves right along with:

"Tell me. . .looking back on all the films you've made. . .which hairdresser has influenced you most?''

Nonetheless, a valuable technique for attempting to steer an interview along more promising lines is to wind up an answer with a provocative statement that cries out for a follow-up question, if the interviewer is interested:

". . .which is why, of course, I then completely changed our approach to incentive compensation.''

Your interviewer ought to be tempted to ask what kinds of changes you made and what resulted. But if he's not, at least you haven't been rude or boring, and you haven't wasted time on a topic he's apparently not interested in. The bull doesn't always run after the red flag.

And that's it. Questions and flagged answers are the two polite ways you can attempt to steer an interview toward topics you'd like to discuss. The advantage of both is that they merely suggest. . .they don't force. . .a change of direction. They both leave control of the interview in the hands of the interviewer, which is what you will normally want anyway.

Out of Town Tryouts

Most people find that, in interviewing, "practice makes perfect." By the time they're in their third or fourth interview, they're very effective. But what if you haven't interviewed for quite awhile and you suddenly face an unexpected "biggie"? Or if you look forward to a series of interviews and don't want to waste the first one or two? Then try your show in Philadelphia and Boston prior to opening night on Broadway.

"Role playing," of course, is the answer. A social friend or your spouse can sit in for the interviewer, perhaps asking questions from a random list you've prepared. Better yet, try to set up a real grilling by a business friend from the right industry. Choose someone who can come up with his own tough questions, and who will give you a clear-eyed critique afterward.

The Danger of Being Prepared

There's no such thing as being over-prepared. There always is, however, the danger of being over-eager to play back what you've worked on. And by recommending "capsules," I certainly don't mean to encourage that tendency.

Occasionally I come across people so anxious to deliver the thinking they've developed that they don't listen carefully to the question and conform their answer to it. These people are extremely rare. . .only one of them for every 50 or 75 who fail to come up with clearly focused, brief, and factually explicit answers to questions they certainly should have anticipated.

You're too alert to make either mistake.

Engines Ready. . .Contact!

Prepared as you are, you have absolutely nothing to fear as you take off into the sunrise. If you've got anything close to the right stuff, your interview will demonstrate it.

However, let's run through a pre-flight checklist of practical tips:

Check the forecast. If your interview has been arranged by a recruiter, call him the morning or the afternoon before. He may have new information since you saw him last, regarding job content, what's looked for, how long other interviews have lasted, what line of questioning was pursued, and what mistakes other candidates made. Don't betray nervousness by asking about all these items. Just say: "Anything I should know before I go over there tomorrow morning?"

Pack your flight case. Into your elegant attache go extra copies of your resume (just in case your host has misplaced his or wants to pass some along), a yellow pad and a *quality* pen, any charts of figures you may need to refresh your memory if questioning gets detailed, and a *Wall Street Journal* to pull out and read if your host is interrupted or you have to wait a few minutes.

Arrive early and check the equipment. Get there five minutes ahead of time and ask to use the lavatory before being announced. That way you can check for lint on your collar and parsley on your teeth. You'll perform best knowing you feel and look perfect.

Return your salute from the crew. The interview begins in the corridor as your host's secretary greets you and maybe offers to shake hands (be alert for this). She, and through her possibly the receptionist too, will probably be consulted for a report on your poise and personality. Your corridor conversation with her. . .cordial but not presumptuous. . .is the start of your interview.

Don't land prematurely. After your *firm* handshake, I hope your host doesn't feign a landing and then pull up, leaving you discourteously plopped for an awkward minute or two. But he might. It's a fairly common maneuver. Circle gracefully until you get landing instructions, or you clearly see where he's landing.

Warning. There's advice going around...maybe via a book or a psychologically-oriented outplacement firm...not to sit where the interviewer first suggests and, wherever you land, to *move your chair*. This odd behavior is supposed to connote an aggressive personality. I merely find it obnoxious. Unless you've got a bad back, or the sun's in your eyes, why not just sit down where indicated, and relax?

Five-minute warning. Don't go all-business all at once. Get off to a positive, upbeat start on a relatively personal note. Admire something in the office, or the company's convenient location, or the fine weather. Do *not* start off with the lousy weather, a bad commute, or any other "downer."

Hazardous terrain. Enter the Bermuda Triangle with extreme caution, if at all. Avoid such obviously hazardous topics as politics, religion, and sexually- and racially-oriented issues. Beware of trick questions aimed at exposing your negative attitudes on these matters by implying in advance that the interviewer has such feelings. Even sports can be a hazardous topic until you know your host's opinions. Believe it or not, some interviewers will see your failure to share their views on player trades as an indication that you're probably not a very shrewd analyst in the world of business either.

Keep an eye on the radar. Read the interviewer's body language. Leaning back signals a smooth leisurely ride; tapping fingers, fidgeting, and checking the clock call for crisper answers. "Closed position" (tightly-crossed arms and legs) says you're meeting resistance, whereas open, loose limbs say "all clear." And hand-to-face says he...and you...are uncertain, possibly untruthful. Body language can be overrated, but shouldn't be ignored. If you haven't read a book on the subject, you ought to.

Don't go on autopilot. No matter how well things seem to be going, don't let your guard down. The most skilled and subtle interviewer is never the one who treats you roughly. The one who puts you totally at ease is the one who'll find out even more than you'd prefer to tell him.

Debrief promptly. If a recruiter is involved, call soon afterward to debrief. The client will also call, and if the recruiter can play back your favorable comments, they will reinforce the client's good feelings about you. Don't be a sappy sycophant. But don't be coy, either. People tend to like people who obviously like them. And recruiters are more inclined to support candidates who probably will accept, than those who might not.

File your flight report. Why not send a brief "thank you"...two to four paragraphs, using "Monarch" (7¼" × 10½") personal stationery if you have it, otherwise "regular size." While you may refer in some way to what was discussed, this note is *not* a parting salvo of hard sell. Instead, it's a courtesy that says *fine person*...and differentiates you from the vast majority of candidates, who don't bother with amenities. Even more importantly, write down for future reference everything you found out at your interview. Most candidates won't do this either. Therefore, you'll be more on the employer's wave length than they will, at "second round" interviews three or four weeks later.

Answering the Unasked Questions

No interviewer these days is going to invite legal action by asking:

"Do you really think a woman can handle this job?"

"Aren't you a little too old for a grueling position like this?"

"Do people respond to you just like everyone else, even though you only have one eye?"

''With that brace on your leg, I don't suppose you get out to visit the companies in your group very often, do you?''

In an ideal world, these questions would not only be unasked, they would also be unthought. But our present world is far from ideal. If you vary much from the norm...if you're an ethnic or racial minority, physically handicapped, noticeably younger or older than most executives, considerably heavier or shorter...there may be unspoken questions in the mind of the interviewer about your ability to handle the job because of your ''difference.'' The best course is to rebut these objections, even though they're not voiced.

But you must communicate *indirectly*. You can't simply pipe up and say, ''Don't worry about my age; I'm more effective at 59 than I ever was at 30 or 40.'' If by chance the interviewer wasn't thinking of your age as a problem, he'll wonder why you're being so defensive. And if he was thinking about it: (1) he'll be offended that you caught him, (2) he'll be unconvinced by your self-serving assertion, and (3) he'll worry that you may already be hinting at legal action if he doesn't give you the job.

Just as in writing your resume, you can answer such unspoken questions with offsetting information. If you're probably a lot older than the other candidates, casually mention spending your vacation as an instructor for Outward Bound...or that you're leaving in August for two weeks of mountain climbing in Nepal. Or maybe just mention your interest in finding a challenging partner for a few good sets of tennis while you're in town. Make the interviewer think of you as healthy, vigorous, and in your prime. Don't talk about something you watched on television, or how hard you were hit by the flu that's going around. Everyone watches TV and gets sick occasionally, but you can't afford to raise image problems with someone who doesn't know you.

Shatter your stereotype.

Offset *youth* with civic and business responsibilities normally reserved for someone more mature...president of a stodgy country club, trustee of a college, outside director of a bank. (For this purpose, forget ''when-do-you-have-time-for-it?'' concerns.) Fight the *age* problem with evidence of vigorous physical activity and a fast-paced schedule. And if you're a *woman,* stress the fact that you're accustomed to extensive travel, to making difficult decisions, to operating independently. And throw in an anecdote that makes it clear that your household is organized accordingly.

If you belong to a racial or ethnic *minority,* make sure to demonstrate your familiarity and ease with the dominant WASP male culture of the corporation. Defuse the concern that you won't "fit in." And if you're *physically handicapped,* stress your ability to function effectively in the mainstream of everyday life; mention a party you went to recently, grumble about a speeding ticket, talk about your participation in active sports. And if you're *overweight,* stress the fact that you lead a disciplined life in other areas...that you adhere to schedules, work for long-term goals.

What the Interview *Can't* Do for You

For years one of the leading literary agents has been trying to get me to write a book which ought to be called *How To Package and Pretend Your Way Into a Big Job You're Not Qualified For.* Naturally that's not the title he proposes, but it perfectly describes his premise.

Such a concept is not only dishonest, it's ridiculous. No combination of slick resume and glib interviewing can enable you to defeat an array of really excellent candidates and win a job you're not qualified for.

And you shouldn't want such a job. Get it, and your life will be miserable until you lose it...and even more miserable afterward!

However, armed with the knowledge in this book, and the willingness to work as hard as necessary to obtain the position you do deserve, you should be able to fight off the other fine candidates competing against you for any job you fully deserve and can perform.

Good luck. I hope you do.

Negotiating Your Employment Contract...
Getting Plenty, and Making Sure

So you're giving up a fine job where you're comfortably settled, well respected, generously paid, and on a fast track toward bigger and better things. You're seizing an even greater opportunity.

Or maybe you're just winding up an agonizing period of unemployment you feared might never end. You're grasping a life-line.

Either way, the question now is: What are you going to *get?*

The single most important...and the easiest...way to win a very good deal from a new employer is to make him fully aware of what a good deal you have where you are. Then his initial offer should be something you can graciously accept. Bargaining can be minimized or avoided altogether.

Protection is another problem. Probably you're thinking:

> "Boy, I'd like to get an employment contract.
> But most companies refuse to give them."

You're right, of course. Most companies don't want to hand you a document marked "Contract." Nevertheless, these days more and more corporations are putting more and more in writing.

And believe it or not, every time you start a new job, you *can* have an *employment contract*...even if you *don't* receive a paper with that title on it. You and I will make sure that your terms-of-employment are solidly nailed down...and as favorable as they can possibly be.

We'll also define the jargon you may be confronted with. And we'll review how you can pleasantly and reasonably speak up for what you want.

First let's look at the difference between employment negotiations and every other kind.

When you negotiate to buy a house, or a boat, or a car, the object itself stays the same in your eyes, while you haggle over price. Your liking and respect for the seller can drop to zero. But what you're trying to buy remains just as enticing as it was the first moment you saw it.

Unfortunately, when you negotiate for your own employment...and even if someone else "fronts" for you (which I don't recommend)... you're not just selling yourself. You're *being* yourself. You were a "class act" during your interviews. Don't figure it's now safe to turn into a ruthless...or a petty...sleaze, just because the employer has chosen you and begun discussing your terms of employment. As my Granny used to say:

"There's many a slip, twixt the cup and the lip."

If you demonstrate any undesirable characteristics at this point, the whole deal may be off. Anything that seems overreaching or underhanded will be held against you.

So stand by everything you promised, stated, or implied. If you described your current compensation as X, don't suddenly claim its's X plus 35%, just because four friends tell you that's what they're getting for almost exactly the same job you have. And if you initially implied that it would be easy for you to relocate, don't later raise all sorts of costly problems you want your potential employer to throw money at.

He just may decide that you've been less than forthright...or at the very minimum that you're a drag to deal with. And on either basis, you could still lose out to another candidate.

The trick in negotiations is to indicate what a good deal you have where you are.

In the end, you won't move unless you score a significant improvement.

And nobody's going to ask you to. At least *not if they fully appreciate your current circumstances and compensation.*

Responsibility, growth opportunity, and possibly a chance to build long-term net worth...not just a boost in current income...will be your main reasons for any move. But you *do* expect financial improvement, both immediate and long-term. And the only way your prospective employer can know the full extent of what you're now getting is if you tell him.

As an executive recruiter, I always make sure to find out every facet of current compensation, plus any expected changes within the next 12 months. And I communicate all of this information to my client in a detailed written summary *before he meets the candidate.* That way he realizes right from the start that Candidate X will have to get upwards of $190,000, whereas Candidate Y can probably be hired for $130,000 and possibly less.

Face it. Cost/value assessment works exactly the same in hiring executives as in buying merchandise. There will be no reluctance to pay what you obviously cost...a reasonable incentive over what you're making now...if you're evaluated and proven "the one we want" during realistic shopping for alternatives.

But if you allow yourself to be thought of as a $130,000 candidate, when it will really take more than $190,000 to move you, then don't be surprised to receive an "underwhelming" offer. And don't be surprised either, if subsequent disclosure and bargaining can never quite build the financial platform you should have stood on from day-one.

Prepare a written summary of current compensation. It's as helpful as your resume in orienting recruiters and employers.

Take a look at the sort of financial summary I prepare with respect to all the candidates I present. In the illustration on the next page, I've laid out the information as if you were preparing the chart for yourself.

Unfortunately, many recruiters don't bother to dig into current compensation. Moreover, you may be on your own, with no recruiter involved. So, unless you work up a financial review, chances are your proper figures won't be registered in the early stages when they'll do you the most good.

Indeed, you've probably got to do some figuring, just to find out for yourself where you stand. Nine out of ten executives I meet don't fully appreciate their current compensation until I prompt them to think about it in detail. In the end, of course, everyone always figures out to-the-penny what he's now making, in order to weigh the financial offer that accompanies an enticing opportunity. But by then it may be far too late to get the employer to think of you in the right price range.

Here's a sample summary that will give you some ideas. Since it's *informal* (even though precise), you won't put a title on it.

	X Year (Current fiscal/ ends in 4 mos.)	Y Year (Next fiscal)
Base Salary	$97,500	$125,000[a]
Bonus	30,000[b]	50,000[c]
Short-Term Incentive (Cash)	20,000[d]	27,000[e]
Long-Term Incentive (Deferred)	25,000[f]	33,250[g]
Company Car Allowance	14,400	14,400
Country & City Club Dues	2,300	2,300
Approximate Annualized Value of Stock Options	18,000[h]	18,000[h]
Daughter's Tuition Scholarship	6,000[i]	6,000[i]
	$213,200	$275,950[j]

[a]Assumes promotion to EVP/COO in June, and mid-point of $115m to $135m salary bracket for that job. If not promoted, my base will probably rise 8% to $105,300.

[b]Assured; could go to ceiling of $35,000.

[c]Estimate assumes promotion; otherwise $35,000 to $40,000.

[d]Based on achieving personal goals (100% earned in past five years).

[e]Assumes promotion; otherwise approximately $22,500.

[f]Based on Corporation achieving four-year profit goal. Paid in past three years, and currently on-target.

[g]Assumes promotion; otherwise $27,000.

[h]Difficult to predict; however, this is the actual average of the past three years.*

[i]Linda is one of five winners of a company-wide academic high school scholarship competition, granting full tuition to four-year college. Next year is the second-last year of her scholarship.

[j]Assumes promotion; if no promotion, I expect $233,000, based on these figures in Y year: $105,300[a], $37,500[c], $22,500[e], and $27,000[g].

---

*Alternatively, you can estimate future value of options by obtaining a forecast of growth in earnings-per-share (for example from Value Line), and multiplying future EPS by the current multiple. If that theoretical price is higher than your option price, you have an approximation of future option profit.

Keep your summary as simple and objective as possible. Only discuss cash. Don't bring up FICA, insurance, medical, and other ordinary employee benefits that are likely to be comparable, wherever you go. That makes you look petty. If you get $110,000 straight salary and nothing else, say so.

But if you've got money coming at you from several directions, point out and add up *everything*. If you expect a raise or a promotion within the next several months, be sure the recruiter and the employer know what's coming. Your incentive to move must be figured on top of what you'll soon get where you are...not just on top of what you have this very minute.

Even if you're unemployed, you want your prospective employer to realize what you're *accustomed* to getting. If he's sensitive and smart, he won't want you to feel that your duress has been taken advantage of. And, since you'll be nervous about asking more than he offers, you'll want to make doubly sure that his initial offer is as high as possible.

When do you hand over
your compensation summary?

Maybe never.

The recruiter or the employer will surely ask, "What's your current compensation?" Answer with an approximate figure justified by your summary. At that point he may say:

> "Well, that's in our ballpark. We can certainly come up with an attractive incentive."

If so, don't go further. Pocket your summary and never pull it out. Obviously you're going to get a tempting offer.

On the other hand, your current compensation may spark a reaction like this:

> "Wow! That's certainly more than I would have thought. How do you come up with that number?"

If so, you're prepared to handle compensation in the strongest, yet least disruptive, possible way:

> "Well, I did a little figuring before I came over here. I didn't want to waste your time, if what I already have is close to what you'll be offering. When you have a few minutes, you can look this over and see if it's something you can see fit to improve upon."
>
> *(Hand over your paper.)*
>
> "By the way, are you having any problem with the new import quotas?"

See what your paper does? It lets you register. . .without being at all boastful, obnoxious, or tedious. . .all facets of the good deal you already have. And you do so without skipping a beat in the central conversation that is convincing your host that you're the person who best understands his business and can do the most to build it. . .the person he needs, regardless of cost.

Today executive compensation packages are hardly ever simple and straightforward. They have to be studied to be understood. How any one will fare in years one, two, three, and beyond in leaving X Company to join Y Corp., which has different programs, requires careful analysis.

Chances are, the person you hand your "summary" to won't even attempt to evaluate it himself. He'll have it looked at by his compensation expert, who can authoritatively analyze what you have, in comparison with various proposals he might make.

The result will be an offer your prospective employer is comfortably sure will be attractive to you. Moreover, it will probably be accompanied by a visual aid that clearly showed him. . .and now proves to you. . . what the advantages of his offer are.

The best way to negotiate is to avoid having to do much negotiating at all. Do your homework right away. And let your would-be employer know as quickly and clearly as possible what you're already getting. He's a lot more likely to make you an offer you can't refuse if he's thoroughly aware of what you *can* refuse.

Now let's discuss contracts.

Can you get one?

Yes!

Play your cards right and you can almost certainly put your new employer under a written obligation. And if you're smart, you'll surely try to do so.

As you may recall from your Business Law course in college, a verbal contract is just as enforceable as a written one. *But only if, by its terms, it's to be performed within one year.* This, of course, becomes important if you are looking for a firm agreement of employment to last more than a year.

Indeed, if you only have an oral agreement, it had better not promise anything that can't be performed in a year. Otherwise, the *whole agreement can't be enforced...* even the parts that can be performed within a year.

And of course "time protection" for more than a year is usually the main thing an employee tries to negotiate. When he tells his would-be employer, "I want a contact," he's saying:

> "I want to be sure, before I give up the secure job I have, that you can't casually dump me on the street in no time at all, and for no good reason."

And in his traditional reluctance to provide a written "contract," the employer is saying:

> "That's exactly what I want to be sure I *can* do. I can't *manage* my business unless I'm completely free to pick and change my team at any time and for any reason."

How do these seemingly irreconcilable views get resolved?

By compromise. The executive asks for a four- or five-year "contract," and the employer comes up with two-years, or less. Seldom will a company commit itself for five years to an executive who isn't already on its payroll.

Consider the "termination agreement."
It's better than an X-year "contract"...and easier to get.

The employee wants firing to be permissible only for criminal acts... and maybe also insanity, wanton negligence, or gross incompetence. The employer, on the other hand, wants just about any reason to suffice, as long as time parameters are respected. In the end, the employer will usually get plenty of leeway as to *cause* for firing. The employee will hold out for...and achieve...*time* protection, which is basically all he ever hoped for anyway.

Which brings us to the advantages of a "termination agreement" over a straight X-year "contract." Employers who are unwilling to grant two- and three-year contracts will usually be more amenable to an 18-month...or if you can't do better a 12-month...termination agreement which says, in effect.

"You can fire me at any time for any reason. But you must give me 18-months' notice, or at least keep me on the payroll for 18 months afterward."

This arrangement doesn't tie the employer's hands, and it doesn't box him in for an exceedingly long time. So he's more willing to go along with it.

And for all practical purposes, you receive even better protection than under a two- or three-year "contract." Security under those deals soon elapses to zero. But with an 18-month termination agreement, there's always a year-and-a-half of future paychecks. Even if you become CEO at $800,000 per year, you can still whip out the termination agreement you got when you joined the company as a division manager at $80,000 ten years earlier. You'll collect $1,200,000 during the next 18 months... thanks very much!

> **There are contracts...
> and there are C·O·N·T·R·A·C·T·S!**
>
> **On the one hand, there are handshake agreements,
> written into an "offer letter."**
>
> **And then there are "employment contracts,"
> hammered out by opposing lawyers.**
>
> **If you can get ideal protection from something simple
> and friendly, don't hold out for "big deal" paperwork.**

I've known lots of prominent and highly paid New York lawyers... business-controlling partners in the famous law firms, and General Counsels of America's largest corporations.

Standing head-and-shoulders above them all is the smartest human I've ever met...about 5'2" and hardly 100 lbs. (mostly brain)...who attended law school over 50 years ago and since then has been doing post-graduate work in common sense. He's always practiced independently of the huge law firms. Many corporations use them for routine matters...but bring him in on very important and difficult issues. Moreover, the CEO's of those corporations insist on getting his slant on their personal legal matters.

Interestingly, this legal ninja has a devastating secret weapon that many of the other "super-lawyers" seem almost unaware of:

Simplicity!

Phil (not his real name...but close) would much rather have an agreement embodied in a plainly-worded letter or an exchange of letters than in a 27-page document full of convoluted clauses.

It's not at all unusual to go to Phil asking that a contract be drawn up to formalize an agreement along the lines of a simple letter or an exchange of letters you show him, only to be told:

> "No way! You've got 'em flat-footed on the basis of this *letter*. If they don't perform, we can sue them and get everything you're looking for, plus punitive damages as well. But if we go in and try to negotiate a formal contract with their legal department involved, there's no way in the world we can get language like this."

> "Just write them a friendly reply, saying you're pleased to go ahead as they've suggested, except for that one little change in the schedule that you've both agreed to."

> "And for heaven's sake, don't misplace the letters. They prove what your agreement is, and you could be mighty thankful to have them later on."

You get the idea.

It may be comforting to have a long and explicit document spelling out every conceivable facet and contingency of your arrangement with your employer. But it's not necessary. He and his company are just as bound by what he writes in his offer letter...assuming you accept his offer and go to work relying on it...as if there's a fancy paper marked "contract," which you both sign. And he's equally bound whether he asks you to countersign his "offer letter" or not.

Today almost every company
provides offer letters.

So don't quit your job until you have
something in writing.

You have clout.

You may not have enough leverage to get all the money or all the protection you want. But whatever you do get, you certainly have the power to get into writing.

Just say:

> "Well, Herb, I guess we're agreed on all the really important points. The title will be Vice President - Manufacturing. I'll report directly to

you as President, and I'll be on the Management Committee. Besides the factories in the U.S. and abroad, I'll have responsibility for Purchasing, Manufacturing Engineering, and Quality Control...but not New-Product Engineering.''

''My base salary will be $150,000, and I'll participate in the officer-level short- and long-term management incentive programs... and receive options...as you outlined them to me. I'll also get that $75,000 upfront to make up for not coming under your bonus plan this year, and to help with any moving expenses not covered by your most comprehensive moving package, as described in this booklet. And I'll receive a $1,000 monthly car allowance.''

''In terms of job security, I'll be getting 18 months' termination protection. You can discharge me at any time for any reason. But unless I've done something criminal against the company, you must either give me 18 months' notice, or pay me for 18 months after you let me go. And if you give me some notice but less than 18 months, you'll continue to pay me up to a total of 18 months from the time you give me notice.''

''As soon as I have your offer letter putting all of this in writing, I'll go in and resign.''

That's the way.

Just *assume* Herb will be putting what you and he have agreed on into an offer letter. When he does, you'll resign. And, of course, not before.

How can he refuse? He'd have to say:

''Well, you've accurately summarized what I'm going to do for you if you join us. But I'm certainly not willing to confirm in writing what I've just been telling you. Why, that would help you hold me and the company to it later on!''

No, he can't say that. And when you have your ''offer letter,'' you have your ''contract.'' The essence of your agreement with him is in writing.

About the only resistance he could put up would have to go something like this:

"We do things here on a handshake. There's mutual trust. It's almost like a family. You have my word. That ought to be good enough. And if it isn't, then maybe you and I don't have the right relationship to go ahead on anyway."

Your obvious rejoinder would be:

"Herb, there's no question that *you and I* have exactly the right relationship. I know you'd never break your word to me. But, God forbid, something might happen to you...or me...on the way home tonight, or next month, or a year from now. I know of an instance where that's exactly what did happen. So before I resign, I'd really appreciate a note from you."

If Herb refuses, no matter what reason he gives, you're better off not going to work for him.

Virtually no employer will refuse you an "offer letter."

But many will deny you a "contract."

Yet the two papers amount to the same thing!

Ironic...but true. Ask for an "offer letter" and you'll almost never be refused.

But ask for a "contract," and you'll be refused more than half the time:

"No way, Bob. We just don't *have* written contracts here. Why, I don't have one myself. I can't...and I won't...do for you what nobody's ever done for me. We're not one of those shifty outfits where that sort of thing is necessary. I trust my boss completely to do what he promises me. And he's never let me down. If you can't think of me the same way, then maybe I'm not right for you... or maybe our company isn't right for you."

Now you've confronted yourself with a tough argument to overcome. You've asked for a "contract." You haven't merely *assumed* you'll get an "offer letter"...something virtually every company gives, and something your prospective boss *did* get when he came aboard.

Lots of luck!

Why should your would-be boss try to achieve for you, an unproven newcomer, something he's never received during nine years of loyal service and outstanding performance?

Seen through his eyes, your asking for a "contract" seems presumptuous, if not downright unreasonable. Fortunately, there are several rejoinders you can make, and I'll lay them out for you.

But don't blunder into arguing for a "contract," when an "offer letter" will work equally well, and be vastly easier to get. The trick is to find out in one of your earliest discussions...long before you begin "negotiations"...whether the company uses "employment contracts," and whether they're willing to give you one. If not, don't even bring up the subject later on. Just *assume* your way into an "offer letter" that covers the same ground.

But suppose...for whatever reason...you want to get a mutually-signed document labeled "Employment Contract" out of a company that traditionally refuses to give them. Here are the arguments you can use:

1.   "It's a logical, businesslike approach to a business matter. People die and move on, and memories fade. A written agreement is the obvious safeguard."

2.   "More and more companies *are* writing 'employment contracts' for senior managers these days." Some estimates and surveys suggest that up to 40% of America's largest corporations now enter into formal written agreements with a substantial number of their executives.

3.   "I have an 'employment contract' at my current company, and I appreciate the security it provides. It's just one of many advantages, and I don't feel like moving to another company and getting *less* on any score than I've got now."

4.   "With today's business uncertainties, all executives are more reluctant to move than ever before. I believe that it's

important for your company to re-think its policy against giving contracts. Not only do I want one. But I'll also be trying to recruit other outstanding and well-situated executives to work for me here. Being able to give them the reassurance of a contract will be very helpful.''

5. ''Moreover the company can extract some important concessions from the executives it has under contract. We can put reasonable restrictions on their ability to walk out and leave us in the lurch...to join our direct competitors...to reveal our trade secrets...to be paid for work other than ours in their spare time...and so forth. Besides helping us get people, our contracts can help us get *what we want out of them.*''

There you have your strongest pro-contract arguments. Use them as you see fit.

If you do wind up negotiating a formal employment contract, lawyers will be involved on both sides.

Don't underestimate their prodigious ability to destroy a good deal for you.

I've seen it over and over. An executive gets a once-in-a-lifetime opportunity. In a love-feast of seeing eye-to-eye on absolutely everything, the prospective employer and employee ''let the lawyers take over from here.'' Far from merely ''getting things down on paper'' or ''tying up loose ends,'' as the happily-mated principals expect, the result is total destruction of the deal.

Here are a couple of examples. Names, of course, are changed to protect the foolish.

Len was President of a $175 million group of companies owned by a $9 billion conglomerate. I recruited him to join a far more prestigious $4 billion corporation as President of its $565 million group of similar companies. He wasn't and never would be a corporate officer of the $9 billion company, because his businesses were insignificant to its volume. At the $4 billion company, on the other hand, he'd head one of just four "Groups," and he'd be a corporate officer and a Director.

Len and the CEO readily agreed on everything...salary, duties, directorship, generous participation in incentive programs, and a fist-full of stock options. So the CEO supplied a contract, which Len had a week to check out with his lawyer.

On the second-last day, Len phoned me. He was at the office of a prominent attorney used by his sister, a world-famous entertainer. "I don't know what to do, John. I'm getting way more than at X corporation, but this guy points out that it's quite a bit less than the other three Group Officers make. He wants me to ask for more."

I told Len it was too late. The CEO would tear up the contract, if Len went back on his word. And besides, Len was becoming one of five top officers and a board member. Any inequity would be corrected as Len proved himself through performance, and increased the relative size of his group through internal growth and acquisitions. "Attack any other wording of the contract on advice of counsel, but don't let him make you look sleazy and indecisive," I told Len.

"You're right, of course," said Len. 'But would you mind coming over here and saying the same thing? This fellow is a close friend of our family. He's an expert, and he's charging me far less than he normally gets. So I don't want to just casually dump on the advice he's giving me."

Shocked...and concerned that the CEO and I had both made a mistake in selecting this otherwise brilliant and successful executive...I walked four blocks and took an elevator 38 stories to the intimidating opulence of the great lawyer's office. The guy was a sleaze! And he was encouraging Len to be one, too. Nevertheless, I spoke diplomatically.

Len did not return his contract as he should have the following day. Nor did he call. After the weekend and two days of the next week rolled by, the CEO and I agreed that I should call Len...hear a good excuse if he had one...and if not, tell him the deal was off. Len may have been advised to await a panicky call from us offering more money. That did not happen. And the deal was off.

Less than a year later, Len's conglomerate divested his unit to a company that didn't need his services. He's had other jobs in the several years since. But none as good as the one he was forced out of. And none even remotely as good as the chance-of-a-lifetime job on which he gave his hand-shake acceptance...and then asked his lawyer to check his contract.

Another example is equally pathetic.

I recruited an executive we'll call Bill, who had built the fastest-growing business in its field for Conglomerate X. The CEO of Conglomerate Y wanted him to take over an operation of equal size and much greater potential.

The attraction...besides an exciting challenge...was a contract, which gave Bill a percentage of increased-profit. Moreover, Bill couldn't be fired except "for cause." Salary was well above Bill's current base-plus-bonus, and the deal was designed to more-than-double his pay after a couple years of his dependably excellent management. Within five years Bill...who was enthusiastic about the opportunity...should have earned about $600,000 per year, three times his current compensation.

This time the employer's and the the candidate's lawyers both helped queer the deal. The CEO of Conglomerate Y wanted Bill's contract signed within 72 hours, to provide extra news at a previously-scheduled Monday afternoon meeting of securities analysts. A contract was hastily prepared by company lawyers who, unfortunately, included a clause they use with executives who don't get Bill's deal.

The flawed document was zapped to Bill by facsimile late Friday afternoon. His lawyer pointed out the offending phrase as "bad faith" by the over-eager CEO, who could legitimately be accused of "applying time pressure" toward hasty acceptance. Bill had been invited to call the CEO at home over the weekend with any questions. He didn't. And meanwhile, Bill's current CEO called Bill and pressured him to stay.

Result: Instead of calling his new employer on Monday morning, as agreed, to confirm he'd signed the contract, Bill called to say he was backing out. Shocked, the CEO offered to let Bill's lawyer revise the wording as he saw fit. He also offered to forego the announcement in favor of any more leisurely schedule Bill preferred. Too late. Bill had been wrongly convinced that his prospective employer was looking forward to breaking the contract.

Percent-of-profit deals with no cap and no time limit are exceedingly rare. Bill will almost certainly never be offered another one. Indeed, almost no executive ever gets such an opportunity.

But there's a bit more to this story. Although Bill was thrilled with the opportunity, he and his family disliked moving from the "Sun Belt" to the residential suburb of New York, where the business is located. So his lawyer's advice reinforced other qualms. Ironically, Bill's current company soon promoted him to their Manhattan headquarters. Now he lives in a town very near to where his once-in-a-lifetime opportunity is located. But instead of a five-minute drive to the office, he has an arduous daily train ride.

Meanwhile, a more junior executive has completed his first year in the job Bill could have had. Sales are up nearly 50% and profits are up about 70%. This young man receives only ordinary compensation. Bill, on the other hand, would be earning twice what he docs with his current company, even after a big raise that accompanied his promotion and relocation.

In both incidents, lawyers served as "sounding boards" and "counsiglieri," when excellent executives were emotionally vulnerable. It's one thing to be coldly analytical and decisive when dealing with business problems...and quite another when weighing an irreversible change in your personal circumstances. Then you reach out for...and cling to... the advice of your lawyer. More than at any other time, you're likely to let someone else *help* you decide, rather than merely provide further input for your *own* objective decision.

Interestingly, the lawyers engaged by both executives were personal friends...supposedly eminent attorneys, and supposedly working for far less than their customary fees. How easy it is to give undue weight to the comments of a lawyer who's your friend, and confirms that friendship through a low fee.

I bring all of this to your attention for a reason. *If and when you negotiate an employment contract, chances are you'll turn to a personal friend who's a lawyer for advice.* From experience I know that's what almost every executive does.

Please be careful.

You've experienced the universal tendency of lawyers to screw up every kind of deal. Know right here and now that they...your friends included...will have just as much tendency to screw up your breakthrough employment opportunity.

So much for general advice on negotiating your employment contract.

Now let's quickly look at the topics to cover, and how to handle them.

Re-read this section for ideas, whenever you're hammering out a formal contract.

Despite its seeming complexity and its importance to you, your "Employment Contract" will cover only a relatively few matters:

1. Term of the Contract

2. Your Duties

3. Getting Rid of You

4. Tying You Down

5. Your Compensation, Including Salary, Bonus, Various Stock Options and Grants, Golden Handcuffs, and Golden Parachute.

We'll look at all of these in relation to your self-interest. What would *you* prefer? And what is the employer trying to accomplish?

As you negotiate a formal employment contract, bear this happy thought in mind: Virtually all experts agree that such contracts benefit employees more than employers. You gain more in job security, compensation, and bargaining clout if and when the relationship goes sour, than the employer does in terms of actually preventing you from leaving at an inopportune time and taking your competitively-significant skills elsewhere.

Term of the Contract

When a new employee is brought in under contract, the agreement is likely to run only two or three years. Key employees already on payroll...and sought-after superstars from outside...are usually tied down for three to five years. The more sure the employer is that he wants you, the longer the commitment he proposes.

Automatic renewal can extend the contract indefinitely:

> "This contract shall be extended for additional three-year periods, unless either party notifies the other in writing prior to one year from the end of any such three-year renewal."

Very nice protection if you can get it. A more common provision would be an automatic one-year renewal. Consider, however, how favorably an 18-month termination provision may compare with whatever automatic renewal you're offered.

Your Duties

The statement of duties is extremely important, because it opens the door to the two main ways employers try to get out of their commitment. They either:

1. force you to leave by changing your duties, or

2. fire you, claiming you haven't performed them.

It's tough to defend against these twin assaults. But you've got to try. Can you accept a drastic demotion or an onerous relocation? Can you perform to the full extent of a vague and arbitrary standard? If not, keep a sharp eye on the language that goes into your contract.

Nail down specifics. Title? Location? Reporting to whom? With what operations reporting to you? Are you a member of the Management Committee? The Board of Directors? Try to get a statement that you can't be given a lesser title, lower-level reporting relationship, less responsibility, or relocation away from corporate headquarters.

Watch out for these phrases: *"such duties as may be assigned,"* and *"full time and best efforts."* If you agree to perform whatever duties you're assigned, stand by for some pretty demeaning ones when your boss wants to get rid of you. Try for a modifying phrase such as "of comparable or higher responsibility and status." And if you pledge your "full time and best efforts," look for an attempt to break your contract if you try to do any outside consulting, writing, or speaking in the evening or on weekends. A better promise would be not to do any consulting or other work for any competitor of your employer during non-business hours while on the employer's payroll.

Getting Rid of You

You'd like to tie up your employer so he can only fire you *"for cause,"* as the lawyers say. And very good cause, such as committing a felony against him. Otherwise, you'd like to force him to employ you to the end of your contract, or at least pay whatever severance is specified.

He, on the other hand, would rather employ you *"at will,"* so he can dispense with you at any time, without a reason, and with no financial consequences, just as he could if there were no contract (although these days age-discrimination legislation and sympathetic courts may provide some protection, even without a written contract).

In the end, you'll get a provision that says you can only be fired *"for cause."* But you'll have a tough time getting the statement of what constitutes adequate "cause" worded narrowly enough to give you any real protection. You'll want a lawyer to ponder the exact language. But here are a couple particularly troublesome "cause" statements that you should beware of:

> *"Violations of law and company policy."* Will traffic violations suffice? Taking home pencils and pads to do office work

at night and on weekends? Failure to get your expense report in on time? Failing to prevent your teenage son from taking the company car for a spin? Failing to obey any order of a superior officer, no matter how frivolous or demeaning?

"Failure to perform duties as assigned from time to time by the employer." Which duties? Newly-assigned, frivolous and demeaning? Requiring relocation to the island of Elba? Failure to meet unrealistic goals, budgets, and forecasts?

Obviously you should try to get permissible firing "for cause" as clearly worded and as limited in scope as possible. "Illegality" might be tagged "except for misdemeanors not directed toward the employer." And, if possible, try to require *"prior written warning"* before you can be fired for "violation of company policy" or "poor performance." Might as well get a shot at correcting your deficiency.

And try to insist that your firing "for cause" be done in writing, and accompanied by a *"written statement of the reasons"* for firing. If the reasons are flimsy, the company may hate to put them in writing, and may either be less quick to fire, or more willing to pay reasonable severance.

Also insist on an *"arbitration clause"* providing that conflicts under the contract shall be settled by binding arbitration. Court calendars are backlogged for years and trials are prohibitively expensive...at least from your point of view. Quicker, cheaper justice helps you a lot more than it helps your employer.

And finally, try to get a clause continuing your company-provided *medical and life insurance* until you're employed full-time by your next employer.

Tying You Down

Obviously one of the main advantages the employer receives is your agreement to work for him during the contractual time period. Since he has you signed up for X years, you'll presumably turn a deaf ear to executive recruiters. And certainly none of the time he's paying you for will go into looking for a better job.

Right upfront the contract will say that "the Company employs" and that "the Employee agrees to be employed" from X until Y.

Does that mean you can't possibly leave?

No. As court decisions on these matters often point out, "slavery" ended generations ago. No matter what the paper says, you can't be chained to your desk. The contract gives you various compensation guarantees and some measure of security. But it can't *force* you to work for the employer.

About the best the contract can do for the employer is to try to discourage you from working for any of his competitors. However, that can hurt you. After all, they're more likely than anyone else to want you, and to pay big money to get you. If you're performing brilliantly for your employer, you're able to do the same thing just as brilliantly for them.

Two clauses..."*non-compete*" and "*confidentiality*"...will try to keep you away from your most likely alternative employers. Fortunately, both clauses are hard to enforce by suing you for breach of contract, because the employer must prove *damages* in order to get money from you. And most of the time that's not easy. If you leave and take major customers or clients with you, he probably can prove he's lost profits. But if you merely withdraw your management brilliance and the operation doesn't fall apart the minute you walk out, he's got a very weak case.

The "*non-compete*" clause pledging you not to join a competitor during the term of the contract...and possibly for several years afterward...is particularly interesting because there's a logical "Catch 22," which you can use in bargaining with your employer. If you're so valuable that he has to isolate you from all his competitors, then he should be paying you plenty for your work...*and* for your vow of competitive celibacy. Conversely, if your agreement to stay away from your likeliest future employers isn't costing your employer very much, then it shouldn't be very stringent.

Hard as it may be for your employer to recover damages if you join a competitor when prohibited by your contract, the non-compete clause still has some nasty implications. The employer can sue you. And legal costs and time-consuming aggravation will cause you real pain. To your corporate employer they're not burdensome. Moreover, your appeal to other employers may fade if they know you're being sued by your former employer. Indeed, *they* may even be sued...rightly or wrongly doesn't matter...for "inducing" you to breach your contract.

Even though your employer may not be able to win a cent of damages from you in the long run, he can certainly give you trouble when you try to walk out. And in the end he may make you buy your freedom. He may offer to give up his "rights" under the contract if, in return, you give up some of your deferred compensation, a retirement benefit, or your latest earned-but-not-yet-paid bonus.

On the other hand, if you're a really hot property, you may be able to get protection from the company that's trying to hire you. They may be willing to provide the legal defense necessitated by breaking your contract, and to pay any judgment (unlikely) that's entered against you. Now your former employer has to pick on someone his own size. Chances are, he'll drop his sure-to-fail law suit.

So the bottom line is that you can walk out. But you may not be whistling.

In writing the non-compete clause, the employer will try to make the prohibition as broad and long-term as possible...perhaps shielding you from "any company or organization having any activities or interests competitive to the Employer, during the term of this contract, and for X years afterward." You, of course, will want to minimize the prohibition. Try to:

    1. *Eliminate the clause.* Say you aren't being paid enough to curtail your most likely employment opportunities.

    2. *Void the clause if you're fired,* or if your contract *isn't renewed.* Why should your employer be able to tell you what to do after he stops paying you? Moreover, if discarding you is correct and fair, you'll handicap his competitor. He should cheer you on!

    3. *Limit the clause to **full-time** work for a competitor.* Try

to preserve your chance to do consulting in your industry after retirement or firing.

4.   *Narrow the coverage to business units that are directly competitive.* When only one subsidiary of a conglomerate competes with your employer, the rest of it shouldn't be off-limits. Try to get him to name the two or three competitors he's most concerned about, leaving you a chance to make a future living with the rest of the industry.

The *"confidentiality"* clause pledging you not to reveal your employer's trade secrets is the Siamese twin of your promise not to work for his competitors.

Every business has some information it doesn't want outsiders to know... product formulae or diagrams; R&D, manufacturing, marketing, and advertising plans, methods, and breakthroughs; customer identities and buying patterns; incentive compensation schemes; acquisition and divestiture strategy and plans. The list could go further.

The need for confidentiality is legitimate. Unfortunately, the wording of the clause probably won't be. It may prohibit you from revealing anything at all about the company while you work there and perhaps long afterward. Indeed, the clause may be so broad that you virtually can't help but run afoul of it. Then whenever the company wants to get rid of you, breach of confidentiality will come in handy as one among several trumped-up reasons.

The employer's strategy is strictly legal harrassment. Damages could never be proven for divulging unimportant information that was probably already widely known. But the lawyers could try to claim a "cause" for your firing, as they chip away the protection the contract is supposed to give you.

Your strategy, on the other hand, is to whittle down the outrageously broad language. Try to *eliminate* the clause. And, failing that, try to have it cover only:

1.   intentional (not accidental) disclosures that

2.   could be harmful to the company.

In the long run you needn't fear this clause much. But you know why the employer wants it worded to take in the whole blue sky. So do your best to get it worded sensibly.

Your Compensation

You'll try to get everything you possibly can, and you'll make sure it's all written into your contract: substantial base salary, maximum bonus opportunity, and maximum participation in all of the company's most lucrative stock-related and deferred-compensation programs.

Go for it!

If you'll report just one or two layers below the Chief Executive, be sure to study the company's 10-K and its Notice of Annual Meeting/Proxy Statement, listing compensation arrangements at the top of the pyramid. And do it *before* your compensation is discussed. The best indication of what you can try for now...and work toward in the future...is to find out what your boss is making, or failing that, what his boss is making.

Chances are, the biggest biggies are covered by programs that don't extend much lower. But you might as well ask whether you're in on a lesser share of the same deals they get. If not, the deal just below theirs? Or a third-level deal? How many people qualify for the highest-echelon incentive compensation program you will participate in? The top 15...or 50? Or the top 5,000?

Despite all the glowing words about how important you'll be, nothing is a clearer indication of where you *really* rank than the echelon of the compensation programs you do-and-don't qualify for. Moreover, some polite pre-employment curiosity may get you included in higher programs, if the goodies your prospective employer is planning for you don't quite match the flattery he's handing out.

When it finally comes to writing your compensation into your formal "Employment Contract," there are virtually no pit-falls. *Without your having to argue and push, the document will fully and firmly state what you're getting.*

Why not? After all, the spotlight is on your compensation. It's the star of the show! It's your inducement to sign the rest of the document. It's what the magician *wants* you to see; whereas up to now we've been on the lookout for what he might be doing with his *other* hand...possibly tying a slip-knot on the contractual straightjacket you're lacing him into.

Since your compensation will slide effortlessly into the contract, the best I can do at this point is to give you a hand with the jargon you may encounter. Plus a few comments, wherever I think they might be helpful:

Base Salary should be upwardly open-ended..."at least X." And "to be reviewed annually," if escalations aren't pre-negotiated.

Bonus should depend to a reasonable extent on *your* performance, or on a smaller unit you'll influence in a major way...not just a huge entity you won't make much difference to.

First-Year Guarantee. Make sure that...at least during the first year...you're assured of making 20% to 30% more than if you stay where you are. Maybe your new salary alone will cover the incentive to move. If not, you can probably get first-year's bonus "guaranteed" by pointing out that, after years of experience, you know almost-to-the-penny what your bonus will be where you are. Obviously, you're far less certain of the new situation. In the second year, of course, you're happy to be treated just like everyone else.

"Signing," "One-Time," or "Special" Bonus. To make up for not immediately coming under intermediate- and long-range compensation programs, and to make your relocation more painless than under standard policy...while still not putting your base-and-bonus out of line with other executives at your level...you may be given a "signing bonus," which occurs only "one-time." It's a sensible solution to an obvious problem. Unless you're the executive equivalent of a sports star "bonus baby," don't expect a bonanza.

Stock Option Plans differ from company to company, and the same company may have more than one plan operating simultaneously.

Incentive Stock Options...often referred to as "ISO's"...used to be highly attractive to employees because the profit they generated could be treated as a *capital gain,* rather than ordinary income. However, the Tax Reform Act of 1986 equalized the rates on ordinary income and capital gains, thereby eliminating this advantage. There's *no tax due* when you *buy* your shares at the less-than-market option price, and this is the primary remaining advantage of an ISO.

To enjoy this advantage, however, you will not be permitted to exercise these options until two years after they were granted, and the price-per-share at which your options are pegged must be 100% of fair market value on the day they were granted. Moreover, on ISO's granted after 1986, you can only exercise options worth up to $100,000 (valued at grant) per year. You should also be aware that ISO's may create alternative minimum tax.

Nonqualified Stock Options. These options don't "qualify" for capital gains tax treatment by the employee; hence the term "nonqualified." However, since the Tax Reform Act of 1986 equalized rates on ordinary income and capital gains, this disadvantage has disappeared. "Nonqualified" options are extremely attractive in several ways. Price needn't be 100% of market value, so they can be granted at below-market prices...for example, at or below book value, at some fraction of market value, or even at $1 (or less) per share. There's also no limit on how many options may be granted; exercise can be sooner than two years after granting; and there's no need to hold the stock for any particular period after exercise. However, unlike ISO's, you pay the tax when you exercise the option.

Because the "nonqualified" option may put stock under the control of the employee at a less-than-publicly-traded price, the employer is entitled to deduct the difference between option price and fair value as a business expense for tax purposes (conversely, the employee pays ordinary income tax on the difference).

Further, all of the employee's profit is a tax deduction for the company. These favorable employer deductions are *not* available for an ISO. Therefore, most compensation experts are predicting that "non-qualified" options will become even more popular, and ISO's will become less popular.

Stock Grants and Restricted Stock Grants. You don't buy the stock. The company *gives* it to you...usually as a reward for staying with them and/or meeting certain performance goals, in which case your grant may be called a *"Restricted Stock Grant,"* because of the time "restriction" which must elapse, or the goal which must be met, before you actually own the shares. For example, a 1,000-share grant may vest at the rate of 250 shares every year for four years. You have to stay four years to get it all, and you pay ordinary income tax on each 250 shares according to their value when you actually receive them. While you're waiting for vesting, you may receive dividends on all 1,000 shares, and you may have the right to vote the stock.

Restricted Stock Units. The concept of "units" gives the employee even greater flexibility and hence more different ways he might profit. "Restricted" as to time, the employee can...after the specified waiting period...exercise his units in a variety of ways as specified by the particular plan. Usually, he can take a share of stock for each unit; or he can get *cash* equivalent to the difference between the value of a share when the unit was granted and the market value when he "exercises"; or he can take some shares and the remainder in cash. With *units,* the employee usually gets dividends while he's waiting to exercise, but doesn't get voting rights.

Stock Appreciation Rights give the employee the right to receive...after a minimum waiting period...the difference in market value between a certain number of shares at the time of granting and at the subsequent time of "exercise." Under most plans he can receive that amount in shares, or cash, or a combination.

Phantom Stock Options are almost the same as Stock Appreciation Rights. After the initial waiting period, the employee has several years during which he can pick his own time to receive the stock value-differential in stock or cash. Meanwhile, of course, he gets dividends on the "phantom stock." The only extra wrinkle Phantom Stock Options may have that Stock Appreciation Rights usually don't have is a chance to get company stock at a discount, if the employee chooses stock when he "exercises."

Stock Appreciation Grants. Similar to Stock Appreciation Rights, except that there's a finite time period. On the terminal date, the employee gets the value of the differential in stock or cash. He doesn't have the "right" to choose the date on which he "exercises."

Stock Purchase Plans. Some companies allow employees to purchase a limited amount of stock at a discount from the public market price...often at book value. Or the company may enable the employee to purchase company stock at market price, and then "match" the employee's purchase with additional stock dollar-for-dollar or at 50 cents...or some other fraction...per-dollar. Usually stock purchased under these plans goes into a tax-sheltered fund similar to an IRA, so that the under-the-market purchase differential and accumulating dividends won't be taxed until the money is withdrawn. Otherwise, the employee would have to pay income tax on the under-market price differential.

"Qualified" Plans. This general term applies to all benefit plans which are given special tax advantages if they "qualify" under IRS rules. These plans take many forms, such as savings, "401(k)," profit-sharing, stock purchase, and pension plans. The qualifying rules have to do with such matters as broad-based eligibility, benefit formulas that don't favor the highly-paid, and limitations on high amounts. Because such plans encourage people to provide for their own retirement, the IRS bestows certain tax advantages on participants in plans which satisfy IRS rules.

One central advantage of any "qualified" plan occurs when you terminate employment and receive payment from, for example, your savings or profit-sharing plan. Unlike a payout from a deferred compensation plan, which is taxed currently, you may often continue to defer taxes on your "qualified" plan by rolling your account into an IRA or into your new company's qualified plan. Or you may pay taxes currently but, under certain circumstances, you may qualify for special tax treatment, which lowers the tax bite substantially. The company you're leaving must give you a detailed written description of these tax treatments. And you should, of course, discuss these choices with your tax advisor.

Deferred Compensation. Many highly-paid executives have historically preferred to defer some of their current pre-tax income for payment after retirement. Or on some other agreed-upon date. These arrangements, called "non-qualified deferred compensation plans," allow you to defer payment of taxes until the income is actually received, when you may be in a lower bracket.

However, with the dramatic decreases in personal income tax rates in the 1986 Tax Act, the attraction of deferred compensation arrangements is diminished, at least until tax rates go back up again. Try to guess future government tax policies. Recognize that, if you participate in your new employer's plan now, you may be deferring income into a higher tax bracket in the future, than the one you're deferring it out of now.

Also, if you're participating *now* in your *current* employer's plan, be careful to find out what happens to your deferred compensation accounts when you quit. These plans almost invariably change the payout rules upon termination, and the amount of interest you receive often changes, too. Also keep in mind that the amounts you receive from a non-qualified plan are subject to current income tax at ordinary rates, and cannot be rolled over to an IRA or to another company's plan.

Interest-Free or Low-Interest Loans. If you get a loan from your employer at a considerably lower rate than any other lender would provide, the IRS will want to tax you on what you're saving. And your employer may insist that the loan becomes due if you try to leave...a form of "Golden Handcuff." You're probably better off getting him to strong-arm a bank into loaning you the money.

"Golden Handcuffs." Any compensation program that makes it costly for you to leave the company. Various options, stock appreciation, and incentive compensation schemes make you stick around in future years to get the benefit of what's "granted" now. Click go the handcuffs!

"Golden Parachute." Any compensation arrangement that generously takes care of you, if you're thrown out or demoted because of a corporate merger or takeover. You'll have to be one of the top handful of corporate officers to get a "parachute." But you'll probably land ever so softly in the lap of luxury, with one to five years of your highest-ever base-plus-bonus annual compensation (your choice of lump-sum or continuation payments), immediate vesting of all "granted" stock, immediate exercisability of all options, immediate payment of all performance-contingent sums under incentive programs, immediate vesting of your pension benefits, and continuation of your company-paid medical and life insurance for the same duration as your compensation, or until you join another corporation full-time.

> Notice that you immediately get your hands on lots of stock. Letting the jackals have it at their inflated takeover price will be sweet revenge. And even if you're not high enough on the pyramid to enjoy a "parachute," you'll probably get control of a lot of your "granted" and "optioned" stock, when the corporation that promised it to you goes out of existence. You, too, will probably enjoy immediate payment at what will surely be a near-term, and maybe an all-time, high price.

And there you have the jargon of compensation, as it relates to your employment contract.

Unless you're headed for the very apex of the corporate pyramid, you'll have to content yourself with the compensation programs that serve you among many other executives. But make it a point to find out what programs the company *has,* and try to get yourself included in the highest-level ones you can possibly qualify for.

At this point, I've done all I can to help you reach for a wide slice of the corporate pie. Knowing the terms and techniques we've discussed will help you press for the best possible deal...and to document that deal as firmly and cordially as possible.

We've wound up by talking about what you may encounter in negotiating and drafting a formal "Employment Contract." But don't forget that you can also get good written evidence of your employer's commitments in your "offer letter," and in various other letters and memos that will pop up over the years. Save everything in writing that makes a promise to you. And in this regard, one final tip:

> Be sure to ask for *and save* the employer's printed "new employee" literature, personnel manuals, and statements of policy.

Sure, you're a big wheel, and that sort of material is mainly intended for little cogs in the corporate machine. However, courts and juries these days tend to read that stuff as a literal promise by the employer. He may think he's employing you *"at will"*...meaning he has the right to fire you at any time and for any reason. But some of his printed material, which you can readily pick up and save, may say something like this:

> "When you join the XYZ Company, as long as you perform satisfactorily, you are going to be part of our family."

If so, you can argue:

> "See? This isn't employment at will. You can only discharge me for cause. And you haven't shown cause. Therefore, you can't discharge me."

Farfetched? Possibly not. In many instances these days, corporate employers are losing law suits and paying damages in such cases. And alert personnel departments are working overtime to purge their literature. But if you can grab such printed statements on the way into the next corporation you work for, save them. You may have valuable *"collector's items"* in more ways than one.

Special thanks to Gary Thompson and Ira Kay for helping to dispel the fog imparted by the Tax Reform Act.

How To Find a Job by Not Looking for One

Believe it or not, one of the best ways to find an excellent job working for someone else is to try as effectively as you can to go off on your own.

Ironic? Indeed, but true.

Self-employed...or striving to be...you become attractive to people who'll want to put you on their payroll.

Work hard toward self-employment, and you can virtually count on getting some tempting job offers as a by-product. But proceed half-heartedly as a phony job-seeking gimmick, and you'll get nothing.

So read on *only* if you truly would like to be your own boss...and are willing to do what it takes to achieve that goal.

Not only will you *not* have to give up your search for ordinary employ-ment while you seek self-employment, you'll *heighten the impact* of

your search for a regular job by packaging it inside your quest for independence.

Who knows which option you'll end up with? Fortunately, it's "heads" you win..."tails" you win.

There are only 3 basic ways to become your own boss.

Fortunately, pursuing 2 out of 3 will generate job leads at the same time you declare your independence.

If we dispose of such unlikely ways of becoming self-employed as inheriting a business, or marrying into the owner's family, or striking oil on that acreage behind your cottage at the lake, we're left with only three ways to make it happen:

1.　Become a consultant.

2.　Start a business.

3.　Buy a business.

Two of the three...consulting, and attempting to buy a business...can be aggressively pursued while subtly seeking a payroll job.

Starting a business can not. If the startup is modest and readily attainable...an antique store, a restaurant, or an inn, for example...any $100,000+ executive should certainly be able to accomplish his goal. No need for a "fall-back" objective.

Businesses that begin very small can become very large...Apple Computers, McDonald's, and Kentucky Fried Chicken come immediately to mind. But such wonders of capitalism are not wrought by entrepreneurs who "hedge" their bet by keeping an eye peeled for salaried employment.

On the other hand, the prospective clients you must solicit to establish a consulting practice, and the people you must contact to find a sizable business to buy and raise money for the purchase, are the same ones you'd want to reach when job-hunting through personal contact and networking.

Moreover, these influential people are likely to react far more favorably when contacted about an intriguing consulting proposal, or a potentially profitable business deal, than when hit for the 500th time with the dreary "I'm in the process of making a career change and would like to have the benefit of your thoughts and advice."

Should you try to be a consultant?

Becoming a consultant is easier and quicker to achieve than buying a business, so let's look at consulting first.

And let's be very clear on what we're talking about. We're not discussing the common resume cover-up of a gap between jobs with an entry that says "Self-employed Consultant," even though the writer didn't aggressively seek assignments, and didn't handle any worth mentioning. We're talking about actually trying to sell consulting engagements, with the intention of doing a fine job and, hopefully, building a lucrative practice.

Only if you really *want* to become a consultant, will your solicitations have any credibility. If you ask for an appointment to discuss consulting and then come in and try to wheedle your way onto the payroll, you'll have zero credibility...both as a consultant and as a potential employee.

So don't even consider the consulting option unless you:

1. have *expertise* that would benefit clients;

2. have the *skills and personal characteristics* to be a consultant; and

3. are willing to *accept the advantages and disadvantages* of a consulting career.

We'll consider these three issues separately. Then if "all systems are go," we'll take a look at how trying to become a consultant not only won't encumber your search for a salaried position, but may in the end lead to the happy dilemma of self-employment *and* tempting on-payroll offers.

What expertise do you have that can lead to successful consulting engagements?

Almost every $100,000+ executive has knowledge that could be valuable to clients. Analyzing problems and opportunities, and figuring out what action to take, are what every executive does. Consulting merely applies those processes to someone else's problems.

However, the most successful consultants...especially *individuals,* in contrast to the huge generalist outfits like McKinsey, Cresap McCormick & Paget, and Booz Allen & Hamilton...generally have a *personal specialty,* which they obviously know more about than a crew of MBAs from one of the giants.

To illustrate, here are three enormously successful individuals who now consult for a living, after leaving the payrolls of large corporations:

1.   Mr. X headed Marketing for one of America's leading magazine-publishing and direct-marketing companies. Deposed along with his boss, the Chief Operating Officer, in a political upheaval more than ten years ago, Mr. X immediately offered himself as a consultant to all the other large print media and direct marketing companies. Then only in his 30's and already making a six-figure salary (and we've probably had 200% inflation since), he immediately earned more money consulting than he ever made on payroll. Today he still works out of his home with only an answering machine to take his calls. And, although they might not admit it publicly, many of his former competitors now support his handsome lifestyle as consulting clients.

2.   Mr. Y was Chief Executive of a medium-sized public company (9-figure sales), which he led through a very suc-

cessful decade of growth, both by internally-generated new products and through acquisitions. Deposed by his Board, not for poor performance but allegedly for a drinking problem, Mr. Y became a consultant to a competitive corporation with the sole mission of scouting small companies for acquisition. Operating on an annual retainer discountable against brokerage fees on the deals he arranges, he's now "earning double what I did as CEO."

3.   Mr. Z retired as a senior scientist with a major chemical company while still too youthful to become inactive. Today he helps foreign chemical companies avoid transgressing U.S. patents, and advises them on whether technology they have developed may be patentable in the U.S. He does no work that requires an expensive laboratory or a research staff. He merely draws on his personal expertise and the resources of a public patent library.

Notice that each of these successful consultants offers a personalized specialty. None is a jack-of-all-trades in competition with the large national consulting firms. What comparably special contribution could you make...and to whom? Only you can say. But here are some possibilities:

1.   CEOs and Division heads of companies in your field might value a "second opinion" on basic issues. Or they might welcome "take charge" handling of special projects.

2.   Perhaps there are companies in fields *related* to yours, that should consider diversification into categories you know more about than they do.

3.   If you're from a large company, you may have sophistication that smaller firms can't afford to keep on payroll. Offer project assistance. Or perhaps one-day-per-week on an annual retainer.

4.   Foreign companies wanting to penetrate the U.S. market might need your help.

5.   Conversely, domestic companies might benefit from your international experience.

6.   And if you're on the leading edge of any specialty, there are always "trailing" edge companies, who are potential clients.

Do you have the skills and personal traits to be an independent consultant?

Okay, let's assume you've figured out how your expertise *could* help corporate clients. There's still the question of whether you have the right *personal attributes*. Working for Cresap, Booz, or McKinsey is just another payroll job. To succeed independently you need everything "large-firm" consultants have...and more:

Salesmanship. Except for "repeats" and referrals from current clients...and starting out you won't have any...every assignment will be one you've had to sell. If you can't approach new people, and can't tolerate rejection, don't go into consulting.

Analytical, Bright, Logical Mind. Clear, insightful thinking is...along with your special expertise...what you're selling.

Written and Oral Communication. Sometimes you'll present informally. But expect to deliver written reports and chart/slide presentations. If your pen and platform skills aren't good, don't enter consulting.

Self-Start and Self-Discipline. Performing *what* you promise *when* you promise is mandatory. And no supervisor will check your progress toward deadlines.

Creativity, Openmindedness, Resourcefulness, Versatility, and Adaptability. Being able to invent, improvise, ad lib, and generally deal with the unexpected and unfamiliar is essential. "By-the-book" people have little to offer as consultants.

Common Sense, Practicality, and Pragmatism. Down-to-earth, easy-to-implement recommendations are the best kind.

Service Attitude. Unfortunately, consulting is a service business. If you'd much rather be accommodated than accommodate, consulting is not for you.

Ability To Cope with Financial Insecurity. There's feast and famine...no regular payday.

Fortunately, traits that may handicap you in large organizations are tolerated...and even desired...in an independent consultant.

Do you have these characteristics? If so, you may be more welcome on retainer than on payroll.

Obvious Personal Brilliance. The same superior who feels threatened by a subordinate with an off-the-chart IQ is delighted to find such brain-power in an outside consultant.

Strong Self-Assurance and Matching Ego. Same goes for a strong, sure touch and lack of self-doubt...scary in a subordinate or a peer, but excellent in a consultant who can be summoned and dismissed at will.

Task Orientation and Political Aloofness. A consultant must be politically sensitive. But he can concentrate on his work, safely ignoring the day-to-day skirmishes that can undermine the too-task-oriented corporate employee.

If you're not average, not a team player, don't care about petty politics, don't suffer fools (other than paying clients) gladly, and tend to challenge authority and to be outspoken...then perhaps you can do the corporation, and yourself, more good as a paid observer than as a salaried participant.

Indeed, even if you have patently undesirable characteristics from a corporate point of view, you may be able to get by with them as an outside consultant. Maybe you like to work three 18-hour days and take a week off. Maybe you have a drinking problem but can discipline yourself to keep critically important commitments. Maybe you're brilliant, but have a loathsome personality and are insufferable as both a boss and a subordinate; yet you're capable of exquisite charm when you choose to display it. Show your clients only the good side of your Jekyll & Hyde personality, and you can succeed as a consultant.

Don't get into consulting unless you can endure some very negative aspects.

The withdrawal pangs are excruciating!

As a $100,000+ executive, you're used to having power. People at your beck and call. The prerogative to decide. Even when you have to seek higher endorsement, *you* determine what is or isn't considered.

Every executive who's had power and suddenly becomes a consultant is shocked by the role reversal. Nothing I say can adequately prepare you.

As an executive, you can call meetings to which any number of people must come...some of them perhaps far more prominent and wealthy than you are. And you preside. One by one the participants tell what they've done to further your objectives since the last meeting, and what they propose to do in the future. Finally, you assess their contributions, and you assign further work in preparation for the next meeting.

How different when you become a consultant.

You can still call a meeting. But this time it's probably a fact-finding session, at which *you* take notes. And if a report has to be written, *you* write it.

Maybe, on the other hand, your meeting is a "progress report" to your client. Elapsed-time-pressure was building up, and you called him before he called you. But now you're the supplier. What have *you* accomplished since the last meeting? And what will *you* do prior to the next one? The shoe's on the other foot. And until you get used to it, it *pinches!*

Moreover, what you produce will be analysis and recommendations. You don't control whether...nor how well...your advice will be carried out. And you may become very frustrated that lots of your time and hard work produces minimal benefit. *Welcome to the world of consulting.* You merely study and suggest. You no longer decide.

Another pain will be the lack of big-company support services. You can probably afford a secretary from the outset, although perhaps not. But you'll miss the research department, and the reproduction and mailing departments...not to mention all your capable subordinates. Indeed, you'll even miss the social interaction and the sounding board for ideas that was afforded by the sheer numbers of people around you.

And of course there's the fundamental insecurity of not having a predictable paycheck. Every dollar you get is for a consulting engagement you've sold, and for work you've done...or as general contractor farmed out to others, verified, and submitted to your client. No selling? Then no engagement...no money. Poor performance? Then no repeat business...no referrals...no money. The marketplace is a stern and objective judge. Submitting yourself to it is a gutsy move that shouldn't be taken lightly and, indeed, shouldn't be taken at all by most people.

On the other hand, there are some very real advantages to being a self-employed consultant.

True, you don't have a scheduled paycheck. But then you can't be fired. You can lose clients and you can go broke. But through lush and lean, you have a job. There's some security and self-confidence in having even that much control over your life.

And when you make money, only you and the IRS decide what to do with it. Moreover, since you and your accountant will set up an advantageous corporate vehicle and tax-deferral programs, you'll build net worth faster on your own than on a corporate payroll, if your gross profit matches your former salary.

You will, of course, be wallowing in trivia as you set up your office and begin to generate paperwork. On the other hand, your contacts as a consultant will tend to be at *very high levels,* probably CEOs and heads of divisions and functions. And you'll mainly be dealing with major issues.

Also, for some unfathomable reason, outside consultants seem to be treated with more courtesy and respect than subordinates and peers on the corporate payroll. If you're successful and can revel in prestige-without-power, you won't feel you've gone down in the world.

The freedom and flexibility of a consulting lifestyle is another "plus." You can probably do much of your work at home, or at your place in the country or at the shore. And working hours are entirely up to you.

Moreover, consulting is the one form of self-employment that won't risk your life savings. Your first office will probably be at home, and you can equip it with first-class word-processing and copying equipment, stationery and cards, for $10,000...maybe less. And if you're extremely tentative about your commitment, you can use a public stenographer and not invest in equipment until you're encouragingly underway.

If you've ever wanted to be a consultant, the time to "go for it" is immediately after you become unemployed.

To the $100,000+ executive, loss of job...regardless of reason...is a crushing blow. He feels worse if his boss simply wants to replace him, than if his company is acquired and there's no need for two Chief Financial Officers. But not much worse. Either way he's devastated.

Even if he's protected by a generous severance, the worst of the situation is the uncertainty. What next? He does everything possible as fast as possible. Yet he still worries, "How long until my next job?"

But suppose that our former CFO has thought about services he might offer as an independent consultant, if he ever gets an opportunity to become one. He has some intriguing ideas that should appeal to CEOs and CFOs of mega-companies at the top of *Fortune*'s list. And he also has some concepts that might interest the CEOs of relatively unsophisticated companies in the $20 to $50 million range.

In walks the grim reaper, just as before. But this time our hero is ready. Even before negotiating his final severance arrangement, he visits the printer to order stationery, cards, and a simple but elegant, triple-folded $8\frac{1}{2}'' \times 11''$ brochure. Day one of his "unemployment" becomes the first day of his consulting practice.

"Death, where is thy sting? Grave, where is thy victory?" Far from being traumatized and immobilized, our new consultant is *busy*. He may still be receiving money from various sources as a result of his "unemployment." But he's also developing a new income stream. Today he's his own boss...hard at work for a sensible, pragmatic task-master. Yes, he feels pain, disappointment, and self-doubt. But far less of it than most other people in his circumstances, because *he hasn't taken time out to be unemployed!*

If you're going to try consulting, don't waste your "personal contact" and "networking" opportunities on ordinary job-hunting.

Some people solicit consulting assignments only as a desperate "stop gap" measure *after* they've tried several weeks of personal contact and networking in an effort to get another job. This is entirely the wrong sequence for two reasons:

1. Their approach has been *unnecessarily weak and vague.*

2. Having labeled themselves job seekers, they've *destroyed their credibility* as consultants.

Let's look at the "job-applicant-first" scenario. Here's what's said to the *personal contact* by the applicant who *hasn't* read Chapter 4:

"Have you got a job for me, Barbara? I'm leaving X Corp."

If the applicant *has* read Chapter 4:

Barbara, I'm leaving X Corp., and I wonder if you might be a reference for me on our years together at Y Corp."

And to the *networking contact,* following the classic script:

"Mr. Kindly, I'm in the process of considering a career move, and I wonder if I might have just a few minutes of your time to get the benefit of your thoughts and suggestions."

Now imagine going back to these same people weeks or months later and professing to be a consultant. Whether they'll bluntly state it or not, people previously contacted by the job-seeker will think:

> "So nobody would hire you. And now you're trying for part-time work!"

Failure to find fulltime employment doesn't enhance anyone's credentials. Why even *consider* someone who's a consultant only because he couldn't get a regular job?

A timely consulting proposal
shows you off as a potential employee.

Generally speaking, a sales call as a consultant is a much better "showcase" for your abilities, experience, and achievements than an ordinary "personal contact" or "networking" call as a job-seeker. Consider these advantages:

High level contact. Your consulting targets are *at the top*...CEO, Division President, Group Officer, or VP Chief of Function. Networking, unfortunately, takes you randomly to whomever your preceding contact happens to know...maybe the ideal person to evaluate and "sponsor" you, and maybe far from ideal.

Something meaningful to talk about. The most pathetic aspect of a networking appointment from the job-seeker's point of view...and the most irritating from his host's...is the flimsiness of purpose: "a chance to get your insights and suggestions." People worth seeing are busy. Probably your half-hour no-agenda meeting will cause your host an extra half-hour of homework. How much better to discuss a consulting proposal geared to his needs. He'll feel more interested and receptive...less manipulated and imposed upon.

You MUST show your credentials. When offering to do consulting, you have to hand out and discuss something on paper that states your services and qualifications. Your expertise is what's being sold. And after presenting your consultant's "puff" piece, you can also provide your chronological "sales representative" resume, as a more forthright disclosure than most consultants are willing to make. But be sure there's no "Position Desired" or "Descriptive Summary" that implies ordinary job hunting.

You operate in a "selling" format. And on a sales call you're *much more in charge* of your presentation than you are in the "social conversation" of an interview, and the "brain picking" of a networking call.

You have greater opportunity to "sample" yourself. Provide a specific proposal that's written as well as oral. If well done, it's a persuasive *free sample* of your work. You submit it as a consultant. But it also demonstrates what a good conceptualist you'd be as an employee.

You don't have to be said "no" to. "Personal contact" and "networking" visits cry out for a disclaimer from your host:

> "I wish, Sandra, that we had a position for you here. Unfortunately, there isn't anything right now."

On the other hand, your consulting presentation tends to get the standard reaction we always give to salesmen...a courteous hearing and a non-committal answer:

> "Well, I don't know. *Let me think about it.*"

The psychology is just like asking a personal contact for a reference instead of a job. Your listener is left with a matter that's still *somewhat open in his mind.* And you have *an opportunity to come back* with another proposal, based on what you learned at your meeting.

You're easy to say "yes" to. Hiring you as a consultant is low-risk, compared with putting you on payroll. Your assignment is like a *"budget-priced trial size"* of a consumer product. There's enough to measure performance, but no big investment to lose if the product is disappointing.

Without disrupting his current organization, your client can evaluate your performance, and how he enjoys working with you. He may "make you an offer you can't refuse." Or he may pay for your project...which has probably been worthwhile in any event... and say goodbye.

When do you get your job offer...
when you "pitch," or after you've performed?

Obviously, an offer could come at either time.

However, I can't caution you strongly enough not to go in with a phony offer of consulting services, which is really a thinly disguised request for employment. If that becomes your game, it's dishonest; it's transparently obvious; it deserves to fail; and it almost certainly will fail.

Frankly, if a prospective client is going to offer you a job, you're better off if the marriage comes *after* a successful consulting engagement, not before. By then your prospective boss knows you and your work. There's less chance that he'll pre-empt your independence, only to become disillusioned and discard you later.

Meanwhile, you've also found out some beneficial information. You know lots more about your client and his company. You know whether you enjoy consulting. And, after your "firm's" pension and profit-sharing plans are in place, you know how much more you're salting away when working for yourself, rather than for a large corporation. This is probably your one-and-only shot at independence. Don't toss it away casually.

On the other hand, your earnest pitch for a consulting assignment will show you off to advantage. Therefore, it very possibly may lead to an excellent employment offer, instead of a consulting contract. If so... and if you accept...congratulations and best wishes! You've found a job by not looking for one.

Now let's consider the other way
you may find a job by not looking for one:
attempting to buy a business.

Here we're not talking about trying to buy a *small* business. Any $100,000+ executive who wants to exit the corporate arena by purchasing something small...restaurant, store, inn, motel, marina...

should have no difficulty doing so, and wouldn't have read this far in this book, anyway.

No, now we're talking about a big deal...something with annual sales above $5 million, and perhaps $50 million to $100 million or more. Maybe $4 to $25 million is most realistic for an individual to pursue.

You may feel that, for personal fulfillment, you must be at the helm of a sizable business. If so, don't even consider becoming an independent consultant. But don't give up the idea of becoming your own boss, either. If you're a $100,000+ executive, and you're willing to risk whatever money you now have, you can attempt to buy a very substantial business.

Surely you've seen Victor Kiam's TV commercials for Remington Electric Razors:

> "My wife introduced me to this Remington electric shaver,
>   and I liked it so much I bought the company."

It's a true story.

And here's one from my own experience, which proves that just about anyone can do a deal. In 1966, newly married and with only $8,000 in my pocket, I raised $350,000 to buy a radio station (5,000 watts AM and 250,000 watts FM) in Minneapolis-St. Paul, then America's #12 market. Total price of the station was $1 million, with 29% down and the rest earned out over 5 years. Unfortunately, when I met the seller's terms, he refinanced the station and refused to sell it to anyone.

I pursued that deal while happily employed...working nights and weekends on brochures and payout plans, and using vacation days, lunch hours, and a minimal amount of "on-payroll" time for meetings with lenders and venture capitalists. In the process, I found a lot more people in the financial community who wanted me to work for companies they were involved with, than who wanted to put up the cash I needed.

The best job offer was VP - Marketing of a young growth company which had been financed as a startup by the venture capital subsidiary of a famous Wall Street firm. It has since grown to sales of over $100 million, and is listed on the New York Stock Exchange. I would have made a bundle!

Almost all the people I met, even though they didn't provide money, were extremely kind and helpful. Virtually every meeting ended in classic "networking" fashion with suggestions of other people to see, and additional ways to further my project. Finally the head of the venture capital subsidiary of a large New York commercial bank suggested I take my brochures and P&L's to Minneapolis, where my deal would seem larger and more tangible. I did, and immediately got all the money I needed from a local venture capital firm.

Unfortunately, after that deal fell through, I never found another attractively-priced broadcast property, although I did investigate several other businesses...some much larger, but none worth raising money for. However, the fact that, except for the seller's withdrawal of his listing with the broker, I succeeded with the radio station deal convinced me that other people with more sophistication, more money, and more contacts than I had in those days could surely do a highly leveraged deal.

So when I became an executive recruiter several years later, and was asked by clients to do them the favor of "counseling" their senior-executive friends seeking jobs, I began asking the most enterprising-appearing ones why they didn't consider trying to *buy* a company. To most executives in the early '70's when I first started making this suggestion, it seemed a pretty radical idea. Not today!

What happens when you try to locate a company to buy, and try to arrange financing?

Obviously, two things could occur...one a long shot, and the other a certainty:

1. You *may* find the right company, raise financing, and wind up owning much or all of it.

2. You will *undoubtedly* meet and favorably impress lots of

influential people, who know what's going on in lots of companies.

Since 1971, dozens upon dozens of executives have thanked me profusely for suggesting they "network" their way through the investment and commercial banking communities, looking for a company to buy and financing for the deal.

Only a few actually wound up with their own companies. The reason the rest were so grateful: contacts made while attempting to do deals led to excellent employment offers with companies the financial institutions introduced them to.

How do you go about identifying a company and setting up financing?

It's far beyond the scope of this book to discuss in detail how to find a company and do a deal for it. However, the basic idea is all you need to get started. To look for a company, there are basically three channels:

1. Business Brokers

Every major industry has specialist brokers, who advertise in its trade publications. That's how I found the radio stations. Moreover, every major city has general business brokers listed in the "yellow pages." In centers like New York, Chicago, and Los Angeles some of these brokers will know of opportunities all over the country. Most, however, are locally- and small-business-oriented.

2. Investment and Commercial Banks, and Venture Capitalists

Bankers...both investment and commercial...are absolutely your best informants on companies to buy, and also your most productive networking contacts toward by-product employment opportunities.

Naturally you'd expect the great *investment* banks of Wall Street to be tuned in to a huge amount of acquisition and divestiture activity. And they are. But most of their deals, unfortunately, are beyond the participation of individual executives. However, those firms usually have certain members or a department specializing in smaller situations and "venture capital" projects.

Surprisingly, *commercial* banks in virtually every city are perhaps your best source of leads toward "smallish" companies to buy...properties with annual sales of $5 million to $25 million. And commercial banks also produce lots of by-product employment leads. Most people don't realize it, but *every* commercial bank, even a small suburban one, has someone...possibly even a department in larger banks...handling the bank's involvement in businesses that are in transition and/or potentially for sale. If your phone call asking for "the head of your investment banking department" gets you nowhere, just ask for the secretary to the President and tell her:

> "I'm an investor looking to buy a business in the $5 million to $25 million range, and I'd like to talk to the person in your bank who has the best knowledge of any such businesses the bank is aware of that might be for sale."

Right then...or with a call-back later...she'll get you hooked up with the proper person.

Venture capital firms...either independent, or arms of large financial institutions...specialize in financing relatively small deals of the type you might have a shot at doing. Generally speaking, however, they expect you to walk in already having a very specific deal you want them to back. You're far less impressive if you arrive empty-handed, asking for both a concept *and* backing.

However, in preparing this chapter I spoke to one of my favorite venture capitalists, who said:

> "Even so, John, don't discourage your readers from checking with us fairly early in the game. If a really outstanding guy with the right background came in here today, I've got a couple sick little companies that I might let him invest his $100,000 or $150,000 in, and run them. Or I might have an idea in my inventory that I haven't found the right guy for.

And of course, if I'm impressed with a guy but I don't like his deal, I may try to get him to join one of my 'investee' companies.''

3.   Owners of the Businesses Themselves

In these difficult times, most sizable companies...and even the large divisions of major corporations...have specifically earmarked businesses and product lines that ''no longer fit the corporate purpose.'' Possibly something they're tossing out could be your ''chance-of-a-lifetime.'' Vic Kiam bought the Remington Shaver Division from giant Sperry Corporation. To smoke out such possibilities, write to the Chief Operating Officer of the corporation, who'll probably turn you over to someone in Corporate Planning or Finance.

''But John, isn't it totally unrealistic to imagine that I could raise the money for a major deal?''

No. It's easier to find money to back an exciting deal than it is to find a really attractive deal to seek money for.

However, bear this brutal fact in mind: Whoever puts up the money for something far bigger than you can personally finance is going to want you to put most...and perhaps all...of your personal net worth into the deal. That guarantees you'll try desperately hard to make the venture work. You'll succeed...or you'll probably walk away broke.

And of course you won't own the whole company, if it's a sizable deal. Specific arrangements will vary widely. But here's some idea of how things might go if you finance through a venture capitalist. You and any other ''risk'' investors you bring in will put up significant money... maybe 5% to 35% of what's needed. The venture capital firm will come up with the balance (from its own funds, insurance companies, etc.).

The money you receive will be treated as an interest-bearing *loan,* to be repaid from profits. In addition, the capital firm and its ''partners'' will get an ''equity kicker,'' outright ownership of anywhere from perhaps a quarter to more than half of the company. The larger the percentage-of-capital you provide, the smaller their "kicker" will be.

Assemble your "nut" of risk capital
before you begin contacting the financial community.

The reason I was able to offer the requested downpayment of $290,000 (29% of $1 million) to the owner of the Minneapolis radio stations when I personally had only $8,000 way back in 1966 was that I had the backing of Midwest Capital Corporation. In fact, it was Alan Ruvelson, the President of Midwest, who called the owner and told him we were ready to buy the stations according to the terms the owner was asking. I would never have got the backing of Alan and his Board member Leonard Dayton, who was also active in analyzing the deal, if I hadn't had four essentials:

1.   A deal that made excellent financial sense;

2.   A manager they believed could do the job;

3.   A persuasive written prospectus that demonstrated points 1 and 2; and

4.   A "nut" of risk capital that was at least significant, even if far below the total needed to swing the deal.

Although my contribution was a miniscule $8,000, the "nut" I brought to the table was $60,000. . .a little over 17% of the $350,000 cash needed for the downpayment plus a modest amount of working capital. (The stations were operating at about break-even and I, Alan, and Leonard all believed they could quickly become very profitable.) Besides my $8,000, the rest of the $60,000 "nut" came from four of my friends in the advertising business, whose agencies had just "gone public."

Clearly part of my credibility as I wandered along Wall Street collecting helpful advice and employment overtures, and as I ultimately persuaded Midwest Capital to finance the deal, was the fact that people who knew me were willing to risk their own money in a venture I conceived and headed.

Don't even approach the financial community until you've assembled a respectable ''nut'' you're putting at risk. It can be your own cash. Or it can mostly come from others. And the financial institutions won't insist on *seeing* your funds until they're ready to go ahead with you. But don't expect cooperation. . .or even attention. . .until you can give a reasonable answer to this question:

''How much money have you got?''

Also, don't try my old 1966 numbers. Ice cream cones cost a dime to a quarter then. Now they're *upwards* of a dollar. Credibility today probably begins at $250,000. . .maybe $100,000 for a very small deal. Incidentally, today you couldn't touch those AM-and-FM stations I tried to buy in Minneapolis-St. Paul for less than $20 million.

Here's the bottom line. The venture capitalist will want to make sure you've got *a large part of your own net worth* tied up in the deal. As my venture capitalist friend says:

> ''I'll listen if a really good person walks in with only $100,000. . .or even $50,000. . .as long as the amount he's risking is meaningful to *him*. But he's got to be willing to tie up a large portion of his net worth and his liquidity. And if he doesn't have liquidity, he should second-mortgage his house and get some. He should show me he's dedicated.''

Nobody ever said it's easy to become an entrepreneur!

But even if you fail to consummate a deal, you'll make a wealth of valuable contacts as you attempt to put one together.

Okay, let's assume you're really committed to looking for a business to buy, and you've got a ''nut'' of money.

Now let's consider the superior quality of the contacts you'll make by ''networking'' bankers, corporations, and brokers.

The meetings you arrange while looking for a business to buy, and putting together financing, show you off far better than traditional "networking." You're not just another unemployed executive, who drops a familiar name and makes a familiar plea.

Consider these advantages:

Most appointments are NOT granted out of obligation. You reach people in the regular course of their work. . .not because someone imposes you on them.

You have legitimate business to discuss. You propose a money-making deal. . .purchase of a business on which a fee can be earned, or a bad loan worked out. You don't display an out-of-work executive to someone who doesn't need him.

Your managerial competence is a real issue. Far from just a tedious obligation, discussion of your managerial prowess is mandatory. Your experience and achievements would be probed, even if you didn't volunteer them, because they determine whether you're an appropriate purchaser of a business.

You provide an actual demonstration of your ability. You're in a business meeting. If you've already identified your target, you bring a well-thought-out written presentation. And even if you're still looking for a property, your acumen is demonstrated by your realistic objectives, and your reactions to questions and suggestions.

You arrive with a meaningful endorsement. Your "nut" of risk capital is a lot stronger recommendation than just the dropped-name of a prior networking contact. He may not be willing to lend you cab fare to your next appointment. But when you walk in to buy a business, your co-investors in the "nut" are "putting their money where their mouth is."

You talk to knowledgeable, well-connected, and powerful people. Proponents of conventional networking point out that even your dentist or clergyman may introduce you to the chief executive of a major corporation. Perhaps. However, if I were the CEO and got very many such referrals, I'd think seriously about changing both my dentist and my religion. Moreover, the CEO's need for an executive like you isn't something he normally communicates to his dentist or pastor. On the other hand, that need may be glaringly apparent to his banker, even when the CEO is reluctant to acknowledge it.

When trying-to-buy-a-business results in an employment referral from a banker, it may be even stronger than one from a recruiter.

A financial contact who has no "deal" to suggest knows that the odds are overwhelmingly against your eventually acquiring a company. Therefore, he may try to help a company he's close to by suggesting you as a potential employee. For several reasons, his referral can be even more valuable than a recruiter's:

> **You arrive without a "price-tag."** Unlike an unasked-for referral by any type of recruiter, the banker's introduction carries no $30,000+ impediment.

> **Your credibility is enhanced.** With no fee at stake, the banker has sent you only because he feels you may be helpful. He probably has money in the company, and wouldn't jeopardize it by sending a dud.

> **There's clout attached to the referral.** CEOs pay attention to suggestions from their key financial contacts. And if you're referred to a "young growth company," it may even be controlled by the financial institution.

> **You arrive alone.** You're not part of a recruiter's "slate." If you're excellent, nobody will go out looking for additional candidates.

> **Inducements may be offered.** You're being asked to forego your quest for independence. Not being a job seeker, you're not quite treated like one. Chances are, you'll be offered *more* equity participation *sooner* than an ordinary candidate for employment would be.

Trying to buy a company is a great adventure, which every red-blooded All-American Executive may want to try at least once. It's hard work. But it's exhilarating. And if you're smart and lucky, the rewards can be fantastic.

Maybe you'll wind up with your own company. Probably you won't. Regardless of the outcome, chances are you'll generate just as many employment opportunities...and probably better ones...than you will with ordinary job-applicant networking.

Who knows? You may find your ideal job by *not* looking for one.

The Rites of Passage:
What, When, and Whether

We've come a long way in examining *Rites of Passage* within the executive subculture.

We've studied the tribal rites of the headhunters. And we've looked beyond those classic rituals, to every other method by which senior executives move from company to company.

You know *what* to do.

Now let's consider *when* and *whether* you should take advantage of the techniques we've discussed.

You'll use different methods at different times, depending on your circumstances. And if you're willing to invest some effort when you're not about to change jobs, you can put yourself in an exceptionally favorable position to hear of attractive opportunities throughout all the rest of your career.

You know the saying:

> *"An ounce of prevention is worth a pound of cure."*

No question about it. Consider this corollary:

> *"An ounce of preparation is worth a pound of panic."*

And this one:

> *"An ounce of promotion is worth a pound of patience."*

Most people can agree with the logic of statements like these. Yet few can bring themselves to act on them. If you're one of the exceptional few, you'll gain a lot from this chapter.

Knowing the available techniques, let's apply them to the three degrees of job-changing interest you may have throughout the rest of your career:
1. Happy where you are,
2. Unhappy...but you can't show it,
3. Unemployed.

There's no free lunch. The most helpful techniques are also the most work. And the best time for some of them is when you don't have to do them at all.

Sorry about that!

But you're no stranger to hard work. The trouble is you're doing 100%

of it for your employer. Divert some to building a career investment in yourself.

If now's the time to move, do everything you can to make the best possible move. Every subsequent job...by promotion or by stepping outside...will build on your next one.

On the other hand, if everything's going great, now's the time to make yourself known. You won't be called and tempted with leap-ahead opportunities, if the most relevant people in the world outside your company don't even know you exist.

1. What To Do Now, When You're Happy and Not Looking

Connect yourself with the outside world. Tap into the communications system. Prepare yourself to receive *incoming* calls.

You're Happy: Begin work on your retainer recruiter network.

Would you like to have the leading firms doing the most good they possibly can for you from this day forward? Invest some speculative effort now when you're not under pressure, and you can go a long way toward that goal. If you insist on waiting until you do want to change jobs, there's no way you can accomplish anything comparable.

Here are the five obstacles that block you from getting what you want from the world of retainer recruiters. Even though not removable, all five can be minimized through foresighted action:

1. Any firm that can readily fill its assignments without looking for you won't bother to do so. Partial solutions:

> *Identify yourself to many firms,* so that statistical odds will favor an occasional call from one of them.

> Become a *personal favorite* of individual recruiters in those firms, so that you'll get more than your share of the firm's calls.

2.   Each retainer firm will show you only one job at a time, blocking you from all the others it's handling. Partial solutions:

> ***Become known to many firms,*** so that sporadic single opportunities from just a few will be all you need.

> ***Forge trusting relationships*** with recruiters, so that they may be willing to break their rules to help you.

3.   Firms that have your company as an "off-limits" client won't show you anything. Partial solutions:

> Become known to *lots of other firms.*

> ***Wait a while.*** Two-years go by in a hurry. By then your company may have shifted its recruiting business elsewhere.

4.   Mailed-in resumes are presumed to come from executives who are unemployed or in difficulty. Disprove the presumption:

> ***Refuse to consider several unattractive offerings*** over a period of years.

> After widespread distribution of your initial resume, ***merely send updates,*** not complete new resumes.

5.   Some recruiters in each firm are much better than average, and others may be beginners and potential "flunk-outs."

> ***Curry the good ones*** and discourage the others.

You're Happy: Prepare a "sales representative" resume.

Every executive should take time out to develop an outstanding resume. Follow all the suggestions in Chapter 12. You want about 3 to 6 pages that, because of format, can be scanned in 20 or 30 seconds and then...in the rare instances when interest develops...can be devoured by the "scanner" who becomes a "reader," wanting to know more.

You'll probably spend several weekends and evenings developing this compelling "credential." Consider it a "dirt cheap" investment, compared with any other self-advancement program you can undertake. Prepared to perfection, your resume can be used now for your

"Here-I-am" mailing to the retainer executive recruiting industry, and merely updated in the future.

You're Happy: Mail your resume
to *many* leading retainer recruiters.

Get into the files of every retainer firm that may someday benefit you. And do it now, while you're strong where you are. . .and not looking.

Don't sit back and wait, expecting the retainer firms to bump into you on a search. It will seldom happen. If you don't act now to build an ideal "presence" in the files of all these firms, you won't be handy when one of them gets a search you'd love to know about.

Forget the disadvantage of knowing only one-job-at-a-time and the fact that it may not be the right one. If a firm doesn't know you at all, chances are you won't hear about any job they're handling. They might look around and discover you. But if they're busy, and have plenty of others like you in the files, they won't look for you at all.

The greatest irony of your involvement with the retainer recruiting business is the blessing and the curse of the files. For upper-middle-level jobs. . .often near and above $100,000 these days. . .the busy recruiter may not bother to look beyond the files.

And yet when he does "check the files". . .especially at top-management levels, where candidates are least numerous. . .he may find that the most outstanding executives are already assigned to other recruiters and thus beyond his reach. You can't avoid being out-of-reach within any retainer firm. But you can increase the number of opportunities you'll see, by becoming known to many firms.

Therefore, you'll probably want to send your "Here-I-am" mailing to all of the prominent retainer firms listed in Appendix II, and perhaps to several others in your home town, who have a good reputation.

Don't worry about being inundated with job-opportunity calls just because you send your resume. It won't happen! Executives who are out of work and desperately hoping for a flood of calls mail simultaneously to these firms *plus hundreds more,* and they only get a handful of calls. . . perhaps a couple dozen at most during several months to a year of unemployment. With your relatively short list, which is only the cream of theirs, you'll get far fewer. However, two and three years later, you'll still be pleasantly surprised by an occasional "first call" from a firm that had no reason to call sooner.

You're Happy: Take your once-in-a-career-risk now, while it's minimal and you can afford it.

The risk of disclosure when you mail to all the top retainer firms is very small. And the earlier in your career you send your mailing, the less risk there is.

Even if several recruiters in the retainer firms are close friends of your boss, your nastiest rival, or your company's president, it would be highly unethical for them to call and say, "Guess who just mailed in his resume?" That's just as verboten as "floating resumes." And it's even less likely, because there's no money in it. Disclosing your resume to a potential employer might net $30,000+. Disclosing mere *receipt* of it to your current employer would earn no fee. All it would produce is a reputation as a gossip...deadly in the recruiting business.

Several years ago a contingency recruiter serving the advertising industry offered, for an annual fee, to inform subscribing employers whenever she received a resume from one of their employees. Public outcry forced her to withdraw the new "service," a few days later. Employers, interestingly, expressed as much outrage as employees.

Face it. You *do* want to start career-long "awareness" relationships with a wide cross-section of retainer recruiting firms. Sooner is better than later. Even if word should accidentally leak out of one firm, wouldn't you rather deal with that now, when you're "riding high," than in the future when you might be in jeopardy? Wouldn't you rather "explain" to your current boss who's just promoted you, than to his replacement who may be looking for an excuse to fire you?

You're Happy: Get the unattractive job suggestions out of the way now.

Regardless of what you say in your covering letter, every retainer firm you mail your resume to will assume you're either out of work, or afraid you soon will be. That's when and why people mail resumes.

Inevitably, therefore, the first opportunity you hear about from each retainer firm you write to will probably be no better than lateral in responsibility...and possibly unattractive in other ways, too, such as compensation, location, and prestige and stability of the company involved.

Indeed, whenever a particularly unattractive assignment comes in, the recruiter handling it always alerts the research clerk to *"comb the write-ins"* looking for someone unemployed who might want the position, since nobody happy and secure in a comparable position at higher compensation, in a nicer location, or with a better company would even consider it.

Time and *refusal* are the only rebuttals to the ''out-of-work-or-in-trouble'' presumption that dogs every ''write-in.'' If the firm doesn't call you until a year or two after getting your resume, and you're still at the same company with the same title or better, they'll know you're secure. Your letter stated the truth. Similarly, if they call shortly after you ''write-in,'' and you refuse a position comparable to your current one, this too will confirm you're ''solid.''

The recruiter's phone conversation with you will be duly noted in your file. And even though you ''wrote-in,'' instead of waiting to be ''discovered,'' you'll henceforth be regarded as a secure executive who can't be tempted with anything that isn't a substantial advancement. Let's see what a recruiter writes in your file after such a ''first conversation'':

> ''Called him'' (date) ''to propose VP - R&D of Tacky Technology Corp. Not interested, since he already heads 150-person section of the corporate lab, and is moving up fast, at Blue Chip Corp. *Very impressive* on the phone. Sent in his resume 'just to get acquainted.' So he's ambitious and probably will move for the right thing—*but it better be good!''*

The next suggestion you receive from this recruiting firm will be far more interesting.

You're Happy: Help the impressive recruiter.

At the same time the recruiter was sizing you up, you were evaluating him. He quickly understood that you're secure and won't move laterally. Then he agreed with your realistic assessment of the job he presented, and asked you for recommendations. He wasn't dense. He didn't try "high pressure." Indeed, he seemed professional, pleasant, straightforward, and down-to-earth.

As a result, you went out of your way to be helpful. You listened carefully and came up with several potential candidates, plus another person who wouldn't be interested personally, but might identify candidates. Accordingly, the recruiter made an additional notation in your file:

> "Helpful source."   WP

Congratulations! You're well on the way to becoming what they call in the business a "hot file"...someone every recruiter in the firm tries to get his hands on the minute he undertakes something relevant. You'd be a great candidate...and if not, a great help.

Do not, however, help all recruiters equally. If the guy sounds like a dope...and some may, even from the most prestigious firms...don't open up to him. Any firm may have new and/or inadequate recruiters on payroll, who will ultimately flunk out. No point in going out of your way to help them.

Be most helpful to the most impressive. In each firm, they're the ones you want to have knowing how good you are, and fighting for the right to call you up. They'll be the most discreet with the information you give them. They'll appreciate it most. And they're the most likely to be handling the bigger and better jobs that will interest you in the future.

You're Happy: How much help is too much?
Should you identify people in your own company?

First let's consider prospects who are above you. If you're in a relatively small firm which might be hurt by the loss of a potential candidate, keep quiet. The company would be hurt, and you would also be hurt.

But if the company has several layers of good management, it probably won't be hurt, and a promotion to fill a vacancy above you may "domino" into a promotion for you, too. Figure that a really good recruiter will dig to find out what he needs to know. If you won't tell him, he'll just keep asking until someone else does.

Even when the recruiter's opportunity could be a career breakthrough for one of your subordinates, you may decide to identify your person and let him know that you're his benefactor. One of the most senior and respected executives at General Electric (now retired) always recommended his best subordinates to me. Several became candidates. But every single one that wound up getting an offer from one of my clients ultimately refused to leave GE. They just couldn't walk out on a boss...and because of him a company, too...with such obvious concern for their welfare.

Of course, the best way to shield your subordinates and others in your organization is to suggest lots of ideal candidates from other companies. That way, the recruiter has less need to probe your place. If you're extremely helpful and he likes you, he'd rather not cause you grief, even though circumstances will sometimes force him to do so.

You're Happy: Keep records on recruiters.

Start your own file on every retainer firm you have any contact with. Begin with copies of the initial letter and resume you send out. Then update each firm's file whenever one of its recruiters calls. And start a new file whenever someone calls from a firm you haven't written to.

Years go by and memory fades. You want to know who called from each firm, when, what position was discussed, who you recommended if you weren't interested, and *your evaluation of the caller*. Armed with this information, you'll always know who is at least vaguely aware of you at each firm. If more than one person from the firm has called, you know who sounded the most competent and with whom you had the best rapport. And if you suggested people who filled the recruiter's jobs, you can later remind him who they were.

Let's see what you wrote down after the conversation on Tacky Technology. It's the first entry in your file marked "Gordon, Rossi & Boodles":

> Will Pickham, VP, called to suggest VP - Engineering job at Tacky Technology. Shaky-sounding company. Only 55 engineers. Seemed to think I was in trouble and would jump. But then became interested in how well I'm doing, and what it would take to move me.
>
> Told him *"no way"* on Tacky, and recommended Dan Daring and Ron Ready at Raytheon and Fred Fearless at Rockwell. Also Stan Swinger and Peter Plunge. Loved the idea of Stan—said, "Mr. Tacky would flip for someone from Bell Labs." Will was fascinated that 5 years after leaving, I'm keeping current with their people to staff my department here, and could name a young risk-taker over there. Also surprised I'd name one of my own best subordinates, and he let *me* tell Pete to call him about Tacky, so I could stress having Pete's interests at heart. I also told Will to use my name and call Ed Entrepreneur for ideas, because Ed's company is in the same field as Tacky.
>
> *Liked Will!* Very professional, yet down-to-earth. Restoring a Model A roadster. *Excellent GR&B contact.*

Your conversation with Will Pickham has been well documented on *both* sides. Before we move on, let's look again at the last couple words in Will's notation:

"Helpful source."   WP

That modest description hardly conveys Will's full enthusiasm for you. In one phone call, you've gone from "just a write-in" to someone Will won't forget when he has another search in your field. Meanwhile, of course, you may be hearing from other recruiters at Gordon, Rossi & Boodles...some of whom you'll like, and help, as much as you did Will. But until someone else comes along that you like even better, Will's your key to GR&B.

You're Happy: Update the records
that recruiters are keeping on you.

From now on, whenever you receive a promotion or change companies, send a brief letter to the recruiter with whom you have the best relationship at each retainer recruiting firm.

Or maybe just write something like this across the top of a copy of the official announcement:

Will —
An exciting challenge
Is the roadster finished?
Regards
Paul

Will's secretary will see that what you send gets into your file. As a result, his firm stays continually up-to-date on you without your ever sending a new resume...and therefore without your ever reassuming the "out-of-work-or-in-trouble" presumption.

Chances are, however, that by the time you're announcing your next promotion two or three years after your initial mailing, you still won't have heard anything from four-fifths of the firms you originally wrote to. They:

1. Haven't yet needed anyone with your background;

2. Didn't get around to calling you when they did have a need; or

3. Threw away your resume because they had no need when you originally wrote.

"Update" these non-responding firms with a letter that avoids the "out-or-in-trouble" presumption. Refer to your original mailing, and enclose both a copy of the promotion or new-appointment notice, and an up-to-date resume. Say something like this:

(Use personal letterhead)

Mr. Powers Prominent
President
Prominent Associates, Inc.
925 Park Avenue
New York, New York   10025

Dear Mr. Prominent:

Since I originally submitted my confidential resume for
your records in November 1986, I've continued to
receive additional responsibility at Blue Chip Corporation, which last month promoted me to Vice President - Engineering.

Sincerely,

Paul Crane

Enclosures: Announcement
              Resume

And there you have it...a program designed to bring you maximum personal advantage from the retainer executive recruiting industry, throughout the rest of your career.

A modest investment of effort now, while you're happy, may pay an incredible dividend in future years. It could be as valuable as a lottery win, if it lets you know about a break-through career opportunity you wouldn't have had a shot at otherwise. Even if it only reveals a sporadic series of lateral moves you might make, it could be as good as a lottery win...if it comes at the right time to spare you the unforeseeable future pain of job-hunting while unemployed.

One more thing to do right now:
Buy some elegant personal stationery.

Every executive should have genuine *engraved* stationery listing home address and phone. Kept in the office and at home, it lends a personal touch to congratulations, condolences, gift enclosures, RSVP's, and correspondence in support of charitable and cultural causes.

Order some right now, and get the 10-week production period out of the way. Ignore stationery and jewelry stores, and shop the "Yellow Pages" under "Engravers." Take advantage of the low prices lawyers and accountants enjoy. You may not want to buy...or store...enough for an emergency job campaign (at least 2,000 Monarch and 500 standard letterheads; plus 500 Monarch and 2,000 standard [#10] envelopes). If so, just get the engraver's "minimum" order...probably 1,000 Monarch sheets and envelopes. Your "die" will be cut and kept on file. Thereafter, you can get additional quantities in just two or three weeks.

For less than $250 (including die) your minimum order will provide enough stationery to be a "class act" for the next ten years. And with your die on-file, you'll have an insurance policy against the "outplaced look" for as long as you have your current home and phone, and the engraver remains in business. (If local suppliers are expensive, try Dewberry Engraving, Birmingham, AL.)

2. What to do when you're unhappy... but you can't show it.

Too bad you didn't establish "resume contact" with a wide cross-section of retainer recruiting firms two or three years ago, when you were well situated. There's no better remedy for "unhappy-but-I-can't-show-it" than an opportune call from a recruiter. A maximum program then wouldn't be bringing a flood of calls now. But a few welcome calls would be trickling in...maybe five or six a year, and that might be enough to solve your problem.

But let's skip the "I-told-you-so's." Now we'll swing into action... *but cautiously.*

Secretly Unhappy: You can still contact retainer recruiters. But now you must be far more careful to avoid the ones your employer uses.

If you think your employer may be as unhappy with you as you are with him, then you've got to be especially careful not to send your resume to the recruiters he uses. Ordinarily you could accidentally contact those recruiters and there'd be no problem. Professional ethics would prevent their calling your employer and saying, "Guess who I just got a resume from?"

Now, however, circumstances are different. Your employer may have confided his concerns about you to one or more of the firms he uses. Clients usually *do* discuss key managers' strengths, weaknesses, and probable destinies with trusted recruiters. And after that happens, recruiters *will* disclose receipt of a resume from an employee previously described as not up-to-par:

> "You mentioned last week that after we finish the Director of Engineering search, you want us to work on the VP - Manufacturing slot. And maybe early next year, if he doesn't get on the team, you may want to think about a replacement for your head of R&D. Well, I feel a little awkward telling you this, but under the circumstances I feel I must. Today we got a resume from your VP - R&D. Maybe we should proceed immediately on that search, too. What do you think?"

Of course you can't be forewarned if your employer is having secret discussions with a recruiter the company hasn't used before. But stay away from any that he and the rest of the company are known to use.

How can you determine which to avoid? Probably only three or four should concern you, and you may already know them. However, before you mail, make some discreet inquiries. And if your secretary is tight-lipped, subtle, and loyal, send her on reconnaissance, too. Provided with a good "cover story," she may get better information than you will.

Moreover, since your situation now is particularly ticklish, you may want to boldly mark both your covering letter and the front page of your resume:

CONFIDENTIAL;
I AM NOT UNEMPLOYED.

This shouldn't be necessary, and looks a little paranoid. Also, *it won't prevent disclosure by a recruiter your boss has already talked to about possibly replacing you.* But it may offer a slight margin of added protection against accidental mishandling. Probably it will make you feel more comfortable, if nothing else.

Secretly Unhappy: Talk to your best personal contacts.

Obviously, your personal contacts can be trusted. Explain that everything is "hush, hush," but you're beginning to look around. Will they serve as a *confidential reference*? As we discussed in Chapter 3, this request will announce your availability just as clearly as asking for a job or job leads. Yet it avoids the up-front final negative, "Sorry-I-don't-have-anything-and-don't-know-of-anything."

Secretly Unhappy: Consider "targeted networking."

Ordinary networking is obviously out of the question when you're trying to maintain confidentiality. However, if there's a specific target person you want to reach...perhaps a CEO who has a key executive nearing retirement with no obvious successor...you may be able to reach that CEO as suggested in Chapter 4.

A word of warning, however. CEOs and other executives aren't as sensitive to your need for confidentiality as most first-class recruiters are. These executives aren't malicious...just less accustomed to professional caution. Try to reach your "target" with *no more than one trusted intermediary* who knows your "target" personally and will be sure to stress your need for secrecy.

Secretly Unhappy: Your best shot is
a secretive direct mail campaign.

When you absolutely must get into action in a hurry...and do it secretly...there's no substitute for direct mail, with a "sponsor" signing the letters and getting the replies. The method described in Chapter 13 can reach upwards of 1,000 potential employers within 2 to 4 weeks and locate the approximately 3 to 6 among them who, according to realistic statistical odds, currently may need you.

Usually about 1 to 3 of the 3 to 6 will be sufficiently impressed when they meet you to extend an offer. But if you're fighting any handicap in experience, background, track record, ability to express yourself, appearance, age, or anything else that might tilt the odds against you as compared to an "ideal" candidate, consider doubling or tripling the 1,000 mailing to assure equivalent results.

---

3.   Unemployed!

A rough time. But at least there's no need
for secrecy; all options are open to you.

And knowing what you do now, you'll find a new job
far more efficiently than you would have before.

The reason many executives have agonizing difficulty finding another job that fits their talents, background, and compensation requirements is that they don't know what you do.

They're able. And not lazy. Indeed, they work desperately hard.

But they misallocate their efforts, spending huge amounts of time on activities where they've long since passed the point of diminishing returns. Meanwhile they mistakenly neglect other techniques that could be highly productive, because they consider them of little value or even counterproductive.

Unemployed: Approach executive recruiters realistically.

Executive recruiters are the most misunderstood and misused job-hunting resource. Be sure you use them wisely.

Many unemployed executives spend lots of time early in their search hoping to find a recruiter who'll offer to "help." If they're attractive and readily employable, these executives eventually find the harmful "help" they seek...mailing of their resumes to their likeliest employers with a price-tag attached.

You'll deal knowledgeably with contingency recruiters, restricting yourself to the fine ethical firms you're confident will never send your resume or refer your name to *anyone* without contacting you first and getting your authorization for that specific referral. You'll also keep a knowing eye peeled for suspiciously "helpful" behavior by retainer recruiters.

The commonest and saddest of all errors made by senior executives is wasting precious time by haunting the halls of the largest retainer firms, trying through networking and other cajolery to meet yet another of the firm's recruiters in yet another office. Vainly they hope to find out about more than one-job-at-a-time, among the dozens or even hundreds of appropriate openings a firm of that size is always in the midst of filling. You know that this strategy is impossible, and you know why.

Sadly too, many unemployed executives fail to send their resumes to many reputable retainer recruiters, hoping by such misguided "selectivity" to enhance their appeal and usefulness to the small number of firms they choose.

You're aware of the "selectivity" pitfall. So when you're unemployed, you'll routinely submit your resume to every retainer firm you haven't yet sent it to...knowing that no two such firms will ever be working simultaneously to fill the same opening, nor will they ever ask or care which other *retainer* recruiters you've sent your resume to.

If any retainer firm is already showing you an opportunity, you realize that they're as involved with you as they can possibly be. You won't try to pressure them further. But you will call up the one or two most impressive people you already know at each retainer firm where you seem to be dormant. You'll tell them your current circumstances, and mail them an updated resume.

And when you want to push aggressively into the consciousness of retainer firms that don't already know you, you'll force an appointment by using the clout of someone who spends money with them or who's been a candidate or a helpful source. You won't invoke the name of a competitive recruiter. You also won't waste time on more than one "door-busting" visit per firm, and you won't storm multiple offices of the same firm.

Above all, you won't devote the overwhelming preponderance of your time to recruiters, as so many ill-informed executives do. As you fully appreciate, your main mission is to break through to the vast number of jobs the retainer firms are withholding from you, not merely to pursue the one-in-3-or-4-months that each firm may actually show you.

Unemployed: Use personal contacts effectively.

Needless to say, you'll call your closest contacts immediately...and perhaps get together with the best-situated ones. They'll be surprised and pleased when you merely ask them to serve as a reference. Relieved that you haven't asked them for a job, as most unemployed executives do, their long-standing esteem for you will rise even further.

And reminded of what they already know you've done, and apprised of your latest accomplishments, your contacts will think about how they or someone else in their company may be able to use you. Here, too, you've avoided a serious mistake most executives make, by not forcing a closed-issue "unfortunately-we-don't-have-anything" answer.

Unemployed: Use networking. But keep it in perspective.

Now that you're out of work, you can openly indulge in networking.

But don't over-emphasize it to the neglect of other important techniques. Lots of executives have been making that mistake. . .especially since the burgeoning growth of outplacement.

Nowadays I can never see or hear the word "networking" without recalling an offhand remark by one of the legendary cynics of the "people business," as he boasted to me several years ago about how much money he was making since he shifted his firm into outplacement. When I asked how he actually helped his "outplacees" find jobs, he laughed and said:

"I tell them to go *network* themselves!"

A totally different calibre of person in the "people business" is a psychologist in a fine firm that offers outplacement among its many other services and, likewise, endorses networking as the optimum method. When he and I discussed the plight of unemployed executives recently, he cited one of his close personal friends as a successful example. A very high-level executive of a top company in a huge industry, the psychologist's friend lost his job when two giants in that field merged:

"Fortunately, networking saved him. After being 'out' for more than a year, he finally found a job as executive director of a trade association in a totally different field. He makes a lot less money than he used to. And I don't think he likes his new work very much. At least I know he's unhappy not to be in his regular field. But without networking, he wouldn't even have the job he's got. Networking saved his life."

Did this man launch a direct mail campaign?

"No, I advised him not to bother. You get very limited response from that."

Did he try to *buy* a smaller company in his field? There are hundreds of them around. . .many of them in difficulty these days.

"I don't think so."

Did he try to launch a consulting practice in his specialty? As former head of a large portion of one of America's leading companies, he'd be considered an authority.

"I don't know."

What a classic example of networking! This man got the kind of job you'd expect him to get eventually, if he continued long enough meeting and questioning kindly people in the large city where he lives. . .a job uncovered virtually at random, which has nothing to do with his prior background and current preferences.

If this fellow had spent "more than a year" marketing himself to his regular industry, chances are that's where he'd be working today. Random local networking is ideal for lower- and middle-managers, whose non-specific skills and moderate compensation fit a broad spectrum of jobs. It's far less appropriate for the $100,000+ executive who wants to capitalize on years of experience in his current specialty.

If you're ever unemployed, you'll use networking too. But only when it serves your purposes better than the other available techniques. For example, *if you strongly want to avoid relocation, and your skills fit well into a wide variety of companies, and your compensation isn't unusually high,* then networking is an excellent way to look for a hometown job.

Let's say you're a financial officer who's been CFO, controller, and chief of internal audit in various size companies at various stages of your career, and there are reasons why you must stay in Cleveland. Obviously, you can be useful to a wide range of companies and non-profit organizations. Meeting business people all over town and getting each of them to refer you to two or three others is one way of finding out about all the potential local opportunities.

However, a much quicker way would be a direct mail campaign, based largely on the *Ohio Directory of Manufacturers* published by Commerce Register. This book lists about 14,000 companies, either headquartered in Ohio, or Ohio-based divisions and subsidiaries of larger corporations headquartered elsewhere. It doesn't include retailing, wholesaling, travel and transportation, communications, financial, media, advertising, construction, maintenance, entertainment, hospitality, hospital/medical/nursing, education, cultural and other non-profit entities, etc.

Using Commerce Register's *Ohio Directory,* you can identify several hundred local Cleveland *manufacturing* companies. After phoning to confirm name and title of their CEO and their address (see Chapter 13), you can have your letter and "sales representative" resume in the hands of all those potential employers within two or three weeks. If companies with sales of less than $10 million...or some other figure...don't interest you, you won't mail to them.

Moreover, just by scanning the Yellow Pages, or any other directories your public librarian may suggest, you can probably come up with another couple hundred *non*-manufacturing entities large enough to have a role for you. These possibilities can be phone-checked for name/title-of-CEO and mailed within the next week or so of your all-out job campaign.

After letting the appropriate person in hundreds of local organizations...as many as you can identify...know about you within just two or three weeks, you can then settle down to the leisurely pace of networking. Two- or three-a-day networking appointments don't seem so creakingly inefficient *after* you've used your spy-in-the-sky satellite to scan the terrain. Now a ground-level search for clues on foot and by taxi is a perfectly logical next step.

Indeed, your fast preliminary direct mail scan will help target your follow-up networking campaign. Chief executives who take the time to send you a personal letter saying they have nothing for you...and some will...can be phoned for the usual "a-few-minutes-to-get-your-thoughts-and-suggestions" appointment. Occupying high-level business positions, and having demonstrated kindness and courtesy, these CEOs will be ideal networking contacts to augment the list of people you already know.

No question about it...meeting you and liking you, some networking contacts who minutes before were complete strangers may feel like digging into their minds for ideas and their address books for contacts.

The CEO who doesn't need you as his CFO or controller may suddenly realize that you'd be the perfect business manager for the symphony...

and as a member of its board, he can propose you. Or he may send you to his multi-millionaire golfing buddy who owns 18 McDonald's franchises in Ohio...someone who can use and pay appropriately for your talents, but whom you'd never have identified by looking through directories for large Cleveland businesses.

However, if you're a $100,000+ executive with specific background and interests you want to exploit and with a nationwide or global scene to scan, classic networking visits around town are not for you.

Targeted networking, on the other hand, may be. Perhaps you want to meet a CEO in your industry who just lost a divisional president to another company and has, in your opinion, no suitable internal replacement. Now that you're unemployed and have no fear of disclosure, you can freely forge a chain of personal introductions leading to your "target," according to the suggestions in Chapter 4.

Unemployed: Don't be afraid to use direct mail.

Unemployed...or at least out from under any secrecy restraints...you're free to orbit your spy in the sky satellite. Moreover, it can be as blatantly identified as the Goodyear blimp. Scour the whole country, or the world. No need to hide behind a "sponsor." No danger that you'll lose your bird-in-the-hand job as you check out the bush.

When you think in terms of your ability to work full-time openly seeking the best possible job for the next stage of your career, unemployment almost seems desirable. And indeed it can be, if you use it knowledgeably and creatively. Unfortunately, most people don't.

I often run into excellent $100,000+ executives who've been out of work six months or longer and remain totally frustrated in their search for another job. They've long since given up hope of finding a *better* job. I ask them if they've conducted a comprehensive direct mail campaign:

> "Oh, certainly not. I didn't want to cheapen myself in the marketplace."

These very words come back to me again and again from executives who should know better. Not long ago I got a call from a former VP - Corporate Controller of a recently-merged Fortune 500 company, who'd already been "out" seven months. He answered my question about direct mail with. . .word-for-word. . .the #1 cliché on the subject (above). And before I could respond with even a syllable of rebuttal, he plunged right ahead with cliché #2:

"I didn't want to meet myself coming around the corner."

This guy would be unbeatable on TV's *Family Feud.* "The #1 and #2 most popular answers," as the MC says. And. . .bang. . .bang. . .in that order! Both of these classic "reasons" for an unemployed executive not to conduct an all-out direct mail campaign are not only erroneous, they both seem subtly related to a common practice most mature young adult males and females engage in: going to college.

"I-didn't-want-to-cheapen-myself-in-the-marketplace" clearly relates to Econ IA, and its "Law of Supply and Demand." After they become leaders of American Capitalism, formerly proletarian college students confuse increasing potential *demand* (more would-be purchasers who are aware of the product) with increasing supply (multiple clones of the VP in question).

Erroneously they figure that increasing demand will drive the price down. What the professor actually told them, of course, was that increasing *supply* would do that. Indeed, the professor suggested advertising as a means of making more potential buyers aware of the product (increasing demand) and thus (or so he claimed) driving the price *up.*

For years I've wondered how so many American executives arrive at the identical misunderstanding of the "Law of Supply and Demand" when applied to the sale of their own services. After all, these are the same people who spend millions of dollars on advertising to increase demand for commercial products and services.

Moreover, I suspect that even in other personal economic matters, these same people would not make the same mistake. Suppose they owned a house or a boat and decided to sell it at auction. Would they try to restrict the number of people aware of their property's advantages and availability, so as "not-to-cheapen-it-in-the-marketplace"? Would they try to suppress news of the auction in order to assure a small crowd and thus higher prices? I don't think so.

Why then do these executives get "Supply and Demand" confused only as it relates to *themselves*. . .and not with respect to goods and services, both commercial and personal?

My latest theory is still predicated on the pernicious effects of college. However, I've stopped looking for ineffective pedagogy in the Economics Department. The faulty curriculum, I'm now convinced, is not Professor Greybeard on "Supply and Demand." It's *Mom's* advice on *dating.* She's repeatedly quoted as saying, *"If you seem easy to get, they won't want you so much."*

Mom's advice clearly presages and parallels the "I-didn't-want-to-cheapen-myself-in-the-marketplace" rationale for not getting in touch with *any* companies, and likewise being careful to reach only a selective few retainer recruiting firms. Moreover, Mom's principle is adhered to even though the executive knows that no two retainer firms will ever be working on the same job; hence, every firm shunned is potentially a job shunned.

Incidentally, Mom's corollary concern about not getting a "too-available-reputation" can readily be seen as the root logic behind the more colorful, yet enigmatic: "I-didn't-want-to-meet-myself-coming-around-the-corner." Admittedly, that spectre is most disturbing. However, like "cheapening-in-the-marketplace," it's impossible. If you have any lingering concern, check the last half of Chapter 11.

Unemployed: Consider the "Underutilized Asset Discussion" ...an ideal door-opener, if consulting and purchase of a business are part of your exploration.

Absolutely the best way to get an appointment with a chief executive or with any other corporate decision-maker is to have something specific and highly interesting to discuss. Virtually nothing fits that description better than an underutilized asset. . .a business or other resource he has, that could be put to new, better, or additional use, or could be advantageously sold off.

During the years that you've worked for one company in your industry, you've undoubtedly noticed competitors who aren't making the most of something they have. You've probably even noticed similar examples within your own company, but for political reasons, you haven't been able to pipe up.

As an independent consultant or a prospective purchaser viewing the matter from outside, you have no such inhibitions. You can go straight to the CEO of any company with a letter and follow-up phone call outlining your thoughts. And if you make sense, he'll probably be interested enough to invite you in for a hearing.

Typical languishing assets you might identify:

Division or product line underperforming for reasons you'll explain. Or appropriate for divestiture or contribution to a joint-venture you can visualize.

Trademarks that could be used for quick penetration of new markets, or licensed to other users.

Products of overseas subsidiaries that could be profitably imported. Even as America drowns in imports, U.S. multinationals fail to think of bringing in their own unique overseas lines.

Sales forces and distributor networks that could handle related lines.

Patents, technology, and know-how that could be licensed to users in other industries or spawn advantageous entry into other fields. Or possibly even be shared profitably with competitors.

Under-exploited real estate, air rights, timberland, mineral rights, etc. Also unused plant capacity that other companies might need.

Before you blurt out your analysis which, after all, lacks inside knowledge that only the company itself has, make sure you're on firm ground. Ask questions. Confirm your assumptions, and modify your presentation accordingly. Then show that you've thought more deeply and creatively about the asset than the CEO's own people. Perhaps no one has devoted proper time to it. Or maybe it hasn't had the priority you now demonstrate that it merits.

Propose a consulting engagement. Phase I will be a study of the issues you've pointed out. Phase II, if warranted by Phase I, will implement the recommendations of Phase I. You're prepared to handle implementation totally on the outside, or drawing on inside personnel. Or... *stand by for a job offer.* The CEO may prefer implementation by internal personnel...with you leading the team.

I can't even begin to count the number of executives I've come across over the years who've moved from one corporate payroll to the next, by doing a consulting project so impressively that their client hired them as a permanent employee.

On the other hand, if the CEO is *not* interested in more aggressive use of the asset you point out...and if that asset is severable and salable... maybe he'll entertain an offer from you to purchase it.

If so, you have something tangible to discuss with investment bankers and venture capitalists. Start making appointments with them!

Rites of Passage

Well, that's it. That's everything I wanted to impart on the subject of changing jobs at $100,000+.

We've looked at the employment process from every angle. If you really want to accelerate your career, you've got several important steps you can take right now, while you're happy and challenged in your current job. You can even get extremely aggressive while staying under cover.

And if you should ever find yourself out of work, you know everything you can possibly throw into an all-out campaign.

Someday you may face difficult times. Most of us do at least once or twice in a career. But you'll never have to make the pathetic statement we've all heard so often from previously dynamic executives after months of unemployment, with no leads in sight:

"I feel so helpless. I just don't know what to do."

You know what to do. And at a time like that, you'll be busy doing it, not sitting around wishfully waiting for the phone to ring with news that someone else has done it for you.

You also know what not to do. You'll never make the rounds of recruiters until you find one who says:

> "Let me see what I can do to help you."

Nobody will price-tag your head and get to your most likely employers before you do, blocking those casual exploratory sessions your own straightforward contact might otherwise have brought about.

Moreover, you won't waste an undue amount of time on naively ardent courtship of retainer recruiters. You'll get to the most jobs you possibly can through them. And you'll also get *past* them to far more jobs than they're permitted to show you.

From now on, whenever any headhunter calls, you'll deal with him in precisely the way that best serves your self-interest. And over the years, you'll build mutually-trusting relationships with the best retainer recruiters...perhaps even to the point that they'll be willing to suspend their rules to assist you when you urgently need help.

How many and which "Rites of Passage" await you in the years ahead? Almost certainly *interviewing*. Definitely *writing a resume*, and maybe a *covering letter* to go with it. And very likely *negotiating an employment contract*, too. Maybe *outplacement*. And without a doubt plenty of *personal contact, networking*, and *dealing with recruiters*.

Come what may, there'll be more method...and less mystery...in your approach to the potential passages that are always open to you in the world of employment outside your current company.

As a result, I hope you'll feel free to pursue what's best for you...not just what's handed to you.

Expand Your Career by Expanding Yourself

Rites of Passage has been about your career. I'd never presume to offer advice on anything else.

However, a successful career affects you far beyond the workplace and the workday. Greater self-esteem, more money, and a higher spot on the totem pole perk up the non-work aspects of your life, too.

Conversely, who you are and who you know and socialize with *away* from your company...both within your industry and within the community-at-large...can foster your career.

Some people ignore the outside world until their career runs into difficulty. Only then do they launch a frantic program of polishing old contacts and networking new ones. **Don't make that mistake. Learn to live your life so that you continually renew and expand relationships outside your company.**

The legitimate claims on your time and attention made by your family and close personal friends, added to what every employer expects from an upwardly-mobile executive, leave very little time for career-enhancing contact with people you don't see at work.

But you do have a few minutes. This chapter suggests ways you can leverage that small fund of time, so that it will pay large dividends in both career progress and personal satisfaction.

Raise your profile.   Know and be known!

Again and again you've heard the cynical old saying:

> "It's not *what* you know, but *who* you know that counts!"

Unfortunately this cliché is usually spoken bitterly by one of the many losers of the world. He's simultaneously making an excuse, and framing an accusation, as to why someone better-connected or more widely well-thought-of has just received a promotion or a new job he feels he should have had.

How sad!

Not sad that the loser didn't win. But sad that, knowing one of the many perfectly legitimate reasons winners do win, the loser took no steps to foster his own valuable network of personal contacts.

The business world...and society in general...is not a meritocracy in which the wisest and most virtuous person will be sought out from obscurity and escorted to a position of leadership.

Far from it. We all tend to give opportunity and responsibility to people we already know and like. We also tend to give consideration to people warmly recommended by others we know and trust. And we give more attention to strangers who are prominent in their field, than to anonymous strangers who may be equally- or perhaps even better-qualified.

Accordingly, these observations and suggestions:

Trade associations provide a wealth of contacts.

Don't pass up the chance to represent your company in trade association activity. In many companies, association functions are looked down upon, and second- and third-echelon people are often sent because higher-ups are "too busy." Resist any status-minded temptation to be "too busy."

Go. You'll come back knowing people who work for your competitors. If they're high-level and highly impressed with you, someday they may be sources of career opportunity. And if they're lower-level, but able, they may be prospective employees you can hire later on. Even if they're lower-level and unimpressive, you may suddenly find that you need information, and they'll be willing to supply it.

You should always be able to check your phone book or cardfile and identify someone you can phone within every competitor. Wherever your contacts aren't yet ideal, keep upgrading as the years go by.

Seminars and Conferences

Not only does it make sense to attend seminars and conferences as a means of collecting valuable contacts; you can benefit even more from participating. Accept invitations to appear in forums and panel discussions. That may be the quickest possible way to become well known in your industry.

And don't "hang back" waiting to be invited to be a panelist. When you're still young and have most reason to want the publicity, you're least likely to be asked.

After this year's event, and before work on next year's gets underway, write or phone the president of the association and/or the designated chairman of the next meeting. Say what you thought were this year's highlights. And then describe a unique new subject area, or a new twist for a traditional event, which you feel would greatly interest the membership. If you phone, follow up with a written description, which can be conveniently circulated to gather opinions and support.

Creative ideas for association meetings are extremely hard to find, and few people are willing to help. If your attitude is helpful, rather than pushy, chances are the powers-that-be may like your idea and may ultimately ask you to execute it. Even if they go ahead with someone else in charge, you'll probably be one of the key participants.

If you become the leader, you've got a license to make very high-level contacts in soliciting panelists...possibly even CEOs. Even as a participant, you gain exposure and make fine contacts. No longer just a face in the crowd, you're on your way to prominence.

Consider starting your own association.

An outrageous idea? It's done all the time. People and companies who have something to gain by it start a new association.

When companies do it, they usually promote an organization of users and potential users of their products or services. Once identified by association membership, these prospective customers are easier to reach with direct mail campaigns to the general membership list, with ads in the association's publications, and with booths at conventions, etc.

Examples: a leading computer manufacturer has fostered organizations of EDP professionals within various industries, such as insurance and accounting. And an insurance company very successfully launched a national association of retired people in order to promote its policies for people over 65.

When a group of individuals promotes a new association, there's often a double agenda:

1. They see a valid purpose for the organization...essential, or it won't attract membership, and

2. They see themselves acquiring professional prominence by being the instigators...and probably the initial officers...of an association representing their field. Instantly they appear to be acclaimed by their peers as top-echelon people.

Executives who wouldn't for years be considered industry leaders join together to proclaim a new and differently-focused professional association. As founders, they become President, Executive Vice President, Chairman of the Executive Committee, etc. There are enough impressive titles to let each of the founders have one.

Amazingly, I've never seen a group of reasonably-credentialed executives fail in an effort to start a new association. On the other hand, I've never seen anything but failure when one self-seeking individual tries to start an association, just so he can head it. A solo grab for status is too obvious and obnoxious to attract a following.

Frankly, I could list at least a half-dozen thriving associations started by groups of founders who stardusted themselves, while setting up useful organizations that have survived and thrived. How deliberate and how accidental was the personal advantage? No one can say. The fact is that all of these people achieved something valuable for their profession. If they simultaneously gained something for themselves, it was a fitting reward.

Although I can't name the current crop of organization-starters in this context without offending some of them, I'll share one example which is now ancient history.

In the mid-60's a handful of self-proclaimed "young influentials" in the field of consumer products marketing named themselves "Cabal" and "by invitation only" attracted one or two other such rising "superstars" from each of the most prestigious New York-based consumer products manufacturers and advertising agencies. Purpose: "To meet and hear off-the-record talks" by chief executives of leading companies and agencies.

Despite skepticism about both the premise and prospects of the new organization, I accepted my "invitation." What followed were three years of fascinating monthly luncheons at the Harvard Club, as one after another of the CEOs of America's largest corporations and agencies showed up to address less than 40 middle managers. And during that whole time, the same five or six people who conceived the project held the offices of the group, contacted the speakers, greeted and introduced them, and sat with them at the head table.

So if the Trilateralists, the Council on Foreign Relations, and the leading trade association in your industry haven't beckoned, you might consider joining with several congenial co-founders to start a new association.

Write your way to prominence.

Perhaps you can be one of the lucky few to author an article of interest to the *Harvard Business Review,* or some comparably eminent publication. But even if your expertise is too specialized and your profile as yet too low for such a celebrated journal, you can probably come up with something for a trade paper in your industry.

Once you've seen yourself in print, it's an experience you'll want to repeat. And each time the writing will become easier. Moreover, having appeared as a published "authority," you'll be called for quotable commentary by professional writers and reporters who prepare for their articles by reading prior ones.

Indeed, if you really have something to say, maybe you should write a book. A couple individuals I know wrote books on the principles of their industry while still only upper-middle managers. The books were successful, and helped widen the distance between them and their peers. Today both have the title President. One heads the company he joined fresh out of business school. And the other is a man I recruited as president of a small entrepreneurial company, which he has since built into the number-one company in America in its field.

Outside board memberships provide contacts and prestige.

Obviously, you'd be delighted to be asked to join the board of a major NYSE-listed corporation, and maybe someday you will. Certainly that's more likely if you rise to the top of the company you're working for, and if you continually take steps to broaden your network of personal contacts.

Meanwhile, however, an excellent interim career-development move would be to join the board of a small growth-oriented company. Such an opportunity is well within the reach of virtually every $100,000+ executive who makes a point to be as widely connected as possible. Chances are, you already know several presidents of smaller and medium-sized companies, who might be inclined to think of you for their boards, if they only had an inkling of your interest.

And why not a non-profit directorship? There are many relatively young and struggling charitable and cultural organizations which, unlike the venerable institutions, aren't yet dominated by mega-donors and directors from the second and third generations of the same families. Not only can you be a more significant and higher-level supporter of a young institution, you may even find its mission more pertinent and exciting.

Don't shirk fund-raising duty.

The valuable contacts you'll make as a supporter and potentially a board member of a charitable or cultural institution won't be limited to other supporters and officers. In all likelihood, you'll be pressed into service trying to line up contributions from corporations and wealthy individuals. Don't resist.

Awkward as fund-raising may initially seem, it will gradually fill your address book with some prominent contacts. . .particularly if you stress the corporate side, and try to get the business leaders you approach to participate in the institution, rather than just add it to their companies' "contributions" list.

Club your anonymity to death!

Probably you already belong to a respected country club and a city luncheon club. If not, you certainly should. But if you're like most of us, you probably spend very little time at either place. And when you do go, you're usually entertaining an outside guest.

From now on, make it a point to participate in the annual golf or tennis tournament, and other general-membership events, as a means of knowing more of your fellow members. And when you don't have any other lunch date, try sitting at the "club table" of your city club. Sure, you'll meet some dull old fogeys. But you'll also meet some very interesting people you'd never have become acquainted with any other way.

Also consider moving some of your otherwise solitary, or socially "throw-away," pursuits to a prestigious athletic club. Instead of taking a lonely morning jog along the road near home, why not come into the city early and, using the club as your base, run in the park? You'll join other executives in this ritual, and several may turn out to be valuable business and social contacts. Same goes for your thrice-weekly workouts with Nautilus or free weights, and your lap swimming, which you can readily switch from a commercial or community gym to a club frequented by the prominent and powerful. And when you're at the club, why not substitute basketball, handball, squash, or paddleball for your usual workout whenever the opportunity presents itself? You'll get to know a lot more people that way.

One very successful and athletically-inclined CEO of a New York-based Fortune 500 corporation can almost always be found both before and after his 9:00 to 5:30 workday at a prestigious athletic club engaged in strenuous competition with other members of his management team. In fact, over the past decade or so of his presidency, his key aides have been winnowed by Darwinian selection into a group of brainy jocks, who can not only challenge him intellectually in the office, but also athletically at "the club." More than one fine athlete from "the club" has found employment in the corporation. And, except for one woman, all of the top-level executives he's recruited have been macho men who perform impressively at "the club."

One final suggestion: If you travel to the same city fairly often, consider a non-resident membership in one of its leading clubs. Or maybe your present city club has reciprocal privileges. Your athletic routine can be accommodated better than at a hotel; you'll probably make some valuable contacts; and reservations will be less of a hassle when trade shows and conventions clog the city. Accommodations may be spartan, but certainly not unacceptable.

Take the initiative in meeting people who interest you.

At your current level of achievement and prestige, you're already in a position to make overtures toward people you think may share a mutual interest. Don't hesitate. The worst you'll suffer is rejection...something you should learn to accept, if you haven't already.

When you read an article about someone who's just pioneered a new technology that may have future application in areas you deal with, write a note of appreciation and follow it up with an invitation to lunch. Introduce yourself to the conference speaker whose point of view seems so congenial, and suggest meeting later for a drink. Set up an appointment to meet the dean of a nearby business school; perhaps some of your business problems can become his graduate students' research projects, with mutual benefit. If you've admired the work of a sculptor, or a novelist, or a conductor, call or write to say so. You may establish an acquaintance that can broaden your horizons and give you a new perspective. If not, what have you lost?

And if there's someone you particularly want to know, don't hesitate to use your skill at networking to make contact. Gaining a personal introduction through networking is a technique that needn't be reserved just for job-changing.

Personal contacts are one of your most valuable resources.

Let's go back to our cliché:

"It's not what you know, but who you know that counts."

We heard that as a rationalization for not getting a promotion or a new job the speaker felt he should have had. Totally wrong-headed, in my opinion.

Don't let the career orientation of this book and the usual meaning of the "who-you-know" cliché obscure the greatest value of a strong and constantly-expanding personal contact network. It's not just a set of "connections" that may help get you hired. After all, you'll change jobs only a few times during your career. Meanwhile, your personal contacts are useful to you...and you're useful to them...every single day, and in every facet of your life.

The nearest analogy to a strong and wide-ranging network of personal contacts is a good education. Someone very wise said this about education:

> "It's not what you know, but what you can *look up.*"

Following that line of reasoning, a good contact network is far better than a good education. For when you have others to whom you freely lend your knowledge and who freely lend you theirs, then you literally have the benefit of hundreds of different educations, career specializations, ethnic and cultural backgrounds, creative insights, and general data banks from experience and life. The limits of your knowledge and ability to cope are infinitely expanded.

Hence, a good contact network operates just like a good education:

> "It's not what you know, but who you can *ask.*"

Do you want to find out about the performance of a potential supplier or distributor, about the attitude of a governmental agency, or about the most respected authority on an emerging technology? With a good contact network, answers are a phone call away.

Or do you want to know which heart surgeon the best doctors in your city would choose if they were being operated on, or which local contractor has the best reputation for building swimming pools that withstand your area's harsh winters, or where to send your son to college to study international trade? Again, an authoritative answer to each question should be just one or two phone calls away.

In so many ways:

> "It's not what you know, but who you know that counts."

Whatever else you do in your career...and in life... don't curse this idea. Be someone who knows others, and whom others consider worth knowing. Have good contacts, and be a good contact.

The Challenge: To Keep in Touch

It's not only a pleasure, but also a great benefit, to know more and more people. People you can call on for assistance and expertise, and people who know they can call on you for the same favors.

The great problem is how to keep in touch with so many people, when you hardly have time to see and enjoy your closest friends. Indeed, as a busy and upwardly-mobile executive, you may sometimes be forced to give your own family less time and attention than they deserve. How, then, can you hope to keep in touch with business and social contacts? Must you always approach them like this?:

> "Jim, I'm almost ashamed to call. It must be four years since we talked, and then I was phoning to get your ideas on the Peroni acquisition which, incidentally, were very helpful. Gosh, it seems like the only times I ever get in touch are when I want something. But I wonder if you could help me out with some information..."

You can't go on forever, getting in touch only when you want something. Or at least you shouldn't. But what can you do?

Well, one thing's certain. You can't keep in touch with leisurely lunches and long, chatty phone calls. You just don't have the time...nor does the other person, in most cases. And often the connection isn't intimate enough for such a strong dose of togetherness, anyway.

So what's your strategy? Obviously, something thoughtful but less time-consuming. Here are some suggestions:

Make quick, spontaneous phone calls.

When you see something that reminds you favorably of one of your contacts, grab the phone and say "Congratulations," "Bravo," "Well done."

Maybe it's a shrewd acquisition, an ingenious sales promotion, a terrific new commercial, a compelling speech, a scholarly journal article, a quickly-settled labor negotiation, a successful stock offering, a newly-issued patent...or maybe just an unusually handsome new paint job on the house, a rare second-place finish in "Class B" golf at the club, a 12-inning Little League win, or a daughter's acceptance at Yale Law School. The fact that you noticed...and smiled to yourself...is enough reason to call. Give *voice* to the thought!

And with a secretary answering the phone, your brief "thought-of-you-and-decided-to-call" call will probably wind up brief indeed. Chances are you won't get through. That's okay. Just leave your message:

> "No need to have him call me back. Just tell him I called to congratulate him on his son's making All-State."

Shouldn't that have been your previous call, rather than another request for free legal advice?

Let the Postal Service help.

Some of the most successful executives are those who've learned how to use the mails to keep in touch with large numbers of business and personal contacts. This method of renewing acquaintance needn't take a large investment of time, since your secretary does most of the work. Nonetheless it's extremely effective, because you can periodically cover your entire list of contacts, to make sure that nobody gets left behind.

Indeed, annually mailing something "first-class" to all your contacts insures you against inadvertently losing anyone you haven't been in touch with recently. If some of your contacts have moved, the Post Office will probably forward your mailing, and you'll provoke up-dates from whoever you're not current with. And if the time for postal forwarding has elapsed, your envelope "returned-to-sender" will alert your secretary to get on the phone and track the person down.

Send holiday cards.

A lot of people are delighted to see the recent decline in the custom of sending Christmas and Chanukah or New Year's cards. That's an understandable feeling, if you're a young mother with a ten-room house and three children between the ages of 4 weeks and 5 years to take care of. But if you're an upwardly-mobile business executive with a private secretary, maybe you should think again.

Renewing valued associations at least once a year is a small price to pay in gratitude for past courtesies and in anticipation of possibly asking favors in the future. How many years can legitimately go by without a note or a phone call, before it becomes more awkward to call up a former friend than a complete stranger?

Actually, with fewer cards being sent, your card...if you choose to send one, and I suggest you do...becomes a more meaningful gesture. You took the time when you didn't have to!

If you do decide to carry on this gracious custom, don't make the ridiculous mistake quite a few senior executives make. Don't have the envelopes hand addressed and stamped, and then merely put an unsigned, printed card inside. That way the recipient's secretary throws the human touch into the wastebasket. What she hands over is a printed folder that's less personalized than your American Express bill. Word-process the envelopes, and put them through the postage meter. But personalize the card. At least sign your name over the place where it's printed. And if the card goes to someone you've really been remiss in not contacting for a whole year, write a few words of greeting.

Distribute your annual report.

Mail copies of your company's report to any business contacts who might be professionally interested. Attach your card, and add a very brief personal message, such as:

Bob —
Hope you had a good year too
Fred

Let your scissors do the talking.

One of America's most prominent and successful businessmen...and also one of the ablest at selling himself and the company he heads... has an extremely gracious habit that sporadically reminds me and his literally hundreds of other friends that we're on his mind and have his good will.

As he does his voracious reading of periodicals on virtually every subject from all over the world, he clips articles that would interest his friends and has his secretary mail each clipping with just a simple typed note, which he signs:

> John,
>
> Thought of you when I saw this.
>
> Hope all goes well.   *Tony*

You can do the same thing...as I try to, when I think of it. When you do your regular reading of newspapers and periodicals, keep an eye out for articles of interest. For example, you may know that one of your business contacts collects original Audubon prints, coaches a Little League team, cross-country skis, restores antique furniture, or toured Alaska with his wife on vacation last fall. When you run across an article on the appropriate subject, clip it and send it, along with a similar short note:

Dave,
Thought this might interest you.
Susan

Don't worry about whether Dave's already seen the article, or has long since known the information in it. The point is that you remembered his interest and you cared enough to clip the article and send it to him.

Interestingly, you can show personal thoughtfulness with this sort of gesture, when almost anything else would seem blatantly presumptuous. Consider this example: You're three levels down from the CEO on the organization chart, so you wouldn't dream of suggesting a lunch date, even though you occasionally have a few moments of conversation with him while waiting for the 10th floor elevator. It would be a gracious and appreciated gesture, however, for you to send him the article on scrimshaw from your latest *Connoisseur* magazine. You know he's a collector, because he has a lighted vitrine full of it in his office. And of course, if you also happen to be a collector, he may even signal a willingness to talk more freely on the interest you both happen to share.

Indeed, some lower-echelon adventurer who didn't know the CEO even remotely as well as you do could also have sent the article to a Chairman whose hobby is so openly displayed to the entire company. Many CEOs like to feel that they have rapport with more of their executives than just the six on their Management Committee. No matter what your current echelon, why *not* be someone the CEO can speak to, when he wants to break an awkward silence in the presence of several employees?

Early in my career, I watched with awe and respect as a newly-recruited MBA from an unpretentious Midwestern university made five years' progress in two, after ''discovering''' during his first week on the job that he and the CEO of J. Walter Thompson Company ''shared'' an interest in collecting antique Wedgwood china. As this clever young fellow so aptly put it:

''I've got nothing to lose but my anonymity.''

Incidentally, when people are mentioned in the press, they often appreciate having an extra clipping. And regardless of whether they'll send the item along to Mom for her scrapbook, they're pleased to know that someone *noticed*. I'm occasionally quoted in out-of-town papers and would never even know it, if not for the clippings friends send me.

Respond immediately to any piece of good news you read, or hear on TV or radio, about one of your contacts. If you see in the paper that someone you know has published a book or a journal article, led his company to a record sales year or his partner to victory in the country club doubles tournament, married off his daughter in style, or been invited to dinner at the White House, clip the article. Attach it to a short note of congratulation and put it in the mail. Surprisingly few people comment on such out-of-the-ordinary events, and the ones who do are warmly remembered.

Don't waste any opportunity to be thoughtful.

Be as lavish as possible with every kind of invitation. Put your key business contacts on every guest list for cocktail parties you give at home and at the office. When an organization of which you're a director or trustee has a special event, even if it's just a Sunday afternoon open-house at the local nature center, ask for additional invitations to be sent to business contacts who might be interested.

And never let a pair of tickets for anything, from a hockey game to a fashion show, languish unused on your desk. If you're too busy to attend, send them immediately to someone you think might enjoy the event. He or she may also be too busy to use the tickets, but you can be sure they'll appreciate your thoughtful gesture.

If you're anywhere near my age, you'll never forget the black-and-white TV image of John F. Kennedy standing hatless and coatless on that cold day in January 1961, saying:

> "Ask not what your country can do for you; ask
> what you can do for your country!"'

Somehow his exquisite skill with words renewed a logic as old as the Golden Rule.

A lot of people figure they can network their way through life, asking for time, ideas, knowledge, and sponsorship, with no corresponding impulse to do anything in return, except perhaps to say "thank you." Then, without so much as a backward glance, they're off to scavenge from someone else...always with asking and getting clearly in mind. Meanwhile, helping, sharing, and caring are pretty much forgotten and discarded.

That is *not* the way the most influential and successful people I know operate. They treasure the very special values of friendship. And they warmly appreciate their relationships with kind and helpful people they know less well. Their philosophy would parallel JFK's:

> "Ask not what your contacts can do for you; ask
> what you can do for your contacts."

A Parting Word

Here's where I leave you.

For now at least, I've conveyed everything I can think of that could possibly help you negotiate the inevitable "Passages" of a successful executive career in the realm of $100,000+ .

Over the years I've had the pleasure of knowing and observing many of America's leading executives. You and I both owe them a "thank you," because much of what we've covered has come from them. The rest has come from 17 years on the opposite side of the recruiter's desk from the one you face...a perspective it's my pleasure to share with you.

But now we part company. You go back to being an executive, and I go back to identifying and attracting the most appropriate ones to meet the needs of my clients.

Let's hope that someday I may have reason to call you as one of the four or five best candidates in America for a specific CEO position that I've been engaged to fill. Or that you rise so far above $100,000 that you have executives well over $100,000 reporting to you, and I can help in their selection as a means of further helping you.

Until then, thank you for the time we've spent together. And very best wishes for an outstandingly successful career.

Sincerely,

John Lucht

APPENDIX 1

Sources of Information
for a Job Search

1. General Information on Companies and Their Executives; on Industries and Geographical Areas; and on Prominent People

America's Corporate Families (formerly *The Billion Dollar Directory*). Dun's Marketing Services (Corporate Center 2, 49 Old Bloomfield Avenue, Mountain Lakes, NJ 07046; 800-624-0324 in NJ, 800-526-0651 elsewhere). Annual. One hard-cover volume, 3,600+ pp., $395/year lease (no credit cards).

> Information on more than 8,000 U.S. parent companies. Address, phone, sales, no. of employees; primary bank, accounting, & law firm; stock exchange(s); lines of business; S.I.C. codes; and officers and directors. Also 44,000 U.S. subsidiaries/divisions of these companies (listing chief officer only). Three large indexes: (1) subsidiaries/divisions alphabetically, indicating parent company; (2) S.I.C. categories; and (3) geographic (by state and city).

Commerce Register's geographical directories of manufacturers, such as *Ohio Register of Manufacturers* (14,000 companies, $82.50). *Metro New York Directory of Manufacturers* (10,000 companies, $82.50), etc. Commerce Register, Inc. (190 Godwin Avenue; Midland Park, NJ 07432; 800-221-2172) continues to introduce new state/regional directories. Already published, besides Metro New York and Ohio, are: Maine/Vermont/New Hampshire (4,500 companies, $52.50); Connecticut/Rhode Island (7,000 companies, $62.50); Pennsylvania (12,000 companies, $82.50); Massachusetts (7,500 companies, $62.50); Upstate New York (5,000 companies, $52.50); and New Jersey (12,000 companies, $82.50). Annual, soft-cover. (Major credit cards.)

> Information on manufacturers with more than 5 employees within the state/region. Organized by city. Each company lists address, phone, products, incorporation date, employees, sales, plant size, officers and titles, pri-

mary bank, accounting, and law firm. Companies indexed (1) alphabetically and (2) by S.I.C. category.

The Corporate 1000 and **The International Corporate 1000.** Monitor Publishing Company (1301 Pennsylvania Avenue, N.W., Suite 1000; Washington, D.C. 20004; 202-347-7757). Annual. Each one soft-cover volume, 600+ pp., $95 each, or $150 for both (major credit cards).

> Subtitled "A Directory of Who Runs the Top 1000 U.S. Corporations" and "A Directory of Who Runs the World's Leading Corporations," respectively. Each lists names, titles, and (often) direct-dial numbers for key officers, plus outside Board members and their companies. Four indexes in Corporate 1000: (1) people alphabetically, (2) companies geographically by state, (3) companies by industry, and (4) subsidiaries/divisions alphabetically. Two indexes in International: (1) geographical by country, and (2) industry.

Directory of Corporate Affiliations. National Register Publishing Company, Inc. (3004 Glenview Road; Wilmette, Il 60091; 800-323-4601). Annual. One soft-cover volume, 2,010 pp., $349 (Visa,MC).

> Subtitled "Who Owns Whom." Lists 40,000 divisions/subsidiaries of over 4,000 U.S. public and private companies. Lists assets, liabilities, net worth, approximate sales, officers and Board members of parent, plus chief officer of divisions/ subsidiaries. Indexed geographically (state and city) and by S.I.C. codes. Also summarizes recent mergers, acquisitions, and name changes.

The Directory of Directories. Gale Research Company (Book Tower; Detroit, MI 48226; 313-961-2242 in MI, AK, & HI; 800-521-0707 elsewhere). About every two years. One hard-cover volume, 1,325 pp., $185 (major credit cards).

> Organized by industry/discipline. Describes the contents of over 7,800 publications ("directories, professional and scientific rosters, and other lists and guides"). Indexed by subject and publication titles.

Encyclopedia of Associations. Gale Research Company (Book Tower; Detroit, MI 48226; 313-961-2242 in MI, AK, & HI; 800-521-0707 elsewhere). Annual. Volume 1 (3 hard-cover books, about 2,000 pp.), $220/set; Volume 2 (hard-cover, about 1,000 pp.), $200; Volume 3 (soft-cover, about 200 pp.), $210; Volume 4 (hard-cover, about 500 pp.), $185; plus Updating Services (about 200 pp.), $185 subscription (major credit cards).

> Volume 1 (physically, 3 books) gives detailed entries on more than 19,500 U.S.-headquartered, non-profit associations and organizations of all kinds (business and trade, political, social, fraternal, professional, ethnic, educational, etc.), arranged in 17 subject categories; includes address, phone, top

officer, year founded, acronym, membership, subgroups, activities, committees, publications, meeting schedule, etc.

Volume 2 is a geographical and executive index to Volume 1.

Volume 3 is a subscription to two soft-cover supplements, which update on newly-formed and newly-found associations.

Volume 4 gives the same entries as Volume 1 for international associations located outside the U.S.

The Updating Service, by subscription, periodically updates Volume 1, and indexes new organizations listed in Volume 3.

Encyclopedia of Business Information Sources. Gale Research Company (Book Tower; Detroit, MI 48226; 313-961-2242 in MI, AK, & HI; 800-521-0707 elsewhere). Every other year. One hard-cover volume, 730 pp., $185 (major credit cards), plus $75.00 for periodic supplements.

20,000 information sources on 1,280 highly specific subjects (from Abrasives Industry to Zinc Industry), including encyclopedias/dictionaries; handbooks/ manuals; bibliographies; abstract services and indexes; trade associations and professional societies; periodicals; directories; biographical sources; price sources; almanacs/yearbooks; research centers/institutes; on-line data bases.

Guide to American Directories. B. Klein Publications (P.O. Box 8503; Coral Springs, FL 33065; 305-752-1708). Every two years. One hard-cover volume, 600 pp., $55 (major credit cards).

Describes contents, frequency, and cost (if any) of 6,500 directories in a variety of fields (over 300 classifications), with phone numbers. Covers government, financial, scientific, educational, business, and research sources.

International Directory of Corporate Affiliations. National Register Publishing Company, Inc. (3004 Glenview Road; Wilmette, IL 60091; 800-323-4601). Annual. One soft-cover volume, 1,430 pp., $294 (Visa/MC).

Two sections: (1) Non-U.S. holdings of U.S. parent companies; (2) U.S. and worldwide holdings of foreign enterprises. Includes address, telephone, types of business, S.I.C. codes, sales, no. of employees, and key personnel.

Indexes: (1) company names; (2) international trade names cross-referenced to product (S.I.C.) category and company name; (3) foreign companies by country; and (4) companies by S.I.C. categories.

Million Dollar Directory. Dun's Marketing Services (3 Century Drive; Parsippany, NJ 07054; 800-624-0324 in NJ, 800-526-0651 elsewhere). Annual

(February). Two different versions: (1) a four-volume hard-cover series, listing 160,000 public and private U.S. companies with net worth of at least $500,000; (2) one hard-cover volume, listing the top 50,000 companies (net worth over $1,850,000). 2,100+ pp. in one-volume version, $395 annual lease; 11,000+ pp. in four-volume version, $1,195 annual lease; five-volume combination of (1) and (2), $1,495 (no credit cards).

> Includes address, phone, parent company, divisions, officers, incorporation, no. of employees, sales volume, types of business and applicable S.I.C. codes, primary bank. Indexed by geography and industry.

The National Directory of Addresses and Telephone Numbers. General Information, Inc. (401 Park Place, Suite 305; Kirkland, WA 98033; 206-828-4777). Annual. One soft-cover volume, 1000+ pp., $34.95 (major credit cards).

> Address and phone for major U.S. corporations, presented alphabetically and by SIC category. Also miscellaneous special sections listing address and phone for hotels, banks, agencies, etc. in 50 U.S. cities; county, state, and federal government entities; area and zip codes for U.S. cities; banks; transportation; colleges; etc.

Reference Book of Corporate Managements. Dun's Marketing Services (3 Century Drive, Parsippany, NJ 07054; 800 624 0324 in NJ, 800 526 0651 elsewhere). Annual. Four hard-cover volumes, 6,800+ pp. total, $695 lease (no credit cards).

> Biographical profiles on 200,000 officers of more than 12,000 U.S. companies, arranged alphabetically by company name in three volumes. Fourth volume contains indexes by geography and industry (S.I.C. codes).

Standard & Poor's Register of Corporations, Directors and Executives. Standard & Poor's Corporation (25 Broadway; New York, NY 10004; 212-208-8786). Annual, with quarterly update. Three hard-cover volumes, 3,500 pp. total, $425 annual lease (major credit cards).

> Volume 1 lists 45,000 public and private U.S. and Canadian (plus a few foreign) companies. Address, phone, sales, products/services, no. of employees, stock exchange, S.I.C. codes, officers and directors, principal bank, accounting, and law firm.

> Volume 2 sketches 72,000 key executives (year of birth, education, title/business affiliation, residence (if biographee permits), and directorships/trusteeships.

> Volume 3 contains S.I.C. and geographical indexes of companies; index of

subsidiaries/divisions cross-referenced to parent company; obituary section; index of new individuals added since last publication; and index of companies added since last publication.

Standard Directory of Advertisers. National Register Publishing Company, Inc. (3004 Glenview Road; Wilmette, Il 60091; 312-441-2210 in IL; 800-323-4601 elsewhere). Annual. Two different editions (''Classified Edition,'' organized by product classification, and ''Geographical Edition,'' organized by state and city), plus bi-weekly bulletin and five cumulative supplements. 1,343 pp. plus supplements, $235 per book; $314 for book plus 3 supplements; $469 for book plus updates plus supplements (Visa, MC).

Lists over 17,000 U.S. advertiser companies, with address, phone, sales, no. of employees, primary business(es), key managers, advertising agencies of record, account executives, time and amount of appropriations, and advertising media. Also lists subsidiaries/divisions. Two major indexes: (1) company names and (2) tradenames (over 35,000) cross-referenced to manufacturer.

Thomas' Register of American Manufacturers. Thomas Publishing Company (One Penn Plaza, 26th floor; New York, NY 10119; 212-290-7200). Annual. 19 hard-cover volumes, 30,000+ pp. total. Visit your library.

Profiles 123,000 manufacturers, with their major products and services. Includes 8,000 pp. of catalog material and 102,000 registered tradenames.

Ward's Business Directory. Information Access Company (11 Davis Drive; Belmont, CA 94002; 800-227-8431). Annual, except third volume, every other year. Three vinyl volumes, 4,000 pp. total, $360 per volume, $700 for two, $900 for three (no credit cards).

Demographic and financial business data, organized (1) geographically, (2) alphabetically, and (3) by S.I.C. codes. Volume one: largest U.S. companies; Volume two: smaller U.S. companies; Volume three: international companies.

Who's Who in America. Marquis Who's Who, Inc. (3002 Glenview Road; Wilmette, IL 60091; 312-441-2210 in IL; 800-323-4601 elsewhere). Every two years. Two-volume hard-cover set, 3,900 pp. total, $250, plus $72 for Index (major credit cards).

Profiles over 74,000 leaders, decision-makers, and innovators from a variety of fields (business, government, journalism, art, diplomacy, law, science, medicine, music, education, etc.). Biographies include education; career history; achievements, writings, and awards; civic and political activities; memberships; and addresses. Separate volume contains Index.

Who's Who in Finance & Industry. Marquis Who's Who, Inc. (3002 Glenview Road; Wilmette, IL 60091; 312-441-2210 in IL: 800-323-4601 elsewhere). Every two years. One hard-cover volume, 640 pp., $154 (major credit cards).

> Profiles over 17,000 principal decision-makers from the fields of banking, insurance, transportation, government regulatory agencies, major corporations, etc. Biographies include education; career history; professional and social memberships; achievements; writings and awards; and home and office addresses.

---

2. Information on Particular Industries

Advertising/Market Research/Public Relations

Standard Directory of Advertisers [see listing in Section (1)].

Standard Directory of Advertising Agencies. National Register Publishing Company, Inc. (3004 Glenview Road; Wilmette, IL 60091; 312-441-2210 in IL; 800-323-4601 elsewhere). Three times a year, plus nine supplements. $129 for the three books; $292 for the three books plus nine supplements.

GREEN BOOK: International Directory of Marketing Research Houses and Services. American Marketing Association/New York (310 Madison Avenue, Suite 1211; New York, NY 10170; 212-687-3280). Annual. $50.

Public Relations Register. Public Relations Society of America (845 Third Avenue; New York, NY 10022; 212-826-1750, Ext. 45). Annual (Sept.). $75.

Aerospace/Defense

Aerospace Companies. DMS, Inc. (100 Northfield Street, P.O. Box 4585; Greenwich, CT 06830; 203-661-7800). Updated monthly, $950/year.

Top 500 RD&E Companies. DMS, Inc. (100 Northfield Street, P.O. Box 4585; Greenwich, CT 06830; 203-661-7800). Annual (November), $1,000.

World Aviation Directory. Murdoch Magazines (Subscription Department,

BFG, Suite 310, 20 Brace Road; Cherry Hill, NJ 08034; 800-932-0017). Twice a year (Spring & Winter). $95/book or $160/year.

Agribusiness/Foods

Food Engineering's Directory of U.S. Food Plants. Chilton Company (Chilton Way; Radnor, PA 19089; 215-964-4444). Every other year. $295.

Thomas Grocery Register. Thomas Publishing Company (One Penn Plaza, 26th floor; New York, NY 10119; 212-290-7200). Annual. 3 volumes. $105.

Quick Frozen Foods Directory of Frozen Food Processors. Saul Beck Publications (271 Madison Avenue, Suite 1103; New York, NY 10016; 212-557-8600). Annual (June). $63 (no credit cards).

The National Frozen Food Association Directory. National Frozen Food Association (604 West Derry Road, P.O. Box 398; Hershey, PA 17033; 717-534-1601). Annual. $50.

Fruit and Vegetable Blue Book. Produce Reporter Company (315 West Wesley Street; Wheaton, IL 60187; 312-668-3500). Twice a year (Apr. & Oct., with intervening updates). $300 lease.

Directory of the Canning, Freezing and Preserving Industries. James J. Judge, Inc. (P.O. Box 550; Westminster, MD 21157; 301-876-7150). April of even-numbered years. $90 (no credit cards).

Apparel/Textiles

American Apparel Manufacturers Association Directory. American Apparel Manufacturers Association (2500 Wilson Boulevard, Suite 301; Arlington, VA 22201; 703-524-1864). Annual. $100.

Fairchild's Textile and Apparel Financial Directory. Fairchild Books (7 East 12th Street; New York, NY 10003; 212-741-4280, but no phone orders). Annual (Oct.). $50.

Davison's Textile Blue Book. Davison Publishing Company (P.O Box 477; Ridgewood, NJ 07451; 201-445-3135). Annual (Feb.). $90.

Accessories Resources Director. Business Journals, Inc. (P.O. Box 5550; Norwalk, CT 06856; 203-853-6015). Annual (Jan.). $12 (no credit cards).

Automotive Industry

The Market Data Book. Crain Communications (965 East Jefferson; Detroit, MI 48207; 313-446-6000). Annual (April), in connection with *Automotive News.* $22.50.

Motor Vehicle Facts & Figures. Motor Vehicle Manufacturers Association of the United States (300 New Center Building; Detroit, MI 48202; 313-872-4311). Annual. $7.50.

Ward's Automotive Yearbook. Ward's Communications, Inc. (28 West Adams; Detroit, MI 48226; 313-962-4433). Annual. $140.

World Motor Vehicle Data. Motor Vehicle Manufacturers Association of the United States (300 New Center Building; Detroit, MI 48202; 313-872-4311). Annual. $35.

Banking/Finance/Venture Capital

American Bank Directory. McFadden Business Publications (6195 Crooked Creek Road; Norcross, GA 30092; 404-448-1011). Twice a year (May & Nov.). $150 per issue (no credit cards).

Directory of American Savings and Loan Associations. T. K. Sanderson Organization (1115 East 30th Street; Baltimore, MD 21218; 301-235-3383). Annual (April). $50 (no credit cards).

Directory of Municipal Bond Dealers of the United States. The Bond Buyer, Inc. (One State Street Plaza, 30th floor; New York, NY 10004; 212-943-9427). Twice a year (Spring and Fall). $80/single copy, plus $40/additional copies; $115/year (no credit cards).

Guide to Venture Capital Sources. Venture Economics, Inc. (P.O. Box 348; Wellesley Hills, MA 02181; 617-431-8100). Annual. One volume. $95.

International Bank Directory. McFadden Business Publications (6195 Crooked Creek Road; Norcross, GA 30092; 404-448-1011). Once a year (August). $95 per issue (no credit cards).

Moody's Bank and Finance Manual. Moody's Investors Service (99 Church Street; New York, NY 10007; 212-553-0300). Annual (May), with bi-weekly updates. Two-volume set, plus updates. $895 (no credit cards).

The Rand McNally International Bankers Directory. Rand McNally & Company, Financial Publishing Division (P.O. Box 7600; Chicago, IL 60680; 312-673-9100). Twice a year (June & Dec.). Four-volume set, each issue. $190, one issue purchase; $160, one issue subscription; $300, two issue subscription (no credit cards).

Directory of Institutional Investors. Vickers Associates, Inc. (226 New York Avenue; Huntington, NY 11743; 516-423-7710 in NY; 800-645-5043 elsewhere). Twice a year (Apr. & Oct.) $75/year.

Biotechnology

The Biotechnology Directory. Stockton Press (15 East 26th Street; New York, NY 10010; 212-481-1334). Every other year. $140.

Genetic Engineering & Biotechnology Related Firms Worldwide Directory. Sittig & Noyes (P.O. Box 592; Kingston, NJ 08528; 609-924-1760). Annual. $200.

The Medtech Directory. Medtech Services (44 Wall Street; New York, NY 10005; 212-968-2255). Annual (Feb.). $135.

Chemicals/Plastics

Chemical Industry Directory. State Mutual Book and Periodical Service, Ltd. (521 Fifth Avenue; New York, NY 10017; 212-682-5844). Annual (May or June). $295 (no phone orders, no credit cards).

Directory of Chemical Producers - U.S.A. Stanford Research Institute (333 Ravenswood Avenue; Menlo Park, CA 94025; 415-859-3627). Annual, plus two supplements (Summer & Fall). $900 annual subscription (includes inquiry privileges).

Modern Plastics Encyclopedia. McGraw-Hill Publications Company (P.O. Box 423; Hightstown, NJ 08520; 609-426-5129). Annual. $42 (no credit cards).

Plastics World Directory. Cahners Publishing Company, Inc. (275 Washington Street; Newton, MA 02158; 617-964-3030, Ext. 511). Annual (March). $35 (no credit cards).

Communications

Telecommunications Systems & Services Directory. Gale Research Company (Book Tower; Detroit, MI 48226; 313-961-2242 in MI, AK & HI; 800-512-0707 elsewhere). Annual. $240.

Telephone Industry Directory & Source Book. Phillips Publishing (7811 Montrose Road; Potomac, MD 20854; 301-340-2100). Annual. $97.

[*See also:* Information Processing Industry, and Motion Picture/Broadcasting Industry.]

Consultants

Dun's Consultants Directory. Dun's Marketing Services (3 Century Drive; Parsippany, NJ 07054; 800-526-0651). Annual. $325 lease.

Direct Mail

Direct Mail List Rates and Data. Standard Rate & Data Service, Inc. (3004 Glenview Road; Wilmette, IL 60091; 312-256-6067 in IL; 800-323-4588 elsewhere). Subscription (semi-annual). Visit your library.

Direct Marketing Association Membership Roster. Direct Marketing Association, Inc. (6 East 43rd Street; New York, NY 10017; 212-689-4977). Annual. Not available to non-DMA members; members receive one copy free and may purchase additional copies for $30 each.

Directory of Mail Order Catalogs. Grey House Publishing, Inc. (Bank of Boston Building; Sharon, CT 06069; 203-364-0533). Periodically. $125.

Mail Order Business Directory. B. Klein Publications, Inc. (P.O. Box 8503; Coral Springs, FL 33065; 305-752-1708). Annual. $65.

Electronics

American Electronics Association Directory. American Electronics Association (2670 Hanover Street; P.O. Box 10045; Palo Alto, CA 94303; 415-857-9300). $55 for members; $130 for non-members.

Electronics Buyers' Guide. McGraw-Hill, Inc. (1221 Avenue of the Americas; New York, NY 10020; 212-512-2544). Annual (June). $40 (no credit cards).

Electronic Industry Telephone Directory. Harris Publishing Company (2057-2 Aurora Road; Twinsburg, OH 44087; 216-425-9000). Annual (Sept.). $43.50.

Electronic News Financial Fact Book and Directory. Fairchild Publications, Inc. (7 East 12th Street; New York, NY 10003; 212-741-4280, but no phone orders). Annual (Sept.). $125 (no credit cards).

The Gold Book: Electronic Design Master Directory. Hayden Publishing Company (10 Mulholland Drive; Hasbrouck Heights, NJ 07604; 201-393-6253). Annual. 6 U.S. volumes, $70; 2 Western Europe volumes, $70 (no credit cards).

Who's Who in Electronics. Harris Publishing Company (2057-2 Aurora Road; Twinsburg, OH 44087; 216-425-9000). Annual (February). $93 (no credit cards).

Energy Industry

Brown's Directory of North American Gas Companies. Harcourt Brace Jovanovich, Inc. (HBJ Publications; One East First Street; Duluth, MN 55802; 218-723-9200 in MN: 800-346-0005 elsewhere). Annual (Dec.). $165.

Electric World Directory of Electric Utilities. McGraw-Hill, Inc. (1221 Avenue of the Americas; New York, NY 10020; 212-512-4934). Annual. $275.

The Geophysical Directory. Geophysical Directory, Inc. (P.O. Box 13508; Houston, TX 77219; 713-529-8789). Annual (March). $25.

Moody's Public Utility Manual. Moody's Investors Service, Inc. (99 Church Street; New York, NY 10007; 212-553-0435). Annual (Nov.), with bi-weekly updates. Two volumes. $780.

Oil and Gas Directory. Geophysical Directory, Inc. (P.O. Box 13508; Houston, TX 77219; 713-529-8789). Annual (September). $40.

Oilfield Service Supply & Manufacturing Directory. Pennwell Books (P.O. Box 21288; Tulsa, OK 74121; 918-835-3161). Annual. $95.

Whole World Oil Directory. National Register Publishing Company, Inc. (3004 Glenview Road; Wilmette, IL 60091; 312-441-2267 in IL; 800-323-4601 elsewhere). Annual (Nov.). $139.

World Energy Directory. Gale Research Company (Book Tower; Detroit, MI 48226; 313-961-3353 in MI, AK, & HI; 800-521-0707 elsewhere). Irregularly. $230.

USA Oil Industry Directory. Pennwell Books (P.O. Box 21288; Tulsa, OK 74121; 918-835-3161). Annual. $105.

Executive Recruiting Industry

Directory of Executive Recruiters. Consultants News (Templeton Road; Fitzwilliam, NH 03447; 603-585-6544). Annual (separate Retainer and Contingency sections), one volume. $24.95 prepaid, $28.95 billed.

Forest Products Industry

Crow's Buyers' and Sellers' Guide of the Forest Products Industries. C. C. Crow Publications (P.O. Box 25749; Portland, OR 97225; 503 646 8075). Annual (Mar.). $120.

Health Care Industry

American Hospital Association Guide to the Health Care Field. A.H.A. Services, Inc. (P.O. Box 99376; Chicago, IL 60693; 312-280-6030). Annual (August). $66 for members; $88 for non-members.

Dun's Guide to Healthcare Companies. Dun's Marketing Services (3 Century Drive; Parsippany, NJ 07054; 800-624-0324 in NJ; 800-526-0651 elsewhere). Annual. $325.

Medical and Health Information Directory. Gale Research Company (Book Tower; Detroit, MI 48226; 313-961-2242 in MI, AK, & HI; 800-521-0707 elsewhere). 3 volumes, published one per year in three-year cycles. Volume 1: Names of Medical & Health Organizations & Associations; Volume 2: Where to Get Information-AV Materials, Libraries, Databases; Volume 3: Names & Addresses of Clinics, Treatment Centers, Counseling & Diagnostic Services. $165 each; $410 per set.

Medical and Healthcare Marketplace Guide. International Bio-Medical Information Service, Inc. (8525 S. W. 92nd Street, Suite 3A; Miami, FL 33156; 305-271-7272 in FL; 800-822-3366 elsewhere). Annual. $307.

High Technology

The Corporate Technology Directory. CorpTech (2 Laurel Avenue; Wellesley Hills, MA 02181; 617-237-2001). Annual. 3 volumes. $650.

Directory of Public High Technology Corporations. American Investor, Inc. (311 Bainbridge Street; Philadelphia, PA 19147; 215-925-5083). Annual. 2 volumes. $195.

[*See also specific high-tech categories:* Aerospace/Defense; Biotechnology; Communications; Electronics; Research & Development.]

Hotel/Motel/Resort Industry

Directory of Hotel and Motel Systems. American Hotel Association Directory Corporation (888 Seventh Avenue; New York, NY 10106; 212-265-4506). Annual (March). $29.50.

Official Hotel and Resort Guide. Murdoch Magazines (Subscription Dept., BFG; 20 Brace Road, Suite 310; Cherry Hill, NJ 08034; 800-932-0017). Annual Four Volumes. $220.

Travel Weekly's World Travel Directory. Murdoch Magazines (Subscription Dept., BFG; 20 Brace Road, Suite 310; Cherry Hill, NJ 08034; 800-932-0017). Annual. $97.

Information Processing Industry

Computers and Computing Information Resources Directory. Gale Research Company (Book Tower; Detroit, MI 48226; 313-961-2242 in MI, AK, & HI; 800-521-0707 elsewhere). Every other year (even years). $160.

Data Sources - The Comprehensive Guide to the Information Processing Industry: Equipment, Software, Services, Companies and People. Ziff-Davis Publishing Company (One Park Avenue; New York, NY 10016; 212-503-5393). Twice a year (May & Nov.). $600 for single edition; $795 year.

Directories of Computer Installations. Computer Management Research, Inc. (20 Waterside Plaza; New York, NY 10010; 212-683-0606). Area directories presently published include: New York Metro, $700; New England, $395; and Mid-Atlantic States, $395.

Encyclopedia of Information Systems and Services. Gale Research Company (Book Tower; Detroit, MI 48226; 313-961-2242 in MI, AK, & HI; 800-521-0707). Every other year (even years). Two volumes: U.S., $210; International, $185; both for $370.

ICP Software Directory. International Computer Programs, Inc. (9000 Keystone Crossing; Indianapolis, IN 46240; 800-428-6179). Twice a year (January & July). 10-volume set, $934/year; Volumes 1–6 (Mainframes and Mini-computers), $639; Volumes 7–10 (Microcomputers), $295.

Telecommunications Systems and Services Directory. Gale Research Company (Book Tower, Detroit, MI 48226; 313-961-2242 in MI, AK, & HI; 800-512-0707 elsewhere). Every other year (odd years). $270.

Insurance Industry

Best's Insurance Reports: Life-Health. A.M. Best Company (A.M. Best Road, Oldwick, NJ 08858; 201-439-2200). Annual book plus weekly magazine, $375; Annual book, weekly magazine, and weekly insurance management reports, $490; Annual book, weekly magazine, weekly insurance management reports, and special inquiry service, $680 (no credit cards).

Best's Insurance Reports: Property-Casualty. A.M. Best Company (same contact/prices) as Life-Health Reports, above).

Insurance Almanac. Underwriter Printing and Publishing Company (50 East Palisades Avenue; Englewood, NJ 07631; 201-569-8808 in NJ, 800-526-4700 elsewhere). Annual (July). $75 (no credit cards).

Who's Who in Insurance. Underwriter Printing & Publishing Company (same contact as *Insurance Almanac* above). Annual (Feb.). $75 (no credit cards).

Law

Law and Legal Information Directory. Gale Research Company (Book

Tower; Detroit, MI 48226; 313-961-2242 in MI, AK, & HI; 800-521-0707 elsewhere. Every two years (even years). $280.

Martindale-Hubbell Law Directory. Martindale-Hubbell, Inc. (P.O. Box 1001; Summit, NJ 07901; 201-464-6800 in NJ; 800-526-4902 elsewhere, but no phone orders). Annual. 8 volumes. $160 (no credit cards).

Who's Who in American Law. Marquis Publications (3002 Glenview Road; Wilmette, IL 60091; 312-441-2387 in IL; 800-621-9669 elsewhere). Every two years (odd years). $154.

Mining Industry

E/MJ International Directory of Mining. McGraw-Hill Publications Company (1221 Avenue of the Americas, 42nd floor; New York, NY 10020; 212-512-6158, but no phone orders). Annual (Aug. or Sept.). $90.

Keystone Coal Industry Manual. McGraw-Hill Publications Company (same contact as above). Annual (July or Aug.). $130.

Motion Picture/Broadcasting Industry

Broadcasting/Cablecasting Yearbook. Broadcasting Publications, Inc. (1735 DeSales Street, N.W.; Washington, D.C. 20036; 202-638-1022 in DC; 800-638-7827 elsewhere). Annual (March). $105.

International Motion Picture Almanac. Quigley Publishing Company, Inc. (159 West 53rd Street; New York, NY 10019; 212-247-3100). Annual (Jan.). $62.50; or $99 for both Motion Picture and Television Almanacs.

International Television Almanac. Quigley Publishing Company, Inc. (contact/price indicated above).

Standard Rate & Data publications, including **Network Rates and Data, Spot Radio Rates and Data,** and **Spot Television Rates and Data.** Standard Rate & Data Service, Inc. (3004 Glenview Road; Wilmette, IL 60091; 312-256-6067 in IL, 800-323-4588 elsewhere). Monthly subscription publications. Visit your library.

The Video Register. Knowledge Industry Publications, Inc. (701 Westchester Avenue; White Plains, NY 10604; 914-328-9157 in NY, 800-248-5474 elsewhere). Annual (Nov.). $69.50.

Working Press of the Nation, Volume Three: Radio and Television Directory. National Research Bureau Inc. (424 North Third Street; Burlington, IA 52601; 319-752-5415). Annual. $115 (no credit cards).

Music/Record/Video Industry

International Buyer's Guide. Billboard Publications (P.O. Box 24970; Nashville, TN 37202; 615-748-8100). Annual (fall). $57.

Non-Profit

The Foundation Directory. The Foundation Center (79 Fifth Avenue; New York, NY 10003; 212-620-4230). Directory published odd years, with Supplement even years. $65 for Directory, $35 for Supplement, $95 both.

People in Philanthropy. Taft Group (5130 MacArthur Boulevard, N.W.; Washington, D.C. 20016; 202-966-7086 in DC, 800 345 2228 elsewhere). Even years. $197.

Packaging Industry

Official Container Directory. HBJ Publications (1 East 1st Street; Duluth, MN 55802; 218-723-9361 in MN; 800-346-0085 elsewhere). Semi-annual (spring & fall). $38/issue.

Pharmaceutical Industry

Drug and Cosmetic Catalog. HBJ Publications (1 East 1st Street; Duluth, MN 55802; 218-723-9361 in MN; 800-346-0085 elsewhere). Annual. $15.

Pharmaceutical Marketers Directory. Fisher-Stevens Publications (Campus Road; Totowa, NJ 07512; 201-890-1122). Annual (May). $109.

World Directory of Pharmaceutical Manufacturers. IMS World Publications Ltd. (York House; 37 Queen Square; London WC1N 3BH England; 49-1-831-68-06). Every two years. $175.

Publishing/Information Industry

Gale Directory of Publications. Gale Research Company (Book Tower; Detroit, MI 48226; 313-961-2242 in MI, AK & HI; 800-512-0707 elsewhere). Annual (March). $115.

Information Sources: The IIA Membership Directory. Information Industry Association (555 North J Avenue, N.W., Suite 800; Washington, D.C. 20001; 202-639-8262). Annual (November). $39.95 for members, $79.95 for non-members.

International Literary Market Place. R. R. Bowker Company (Order Dept.; P.O. Box 762; New York, NY 10011; 212-645-9700 in NY; 800-521-8110 elsewhere). Annual (April) $95.

Literary Market Place: The Directory of American Book Publishing. R. R. Bowker Company (same contact as above). Annual (Dec.). $75.

Magazine Industry Market Place. R. R. Bowker Company (same contact as above). Annual (March). $59.95.

Standard Rate & Data publications, including **Business Publication Rates and Data** and **Consumer Magazine and Farm Publication Rates and Data.** Standard Rate & Data Service, Inc. (3004 Glenview Road; Wilmette, IL 60091; 312-256-6067 in IL, 800-323-4588 elsewhere). Monthly subscription publications. Visit your library.

The Standard Periodical Directory. Oxbridge Communications, Inc. (150 Fifth Avenue; New York, NY 10011; 212-741-0231). Annual (Jan.). $295 (no credit cards).

Working Press of the Nation. Volume 1: Newspaper Directory; Volume 2: Magazine Directory; Volume 3: TV & Radio Directory; Volume 4: Feature Writer & Photographer Directory; Volume 5: Internal Publications Directory. National Research Bureau, Inc. (424 North Third Street; Burlington, IA 52601; 319-752-5415). Annual. $115 per volume; $215 for three volumes; $250 for all five.

Real Estate/ Construction Industry

Directory of Real Estate Investors & Commercial Real Estate Brokers.

National Register Publishing Company, Inc. (3004 Glenview Road; Wilmette, IL 60091; 312-441-2267 in IL, 800-323-4601 elsewhere). Annual (March). $177.

LSI Blue Book of Major Homebuilders; LSI Gold Book of Multi-Housing; and LSI Red Book of Housing Manufacturers. LSI Systems, Inc. (11-A Village Green; Crofton, MD 21114; 301-261-6363). Annual. Regional editions of each, $60; National editions of each, $140; all three National books, $345 (no credit cards).

National Real Estate Investor Directory. Communication Channels, Inc. (Book Dept.; 6255 Barfield Road; Atlanta, GA 30328; 404-256-9800, but no phone orders). Annual (June). $32.95 (no credit cards).

National Roster of Realtors Directory. Stamats Communications, Inc. (427 Sixth Avenue, S.E.; P.O. Box 1888; Cedar Rapids, IA 52406; 319-364-6032). Annual (May). $50 for members, $75 for non-members.

Society of Industrial Realtors Directory. Society of Industrial Realtors (925 Fifteenth Street, N.W.; Washington, D.C. 20005; 202-383-1150). Annual (May). Free.

Research & Development

Research Centers Directory. Gale Research Company (Book Tower; Detroit, MI 48226; 313-961-2242 in MI, AK & HI, 800-521-0707 elsewhere). Annual (Nov.) Two volumes. $355 (no credit cards).

Top 500 RD&E Companies. DMS, Inc. (100 Northfield Street, P.O. Box 4585; Greenwich, CT 06830; 203-661-7800). Annual (Nov.), $1,000.

Retailing

The Chain Store Guides. Business Guides, Inc. (425 Park Avenue; New York, NY 10022; 212-371-9400). Annual (month in parentheses), unless otherwise noted. * = available in National or By-State editions. Guides include:
Directory of Department Stores/Mail Order Firms.* (Nov.) $189.
Directory of Women's & Children's Wear Specialty Stores. (Sept.) $149.
Directory of Consumer Electronics, Photography & Major Appliance Retailers & Distributors. (May). $189.
Directory of High-Volume Independent Restaurants. (July). $249.

Directory of Country Clubs. (Nov.). $249.

Directory of Home Furnishings Retailers. (Sept.). $249.

Directory of Hardlines Distributors. (Odd years). $159.

Directory of Men's & Boys' Wear Specialty Stores. (Sept.). $149.

Directory of General Merchandise/Variety Chains & Specialty Stores. (April). $179.

Directory of Discount Dept. Stores/Catalog Showrooms. (March). $189.

Directory of Drug & HBA Chains/Drug Wholesalers.* (Dec.). $189.

Directory of Home Center Operators & Hardware Chains.* (July). $189.

Directory of Auto Aftermarket Suppliers. (Even years.) $169.

Directory of Supermarket, Grocery & Convenience Store Chains. (Oct.). $189

Directory of Cooperatives, Voluntaries & Wholesale Grocers. (Nov.) $179.

Directory of Chain Restaurant Operators. (May). $199.

Directory of Food Service Distributors.* **(June).** $179.

Directory of Computer & Software Retailers. (April). $249.

Directory of Shopping Centers in the United States. National Research Bureau, Inc. (424 North Third Street; Burlington, IA 52601; 319-752-5415). Annual (Oct.). Four regional volumes (East, South, Midwest, West). Lease. $135 each, $285 for the set.

Fairchild's Financial Manual of Retail Stores. Fairchild Books (7 East 12th Street; New York, NY 10003; 212-741-4280, but no phone orders). Annual (Nov.). $60.

Major Mass Market Merchandisers. Salesman's Guide, Inc. (1140 Broadway; New York, NY 10001; 212-684-2985). Annual (July). $80.

Training & Development

Training and Development Organizations Directory. Gale Research Company (Book Tower; Detroit, MI 48226; 313-961-2242 in MI, AK & HI; 800-521-0707 elsewhere). Irregular. $270. Inter-edition subscription to **New Training & Development Organizations,** $105.

Transportation Industry

Air Freight Directory. Air Cargo, Inc. (1819 Bay Ridge Avenue; Annapolis, MD 21403; 301-266-4572, but no phone orders). Bi-monthly. $51/year subscription, or $15 per single issue.

American Motor Carrier Directory. Motor Carrier Directory (5770 Powers Ferry Road, Suite 202; Atlanta, GA 30327; 404-955-3000). Semi-annual. $130/year subscription (no credit cards).

Bus Industry Directory. Friendship Publications, Inc. (P.O. Box 1472; Spokane, WA 99210-1472; 509-328-9181). Annual (June). $40 (no credit cards).

Traffic Management: The Directory. Cahners Publishing Company (275 Washington Street; Newton, MA 02158; 617-964-3030, Ext. 473). Annual (Mar.). $25 (no credit cards).

Who's Who in Railroading and Rail Transit. National Railway Publication Company (Circulation Dept.; 424 West 33rd Street; New York, NY 10001; 212-714-3100 in NY; 800-221-5488 elsewhere). Every three years (including *Quarterly Pocket List of Railroad Officials*). $28 paper; $60 cloth.

World Aviation Directory. Murdoch Magazines (Subscription Department, BFG, Suite 310, 20 Brace Road; Cherry Hill, NJ 08034; 800-932-0017). Twice a year (Spring & Winter). $95/book or $160/year.

APPENDIX II

Retainer Executive Recruiters

Have you decided to cultivate prominent retainer recruiting firms?

Here is a core list of 91 firms you can use as a starting point.

If a firm has multiple offices, the address given is the home office (normally where centralized files are kept), and therefore the best place to send your resume. The name of the firm's CEO (or in some cases its most prominent member) is also listed, so you can address your mailing to an actual person.

Cities having branch offices are also listed (with phone numbers) so you can see if there's one in your city. If so, you can phone to get the address and the name of the office manager, and mail a letter and/or promote an introduction.

If you're in a hurry to make a change, there's no harm in mailing to both the national headquarters and the local office. Your eagerness is assumed when you send to either place. Therefore, if both resumes reach the central filing location, the filer will merely discard the extra copy. It won't occasion notice, notation, or comment.

Many of these firms (marked by *) are members of the Association of Executive Search Consultants (AESC), a trade association of professionally-recognized recruiters. Most of America's largest firms (marked #), however, are not members.

Of course, it's beyond the scope of this book to provide any assurances, but all of the listed firms are expected to deal with you in a first-class manner.

BARGER & SARGEANT, INC.*

5 Warren Street
Concord, NH 03301
(603) 224-7753

H. Carter Barger, President

Also:
Boston, MA (617) 542-2929

BARTHOLDI, DROMESHAUSER & MAZZA

20 William Street, Suite 228
Wellesley Office Park
Wellesley Hills, MA 02181
(617) 235-2120

General Partners:

T. G. Bartholdi
Peter Dromeshauser
Dave Mazza

Also:
Menlo Park, CA (415) 854-4462
Vail, CO (303) 476-0922

BATTALIA & ASSOCIATES, INC.*

275 Madison Avenue, Suite 2315
New York, NY 10016
(212) 683-9440

O. William Battalia, Chairman

BENTLEY & EVANS INTERNATIONAL, INC.

One Penn Plaza
New York, New York 10119
(212) 371-1212

Charles E. Evans, Chairman

BILLINGTON, FOX & ELLIS, INC.

20 North Wacker Drive, Suite 3300
Chicago, IL 60606
(312) 236-5000

William H. Billington, Jr., Chairman

BOWDEN & COMPANY, INC.*

5000 Rockside Road, Suite 120
Cleveland, OH 44131
(216) 447-1800

Otis H. Bowden II, President

BOYDEN INTERNATIONAL*

260 Madison Avenue
New York, NY 10016
(212) 685-3400

Putney Westerfield, President

Also:
Atlanta, GA (404) 261-6532
Chicago, IL (312) 782-1581
Dallas, TX (214) 387-7973

Ft. Lauderdale, FL (305) 491-5949
Houston, TX (713) 626-4790
Los Angeles, CA (213) 622-0411
Menlo Park, CA (415) 854-9090
Morristown, NJ (201) 267-0980
Pittsburgh, PA (412) 391-3020
San Francisco, CA (415) 981-7900
Stamford, CT (203) 324-4300
Washington, DC (202) 293-5560
Wellesley, MA (617) 239-0190

THE BRAND COMPANY, INC.*

12740 North River Road
Mequon, WI 53092-2299
(414) 242-6203

J. Brand Spangenberg, President

BRISSENDEN, McFARLAND & WAGONER, INC.

1111 Summer Street
Stamford, CT 06905
(203) 324-1598

Principals:
Hoke Brissenden
Richard M. McFarland
Robert E. Wagoner

Also:
Somerset, NJ (201) 469-8288

CANNY, BOWEN, INC.

425 Park Avenue
New York, NY 10022
(212) 758-3400

Carl W. Menk, Chairman
Robert A. Howard, Managing Director

Also:
Boston, MA (617) 723-5900

CHRISTENSON & MONTGOMERY, INC.*

466 Southern Boulevard

Chatham, NJ 07928
(201) 966-1600

Managing Partners:
H. Alan Christenson
Robert M. Montgomery

WILLIAM H. CLARK ASSOCIATES, INC.

200 East Randolph Street, Suite 7912
Chicago, IL 60601
(312) 565-1300

Richard A. McCallister, President

W. HOYT COLTON ASSOCIATES, INC.

67 Wall Street
New York, NY 10005
(212) 509-1800

W. Hoyt Colton, President

COOPERS & LYBRAND

1000 West Sixth Street
Los Angeles, CA 90017
(213) 482-6242

Helen E. Friedman, Director—
West Region Executive Search
Consulting Services

Also:
Atlanta, GA (404) 658-1000
Chicago, IL (312) 701-5500
Detroit, MI (313) 446-7100

CORPORATE STAFFING GROUP, INC.

350 South Main Street, Suite 213
Doylestown, PA 18901
(215) 345-1100

Principals:
C. D. Baker
Laurie B. Carey

DEAN, HOWARD & SIMON, INC.

81 Wethersfield Avenue

Hartford, CT 06114
(203) 727-0721

Howard D. Nitchke, President

THORNDIKE DELAND ASSOCIATES

1440 Broadway, Suite 2264
New York, NY 10018
(212) 840-8100

Edward A. Raisbeck, Senior
Partner

DEVINE, BALDWIN & PETERS, INC.*

250 Park Avenue
New York, NY 10177
(212) 867-5235

Robert L. Peters, Jr., President

Also:
Westport, MA (617) 636-6764

ROBERT W. DINGMAN COMPANY, INC.*

32131 West Lindero Canyon
Road
Westlake Village, CA 91361
(818) 991-5950

Robert W. Dingman, President

EASTMAN & BEAUDINE, INC.

111 West Monroe Street, Suite 2150
Chicago, IL 60603
(312) 726-8195

Frank R. Beaudine, Chairman &
CEO

Also:
Dallas, TX (214) 661-5520
New York, NY (212) 486-9655

ERNST & WHINNEY/EXECUTIVE SEARCH

2000 National City Center
Cleveland, OH 44114
(216) 861-5000

Tom Clevidence, Senior Manager

Also:
Atlanta, GA (404 658-9400
Chicago, IL (312) 368-1800
Dallas, TX (214) 979-1700
Indianapolis, IN (317) 236-1100
Los Angeles, CA (213) 621-1666
New York, NY (212) 830-6000
Philadelphia, PA (215) 561-4800
Washington, D.C. (202 862-6000

LEON A. FARLEY ASSOCIATES*

468 Jackson Street
San Francisco, CA 94111
(415) 989-0989

Leon A. Farley, President

Also:
Dallas, TX (214) 969-0370
Washington, DC (202) 887-0666

FENVESSY & SILBERT, INC.

645 Madison Avenue
New York, New York 10022
(212) 755-5050

Violet Opalka, Vice President

FENWICK PARTNERS

450 Bedford Street
Lexington, MA 02173
(617) 862-3370

James Masciarelli, President

FLEMING ASSOCIATES*

1428 Franklin Street
P.O. Box 604
Columbus, IN 47202
(812) 376-9061

Robert L. Piers, Managing
Partner

Also:
Atlanta, GA (404) 641-6050
Columbus, OH (614) 764-1587
Houston, TX (713) 987-3310

Louisville, KY (502) 426-3500
Memphis, TN (901) 767-3924
Metairie, LA (504) 836-7090
Miami, FL (305) 592-0081
Sarasota, FL (813) 366-7979
Stamford, CT (203) 324-1153

FOSTER & ASSOCIATES, INC.*

601 California Street, Suite 2275
San Francisco, CA 94108
(415) 982-0330

Thorne S. Foster, President

JAY GAINES & COMPANY*

598 Madison Avenue
New York, NY 10022
(212) 308-9222

Jay Gaines, President

GAROFOLO, CURTISS & COMPANY*

326 West Lancaster Avenue
Ardmore, PA 19003
(215) 896-5080

Frank Garofolo, President

Also:
Boston, MA (617) 227-0260
Glens Falls, NY (518) 793-1139
Washington, DC (202) 822-0070

N. W. GIBSON INTERNATIONAL

5900 Wilshire Boulevard, Suite
760
Los Angeles, CA 90036
(213) 930-1100

N. W. Gibson, President

GILBERT TWEED ASSOCIATES, INC.

630 Third Avenue
New York, NY 10017
(212) 697-4260

Principals:
Lynn Tendler Gilbert
Janet Tweed Arkush

THE GOODRICH & SHERWOOD COMPANY

521 Fifth Avenue
New York, NY 10017
(212) 697-4131

Andrew Sherwood, CEO

Also:
Greenwich, CT (203) 625-0800
Morristown, NJ (201) 455-7100

GOULD & McCOY, INC.*

551 Madison Avenue
New York, NY 10022
(212) 688-8671

William E. Gould, Managing Partner

GRANT COOPER & ASSOCIATES

680 Craig Road, Suite 301
St. Louis, MO 63141
(314) 567-4690

H. Evans Roberts, Chairman
Byron J. Johnston, President

HALBRECHT ASSOCIATES*

1200 Summer Street
Stamford, CT 06905
(203) 327-5630

Herb Halbrecht, President

HALEY ASSOCIATES, INC.*

375 Park Avenue
New York, NY 10152
(212) 421-7860

James K. Makrianes, President & CEO

HANDY ASSOCIATES, INC.

245 Park Avenue
New York, NY 10167
(212) 867-8444

J. Gerald Simmons, President

HARRIS & U'REN, INC.*

1976 Arizona Bank Building
101 North First Avenue
Phoenix, AZ 85003
(602) 257-1072

Lester U'Ren, President

HASKELL & STERN ASSOCIATES, INC.*

529 Fifth Avenue
New York, NY 10017
(212) 687-7292

Allan D. R. Stern, Managing Director

Also:
Westport, CT (203) 222-1882

THE HEIDRICK PARTNERS*

20 North Wacker Drive, Suite 4000
Chicago, IL 60606
(312) 845-9700

Gardner W. Heidrick, Chairman
Robert L. Heidrick, President

#HEIDRICK AND STRUGGLES, INC.

245 Park Ave.
New York, NY 10167
(212) 867-9876

Gerard R. Roche, Chairman
David R. Peasback, President

Also:
Atlanta, GA (404) 577-2410
Boston, MA (617) 423-1140
Chicago, IL (312) 372-8811
Cleveland, OH (216) 241-7410
Dallas, TX (214) 220-2130
Greenwich, CT (203) 629-3200
Houston, TX (713) 237-9000
Los Angeles, CA (213) 624-8891
Palo Alto, CA (415) 856-3400
San Francisco, CA (415) 981-2854

HODGE-CRONIN & ASSOCIATES, INC.*
9575 West Higgins Road, Suite 904
Rosemont, IL 60018
(312) 692-2041

Richard J. Cronin, President

HOUZE, SHOURDS & MONTGOMERY, INC.*
Peninsula Pointe, Suite 190
27520 Hawthorne Boulevard
Rolling Hills Estates, CA 90274
(213) 377-6400

James M. Montgomery, President

 # WARD HOWELL INTERNATIONAL, INC.*
99 Park Avenue, Suite 2000
New York, NY 10016
(212) 697-3730

Max M. Ulrich, Chairman of the Board

Also:
Chicago, IL (312) 236-2211
Dallas, TX (214) 749-0099
Greenwich, CT (203) 629-2994
Houston, TX (713) 655-7155
Los Angeles, CA (213) 623-7961
San Francisco, CA (415) 398-3900

INTERDATUM, INC.
767 Third Avenue
New York, NY 10017
(212) 980-3800

Dale L. Bennett, President & CEO

Also:
Palo Alto, CA (415) 853-3070
San Francisco, CA (415) 989-8212

INTERNATIONAL MANAGEMENT ADVISORS, INC.*
767 Third Avenue
New York, NY 10017
(212) 758-7770

R. James Lotz, Jr., President

Also:
Farmington, CT (203) 673-2300
Morristown, NJ (201) 898-0060

CHARLES IRISH COMPANY, INC.*
137 Mine Lake Ct.
Raleigh, NC 27609
(919) 847-3999

Charles W. Irish, Chairman
Joan S. Irish, President

JOHNSON, SMITH & KNISELY, INC.*
475 Fifth Avenue, Suite 1402
New York, NY 10017
(212) 686-9760

Robert Smith, Partner

 # A. T. KEARNEY EXECUTIVE SEARCH*
222 South Riverside Plaza
Chicago, IL 60606
(312) 648-0111

James R. Arnold, President

Also:
Alexandria, VA (703) 836-6210
Atlanta, GA (404) 393-9900
Boston, MA (617) 262-2494
Cleveland, OH (216) 241-6880
Dallas, TX (214) 386-8750
Denver, CO (303) 572-6175
Los Angeles, CA (213) 627-0721
New York, NY (212) 751-7040
Redwood City, CA (415) 595-4300
Scottsdale, AZ (602) 994-3032

KENSINGTON MANAGEMENT CONSULTANTS, INC.

25 Third Street
Stamford, CT 06905
(203) 327-9860

Ann M. Fimmano, President

 # KORN-FERRY INTERNATIONAL

1800 Century Park East, Suite 900
Los Angeles, CA 90067
(213) 879-1834

Lester B. Korn, Chairman
Richard M. Ferry, President

Also:
Atlanta, GA (404) 577-7542
Boston, MA (617) 423-4100
Chicago, IL (312) 726-1841
Cleveland, OH (216) 861-5656
Dallas, TX (214) 651-1801
Denver, CO (303) 292-1834
Houston, TX (713) 651-1834
Los Angeles (branch) (213) 624-6600
Minneapolis, MN (612) 333-1834
Newport Beach, CA (714) 851-1834
New York, NY (212) 687-1834
Palo Alto, CA (415) 856-2611
San Francisco, CA (415) 956-1834
Seattle, WA (206) 621-1834
Stamford, CT (203) 359-3350
Washington, DC (202) 822-9444

KORS MARLAR SAVAGE & ASSOCIATES

1980 South Post Oak Blvd., Suite 1580
Houston, TX 77056
(713) 840-7101

Paul Kors, President

Also:
Annapolis, MD (301 268-7800
Los Angeles, CA (213) 553-5102

KREMPLE & MEADE*

1900 Avenue of the Stars, Suite 1170
Los Angeles, CA 90067
(213) 456-6451

Robert Kremple, Partner

KUNZER ASSOCIATES, LTD.*

208 South LaSalle Street, Suite 1508
Chicago, IL 60604
(312) 641-0010

William J. Kunzer, President

LAMALIE ASSOCIATES INC.

P.O. Box 273260
Tampa, FL 33688
(813) 961-7494

Robert E. Lamalie, Chairman & CEO
John F. Johnson, President

Also:
Atlanta, GA (404) 237-6324
Chicago, IL (312) 454-0525
Cleveland, OH (216) 694-3000
Dallas, TX (214) 754-0019
New York, NY (212) 953-7900

LAWRENCE L. LAPHAM ASSOCIATES, INC.*

230 Park Avenue, Suite 923
New York, NY 10169
(212) 599-0644

Lawrence L. Lapham, President

Also:
Fairhaven, NJ (201) 842-8665

LAUER, SBARBARO ASSOCIATES, INC.*

3 First National Plaza, Suite 650
Chicago, IL 60602
(312) 372-7050

Richard D. Sbarbaro, President

LOCKE & ASSOCIATES*
2160 Charlotte Plaza, Suite 2160
Charlotte, NC 28244
(704) 372-6600

M. Fred Locke, Jr., President

ROBERT LOWELL INTERNATIONAL
12221 Merit Drive, Suite 1510
Dallas, TX 75251
(214) 233-2270

Robert M. Bryza, President

THE JOHN LUCHT CONSULTANCY INC.*
The Olympic Tower
645 Fifth Avenue
New York, NY 10022
(212) 935-4660

John Lucht, President

McBRIDE ASSOCIATES, INC.*
1151 K Street NW
Washington, D.C. 20005
(202) 638-1150

John McBride, President

McFEELY WACKERLE & JETT*
20 North Wacker Drive, Suite 3110
Chicago, IL 60606
(312) 641-2977

Partners:
Clarence McFeely
Frederick Wackerle
Charles Jett

HAROLD A. MILLER ASSOCIATES*
P.O. Box 9017

Winnetka, IL 60093
(312) 446-7900

Harold A. Miller, Owner

MITCHELL, LARSEN & ZILLIACUS
523 West Sixth Street, Suite 737
Los Angeles, CA 90014
(213) 489-7120

Partners:
Thomas Mitchell
Richard Larsen
Patrick Zilliacus

MSL INTERNATIONAL LTD.
200 Galleria Parkway, Suite 630
Atlanta, GA 30339
(404) 955-9550

Charles J. Chalk, President

Also:
Chicago, IL (312) 321-0800
Dallas, TX (214) 770-4585
New York, NY (212) 644-5656
Philadelphia, PA (215) 875-2300
San Francisco, CA (415) 543-3950
Washington, DC (202) 467-6405

NORDEMAN GRIMM, INC.
717 Fifth Avenue
New York, NY 10022
(212) 935-1000

Jacques C. Nordeman, Chairman
Peter G. Grimm, President

Also:
Chicago, IL (312) 332-0088

OLIVER & ROZNER ASSOCIATES, INC.*
598 Madison Avenue
New York, NY 10022
(212) 688-1850

Frank G. Oliver, President

#PEAT MARWICK MAIN & CO./EXECUTIVE SEARCH

345 Park Avenue
New York, NY 10154
(212) 758-9700

Dwight E. Foster, National
Practice Director

Also:
Atlanta, GA (404) 577-3240
Boston, MA (617) 723-7700
Chicago, IL (312) 938-1000
Cleveland, OH (216) 696-9100
Costa Mesa, CA (714) 850-4300
Dallas, TX (214) 754-2000
Denver, CO (303) 296-2323
Houston, TX (713) 224-4262
Kansas City, MO (816) 474-6480
Los Angeles, CA (213) 972-4000
Miami, FL (305) 358-2300
Minneapolis, MN (612) 341-2222
Philadelphia, PA (215) 299-3153
San Francisco, CA (415) 981-8230
San Jose, CA (408) 279-2000
Short Hills, NJ (201) 467-9650
Stamford, CT (203) 356-9800

POIRIER, HOEVEL & CO.

12400 Wilshire Blvd., Suite 1250
Los Angeles, CA 90025
(213) 207-3427

Roland Poirier, Partner
Also:
New York, NY (212) 956-4020

DAVID POWELL, INC.*

3000 Sand Hill Road
Building 3, Suite 230
Menlo Park, CA 94025
(415) 854-7150

David Powell, President

PRENG ZANT & ASSOCIATES, INC.

1415 Louisiana, Suite 2500
Houston, TX 77002
(713) 655-1500

David E. Preng, President
Also:
Fort Worth (817) 332-6601

#PAUL R. RAY & COMPANY, INC.

1208 Ridglea Bank Building
Fort Worth, TX 76116
(817) 731-4111

Paul R. Ray, Chairman

Also:
Atlanta, GA (404) 892-2727
Chicago, IL (312) 876-0730
Dallas, TX (214) 969-7620
Houston, TX (713) 757-1985
Los Angeles, CA (213) 557-2828
New York, NY (212) 371-3000
Palm Springs, CA (619) 323-7705

#RUSSELL REYNOLDS ASSOCIATES, INC.

245 Park Avenue
New York, NY 10167
(212) 953-4300

Russell S. Reynolds, Jr.,
Chairman
H. Leland Getz, Vice Chairman
Ferdinand Nadherny, President

Also:
Boston, MA (617) 523-1111
Chicago, IL (312) 993-9696
Cleveland, OH (216) 575-1750
Dallas, TX (214) 220-2033
Houston, TX (713) 658-1776
Los Angeles, CA (213) 489-1520
Menlo Park, CA (415) 854-3330
San Francisco, CA (415) 392-3130
Stamford, CT (203) 356-1940
Washington, DC (202) 628-2150

ROBISON & McAULAY*

3100 NCNB Plaza
Charlotte, NC 28280
(704) 376-0059

John H. Robison, Jr., President

ROPES ASSOCIATES, INC.*

One Financial Plaza, Suite 1404
Fort Lauderdale, FL 33394
(305) 525-6600

John Ropes, President

SCHWARZKOPF CONSULTANTS, INC.*

15285 Watertown Plank Road
Elm Grove, WI 53122
(414) 781-8000

Ed A. Schwarzkopf, President

M. B. SHATTUCK ASSOCIATES, INC.*

100 Bush Street, Suite 501
San Francisco, CA 94104
(415) 421-6264

M. B. Shattuck, President

Also:
Saratoga, CA (408) 867-5161

SILER & ASSOCIATES, INC.*

5261 Port Washington Road,
North
Milwaukee, WI 53217
(414) 962-9400

David J. Siler, President

SKOTT/EDWARDS CONSULTANTS, INC.*

230 Park Avenue, Suite 1532
New York, NY 10169
(212) 697-7640

Edward W. Golden, Chairman
Skott B. Burkland, President

Also:
Rutherford, NJ (201) 935-8000

SMITH, GOERSS & FERNEBORG, INC.*

25 Ecker Street, Suite 600
San Francisco, CA 94105
(415) 543-4181

Senior Partners:
Ronald G. Goerss
John R. Ferneborg

PAUL STAFFORD ASSOCIATES, LTD.*

45 Rockefeller Plaza, Suite 670
New York, NY 10111
(212) 765-7700

Norman F. Moody, Chairman
Robert M. Flanagan, President

Also:
Atlanta, GA (404) 522-4677
Chicago, IL (312) 346-0655
Princeton, NJ (609) 987-2704
San Francisco, CA (415) 788-4800
Washington, DC (202) 331-0090

S. K. STEWART & ASSOCIATES*

The Executive Building
PO Box 40110
Cincinnati, OH 45240
(513) 771-2250

Stephen K. Stewart, President

#SPENCER STUART & ASSOCIATES

401 North Michigan Avenue
Chicago, IL 60611-4244
(312) 822-0080

James J. Drury, Managing
Director

Also:
Atlanta, GA (404) 521-2900
Cleveland, OH (216) 575-0500
Dallas, TX (214) 880-0400
Houston, TX (713) 225-1621
Los Angeles, CA (213) 620-0814
New York, NY (212) 407-0200

San Francisco, CA (415) 495-4141
Stamford, CT (203) 324-6333

TASA INC.*

875 Third Avenue, Suite 1501
New York, NY 10022
(212) 486-1490

Klaus Jacobs, President

Also:
Miami, FL (305) 662-5500
Palo Alto, CA (415) 323-0202

WILKINS AND THOMAS, INC.*

100 South Wacker Drive
Chicago, IL 60606
(312) 930-1036

Edwin N. Wilkins, Chairman
John T. Thomas, President

WILKINSON & IVES*

23 Altarinda Road, Suite 101
Orinda, CA 94563
(415) 254-2770

Partners:
William R. Wilkinson
Richard K. Ives

Also:
San Francisco, CA (415) 433-2155

WILLIAM H. WILLIS, INC.*

445 Park Avenue
New York, NY 10022
(212) 752-3456

William H. Willis, Jr., President

WINGUTH, SCHWEICHLER ASSOCIATES, INC.

24 California Street, Suite 750
San Francisco, CA 94111
(415) 495-8255

Erwin W. Winguth, President

WITT ASSOCIATES, INC.*

724 Enterprise Drive
Oak Brook, IL 60521
(312) 574-5070

John S. Lloyd, President

Also:
Dallas, TX (214) 770-2070
Newport Beach, CA (714) 851-5070

YELVERTON & COMPANY*

353 Sacramento Street
San Francisco, CA 94111
(415) 981-6060

Jack R. Yelverton, President

ARTHUR YOUNG EXECUTIVE RESOURCE CONSULTANTS

277 Park Avenue, 17th Floor
New York, NY 10172
(212) 407-1515

Bart DiChiara, Principal

Also:
Chicago, IL (312) 645-3065
Dallas, TX (214) 969-8768
Hartford, CT (203) 527-8000
Los Angeles, CA (213) 977-3473
Minneapolis, MN (612) 343-1000
San Francisco, CA (415) 951-3000
Washington, DC (202) 838-7190

EGON ZEHNDER INTERNATIONAL, INC.

645 Fifth Avenue
New York, NY 10022
(212) 838-9199

Daniel Meiland, Regional Director—North America

Also:
Atlanta, GA (404) 231-0000
Chicago, IL (312) 782-2846

APPENDIX III

Behind the Scenes with the Retainer Executive Recruiter

Up until now, your side of the executive recruiter's desk has never been the one with the drawers on it.

Too bad. Because changing jobs through a search handled by one of the retainer firms is perhaps the single most important "Rite of Passage" for the executive at, or reaching for, $100,000+. And how the process really works will never be entirely clear to you until you've seen it from the recruiter's perspective.

Which is why you and I are now going to take a look at what happens inside a retainer recruiting firm during a search...and also what happens to all the executives who are involved, whether they realize they're involved or not.

The Drama Begins

And now for your amusement and amazement, here's your initiation into the victories and defeats, the passion and pathos, of retainer executive recruiting. Silently and secretly we penetrate the posh New York offices of Gordon, Rossi & Boodles, one of America's very large retainer firms. The nameplate on the mahogany door we're entering says "Will Pickham." And as we slip inside, the phone rings.

Our hero answers promptly. He's a genuinely nice guy...a boyishly handsome former preppie and former executive, with a quick smile. Tanned, and trim, he's aging elegantly into his mid-forties, and he's pleased with executive recruiting as his second career.

"Will Pickham here."

"Hello, Will, this is Sherm Summit at Integrated Standard Corporation."

Wow! thinks Will to himself, *it's the CEO in person. I've never dealt with him before. I wonder what's up.*

As he and Summit exchange pleasantries, Will quickly recalls his dealings with ISC, a $1.2 billion conglomerate. Almost exactly two years ago, Will was retained by the then-President of the Food Division, Bill Beane, to find a replacement for his Vice President of Marketing. Bill hired another food man, Graham Rusk. And since then, Will has stayed close to both Bill and Graham. But so far there's been no new business for Gordon, Rossi & Boodles.

Bill Beane has since been promoted to EVP of the whole conglomerate, in charge of five of its eight divisions, including its large and thriving Food Division and its much smaller...and languishing...Proprietary Drug Division. He's thought to have the best shot of anyone in the company at becoming President and COO fairly soon, and CEO when Summit reaches mandatory retirement in five years. Recently, Rusk moved up to replace Beane as head of the Food Division. There've been a couple management openings at ISC recently, but they've been filled from inside. So in the past two years, no searches.

This history is fresh in Will's mind. With time running out, and over 1,000 other client companies off-limits to GR&B recruiters, *We'd soon have had to enter ISC,* thinks Will. *I'm glad they've called. If we'd gone in there, my relationship would have been ruined..*

And now the Chairman on the phone. Fantastic!

"Bill Beane has told me about you," says Mr. Summit, "and your great work in finding Graham Rusk. In fact, Bill partly owes his promotion to you, since Graham did a fine job in marketing, and was ready to take over from Bill as President of Foods. This year we're up 40% in that Division, and I give Bill and Graham the credit."

Will murmurs something modest about how it doesn't take a genius to recognize real talent when you see it. And Summit continues as if Will hadn't spoken.

"Now I've got another project I think you can help us with. I'm taking care of this one personally, since Bill's tied up with our tender offer to the Deli-Shoos Foods people...you've probably read about that in the paper. While he's handling that, I'm holding down the fort here; I like to get my hands dirty every now and then. And our Senior VP of Human Resources, Al Umans, won't be around much either. He and his IR man are coping with a union-organizing drive, which looks like it'll come to a vote in all nine of our Western plants within the next three months. So this is going to be basically you and me."

There's a pause, while Summit swigs Diet Pepsi from a deeply-cut Baccarat glass.

"Now what we want is a new President for our Proprietary Drug Division... the products that sell over-the-counter without a doctor's prescription. And I want someone who can walk right in and take charge."

"So it's got to be a fairly senior executive, with solid experience in proprietary drugs," muses Will.

"That's right. With real strength in marketing. We have a good R&D person, and our manufacturing and distribution are the most efficient in the industry. What we need is somebody who can sell the hell out of our stuff. That's the name of the game in over-the-counter drugs anyway," Summit continues. "The products are all pretty much alike; your success depends on how you position them in the market."

"What do you feel the job should pay?" asks Will nonchalantly. He holds his breath as he waits for the answer...which of course determines what Gordon, Rossi & Boodles' 33% fee will be.

"I plan to offer about $185,000. I'd like to hold it a little under what we're now paying Graham."

An exultant voice in Will's head begins to shout, *Ohhhhkayyy! That's a fee of more than $60,000. Not bad at all. In fact, it's damned good!* Without noticing it, Will has jumped to his feet and...phone in hand...is happily pacing back and forth.

Will's thrilled. But there's a cloud forming on his horizon. Summit continues.

"Now I hope you've had some experience in the proprietary drug field." Obviously he expects a positive reply.

"Oh, yes. Less than a year ago, we put in the new President of Compu-Medic. You've probably noticed it's been one of the industry's most exciting turnarounds." No false modesty for Will at this point.

"Yes, I know. They've become tough competitors. Your firm did that?" Summit sounds almost accusing.

"I personally handled the search, and recruited the top executive of Better & Best. Another search I handled was the President of Orchid."

Summit replies, "Well, there was a lot of talk about that one." His tone makes it clear that the talk wasn't entirely favorable. "I hear he came from

Alphanetics...not exactly a major force in the drug field! Is it true that he was only a Marketing VP in one of their smallest divisions?'' There's an obviously critical note in his voice. ''You did that?''

Yes, thinks Will, *and not necessarily by choice. We have so many client relationships that most of the big and successful drug companies were off-limits to me. So when I found this really good guy, even though he was relatively inexperienced and came from a place like Alphanetics... But he is a sensational talent.*

Will answers calmly. ''You can't really associate him with Alphanetics' record, because he was only there for about eighteen months. He's been moving up like a rocket in the industry, and he went to Alphanetics after four years of heading the Prestige Panacea account at PanGlobal advertising agency. Of course, the jury's still out, but he's already got a lot of things moving over at Orchid. Did you notice the introduction of their new pain reliever aimed specifically at lower-back pain?''

''Oh, that was him?'' says Summit, with a note of admiration in his voice. ''I'm beginning to see your reasoning in putting him in at Orchid. I see those ads on TV all the time. They're obnoxious, but the product's already earned almost a 4% market share of the entire headache-and-pain-relief category. I have to admit I'd much rather have their new product for backs than our thirty-year-old remedy for menstrual discomfort, which has been dragging along at a 2½% share for about the past seven years. The thing is, their *product*'s nothing new. It's the ad campaign that's moving it.''

''That's right. His ad background is what Orchid really needed,'' says Will confidently. ''And he headed all the marketing and sales at that division of Alphanetics.'' *And if he hadn't come from a place like Alphanetics, I'd have had a lot more trouble reaching him, with most of the biggies off-limits to Gordon, Rossi & Boodles,* thinks Will.

''Well, it sounds like you've done some good work in the drug field,'' concludes Summit more genially. ''By the way, any other success stories I should know about?''

Will thinks fast. He's learned to beware of all questions introduced with a casual ''By the way.'' He must find the right balance. On the one hand, Summit wants the reassurance of prior experience. On the other hand, wily old fox that he is, Summit may also be probing the extent of GR&B's client conflicts. The more drug companies they've worked for recently, the fewer they can go into now to look for candidates.

So Will adds carefully, "Yes, we did a job recently for Biopharm" [a small firm on the fringe of the market]. "And we found the Chairman of the Board at Gastrix...you know, the company that makes nothing but that very successful line of indigestion remedies."

Will does well. He gives Summit the additional assurance he seems to want, without identifying any other major companies as "off-limits." And Summit arranges an appointment the following Wednesday for Will to come to the home offices of ISC in Lovelytown, N.Y., thirty miles outside of New York City, to get further details about the position and the type of person ISC is looking for.

Will hangs up and conveys the good news to his secretary, Wilma. On a high, he heads down the corridor to tell his buddy, Buddy Young. For months, Buddy has been urging Will to go into ISC himself, and open it up to Buddy and the rest of GR&B. So Will can't wait to let Buddy know how well things have turned out because of his patience. What are friends for, if not to suffer a few "I told you so's"?

Will arrives just as Buddy is saying goodbye to an executive he's been interviewing.

"Hi, Will, how're ya doin'? Meet Sam Sage, who's here to talk to me about that Expodex job. Go on into my office and sit down, Will. I'm just seeing Sam out to the elevator."

When Buddy returns, he's duly impressed with Will's news, and suggests a drink after work at the Four Seasons to celebrate.

So Will's day ends on a high note.

We Live in an Imperfect World

Early the following week, Will makes time to start the groundwork for his upcoming meeting with Summit. He asks Gordon, Rossi & Boodles' chief researcher in the New York office, Gloria Monday, to check out the top ten companies in the proprietary drug field. He might as well find out how many are going to be off-limits for the ISC search.

Gloria walks into Will's office at quitting time on Wednesday afternoon. Unfortunately, her report is just about what Will expected. Here's what he has to contend with.

Top Ten Firms

(* indicates ''off-limits'')

*CompuMedic: Off-limits, as Will has already told Summit.

*Parker Laboratories: Off-limits, a fact unknown to Summit.

Better & Best: Open. But after Will took a key man out for the Compu-Medic job, a highly-disliked successor was promoted; other execs have also departed, and now there's no one left that Summit is likely to favor.

*Orchid: Off-Limits, as Summit knows.

Maxi-Medi-Marketing: Open.

*National Anodyne: Off-Limits, which Summit doesn't know.

Right Remedies: Open.

*Prestige Panacea: Off-limits, unbeknownst to Summit.

*Coca Nostrumoi Off Limite, aloo unbeknownot to Summit.

BioDynamics: Open.

In other words, six out of the top ten firms are off-limits to all Gordon, Rossi & Boodles recruiters...although Summit has learned about only two of those six. Of the remaining four companies, Will knows that one is extremely unlikely to have anyone that Summit would consider presidential material. So there are really only three of the ''top-ten'' proprietary drug companies where Will can find ISC's new division head. Will hates to think of the sweat and blood this assignment probably will require.

Still, as an experienced, executive recruiter, Will's faced worse before...and he'll cope again this time. He's good at his job.

Nonetheless, Will is pleased to look up and see Buddy...briefcase in hand... poised in the doorway, beckoning.

''Knock it off, Will. If I don't catch the 6:12 tonight, Linda will have a fit. So let's slip over to the Four Seasons while we can still get a seat, and celebrate. You got a new assignment from ISC, and this afternoon I finally completed my PhantaSee! Fashions search, which has really been the pits!''

Two friends...co-workers in a demanding, but also an intellectually stimulating and financially rewarding, business...unwind together at the end of a tough day. They nab two well-placed seats...and inhale the top third of their drinks. Then, they settle down and slowly savor the rest until train time for Buddy. Soon Will brings up a familiar subject. And although Will and Buddy, their searches, and their employer are fictitious, the information they discuss about recruiting firms in the real world is from published reports and recent estimates.

"Darn it," says Will, "even though I'm thrilled to get the ISC search, it looks like it's going to be a bitch. Gloria came in this morning with the rundown. Six of the top ten proprietary drug companies are off-limits. It's a presidency, for heaven's sake! Why, practically every VP - Marketing would be willing to consider a presidency. In the end he or she might not move, but they'd certainly be happy to meet the client and talk. *But I can only go into four of the top ten companies.* And a lot of the smaller ones will be off-limits too. I can't remember the last time I was able to go everywhere in my client's industry and look for the *best person.* All I can do is try to find some good people who don't work for one of our other clients. *And we've now got way over a thousand clients!"*

"Know how you feel, my lad," says Buddy, who's had five years in the business...only one more than Will. "Part of the reason I came to GR&B from Randall Radley Associates two and a half years ago is that GR&B was only half their size then. So with GR&B I could search more places for my candidates... and do it much more easily...because there weren't so many companies off-limits. But we've been growing 20% a year, and we're now almost as big as they were then. By the end of my third year here we'll be *exactly* that size. And if they had off-limits problems at Radley then, imagine what they must have today, because they're growing too!"

"The real problem," says Will, "is the number of recruiters on staff. Not only do I have to protect *my* clients...that wouldn't be too bad, because I've only worked for 20 or 30 clients within the past two years. But I've also got to protect *your* clients too, Buddy. And *the clients of 48 other guys!* That's why there are way over 1,000 companies I can't go into...none of us can...at GR&B."

"Yeah, but would you be any better off at any of the other large firms? I don't think so," Buddy interjects.

"That's the point," Will continues. "There's always been a big problem. Way back in October '78, when *Fortune* did a study of the recruiting industry, Heidrick & Struggles then had 75 recruiters and 2,000 client companies off-limits...an average of almost 27 per recruiter, and about in line with my experience. Look at the chart I found in Gloria's 'Recruiting Industry Information' file. It's recent. In 1987, she estimated sizes of some of the biggest search firms according to approximately how many recruiters each one had working domestically in the U.S. The number of recruiters they have in foreign countries doesn't matter, because they don't protect a client company in the U.S. unless they serve it domestically.''

APPROXIMATE NUMBER OF RECRUITERS OPERATING IN U.S.
WITHIN LARGE RETAINER FIRMS*
(1987 Estimate)

Korn/Ferry International	154
Russell Reynolds Associates, Inc.	80
Heidrick and Struggles, Inc.	67
Peat Marwick Main & Co./Executive Search	50
Boyden Associates, Inc.	45
Spencer Stuart & Associates	43
Ward Howell International, Inc.	39
Paul R. Ray & Co., Inc.	33
A. T. Kearney Executive Search	29
Fleming Associates	26
Ernst & Whinney/Executive Search	25
Interdatum, Inc.	25
Coopers & Lybrand	24
Arthur Young Executive Resource Consultants	21
Skott/Edwards Consultants, Inc.	20
Witt Associates, Inc.	20
Lamalie Associates, Inc.	17
MSL International Ltd.	17
Paul Stafford Associates, Ltd.	16
Canny, Bowen, Inc.	15
The Goodrich & Sherwood Company	15
Handy Associates, Inc.	15
Egon Zehnder International, Inc.	15
Garafolo, Curtiss & Company	12
Haley Associates, Inc.	11

*Only recruiters stationed in the U.S. are estimated, because clients served elsewhere are not off-limits in the U.S.

"Yeah, Will," says Buddy, "it cuts both ways. We've got our client list off-limits. And on top of that, we also have to stay away from every executive that anyone else in GR&B has permission to talk to."

"Exactly," says Will. "I have to stay away from every executive who works for 1,000-plus client companies. And I also have to stay away from all the non-client executives who are among the 85,000 that we keep tabs on, unless I've checked in advance to make sure that I...and not one of our 49 other recruiters... have exclusive permission to call the guy up. *That means I get one-50th of what's left, after we bypass all the employees of more than 1,000 client companies!*"

"It's tough," Buddy agrees distractedly, eyeing an exceptionally curvaceous leg dangling from a swag of dark ranch mink on a nearby bar stool.

"And, Buddy," Will continues, "we're certainly not the only ones to track a lot of executives. Why, way back in that '78 *Fortune* article, Heidrick & Struggles and Boyden both said their data banks had 100,000 executives, and the rest of the 'Big Six' firms claimed to have 'between 50,000 and 100,000 names apiece.' In our business the right hand *does* know what the left hand is doing. And if you're in a retainer recruiting firm, you've damned well got to keep out of its way. Sometimes I feel like I've got both hands tied behind my back."

"Now wait a minute, Will," says Buddy. "I can't let you get away with knocking the files like that. Sure, they're the way we keep track of the people you can and can't call. But they're also the way we keep tabs on people we can use to fill assignments. You love the files when you're looking for a top-flight Controller or a VP - Manufacturing, and Gloria walks in and hands you a dozen of those people neatly wrapped up in our manilla folders."

"Yeah, you're right, Buddy. Most of the time I'm damn glad to have them."

"And you're glad, too, that 49 other recruiters have been contributing to those files for the past umpteen years. Quite a few of the files Gloria hands you will be on executives that you, or I, or someone else has interviewed and submitted as a candidate...or worked with as a client...at some time in the past. Ten percent, and maybe more, of those files aren't just mailed-in resumes from people you have to investigate. They're known quantities...all checked out and, if they're interested in your opportunity, all ready to present to your client."

"You're right on that too, Buddy. There's no way in the world that I could handle my heavy load of assignments, if I didn't have the files. They're the beginning-and-the-end on a lot of my searches. In fact, I had lunch Tuesday with Bill Maverick and Allan Keen, who left us last year to start their own firm. They say that the extra speed and freedom they get from being able to call up practically anyone they want to is pretty much offset by the extra grunting and grinding they have to do because they haven't yet built up files like ours that will solve a lot of their searches for them.''

"Another point, Will, about those 49 other recruiters that make your life more difficult. They often make it a hell of a lot easier too. You've probably done favors for most of them...you've come up with candidate ideas when they were stumped...and most of them will gladly try to give you suggestions when the going gets rough. I certainly do. And it was your suggestion of Joan Flannel...thank you very much...that finally wound up my PhantaSee! Fashions search.''

"True, ole Buddy," says Will. "I sure as hell wouldn't help everyone the way I do you...and vice versa, as we've discussed many times. But I do have lots of friends in the firm to exchange ideas with, and that's a great help. Take Bill and Allan. I used to swap suggestions with them all the time. But I probably won't be doing as much of that, now that they've started their own company.''

"Yeah, and what about our offices in seven U.S. cities and four overseas? They come in pretty darn handy when you're traveling. No need to interview in a ditsy hotel room staring at an unmade bed," says Buddy.

"Or to rent a suite that you've got to bill your client for, if it's a high level search and you want to make a really good impression," adds Will.

"And speaking of impressions, Will," says Buddy. "I think you're more likely to get a busy executive to return your phone call right away if you're calling from Gordon, Rossi & Boodles, than if you're calling from an unheard-of little firm like Snerd, Bergen & McCarthy.''

"Certainly potential clients are more likely to call you," says Will. "Name value is very helpful to a Human Resources Officer. His job is on the line when he recommends a search firm to his CEO or to another top officer. Not every search will run smoothly, no matter *who* does it. But when he recommends one of the largest and most famous firms and there's a poor result, it's because the giant firm screwed up. It's not because he recommended a small outfit, that obviously wasn't qualified. The same goes for almost anyone else who chooses a search firm, whether it's a board hiring a CEO, or a division manager going outside for a head of R&D. The decisionmaker can always claim 'due diligence,' when he turns the matter over to a very well-known entity.''

"When you get right down to it, Will, the 'off-limits' restrictions...both client and co-worker...are nothing more than a nuisance for you and me on most searches. Normally, we're just looking for a really good person to fill an opening. He or she can come from almost any company...not just a few leading firms in a certain industry. Only in a situation like the one you've got with Summit, where he's trying to shift the competitive balance of power in his field, does it really matter where you can and can't look. And even then, conscientious guys like us can always get a good result, regardless of the obstacles. Three months from now we'll be back here celebrating your completion of the ISC search.''

''Just like we're now toasting your new President of PhantaSee! Fashions,'' adds Will. ''Drink up, Buddy, and let's hit the road.''

''And all in all, it's a good life, Will. You have to admit that,'' says Buddy, whose wife will be meeting him at the station in their new Mercedes 560SEL, which she just picked up from the dealer this afternoon. ''They're not holding any benefits these days for Will Pickham, are they?''

That's Buddy's exit line, as he takes off for Grand Central, and Will heads for a pre-theater dinner with his wife, a successful pediatrician.

''That's Exactly the Sort of Person You Need.''

The show was a hit. Will and Karen are in a great mood the next morning, as they walk out of their elegant condominium on upper Fifth Avenue. Will may be late this evening. He's driving out to see Mr. Summit.

The interview takes place in Summit's luxurious suite of offices at ISC's headquarters near Lovelytown, New York, with every window framing a breathtaking view of the scenic Hudson River. As Summit predicted, no Bill Beane or Al Umans. From Will's perspective, things go very well. He easily skirts the issue of off-limits companies...without ever having to say anything that isn't literally true.

Summit begins by stressing once again that he must have someone experienced in proprietary drugs...drugs sold to the consumer, rather than prescribed by doctors.

''Of course, I know that anyone from the consumer products field could learn proprietary drugs. But even someone very sharp might take a year or more to get up to speed, and I just can't wait that long. The truth of the matter is, I've already waited too long to get rid of the guy I had in there.''

Summit emphasizes his point by flicking an imaginary piece of lint from the sleeve of his navy pinstripe.

''Now it's essential that I have quick results. So the new person must be experienced in our product lines, and all set to go.''

Will nods. He understands that Summit isn't going to be willing to look at anyone who doesn't have the background he's asking for. *Too bad. . .that makes it even more limiting.*

"Now I understand that you can't go into CompuMedic, because you found their new superstar. But maybe that isn't such a big loss as it seems. Right now that company is so profitable that they'll probably offer whatever it takes to tie down their management team for the foreseeable future. And I suppose you can't go to Orchid either. But I understand your guy brought in a lot of new people, and to tell you the truth, I'd prefer to wait and see if they can really turn that thing around. They're still untested, as I see it, and not a place we're interested in. So where do you plan to look?"

Will can recognize a hot potato when it's handed to him.

"Well, you tell me. Which companies in the proprietary drug field do you respect? Which ones have the kind of managers you feel would fit what you're trying to accomplish at ISC?"

Will's candid blue eyes look straight at Summit.

"Let's see. Well, of course, Prestige Panacea is probably the best-managed of the big firms in the field. . .you couldn't go wrong with the Marketing VP from Prestige. And I think National Anodyne does a consistently good job of marketing. Maxi-Medi-Marketing has one of the hottest growth records in the industry, although I believe part of their success is due to their excellent R&D work. Still, one of their people should know what it takes to get that kind of fast growth. Now, let me think. . .Well, of course, there's Parker Labs. They're an old-line firm, possibly a little bit stodgy, but they've built their brands very solidly, and they have an excellent reputation in the business."

Summit pauses for a moment, steepling his fingers as he gazes fearlessly into the middle distance.

"If I were you, I might take an especially close look at BioDynamics. They're moving into some very promising new areas, and that suggests an alert management with good long-range planning, which I'd like to see more of here at ISC. Oh, yes, and Cosa Nostrums. I've heard their management can be a bit ruthless, but they know how to get cooperation from the retailers. They always wind up with more than their share of shelf and display space. Perhaps a bit of their promotional aggressiveness would serve us well."

"As I think about it now, I really do like the idea of someone from Bio-Dynamics. . .and, of course, Prestige; they're very likely possibilities. . ."

As Summit drones on...repeating again the very limited number of obvious companies on his executive shopping list, Will's spirits are sinking. Four of the six companies Summit has mentioned are off-limits to GR&B...unbeknownst, of course, to Summit. *Where am I going to find my candidates?*

But Will copes with his concern as he answers Summit.

"You've listed some outstanding companies. And there are others too. I'm sure we can find a number of able people. Now at BioDynamics," continues Will, selecting one of the companies open to him, "Lately I've been hearing from our West Coast office that they've got some excellent marketing-oriented general managers in those decentralized proprietary drug divisions they've set up. In fact, I noticed last week in an investor's newsletter I subscribe to that their stock was being highly recommended because the analyst was impressed by their top management and the entrepreneurship those separate profit centers are supposed to encourage."

"Yes, BioDynamics should be high on your list. And I've always liked the sort of people you see at places like Prestige and National Anodyne."

"Yes," Will replies. "That's exactly the sort of person you need."

Summit is satisfied. He pictures Will searching in those companies. Will is relieved. He knows he hasn't committed himself to anything but an expression of blanket approval of the quality of the executives those corporations employ. So both men are in a very good mood as they head for the private dining room and an elegant luncheon whipped up by ISC's corporate chef: grilled sole with a fresh tomato and basil sauce, asparagus puree, and sauteed wild mushrooms that the chef personally collected that morning in the woods at the edge of ISC's property. It's not until they finish the chef's special strawberry sorbet that they go back to talking business.

"By the way," says Summit, reaching into his breastpocket, "I wanted to give you this." It's a neatly typed letter, accompanied by a resume. "I got this in the mail just a few days ago. I never heard of the guy, but it seems that he has the sort of experience we're interested in. Why don't you check him out? From his resume, it sounds like he's been in the right places to get the strong marketing background we're looking for. And, if they're true, his accomplishments are very impressive."

Will's initial response is thankfulness...it's going to be extremely hard to find good candidates for ISC, so he's glad to get one, even from the client. But his feelings change when he scans the resume. It's from Sam Sage...the very same Sam Sage he recently met coming out of Buddy's office...the Sam Sage who's currently assigned within Gordon, Rossi & Boodles to Buddy for his Ex-podex search. *Oh, damn!*

There's no need for Will to tell Summit the immediate reason he's less than enthusiastic about Sam. As he glances at the resume, Will sees something else. "I'm not sure that this background is really what you want. If you notice, practically all of his work has been in *prescription* drugs, not proprietaries. Most of his marketing campaigns have been aimed at the medical profession, rather than the consumer."

Summit takes a quick look at the resume again.

"I see what you mean. But I'm impressed by the depth of his experience in drugs...and by the apparent success he's had. And, after all, he began his career as a brand manager at Promote & Gambol. You can't get much better consumer marketing experience than P&G. Why don't you just check him out?"

Faced with Summit's instruction, Will has no choice but to comply.

"Sure, I'll see about this guy," he agrees, as he puts the resume into the breastpocket of his grey pinstripe. *Maybe I'll be able to discourage Summit from asking any further about Buddy's star candidate, muses Will. And, of course, if Summit does bring up Sam Sage again, and gets at all pushy, that will give me the clout to make Buddy let me also use him as a candidate...an ace in the hole, if I'm as hard up as it looks like I may be.*

Summit goes back to the subject of ISC's needs.

"Now we've talked about a lot of the big companies in the industry. But I don't want you just to pursue the most obvious solutions. I hope you'll look in a few other directions. There are some aggressive young companies coming into the market these days. Some of those hot little ethical drug companies are doing a good job of taking their prescription remedies into the consumer market, now that the FDA has relaxed its rules on what can be sold without Rx...and there are even some rapidly growing firms in the health-food field that are expanding into mass-market proprietaries. You might find somebody at one of those smaller companies."

That may be my answer. It's a darn good idea!

"Yes," says Will, "I'll look very carefully into the smaller companies, too. Sometimes they've got a really outstanding manager who'd love to get into a major corporation."

Will smiles inwardly. He enjoys it when a client indicates some flexibility, and leaves him room for creativity.

"Of course, I recognize we're probably not as attractive as one of the top ten firms," says Summit frankly. "Still, it's an $80 million division. And with the right person at the helm using all the resources of a conglomerate like ISC, growth could be very rapid. We hope that within five years we'll be in the top ten ourselves. I'm willing to spring for acquisitions, if they're brought to me by a *credible* management team that's doing a good job with our own businesses.

"And obviously I know we'll have to make some major changes in what we're doing now," Summit continues. For example, in an effort to make the division profitable, we've done very little advertising in the past few years. That was the policy of the last division head, and I let him get away with it. But I expect to be much more aggressive in the future. If need be, I'll pour lots of money into that division for the next couple of years, to enable them to do all the marketing that's required. We've got a great opportunity for the new President. I hope you find us the person we really need."

The meeting concludes with reassurances from Will that he'll get right to work, and optimism from Summit that he'll soon see a slate of several appropriate candidates. In Summit's mind, Will can search almost everywhere in the proprietary drug industry...whereas, in fact, as Will realizes all too clearly, he's severely limited.

Here are the companies that, following his discussion with Will, Summit visualizes being searched:	*Here is where Will actually can search:*
Prestige Panacea	
National Anodyne	
Maxi-Medi-Marketing	**Maxi-Medi-Marketing**
Parker Laboratories	
BioDynamics	**BioDynamics**
Cosa Nostrums	
"Small up-and-coming companies"	**"Small up-and-coming companies"**

The Struggle Begins

The next morning, as soon as he gets to the office, Will plunges into the ISC search. Better get things moving before his other assignments make new demands on his time.

The first item on Will's agenda is another meeting with Gloria Monday, chief researcher in GR&B's New York office. Since they last talked about the ISC position, she's gone through industry directories and GR&B's computerized files. Today she brings Will print-outs on the four top drug companies that he's able to look into for candidates. Two of these...Maxi-Medi-Marketing and Bio-Dynamics...are on Mr. Summit's mental list. And two others...Better & Best and Right Remedies...while not on that list, are at least sizable enough to rank among the top ten in the U.S.

Through dedicated digging, Gloria has also come up with a list of second-tier companies not currently off-limits to Gordon, Rossi & Boodles recruiters. Will knows that his success rate at these smaller firms may not turn out to be very high. Their top managers usually have substantial equity stakes. So, if the companies are fast-growing and profitable, their managers are unreachable. And if the companies aren't doing well, their executives won't have track records that will impress Summit. Still, Will's thankful at least to have somewhere else to look. Maybe in one of those companies he'll find Mr. or Ms. Right...or anyway, Right-Enough-To-Present.

Gloria also brings Will the files on some proprietary drug company executives known to Gordon, Rossi & Boodles who aren't currently involved in any other recruiter's search. Perhaps one of these people will actually become a candidate for the ISC job. And even the ones who are working for off-limits companies may still be useful as sources of information about good people somewhere else in the field.

Will thanks Gloria for all her help and settles down to do his reading. As he leafs through the pile of folders on his desk, he spots the name of Arthur Applewhite.

Art Applewhite! Of course, I know Art Applewhite...he's PERFECT! Will shouts under his breath, whacking his desk so hard that his Cross pen bounces onto his interviewing chair four feet away. *(Expletive deleted.) Art's exactly the person Summit was describing! (Expletive deleted.) The first thought he came up with was to get the Marketing VP of Prestige Panacea...and that's Art! (Another* *expletive.) I'd forgotten that Art got promoted to VP - Marketing four years ago when Dan Dawson moved up to Senior VP - Marketing & Sales. Why, Art's a carbon copy of Bill Beane, only with consumer drug background instead of food. The chemistry's perfect! Summit would FLIP. . .and so would Bill. Art's always dreamed of getting a shot at running something on his own. And an $80 million proprietary drug company, with strong backing for growth. . .why Art would FLIP, too. It's a gimme! (One last expletive, but less strident, more resigned.) And my hands are tied. . .*

Unfortunately, as Will's silent tantrum reminds us, Gordon, Rossi & Boodles has a strong client relationship with Prestige Panacea. In fact, Applewhite himself was recruited to Prestige by GR&B several years ago. All Prestige executives are off-limits. And, recruited by GR&B, Art is doubly off-limits.

But Art is so perfect for the ISC position that Will even briefly considers going to Mr. Rossi and asking if something can be done to release Art. Then he remembers that one of the reasons GR&B got Prestige as a client was that Rossi plays golf every Saturday with Prestige's CEO. Will knows he doesn't have a prayer of getting Art freed up for ISC.

In fact, if he even so much as called Art to ask for suggestions, Will could be in trouble. It wouldn't do for Art to learn about the open position. . .one he'd be as eager to get as ISC would be to get him. . .because Art might then try to go directly after the job himself. The CEO of Prestige certainly wouldn't take it well if his fair-haired boy ended up with a job that GR&B was searching, *however* it came about. He'd surely complain to Rossi, and Will knows what Rossi would then say to him. And of course the spontaneous appearance of Applewhite on the scene would also create big problems with Summit, who'd either think Will was inept for not identifying Applewhite or less than candid for not stating upfront that he couldn't go into Prestige. No, Will doesn't dare even *breathe* in Art's direction.

Well, so much for Art Applewhite. Put him in the ''No'' pile.

And here's Alice Klasner, over at National Anodyne. Damn, damn, damn!, fumes Will. *Another great person Summit and Beane would love. She's also dying for a shot at general management. But I can't touch National Anodyne. And I'd damn well better not call her for suggestions either. She's a real go-getter. Don't know how she'd manage it, but Alice would be in Summit's office by noon tomorrow. Not quite 31 years old, and she's already had three years as Marketing VP of the sixth largest proprietary drug company. And just look at those new products she's coming out with,* muses Will. *If she doesn't get somebody else's company to run by the time she's 35, she'll probably start her own!* A *nice person, too. She recycles and develops people; she doesn't just dump them on the street. Well, too bad Will, old boy. On the street is where you'll be if you touch Klasner. Anodyne is Sylvia Gordon's client.*

Next, however, Will discovers the file of the financial vice president at Prestige. Will decides it's safe to call him, even though he can't call Art Applewhite, since a finance man is obviously not going to be a candidate for the marketing-oriented division head Will will be inquiring about. This guy's been in the proprietary drug business for a long time, so he might conceivably know of some promising marketing executives who've been at Prestige over the years and then moved on to other companies. Will immediately puts his name on the ''Source'' list.

Painstakingly, Will goes through all the folders. There are no feasible candidates, but he does succeed in compiling a list of possible sources to call. Then he tries to compile a list of prospects. He turns to the photocopied pages of corporate directories Gloria has supplied, to look up the names of marketing people in the three big firms he *can* go into: Maxi-Medi-Marketing, Right Remedies, and BioDynamics. He also checks out the top management of some of the smaller companies. At the moment, these are just names on a piece of paper to Will, but as he calls his sources to ask for their recommendations, he can also inquire about some of the names on the list.

After a few days of making calls, Will begins to feel quite anxious about his ability to put together a decent slate of candidates for Mr. Summit. According to the sources Will's talked to, he'll never be able to put his hands on any but the most junior of the people at Right Remedies, a top-ten firm that's open to him although it wasn't mentioned by Summit as one of his favorites. All of its upper management are beneficiaries of an incredibly generous stock option plan that was set up during a period of crisis five or six years ago. Although the program has since been discontinued, every one of the key people will be millionaires...as long as they stay on a few more years. So Right Remedies is unlikely to yield any candidate.

Another disappointment is the fact that Will has heard very little about good marketing-oriented presidents, general managers, and VP's of Marketing in the smaller companies. If those smaller firms *do* contain a wealth of talent, the people are unknown to Will's informants. Will, and Gloria's researchers, will simply have to phone into those companies and ask for their key executives by title, without knowing anything about them in advance...tedious and usually unproductive work, but necessary in a tough situation like this.

Meanwhile, it's beginning to look like Will's entire list of candidates will have to be drawn from just two places: BioDynamics and Maxi-Medi-Marketing. It's been quite a while since he faced a prospect so bleak.

One Step Forward

Will becomes so concerned about the ISC search that he decides to go see Herbert ("Red") Tapecutter. Red is a senior member of the Gordon, Rossi & Boodles staff, and he's the one charged with working out knotty problems of client conflict. Will pours his tale of woe into Red's ear, and Red is properly sympathetic.

"Can't you find a way to get just one of those companies on the off-limits list unlocked for me? I know I can't go into Prestige, or Orchid, or CompuMedic... our relationships with those firms are much too close. But what about the others? Maybe Parker Labs or Cosa Nostrums? Can you do anything in that direction? I tell you, Red, I need help on this one."

Red promises to look into the situation. Will knows that really means he'll talk to Hamilton Rossi, who usually adjudicates such matters...and get back to Will. In fact, the very next day, Red drops by Will's office to give him some good news.

"Will," says Red, smoothing down the hair that long ago lost the color that conferred Tapecutter's nickname, "I think it will be all right for you to go into Cosa Nostrums. Our relationship with them on the search we did was really not satisfactory. They struck us as very unrealistic and demanding, and they certainly acted like they weren't satisfied with our work. I doubt that they'll use us again...and even if they *did* come back, I'm not sure Mr. Rossi would agree to take any assignment from them. So even though the time limit isn't up, you can go into Cosa Nostrums if you need to."

If I need to. That's a laugh!

"Thanks, Red, I really appreciate the help."

"Any time," waves Red as he departs.

That afternoon, Will at last can look with some satisfaction on his developing list of prospects. As he'd suspected, Better & Best yields no possibilities; there was virtually a complete turnover following the departure of the key executive Will recruited, because his replacement has turned out to be an insecure egomaniac. But Will's heard of a couple people at BioDynamics, and a couple more at Maxi-Medi-Marketing, who sound like good possibilities. He's also going to try some names at Right Remedies, although he's rather doubtful about whether or not they can be lured away. Plus, his research has turned up a couple possibilities at Cosa Nostrums, now happily unlocked. All in all, it's not such a bad starting point.

The next morning, things look even better for the ISC search. Will is able to get through to one of his most carefully cultivated contacts, a senior partner in a major public accounting firm. His contact remembers being impressed with the performance of an aggressive little drug company in Phoenix, called Adam Laboratories. Adam was acquired by a foreign concern, which has since switched Adam to a different CPA firm...the same one it uses for the rest of its U.S. subsidiaries. According to Will's informant, a lot of the credit for Adam Labs' performance goes to their Marketing VP, Charlie Comstock. Will's contact hasn't actually met Charlie, but he thinks there's good reason to believe he might be an excellent prospect.

Will rushes to do a little background research on Charlie, and is delighted to discover that Charlie went to Adam from Parker Labs, where for several years he'd been a senior product manager. It looks like the perfect profile of a young man on his way to the top in the proprietary drug industry. Elated, Will asks his secretary to get Charlie on the phone. Yes, Charlie might be interested in making a move...for the right job and salary...doesn't mind living in the New York area...will send his resume immediately...and can fly in for an interview in the next week or so.

All in all, Will chalks up a good day's work on the ISC job. *I wish I were making as much headway on some of the other things I'm handling,* he says to himself.

But the next day is one that for several weeks hence Will will refer to as Black Thursday. As soon as he's sitting down with his first cup of strong coffee, Gloria pops into his office. She's bearing news...good for Gordon, Rossi & Boodles, bad for Will and ISC.

BioDynamics is now officially off-limits.

"Off-limits!" Will groans. "But we haven't worked for them in years!"

"That was yesterday," says Gloria firmly. Gloria is a practical woman who refuses to cry over spilled milk. "One of the recruiters in our San Francisco office, Ken DeWitt, has been staying very close to the man at the top. And the result is that he's just picked up an assignment to fill the job of head of marketing for their consumer healthcare products group."

"Oh, no," says Will. "That's even worse. Not only does it mean I can't go into BioDynamics to look for my person; it also means that Ken and I are going to be chasing the same candidates.''

Will gets up and starts to pace as he thinks about how he's going to defend his territory against this new incursion.

''Bad luck,'' says Gloria sympathetically. ''But since I realized this new search was going to put you in a hole, I immediately went through all our files and pulled *everyone* I could find who might be of the slightest use to you on your ISC project. . .before Judy, the researcher in the West Coast office, requested them all for Ken.''

Will swivels around and watches in awe as Gloria drops a huge pile of files on his desk.

''There are 26 in all,'' she announces.

''Good work, Gloria!'' says Will. There is real warmth in his smile. *Thank God for Gloria! Am I glad I remembered to get her that Hermes scarf last Christmas; it's the best investment I ever made. If I didn't have her on my side. . .*

Gloria leaves Will's office, her ears still ringing with his words of praise for her foresight. Will immediately reaches for the phone and dials Ken out in San Francisco.

''Ken, you old s.o.b., what are you trying to do to me?''

''Just trying to earn a living, Will. Them's the breaks.''

''That's easy for you to say,'' rejoins Will. ''BioDynamics was my best hope for the ISC search, a real bitch of an assignment, and now you've snatched the company away from me.''

''If you want to talk about snatching, my friend, I've got a few complaints of my own. What about the files? Judy here tells me you've got most of the people who might be of any use to me on the BioDynamics search.''

''So you noticed that, did you?'' chuckles Will. ''Serves you right, you know.''

After a few more minutes of competitive complaining, Ken becomes more serious, and virtually begs Will for help.

''The truth of the matter is that I don't even have a place to start on this search. . .especially since you've got all those files tied up. Listen, Will, can't you at least let me call some of the people you're holding and ask them for suggestions?''

"I don't think I can do that, Ken. Let's face it. You and I are going to be looking for exactly the same person. It's bad enough that I'm going to have to race you to the best prospects, but I sure don't want to give you a head start."

"How about letting me have just *one* of those guys Gloria scooped up for you? You've got the file on Walter Alston, and the man's a personal friend of mine, for god's sake."

"I hate to play hardball with you, Ken, but I need every one of the people I've got. I'm nearly a month into the search already, and right now I have no candidates, and very few solid leads. I've just got to hang on to everything I have."

Ken's sigh is so loud that Will could have heard it without the aid of the telephone.

"You think you've got problems. What about me?" says Ken dejectedly. "I've got exactly the same problem you have, and on top of it, I've lost the few leads open to Gordon, Rossi & Boodles, because of your quick work in getting there first." Ken's groan is heartfelt. "Help me out here, Will."

"I know, it's tough," answers Will sympathetically. *I don't want to cause Ken grief,* he thinks to himself. *In fact I'd like to help him — but I can't give him my files.*

"How about this?" suggests Ken. "If you run across any good people that you can't land because they don't want to move to New York, will you let me have a crack at them? I can pitch them on the climate and the other advantages of San Diego for the BioDynamics job, and maybe I can get them for my search, even if they turn you down for ISC."

Will likes Ken and knows exactly how he feels. And Will may need Ken's cooperation in the future. So he cheerfully agrees.

"Okay, you've got it. Anyone who turns me down flat, for whatever reason, I'll immediately hand over to you. Wilma will turn in each file the same day that happens, and she'll simultaneously sign you up for it."

"Thanks, Will, I appreciate your help. I'd like to do a really good job with this search, because I think I can get a lot more business from BioDynamics. They're doing some reorganizing, and they have an ambitious acquisition program, so a lot of positions could open up in the next few years."

"What happened to the guy who used to have the job you're filling?" asks Will, who thinks *maybe his going somewhere else will stir up the industry in a way that could possibly be helpful to me.*

"They haven't fired him, and they haven't promoted him either. They've moved him into a staff job at the corporate level, something in corporate planning. My guess is that he just wasn't action-oriented and decisive enough for a company that's becoming very aggressive these days. In describing what they want they've kept harping on ability to make timely, independent decisions. Of course, the kick upstairs may just be a graceful way of giving him plenty of time to look around for something else. I think he's been there a long while."

"Hhhhmmmmhh," says Will thoughtfully. "Maybe there's something there for me. Do you think they'd really like to see him go? Maybe they wouldn't mind if I approached him about the ISC job. What do you think?"

"I can't say for sure, but it might be worth a try. I could check it out with the CEO. If it's true that they want to get rid of him, they might even be grateful if we called him up and got him thinking about the outside world."

"It would sure be great for me," says Will eagerly. "It means I'd be able to present a guy from BioDynamics, which is one of my CEO's favorite targets for his search. Not that I'd actually put him in if he's a stiff. But at least I could show that I looked into BioDynamics. And you know, it might even work. If your guy's smart and has a deep background in drugs, he'll appeal to ISC. Maybe it won't matter so much to them that he's a little slow to make a decision, since he'll be reporting to one of the most action-oriented executives I've ever seen...a guy who's also done some great work in developing people. I know of a couple of dead-assed old farts that he's really got up and running. The guy at Bio-Dynamics is probably a hell of a lot better than *they* were when my man started working with them."

"I'll check out the situation with the BioDynamics people," promises Ken.

Losing BioDynamics is a real blow to Will. He'd counted on finding one or two good candidates there...and he knows Summit has been counting on the same thing. Of course, if Ken can swing it, Will may yet present someone from BioDynamics...but he fears it will be largely a matter of window dressing. He still needs to find a really strong candidate to head his slate.

Suddenly, Will remembers the resume of Sam Sage that Summit asked him to check out. A couple weeks have gone by; maybe there's a chance that Buddy can now give him up. *I'd better look into that before Summit raises the issue again,* thinks Will, as he strolls down the hall and walks nonchalantly into Buddy's office.

"Hey, Buddy, you know that guy I met in here a while ago? What was his name...Sam Sage? Is he still a hot candidate for your Expodex search?"

"You bet he is. He's got just the right marketing background, and I think he's going to be one of my strongest runners."

"I was afraid of that," says Will glumly.

He explains that Sam has sent his resume to Sherm Summit at ISC, with the result that Summit has expressed interest in checking Sam out.

"Well, you've got to head that one off," mutters Buddy. "He's mine, and I need him."

"I will if I can, but you know it's not always easy. I already tried to point out that his background is wrong...mainly in ethical drugs aimed at the medical profession...but Summit didn't back off an inch."

"So why don't you tell him you know something...without getting specific...that makes you think he should pass Sam by? You know, say you've got 'mixed reviews' on him, or something like that, and while he might be great in the slower-moving *ethical* drug industry, he wouldn't be the rockem-sockem guy they're looking for to build their consumer business."

"Buddy, that's not the way I operate," Will replies with strong conviction. "Besides, Summit might hear that Sam got the Expodex job, and was recruited there by Gordon, Rossi & Boodles. Then I'd really look like a jerk!" Will shakes his head in concern. "I'm just hoping that if I keep quiet about it, Summit will forget the whole thing."

"Just to be on the safe side," concludes Buddy, "I'm going to set up an appointment for Sam to see the guys at Expodex right away...before I have my complete slate lined up. I'm counting on you, Will, to protect me with my clients. They aren't going to like it if we're selling the same guy to two clients...which is the way they'll interpret it."

"I'll do my best, Buddy," promises Will as he heads back to his own office. But the thought of BioDynamics' new status, plus having to try to keep Sam Sage away from Summit, cause Will to accept, when a favorite client calls with a wild idea. It's a beautiful day. Why don't they use his company's tickets for that afternoon at the U.S. Open Tennis Tournament? Why not indeed!

The First Sketchy Slate

Before the week is over, lucky Will adds not one but *two* candidates to his ISC slate. He hears from Ken on the West Coast, who tells him it's okay to go after the exec who was kicked upstairs. As they had surmised, BioDynamics is pleased at the possibility that Ethan Evans might find other employment. And it comes as no surprise, when Will finally gets Ethan on the phone, that he's equally interested. In fact, on paper he's an excellent candidate: good education, deep experience in the proprietary drug field, long-tenured employment at highly-respected companies. Whatever his flaws may be, they're not readily apparent, and Will is sure Summit will be impressed at seeing a candidate of the caliber of Ethan Evans. And of course he'd damn well *better* see a candidate from *one* of the two companies that seem to be of greatest interest to him...Prestige and BioDynamics.

And then comes a stroke of luck right out of the blue. Will discovers another candidate from the original pile of folders Gloria brought him on Black Thursday...a thin file with nothing but a letter and a resume in it, that had accidentally got shoved under Will's desk calendar. The guy had mailed his resume to Gordon, Rossi & Boodles, where it was received only two days before Gloria scoured the files.

Terrific! exclaims Will to himself...but this time out loud, and Wilma steps in to see what's up.

"Did you win the New York Lotto?" she says.

"Dan Dawson's been fired!" says Will. "Of course his letter says 'disagreed on policy'...whatever. The point is that he was Art Applewhite's boss at Prestige Panacea...Senior VP of both Marketing and Sales. Art just had Marketing. Now I'll bet Art moves up to take over both. Wilma, this is just the break I needed for the ISC search. Now I can present someone from Summit's favorite company. And he can't be *bad*...unless something radical has gone wrong lately... because Art has always spoken well of him. And of course I can easily check out the circumstances with Art. You know, Wilma, I never wish any executive bad luck, because I've been in the corporate world and I know how tough it is. But this guy's problem is a real break for me. And thank goodness for Gloria. If she hadn't grabbed those files, Ken DeWitt would have him."

Will calls Dan right away, and confirms that he was in charge of both Marketing and Sales at Prestige for nearly four years, and was in charge of Marketing for two years before that...ideal experience for the ISC job. On the phone and in his subsequent interview, Dan freely admits he was fired, as Will had guessed. But he stresses that it was due to a policy conflict: he wanted to be much more aggressive than he was allowed to be...wanted to investment-spend on the introduction of some new products, right after making an acquisition that was taking longer to pay out than originally projected to the Board of Directors last year. So he's out. And...yes, Art Applewhite did move up to his job.

Will hears Dan out and pitches the ISC proprietary drug division presidency. Dan is delighted to have a shot at running his own show as president, even though the $80 million business is one-tenth the size of corporate Prestige, for which Dan controlled both Marketing & Sales. Moreover, Dan is happy to hear about a job that doesn't require relocation, because his wife has a lucrative law practice in New York. *Dan's lucky, too, that Gloria grabbed those files*, thinks Will.

Of course Will immediately does some preliminary reference checking to confirm Dawson's story. After all, he was fired. Among Will's reference calls is one to Art Applewhite...ostensibly just to congratulate Art on his promotion and ask the circumstances surrounding it since, despite the promotion, Art would probably give his right arm for the ISC job.

From Art and two other sources Will gets the straight story on Dawson, and it's not really damaging. The acquisition is substantially under-performing the projections Dawson and the President made to the Board, but not so badly that, in the long run, it won't prove a sound diversification. But right now Prestige has got itself into a cash crisis. There have also been some foreign currency losses. And the President just put up a very costly new factory...another good long-range investment...but underutilized now, and raising cost-of-goods. So Dawson's heavy investment spending proposals for new marketing programs...and his blunt outspokenness in support of them...couldn't have come at a worse time. Sensing the Board's frustration, the President seems to have "thrown Dan Dawson to the wolves," says Art Applewhite, "maybe partly to save his own skin."

Will is satisfied that Dawson is basically a competent executive, has no relevant personal faults, and seems to be someone who could be guided and groomed by Bill Beane and Sherm Summit into a successful marketing-oriented company president. His personality, however, won't appeal to them nearly as much as Art Applewhite's would. But Dawson *is* a solid citizen. In fact, Will will be very pleased if every other prospective candidate for the ISC job stands up to preliminary referencing as well as Dawson has.

So at this point, Will has put together a fairly sketchy slate of candidates... not perfect, but at least it's a start:

> **1. Charlie Comstock:**   Even though he's at Adam Labs, a small company, his track record looks good on paper, and he has a stint with a top-ten firm (Parker Labs) on his resume. He may be a promising find.

> **2. Ethan Evans:**   Another candidate who looks great on paper, and, according to Ken, who spoke to him briefly in

person, is very polished with an air of success about him. As someone from BioDynamics, he should impress ISC.

3. Dan Dawson: Although he's just been let go by Prestige Panacea, he has a very good background and seems to be able to handle himself well. And his story checks out.

Not bad. Not bad at all, thinks Will. At least he has a few possibilities now. In fact, he's beginning to think the ISC search might turn out to be the least of his current problems. He winces as he thinks about the troubles on some of his other searches.

And Will still has a few more places to look. He and Gloria's researchers have done their homework on the executives at Maxi-Medi-Marketing and Cosa Nostrums, plus some more of the smaller companies, and Will is ready to get in touch with the most likely prospects, gleaned from corporate directories and from phone calls. And of course, his secretary, Wilma, has already checked the alphabetically-organized computer listing of the 85,000 files Gordon, Rossi & Boodles maintains on all the U.S. executives it has had any sort of contact with in recent years...from being a client or candidate, to merely having sent in a resume.

Fortunately, three of the eight new prospects Will wants to call are people who haven't previously gotten into GR&B's filing system. Wilma has already flagged those three ''no-file'' people on the computer as Will's property; now no other GR&B recruiter can communicate with them until Will gives them up. Meanwhile, he can contact them or not, as he sees fit. Moreover, a fourth new prospect Will hears about is also available to Will, even though he's been tracked in GR&B's system for years. It seems that his file was returned to GR&B's central filing system just a few days *after* Gloria in New York and Judy in San Francisco scoured the files for Will's and Ken DeWitt's respective searches. Unfortunately, the remaining four new prospects are on file at GR&B and out of Will's reach; three files are signed out to Ken DeWitt, and one is signed out to another GR&B recruiter.

The first name on Will's list of prospects to call is Gerry Glib at Maxi-Medi-Marketing. He's corporate Senior VP in charge of Sales and Marketing, and is apparently a heavy hitter. His name appears in several corporate directories, and Will is surprised and delighted to find that he's not yet in Gordon, Rossi & Boodles' files, and hence not yet off-limits to Will or any other GR&B recruiter. *Eat your heart out, Ken DeWitt, out there in sunny California; too much napping by the pool,* thinks Will.

Gerry turns out to be quite enthusiastic about the idea of a job change...so much so that it does make Will wonder just a bit what Gerry's situation at Maxi-Medi-Marketing might actually be. But Gerry sounds like an outstanding candidate, and a brief meeting for cocktails confirms Will's initial impression. Gerry seems to have a lot of ideas for aggressive marketing campaigns for ISC's proprietary drug lines, and it looks like he may be just the person that Will is looking for.

Another candidate from the same company, Frank Finley, Jr., isn't quite so strong. He's one of two Marketing VP's splitting product line responsibility in their Consumer Division and therefore is actually a whole level below Gerry. He's probably a *little* junior for ISC's position. But he seems bright, quick to learn, and very adaptable. And of course, he'd also offer ISC something of a price advantage compared to most of the other candidates. Will decides to put Frank on the "B" list; he's not a top candidate, but he can be introduced to Summit if the "A" list turns out to be too short.

Another candidate is Peter Powers, VP - Marketing of the Proprietary Drugs Division at Cosa Nostrums. He seems to have accomplished miracles in getting distribution for his firm's new products, with extremely aggressive trade promotions...fighting for shelf space chain by chain, and almost store by store. "Cosa's field sales force is the hardest-hitting in the business," Will is told by a prospect in another company, who turns Will down and recommends Powers. For Powers, the ISC job would be a lateral move, but one that he says he's interested in making for personal reasons. He claims to be happy at Cosa Nostrums, and as far as Will has been able to discover, the firm is also happy with his performance. But pressing family matters make it necessary for Powers to move back to the New York area, and his present employer has nothing to offer him there. So it might turn out that Cosa Nostrum's loss will be ISC's gain.

The combination of Powers' experience and his forceful and enthusiastic handling of Will's phone call makes Will add him to the "A" team.

The list now looks like this:

A

Charlie Comstock — Adam Labs

Ethan Evans — Bio-Dynamics

Dan Dawson — formerly Prestige Panacea

Gerry Glib — Maxi-Medi-Marketing

Pete Powers — Cosa Nostrums

B

Frank Finley, Jr. — Maxi-
Medi-Marketing

The very next day brings one of those near-misses that makes Will grind his teeth. He gets a call from Harry Harper, the Marketing VP at Parker Laboratories...which is off-limits to GR&B recruiters. It just so happens that Harry is an ideal candidate for the ISC job. Will, who has met Harry before, thought of him when the search began. But, with Parker off-limits, approaching Harry was out of the question. Now here's Harry on the phone, announcing that he's desperate to leave Parker Labs!

"I want to get out of here, Will. They've appointed a new group executive, a guy I've known and disliked for years. Unfortunately, the feeling is mutual. He's not my *direct* boss, but he's *his* boss; and he's already starting to make my life miserable. This turkey doesn't pass up any chance to knock me, or make me look bad. Maybe he thinks I'm a threat to him...even though I'm two layers down. Of course, by now I'd have been promoted to just one layer down, if he hadn't got his promotion. I just know if I don't get out of here soon, he's gonna cause me real trouble. Will, have you got *anything* for me?"

Will thinks sadly of the ISC job, a perfect match for the experience and capabilities of Harry Harper. But of course it would be as much as Will's job is worth to try to bring them together.

"Harry," he replies, "You know that I think you're an outstanding executive. But we have a client relationship with your employer...and quite specifically with your division, where we put in a head of R&D three months ago. You know the rules. I couldn't possibly show you anything."

"Isn't there some way to make an exception? It's not like you're raiding the place or anything. I've already made up my mind to leave Parker Labs."

"The only time I can make an exception to the rule is when an executive has already told someone in the supervisory line directly above him...his boss, or his boss's boss...that he's looking around and wants to leave."

Will begins to feel a surge of excitement. Maybe he *can* get an ideal candidate for ISC. Absentmindedly, he loosens his tie.

"Could you go to your boss and tell him how you feel about this guy? Explain that you think he's out to ruin your career, and that you intend to start looking around."

"I don't think I can do that, Will," confesses Harry. "My boss and I get along okay, but we're just not close enough on a personal level for me to trust him. And now *he's* also feeling the pressure this guy applies. If he thought I was going to leave soon, he'd probably run right upstairs and suggest they get me out immediately, just to prove he's beginning to think on his new boss's wave length."

"How about going up another level, to Charley Phipps, your CEO?" asks Will. "One time when Mr. Rossi and I were in talking to Phipps about my possibly doing a search that never materialized, Phipps mentioned you to us among three or four younger guys he thought were 'comers' in his organization, but not quite ready yet for what he had in mind."

"I can't do that either," answers Harry dejectedly. "After all, he's the one who promoted this guy...and you can bet the guy is really in solid with him at this point." Harry sighs. "I guess there's no way. I'm trapped. There are only two people to tell, and I can't talk to either one of them."

"I'm sorry to hear it, Harry," says Will sympathetically. *Sorrier than you'll ever know, my friend, since I have the perfect job for you right here in my hand, and I'm straining to find decent candidates.* "But I have to play by the rules over here if I want to keep *my* job. Listen, keep in touch, and let me know if anything changes over there."

Will hangs up with a bang. *That's a heartbreaker! Here's a great candidate, who's begging for the job, and he'd be excellent and it would be ideal timing for him, and in the long run it wouldn't hurt the company either because they'll eventually lose him; yet I can't nail him for ISC.* Will questions...and not for the first time...the wisdom of his decision to earn a living as an executive recruiter.

Will's bad mood is soon to grow even worse. Putting on his suit coat and straightening his tie, he strolls down the hall to share a cup of stomach-destroying coffee with Buddy and commiserate about the day-to-day struggles of their work. In the course of telling Buddy how many things have gone wrong with the ISC search, he eventually breaks down and admits he does have a few promising candidates, among them a guy named Gerry Glib.

"Gerry Glib? Gerry Glib! Gerry Glib!! Hahahahaha!!!" Buddy begins to laugh so uncontrollably that he spills coffee on the stack of resumes on his desk.

"Why are you laughing? What's so funny? What do you know about Gerry Glib?" demands Will.

Buddy finally calms down and wipes his eyes.

"So you got taken by Gerry Glib, huh? Don't let it worry you. It's happened to the best of us."

"What do you mean?" Will finds he's talking through clenched teeth.

"Gerry's one of those guys who's all talk and no action. In interviews, he sounds wonderful. He can sell himself, no doubt about it. But once he gets the job, that's the end of it. One of the big foreign drug companies made the mistake of letting him open up a marketing subsidiary on the Coast to try to penetrate the U.S. market with some of their proprietary items that they got FDA approval to sell over here. They had to give him a lot of rope, and two years later all they had to show for it was a huge stack of bills and an exquisitely decorated office. As far as I know, he never brought in a single dollar's worth of business. Didn't you see the file I made on Gerry? It's all in there."

"Well, I thought Gloria must have checked. She's always extremely careful about procedure."

"Maybe she missed him because he's filed under Gaspar G. Glib, his actual name...did you know that?...but he always goes by Gerry. Also, I made his file when he was still at Messerschmidt, and they're known for their industrial products...most people here don't realize they're in drugs, too. She probably assumed that Gaspar at Messerschmidt and Gerry at Maxi-Medi-Marketing were two different people."

Will's heart sinks as he recalls the glowing description Gerry gave him of that episode in his career...somehow he managed to make it sound like a smashing success.

"I can't believe it," he says crossly. "You mean he's no good at all?"

"No good at all," emphasizes Buddy. "I'm surprised you didn't hear that from people you checked him out with. The guy's a laughing stock of the industry."

Will admits that he didn't bother to check Gerry out very thoroughly...he'd seemed so impressive. And Will was in such need of a good candidate, he just jumped at Gerry when he ran across him in a directory. He was in a hurry, got careless, and made a mistake. He's grateful that he found out *before* he presented Gerry to Mr. Summit...although he wishes he hadn't let Buddy get one up on him like that. He knows it will be weeks before Buddy lets him forget about his own gullibility. *What the hell, it happens to all of us every now and then.* Will crumples his styrofoam cup and heads back to his own office. He has calls to make for another search assignment before the day is over.

First Report to Sherm Summit

The next week, Summit...scheduled to be in the city for a meeting with ISC's investment bankers...has drinks with Will after work. They settle down comfortably at a table in the bar of the New York Yacht Club, and Summit gets right down to the business at hand.

"What have you got for me?," he queries.

"In covering the top companies in the drug field," responds Will smoothly, "I've come up with several people I think you'll find interesting."

"Tell me about them," commands Summit.

"I looked into BioDynamics, one of the companies on your list, and I've got you a real heavyweight. His name is Ethan Evans, and he was just recently promoted from Marketing VP to a job on corporate staff."

"Sounds like coming to ISC as division head would be a lateral move for him," says Summit, shrewdly putting his finger on a weakness in the situation at once.

"That's true. But he's interested anyway because it would get him back into the action."

"What about money?" asks Summit sagely.

"I think he's making about $185,000 at BioDynamics."

"Well, I don't want to pay more than that unless I absolutely have to. Would this guy leave California and come to our area, without some additional monetary incentive?"

"I think so," Will replies, rather tentatively. "I'll talk to him about it. But I have a hunch that if he could be heading a division as president, with a corporation that intends to really back his unit, he'd go for it." *Damned right he'd go for it. It's a lot better than sitting around waiting to be fired.*

"Another company I've already been into is Maxi-Medi-Marketing. There's only one genuine possibility there: Frank Finley, one of two Marketing VP's in one of their divisions. He's a relatively young man, moving rapidly up the ladder, and I've heard some good things about him from other people in the industry."

"Sounds like he might come from the right place for us. What's he making?"

"His taxable income is about $105,000, but they have an excellent deferred bonus program at Maxi-Medi, and at his level he might be getting as much as $30,000 or so additional."

"So he's about ready to step up to our range...maybe a little bit at the low end." Summit takes another belt of his Chivas and water. "What else have you got for me?"

Tough old bastard, thinks Will.

"I've also looked into Prestige Panacea. I find that their top marketing guy... Senior VP of both Marketing and Sales...left a few weeks ago, and his replacement has only been in the job for that short time. He's supposed to be a good marketing executive, but has never before had any experience with sales...never even served any time as a salesman. But I did locate the guy who left, Dan Dawson. He's a seasoned pro in the proprietary drug field, and he might be just the one to step into your job and start running."

"Why did he leave Prestige?"

"I've checked that out, and he comes up pretty clean. It's a bit of a story, which I can discuss with you now if you..."

"No, we'll get to that later, if he's still around when you present your finalists," says Summit. "Anyone else?"

"One of the hottest possibilities is a guy from Cosa Nostrums who has personal reasons for wanting to move back to the New York area. I'm still checking his references, but he looks very promising."

"And is that all?" presses Summit.

"There's also a man from a small company, Adam Laboratories, out in Phoenix. He's got a background with Parker Labs, and I hear the company he's with is doing very well now."

"Never heard of the place, but if he seems to be big enough..."

"I'm seeing him this weekend. If I'm satisfied after an interview, I'll pass him on. Sometimes there's real talent in these smaller companies. People are attracted by the autonomy and the chance to build up an equity stake."

"Well, it sounds like you've come up with a few possibilities," says Summit with a small note of satisfaction in his voice.

And you'll never know how hard I worked to do it! Will pauses to consider the companies he's just discussed, and the gap between the way this interim report has impressed Summit and the more difficult circumstances Will has had to deal with:

"Top Ten" Companies That Appear Searched	*"Top Ten" Companies That Have Been Searched*
BioDynamics	
Maxi-Medi-Marketing	**Maxi-Medi-Marketing**
Prestige Panacea	
Cosa Nostrums	**Cosa Nostrums**

"By the way, what did you find out about that resume I passed along to you?" Summit impales Will with his piercing blue eyes.

Curse the man's memory! Why couldn't he have forgotten?

"I'm checking him out," assures Will. He meets Summit's gaze without the slightest appearance of flinching...but he does call the waiter over to order another glass of Chablis.

"I'll be interested to know what the story is on him," says Summit. Obviously, he's not going to let the subject of Sam Sage die from neglect. Will realizes that he's probably going to have to show Sam the ISC job. Too bad, Buddy. Stand by for a ram!

"Now I hope I'm not throwing you a curve," continues Summit with just a hint of malice gleaming in his eye, "but I've got another candidate I'd like you to check out. His name's Jim Johnson, and he's currently a division head at Daisy Foods."

Will looks up with a surprised expression. Summit has been quite specific about wanting nothing other than a drug background...and now here he is proposing someone from the food industry.

"I know I said I wanted someone with a drug background," says Summit, just as if he'd read Will's thoughts. "I was afraid that someone without plenty of drug experience might take too long to get up to speed, and our situation definitely calls for fast action. But Johnson was recommended very strongly to me by a man I respect, someone who's been on my Board for a number of years. He happened to learn that Johnson has just been passed over for the presidency at Daisy Foods. Apparently, there were several good candidates inside the firm, and another guy just happened to win out."

"I understand that the situation is all very friendly. . .and in fact Daisy wants to keep Johnson if they can," Summit continues. "But he's quietly looking around to see if he can find something with a more open future. I checked Johnson out with Bill Beane, and Bill was thrilled to hear he might be available. He told me, 'He's one of the best guys in the industry. . .why, he may be the only guy who knows more about marketing food than I do!' So with such good recommendations, I think we owe it to ourselves to take a look at Johnson, even though he does come from the food industry."

Will is relieved to hear that Summit's latest enthusiasm comes from Daisy, a company he happens to know is open to Gordon, Rossi & Boodles. This time he can move quickly, and show Summit that he's perfectly willing to act on client-suggested candidates.

"I'll be happy to check him out," answers Will with real warmth. "With any luck, I can get to him tomorrow." *I wish I'd known Summit would take a food guy. It might have made my life a lot easier these last few weeks.*

But in fact Will is perfectly aware that if *he* had approached Summit with this Jim Johnson, or someone like him, Summit would have bridled and reminded Will that he asked for *drug* background only. When a client is paying for a search, he wants to have his preferences respected. Only he can decide to ignore them.

But all in all, Will leaves the Yacht Club a happy man. His five preliminary candidates passed muster, and on top of that, he now has a sixth who comes straight from the client. Six weeks ago, it seemed virtually impossible that Will would be able to find even one decent candidate. . .and now he has a half-dozen that Summit considers appropriate. And the marvel is that four of them come from the top firms in the field, the very ones where Summit wanted him to look. . . a feat Will never thought he'd achieve.

A Recruiter's Work Is Never Done

Wilma locates Al Umans, ISC's Senior VP - Human Resources, in Seattle at the main plant and warehouse of SomeThin Thweet, a $10 million subsidiary that produces low-calorie candy, and gets him on the phone for Will. "Would you believe," says Al, "that this whole big union drive got started in this little shop? How's the Drug Division search coming?" Will gives Al the same optimistic report over the phone that he gave to Mr. Summit.

But Will knows that he still needs to look further for ISC. Although the slate he just presented to Summit is plausible, Will is painfully aware that it's not really quite as good as it looks. Ethan Evans, let's face it, does have a problem making decisions...even though not enough to get him fired during 18 years at BioDynamics. Sherm Summit will almost certainly decide against him during interviews. And if by slim chance he doesn't, Will's final referencing will discourage hiring Evans. *I don't want my long-term relationship with ISC riding on how well they like Ethan Evans three years from now*, thinks Will. Dan Dawson was fired, and Will has seen other clients just as decisive as Summit begin to waver when it comes time to sign up someone a competitor has discarded. Frank Finley is a little junior for the position. Only Pete Powers and Charlie Comstock seem problem-free.

Too bad, Will! Charlie Comstock's clay feet are immediately obvious, when he comes in from Phoenix for his interview at GR&B. Charlie talks too much and listens too little. He gives long, rambling answers to Will's carefully phrased questions. And, worse yet, he never includes any facts and figures that might let Will objectively assess Charlie's performance. By the time their hour-long interview is concluded, Will finds himself in real doubt as to whether Charlie actually has contributed anything to Adam Labs' fine growth in sales and profitability. But whatever Charlie might or might not have done at Adam, he's simply too poor a personal communicator to present to a sharp Fortune 1000 CEO like Summit. Not only would Charlie be shredded during the interview, but Will would surely feel the repercussions as well. Sadly, Will strikes Charlie's name from his list of candidates.

While Will is looking for new candidates, other executives are looking for Will. Lanny Lawrence, a marketing executive at CompuMedic, whom Will placed about seven years ago at a different company, phones Will. Since he now works at CompuMedic, he is of course off-limits. Lanny, an extremely ambitious careerist, speaks with a note of petulance in his voice.

"Will, Lanny Lawrence here. I hear you've been calling around for a guy to go to ISC as President of their proprietary drug division. Why the hell didn't you call me?"

I hate this kind of conversation. "Lanny, I certainly *did* think of you. But you know that CompuMedic is one of our best clients. I can't take people out of there."

"But surely you can make an exception for a good friend. I mean, I'm not desperate to leave or anything, but that ISC job is an outstanding opportunity that comes at the perfect point in my career. I could be here another three or four years before I get a shot at a job at that level. Come on...it'll be okay. I'll tell them I was the one who approached you, not vice versa."

Will spends a couple seconds imagining what Mr. Rossi would say if he heard GR&B had gone into CompuMedic, and winces. He's going to have to think fast to head Lanny off. Unfortunately, Lanny's just the aggressive sort of guy who would go straight to ISC himself, with or without Will's cooperation.

"Lanny, you know that for you I might try to find a way to get around the rules...if I thought the job was really...well...." He lets his voice trail off.

Lanny is obligingly quick to read a meaning into Will's vague remark. "The only thing that might be wrong with that ISC job is that I've heard through the grapevine that in the last few years they've really cut back the advertising budget for their proprietary drug division. It could be a great job. But if the parent company isn't going to back up the marketing effort, well, that's another story."

"What can I tell you?" answers Will thoughtfully. He pauses to let his lack of reassurance sink in. As the silence grows, Will deliberately represses his memory of Summit's crystal clear explanation of how the problem came about *and* how it's going to be corrected.

Finally Lanny says decisively, "Well, I wouldn't want to be put out on a limb like that. I mean, if you're going to be able to make that division truly profitable, you've got to have lots of advertising support. Without it, you just can't make things happen. And I can't afford to let a no-win situation like that louse up my career."

Will sighs as he hangs up the phone. His strategy, unfair though it might have been to Lanny, has obviously succeeded. He didn't lie. And yet there's little chance that Lanny will try to go directly to the ISC job.

But Will still needs one or two more really good people...who are not off-limits for the ISC search. He goes back to his directories, back to his notes, back to his sources. And, wonder of wonders, a new name *does* crop up. Roy Ricardo is a highly regarded U.S. marketing executive who's been working for a South American drug firm, heading their proprietary division, a job he obviously took as a stepping-stone career move. Now he's ready to leave Buenos Aires and return to the States, so he's begun getting in touch with his contacts to see what might be available. One of them...the VP - Manufacturing at Better & Best, whom Roy has kept in touch with since they worked together ten years ago... mentioned Roy to Will.

Will is humming to himself as he checks Roy out. His background is comprehensive and his track record is extraordinary. Bilingual, although born, raised, and Princeton-educated in the U.S., Roy had a meteoric rise to Group Product Manager for all pain-relievers, a $180 million business at Prestige Panacea here in the U.S., by the time he was 30 years old. Then in the hope of getting strong general management experience before age 35, Roy accepted a very lucrative offer to join the Argentinian company as President of a division which he's doubled in size (to $30 million) in just three years. *Wow*, thinks Will, *he'll be gangbusters for ISC!* Optimistically, Will checks out Roy's present employer against his book of client companies that are off-limits at Gordon, Rossi & Boodles. Just as he has surmised, Los Medicamentos is not listed. GR&B has never done business with this South American firm, so it's perfectly okay for Will to recruit its executives.

Almost as an afterthought, Will asks his secretary to check to see whether Roy Ricardo belongs to any other GR&B recruiter. So he's stunned by the bad news. It turns out that there *is* a file on Roy, and it's currently signed out to Doug Abel, one of Will's colleagues down the long corridor at GR&B. Will is concerned, but he doesn't give up hope. He knows that Doug has no assignment that involves anything in the consumer goods industry, much less proprietary drugs, so he assumes Doug is merely using Roy as a source on something involving South America. He hopes a stroll down the hall will enable him to talk Doug into relinquishing Roy, who's tailor-made for the ISC job.

But Will soon discovers that Doug isn't taking so cooperative a view of the situation. He tells Will that Roy is a prospect for his most urgent search a corporate Marketing VP for Brute Force, one of America's leading manufacturers of heavy-duty industrial motors.

"Industrial motors! That's insane. Roy Ricardo is a *consumer* marketing guy, who just incidentally happens to be exactly what ISC is looking for. His proprietary drug experience is going to be wasted in industrial motors."

"You know that, Will, and I know that. But the people at Brute Force don't know that. And they're the ones who are paying their money to get their choice. They want someone with a consumer products background to jazz up their marketing approach.

"But surely the poor guy doesn't want to go into industrial motors...and move to Anthracite Valley to do it!"

"You're probably right that he doesn't especially want to go into industrial motors. But he does want to come back to the States, now that his twins will be entering junior high school in the fall. And he'll probably take the first offer he gets, because he can't run a very efficient campaign from Buenos Aires. Brute Force will pay well...and after all, it's probably the only job he's going to know about...at least the only one from GR&B. Will, I'm absolutely going to keep Ricardo. Do you think it's easy to find anyone in any sort of consumer marketing who wants to go into industrial motors? I searched for *weeks* before I found this guy. And so far he's my only acceptable candidate. I don't want him to know about any other job in the entire universe, and certainly not a presidency in proprietary drugs. No, Roy Ricardo is going to work for Brute Force in Anthracite Valley.''

Will can recognize an immovable object when he sees one. Obviously, Doug is not going to give up Roy Ricardo...and to be fair, Will admits that, in Doug's shoes, he'd behave exactly the same way.

Will's final candidate for the ISC job comes to him from a source he'd thought was exhausted: the talent pool of executives on file at Gordon, Rossi & Boodles. One morning Will's secretary Wilma pops into his office, waving a handful of folders.

''Look what I found!'' she crows. ''I've just been down to Research to return our files from that Consolidated Electronics search,'' she explains. ''And while I was standing there, Renee...that's Glenn Williams' secretary, you know; he's the new recruiter that Mr. Rossi hired a few months ago...came in with a big pile of folders she was returning from his search for the president of a small mail order vitamin company. So I went through them right on the spot, before anyone else could get their hands on them. I pulled out everyone who seemed to have any sort of marketing background.''

''That's wonderful, Wilma. Thanks a lot. Maybe I'll find someone in these files.''

And much to Will's surprise and delight, that's just what happens. Most of the executives retrieved by Wilma are, for one reason or another, unsuitable. But, having physical possession of their files, Will can...and does...study the resume of each of the newly-within-reach executives. And to his delight, one folder gives Will a shot at an ideal candidate.

Mark Matthews is the top marketing executive in a relatively small but rapidly-growing drug division of a large conglomerate...a situation very similar to what ISC hopes to achieve. Data Drugs was purchased about three years ago from its third-generation family ownership, and still retains a family member as President and CEO. Mark Matthews was installed as VP - Marketing shortly after the conglomerate took over. When purchased, Data Drugs had just a couple of old-time small-volume products: a dentifrice for heat- and cold-sensitive teeth recommended by dentists, and an ancient but effective hemorrhoid remedy.

Mark moved into a stodgy operation and made some big changes. At his urging, the company took immediate advantage of the newly-relaxed FDA regulations to bring out a cough remedy containing a very effective ingredient previously sold by prescription only. He also took the firm's old-fashioned hemorrhoid medication, at the time selling only to a few elderly consumers of long-standing loyalty, and gave it new life with an aggressive advertising campaign that managed to capitalize on the product's long history in a series of television commercials that poked fun at the product, while also selling persuasively and remaining in good taste.

With Mark's help, Data Drugs has tripled sales and quadrupled profits in less than four years. But the company for some reason has not rewarded his efforts with commensurate recognition and increased compensation. So he's ready to make a move, and ISC seems like the perfect next step. It would be right for his career, and it would bring him the additional money he's looking for.

Of course, the existence of Mark Matthews in GR&B's filing system had come to Will's attention weeks ago. But Mark was then involved in Glenn Williams' search, so Will didn't look deeply into his background and track record, since he belonged to someone else. Now, however, Mark has become accessible to Will within Gordon, Rossi & Boodles at just the right moment.

A quick phone call, followed by a brief interview, convinces Will that Mark is an exceptionally attractive candidate. As far as Will is concerned, his slate is now complete.

Glenn Williams has already checked Mark Matthews' references, and by this stage Will has done preliminary referencing on all his other candidates. He knows they have the recent job titles and experience, and college degrees, they're claiming, and also that current observers consider them competent and morally upright. Moreover, all candidates know they must submit to Will's intensive final referencing, prior to actual hiring by Mr. Summit. . .if and when both he and they are inclined to take that step.

The Final Slate of Candidates

By the end of his search, Will is very pleased. He has seven attractive candidates for Summit. The finalists are:

> **1. Ethan Evans:**   a senior executive with BioDynamics,
> a top-tier firm. Evans merits consideration, no matter
> what his decision-making problems might be.

> **2. Frank Finley, Jr.:**   an impressive young man on the
> way up at Maxi-Medi-Marketing, also a top firm. He's

definitely a contender, even though his experience is a bit light.

3. **Dan Dawson:** until recently with Prestige Panacea, the top-tier firm that seems to be Mr. Summit's favorite. Even though he's been fired, he definitely gives a good account of himself.

4. **Sam Sage:** his experience has been mainly with ethical pharmaceuticals rather than proprietary drugs, and he's a leading candidate on Buddy Young's Expodex search. Nonetheless he's become a candidate in whom Summit is interested.

5. **Jim Johnson:** highly recommended by a Director of ISC and a favorite of Bill Beane, although his background at Daisy Foods is certainly not what Summit originally asked for.

6. **Pete Powers:** the person at Cosa Nostrums most appropriate for ISC, although more oriented toward field sales management and sales promotion than toward advertising- and image-oriented consumer products marketing.

7. **Mark Matthews:** last, but not least...Will's favorite, from Data Drugs. Here's a rapidly-rising young marketing superstar who, despite being only chief of marketing in a still-small but (thanks to him) explosively-growing-proprietary drug division, has a brief but proven track record in doing just what Mr. Summit wants accomplished. Sales and earnings of the operation Mark joined three and a half years ago had been flat for seven prior years under the leadership of the family-member who's still CEO today. Clearly, it's Mark who's made the difference.

All seven of the finalists are ready for client interviews. So Will personally delivers written presentations on them to Summit, leaving an extra set for Bill Beane. Will also express-mails a set to Al Umans, whom Wilma tracked down at ISC's huge Western manufacturing and distribution center in Denver. Summit decides to handle the screening interviews himself. "That way we don't waste Bill Beane's time on anyone we're not really interested in."

Down to the Wire

Summit's first decision is to rule out Ethan Evans.

"You know," he says to Will in a follow-up phone call, "I suspect this guy was kicked upstairs. He definitely lacks the fire in the belly you want to see in a division head. Corporate staff seems like the best place for him. He's the kind of guy who can tell you the pros and cons of every situation, but I don't think he can go on and make a decision about which risk to take."

"That's very perceptive," responds Will tactfully. "I've heard some things along those same lines, which I would have wanted you to consider if you were interested in going forward with him."

"No, I don't think he's right for us. I liked him personally, and I could see him as a staff analyst or a consultant; certainly he knows the industry. But I don't think he'll deliver in the crunch."

Summit signs off, letting Will know that he's seeing Sam Sage tomorrow afternoon. Twenty minutes later, however, Mr. S calls back.

"Sage just called and canceled his appointment! Seems he just this morning signed the papers to do a leveraged buyout of the Accura Flavors & Fragrances Division of Medica Suisse. Accura is an 80-year-old company...$28 million... in New Jersey. They'd fallen way behind their competitors by the time the Swiss bought them four years ago, and things haven't improved since. Just scraping along...not losing money, but not making anything much either."

"Sage says he's always wanted to own a company," Summit continues, "and this may be the only chance he'll ever get. Sounds on the phone like a *very fine fellow*. I'm sorry to lose him as a candidate. But if I were his age again, and had a chance to go it alone, I'd do the same damn thing. Anyway, I wanted you to know. Can't have this happen many more times, or you've got to rev up that machine of yours and get more candidates over here."

Wow! I knew Sam was working on some deals, thinks Will, *but I never imagined he'd get one to pay off. This is bad news for me. But it'll hit Buddy like a ton of bricks. Sam was his front-runner on Expodex. Hope Buddy's finally got some depth on that search...*

Three days later, Summit calls with another status report. Frank Finley has also fallen by the wayside. Just as Will suspected, Summit finds Frank's experience a bit too light. "In a few more years, he'd be right for us...or we'd take him today in a lower position...but for the presidency right now I have to pass."

Will makes suitable noises, and Summit continues without specifically responding to Will's comments.

"I think we've got four good people left, and I'm going to arrange to have them back for a second round of interviews. This time they'll talk to Bill Beane, and then he and I will get together to make a final decision. I could ask you to set up the dates, but I might as well have my secretary do it, because she knows my...and Bill's...availability better than you would."

More than a week passes before Will hears from Summit again. Meanwhile, Will has been in touch with Al Umans, who's now back at ISC's West Cost headquarters in L.A. Thanks to Al, Will already knows what Summit is going to say.

"At this point we've eliminated Dan Dawson, although he seems competent," says Summit. "We found him to be a little too rigid...maybe a little too insistent on doing things *his* way. He might not be the real team player we need here at ISC. So our final group narrows down to Pete Powers, Jim Johnson, and Mark Matthews. I'll tell you frankly that I favor Matthews, because what he's done for that little company he's in now is just exactly what we want done here. Bill Beane leans a bit toward Johnson...I think, probably, because he's heard so much about him from friends in the food business. That makes Powers our compromise candidate, but neither Bill nor I are really compromisers. Anyway, Bill and I are going to get together on Friday for some squash at the Racquet Club, and afterward we'll thrash out a decision. One more thing...final referencing. Bill has Johnson *wired*. But put young Matthews under your microscope and get back to me by Thursday afternoon." (Mark Matthews' references are excellent, as Will promptly informs Summit.)

Just before lunch on the following Monday, Summit calls one last time, to report their final decision.

"It's going to be Mark Matthews," he announces. "It was a tough call, but I think we'll be satisfied with our choice," he chuckles jovially. "We put it to a vote...and the majority won."

Somehow, Will is not surprised to learn that ISC has selected Summit's favorite candidate.

"But Bill is *very happy* with Mark. Actually, any one of the three would have been good for the job. You came up with some good candidates, and I wouldn't be surprised if we were doing business with you again soon."

Will sighs with relief that it's all over...and that both Summit and Bill Beane are pleased with the result. It's almost 9:00 a.m. in L.A., so Will tries a long distance call to Al Umans and reaches another very happy man. The 2,400-person facility in Denver...Al's biggest worry...voted "No" on Friday, and that outcome is almost certain to be echoed in the remaining five West Coast locations, which vote tomorrow.

Next Will gives a quick call to GR&B's billing department to let them know Mark Matthews' first year's estimated compensation, so that an additional bill bringing Gordon, Rossi & Boodles' fee up to one-third of that amount can be mailed out. Then he buzzes Wilma to tell her the ISC assignment is finished and she can clear up the final paperwork...also please call the Prime-Burger for a rare burger and iced tea. Finally he calls his wife to propose a really special celebratory dinner at the restaurant of her choice (she opts for the main dining room at Caneel Bay on the next long weekend). Then he turns his attention back to the real problem of his existence at the moment: the troublesome search for a chief financial officer for a regional department store chain based in Little Rock, Arkansas.

Victory...and an unending challenge. They're all in a day's work for Super Recruiter Will Pickham.

The Box Score

Now that it's all over, let's take a look at how each of the principals in our little drama has fared. Who are the winners? Who are the losers? Could any of them have done things differently?

Sherm Summit

Our wily CEO is very pleased with Mark Matthews, who has precisely the background Mr. Summit wanted. Moreover, Mr. S is enjoying the good feeling that comes from knowing he had a real choice. He heard about quite a few possibilities, and interviewed six likely candidates...at least three of whom he felt could do the job.

Of course, what Mr. Summit doesn't know is that there were additional people Will knew about but couldn't present, because they worked for other GR&B clients, or were allocated to other GR&B recruiters.

But bear this in mind: although GR&B's two-year off-limits rule against biting-the-hands-that-feed worked against Mr. Summit in this search assignment, that same rule operated to his benefit during the two years following GR&B's

search to bring in Graham Rusk, and now it'll be in force for another two years. Moreover, the rule that kept Will's hands off other recruiters' candidates also kept theirs off Sherm Summit's candidates.

The important thing is that Summit justifiably feels that Will's services were well worth the slightly over $60,000 he paid for them, and he'll probably return to Will at Gordon, Rossi & Boodles the next time he's unable to fill a key position on his own.

Will Pickham

On this assignment, as on most others, Will had his ups and downs.

At the outset, the situation looked bleak. Undaunted, Will threw himself into solving the problem. He had to work to come up with his slate of candidates. But after all, that's what he's handsomely paid to do. Will prides himself on his resourcefulness, and not without reason. He's brought in a sizable fee for Gordon, Rossi & Boodles, and will be getting more business from Integrated Standard Corporation in the future.

Above all, Will has done his very best to serve both his client and his firm. He's happy that he was able to complete the assignment to the eminent satisfaction of Mr. Summit and Bill Beane; glad he was patient about waiting for more work from ISC instead of beginning to take people out; and pleased to have extended a great opportunity to Mark Matthews.

Bill Beane

Since he's Executive Vice President in charge of five of ISC's eight divisions and he's Mark Matthews' new boss, we...and Will...would have liked to have seen more of Bill Beane during the search process, since it's important that he be as pleased with the result as Mr. Summit. There's no reason, however, to believe that he's not. And having twice got a fine executive from Will Pickham, he'll use Will again next time he has a need.

Al Umans

Too bad that the labor emergency has kept ISC's Senior VP - Human Resources from being more accessible to Mr. Summit at this time and more directly involved in the search...particularly at the outset. But all in all, Al too is properly pleased with the outcome, and with the diligence and speed Will has demonstrated. He'll undoubtedly recommend Will to other ISC executives when they need recruiting services.

Arthur Applewhite

Art has no idea he was ever involved in the ISC search. And in a sense, he wasn't, since he was never told about the job, and ISC was never told about him. In Will's mind, however, Art was...and still is...the prototype of what Summit wanted. True, as Will told Summit when he presented Art's unemployed ex-boss Dan Dawson as the logical candidate from off-limits Prestige Panacea, Art hasn't directly supervised a field sales force. But Summit never stipulated that criterion. And Summit didn't know...as Will does...how ideally Art's superior personal characteristics would have fit into an ISC management team that already includes Bill Beane and Graham Rusk. Indeed, mildly negative personal characteristics were what caused Summit to drop Dan Dawson, the executive he *did* see from Prestige Panacea.

So it certainly looks as if Art Applewhite could have been a leading contender for the ISC proprietary drug division presidency...and very likely the winner. But Will's hands were tied.

Nonetheless, Art's weren't.

Right now, as he savors his new promotion to Dan Dawson's job, Art is making excellent career progress...without giving any thought to the "Rites of Passage," which are ever-present in the minds of most exceptionally successful executives. We congratulate Art and wish him well.

However, it will be ironic if tomorrow morning as he scans the "Who's News" section of *The Wall Street Journal,* Art notes wistfully that another man almost exactly his age is stepping up to the presidency of a sizable proprietary drug operation from a far lesser position than Art held even before his recent promotion, and thinks: *What a career-making opportunity...I wish I were in his shoes.* Chances are, Art, you could have been...if you'd made up your mind a while ago that you were ready for a presidency, and if you'd joined us in studying how to precipitate opportunity, rather than just waiting for it to happen.

Alice Klasner

As VP - Marketing at National Anodyne, No. 2 on Mr. Summit's "hit list," Alice is another outstanding potential candidate, who doesn't know what she may have missed. Since she worked for an off-limits firm, Will ruled her out immediately. So Alice continues where she is, without any notion that she could have had an excellent shot at becoming president of a sizable proprietary drug company.

Charlie Comstock

For Charlie, from Adam Labs, the ISC search has been a learning experience. He was thrilled to be contacted by Will, and flown to New York for an interview. He correctly assumed that such attention meant he was beginning to make a name for himself. But since he was never introduced to the client Charlie, no dummy, has concluded that he must have fouled up the interview...which was indeed true.

Therefore, Charlie has decided that if he wants to get ahead, he'll have to learn to do better. So he has signed up for a workshop that videotapes executives in mock presentations and interviews. Now he's perfecting the art of crisp, succinct, factual answers, a relaxed presence, and the ability to really listen to his interviewer. Chances are that when opportunity knocks again, Charlie will be ready.

Dan Dawson

When he got tossed out of Prestige Panacea, Dan took a very logical step, by sending out letters and resumes to every retainer recruiting firm, including our fictitious Gordon, Rossi & Boodles. His reward was a good interview at ISC, where he was one of four top finalists. He lost out only because other candidates with superior credentials or attributes...and (in one case) personal recommendations...were introduced as his competition.

However, Dan's been unemployed almost five months, and Will only got the ISC assignment about three months ago. If Dan had sent his mailing to employers...not just recruiters...he'd have reached Mr. Summit before Will got the search and provided competitive candidates, in addition to Dan. After all, Dan comes from the directly competitive company that was number-one on Mr. Summit's "wish list." Who knows? Dan might have won, if he'd reached Summit directly *and* early.

As an experienced executive, Dan can accept his failure to get the ISC job philosophically. Maybe the next one will be the position with his name on it.

But what he can't understand is why he never hears from anyone at Gordon, Rossi & Boodles again. After all, they obviously thought he was a good enough candidate to introduce to ISC. Indeed, he was called back for a second interview. So Dan knows he must have been a serious contender, as Will reassured him when he phoned to report that Mark Matthews had been selected. Yet there's never a peep from Will, nor any other GR&B recruiter for the next six months.

Eventually Dan gets a job through a networking contact. *But he still shakes his head over the fact that GR&B dropped him totally after the ISC search.*

Dan Dawson may not understand what happened, but we do. Wilma, that pearl of a secretary, quite naturally devotes most of her time to helping Will with his *new* searches...the ones that will bring more money to GR&B and more bonus to Will. So it's months before she finds the free time to clear up the old paperwork and return the files of all the ISC candidates, prospects, and "sources" to the Research Department, where they'll be "logged in"...and thus available to other GR&B recruiters.

Ethan Evans

It was really a stroke of good luck for Ethan at BioDynamics that Ken DeWitt and Will made their deal, in which Ken got a chance to try all the candidates who turned Will down because of location, and Will got a shot at Ethan Evans for the ISC search. Everybody won: Ken got some more people to contact on his search. Will got a candidate who represented an off-limits company. And Ethan got an interview. Although he didn't get the job, Ethan was able to polish his interviewing skills, and he made a couple of very valuable contacts.

Now, Ethan Evans is preparing to go into business for himself as a consultant. When he does, he'll re-contact Summit as a prospective client, and Summit will assign him a comprehensive review of the proprietary drug industry, and ISC's current place and future opportunities in it. "Who cares if he's not decisive," Summit will say to Bill Beane and Mark Matthews. "He certainly knows the industry, and he impresses me as a guy who can identify all the options. Let him gather the information. *We'll* know what to do about it!"

Frank Finley, Jr.

Frank was lucky to be working at Maxi-Medi-Marketing, a company that was open to Will's search, and he was very pleased to be considered for such a high-level position. Since he fully realized that he was probably a bit too junior, he wasn't unduly disappointed when Will tactfully explained that ISC had chosen someone with more experience. And since Frank wasn't actively looking for another job, he didn't notice that nobody at Gordon, Rossi & Boodles called him for another six months.

But when Wilma eventually returned his file to be recirculated in the talent pool, Frank was soon called by another recruiter who had an opening that was just right for Frank. So in the end, he got a job that was an important step up his career ladder...and he got it through GR&B.

Gerry Glib

Gerry has serious problems, and his brief involvement with the ISC search merely highlighted them. Gloria's thoroughness (and Will's desperation) led them both to find Gerry in several corporate directories. Luckily, however, Will's conversation with Buddy revealed Gerry's shortcomings, as referencing would also have done in the end. Had Gerry been a truly competent executive, the result might have been different. But, given Gerry's poor track record, nothing came of his conversation with Will. In fact, Gerry is now on thin ice at Maxi-Medi-Marketing and is quietly beginning to look for something else. Gerry was neither helped nor harmed.

Harry Harper

Because Harry had the bad fortune to work for a company currently off-limits to Gordon, Rossi & Boodles, Will couldn't show him the ISC job, even though it would have been ideal for Harry. In fact, Harry will never be shown any job by any GR&B recruiter...at least not until his enemy has done so much damage that Harry is forced to leave Parker Laboratories.

Yet Harry needn't have been trapped in his unfortunate situation. His mistake was in turning to Will at Gordon, Rossi & Boodles...not understanding that even though Will's a nice guy, he's the last person to be able to help Harry. Harry should have gone to other retainer recruiting firms that had no client relationship with Parker Labs. They wouldn't have introduced him to Mr. Summit; only Will had that assignment. But they might have shown him other attractive possibilities.

Harry, of course, could have gone directly to Mr. Summit through discreet networking. And he could readily have reached Mr. Summit through a secretive direct mail campaign while still preserving the confidentiality of his situation, as we discussed in Chapter 13.

In short, Harry is an executive who needs to learn that, when it comes to looking for a better job, there are more ways than one to identify the right opportunity at the right time. He needs a much better initiation than he's had so far into the "Rites of Passage."

Jim Johnson

Jim handled himself very well in his search for a job with a more exciting future than he has at Daisy Foods, since being passed over for its presidency. By approaching ISC through networking, he got around the obstacle of the executive recruiter. Will would never have presented Jim to Summit, because his background wasn't in the proprietary drug industry, as Summit had unequivocally stipulated. By going directly to ISC, Jim got himself seriously considered for the presidency of a proprietary drug company...and, in fact, very nearly got hired.

Because of his initiative and ingenuity, Jim Johnson's future looks rosy. Summit, very much impressed, is keeping him in mind for future openings and has even mentioned him favorably to the CEO of a soft goods conglomerate, which has nominated Topjob for a seat on its board. Moreover, Will also considers Jim a highly attractive candidate, and will have him in mind for future searches.

Meanwhile, of course, Jim continues his low-profile program of quiet personal contact and very discreet networking. And lately he's having particularly good success by concentrating on the investment and commercial banking community...quietly seeking leads on companies that may be available for purchase. No deal is in the works yet. But Jim's meeting extremely knowledgeable and well-connected people. In fact, one of them is the member of ISC's Board who brought Jim to Summit's attention.

However, having lost out on the ISC opportunity, and becoming frustrated with the unavoidably slow pace of his cautious networking, Jim is now lining up a "sponsor" for a secretive direct mail campaign. Within the next four weeks he'll get his message to virtually every CEO in America who might control an appropriate opportunity. And Jim will do so without ever letting Daisy Foods realize that he's determined to get out as soon as possible. Expect to be reading some exciting news about Jim in *The Wall Street Journal* very soon.

Lanny Lawrence

Lanny is perhaps the only executive in the entire group who really got shafted. He knew about the opening at ISC, and he wanted the job. Moreover, he would have been a very strong candidate. But because Will did what he absolutely *had* to do to protect GR&B's client relationship with CompuMedic, Will was forced to let Lanny draw the wrong conclusion about the open position at ISC.

The moral of Lanny's story is that he should have known better than to rely on Will as his sole informant about the ISC position. And he *would* have known better if he'd been aware of the way the executive recruiting business works, and what Will's needs and problems were. Lanny, too, requires further initiation into the "Rites of Passage."

Mark Matthews

Mark is the obvious winner in this search. He had the right credentials for the ISC job; he was able to convince Will that he had the right credentials; he worked for a company that had no client relationship with Gordon, Rossi & Boodles; and he was not at the moment Will needed him allocated to any other recruiter at GR&B. So Mark was introduced and, in the end, was offered the position.

Mark will never know, however, how close he came to not hearing about the job at all. Luckily for Mark, Glenn Williams is relatively new...in his seventh month...as a recruiter with Gordon, Rossi & Boodles, and therefore not yet assigned the full search load Will and the other GR&B "heavy-hitters" carry. If Glenn's secretary had been as far behind in her search closeouts as Wilma is, Mark's file wouldn't have been instantly returned to the research pool and wouldn't have got there while the ISC search was still going on. And if Wilma hadn't been so diligent and swift, Mark's file might never have come to Will's attention. It could have been checked out by another recruiter...perhaps someone trying to fill a far less attractive position. Lucky breaks can occur anywhere. Mark's happened in the back office of an executive recruiting firm.

Pete Powers

Close...but no cigar for our candidate from Cosa Nostrums.

Pete wound up as one of the top three finalists, but he didn't get hired. Not that he made any mistakes; he didn't. There was nothing he could have done better in order to change the outcome. His marketing bias is toward sales promotion and hard-hitting field sales force activity at the grass roots retailer level, in contrast to big-budget TV campaigns aimed at the consumer. Quite naturally, Pete reflects the philosophy and successful operating methods of the company in which he's gained all of his experience. Unfortunately, Pete's orientation just didn't happen to be what Summit and Bill Beane were buying this time around.

Pete does, however, owe Will Pickham a debt of gratitude for Will's diligence and persistence in appealing to Red Tapecutter, and ultimately clearing away the internal client-protection blockage at GR&B that otherwise would have prevented Pete from finding out about the ISC position. And now that Cosa

Nostrums is no longer off-limits, Pete can expect to hear about another GR&B search. But only after Wilma gets his file back into the central talent pool. And whether that job is in New York...Pete's geographic target...or in Tulsa, will be pretty largely a matter of chance.

Having a desire to move promptly, and into a specific geographic area, Pete really should take matters into his own hands, rather than waiting for the random activity of retainer recruiting firms to solve his problem. Some discreet networking and a secretive direct mail campaign, targeted on the New York metropolitan area, should do the trick...and without triggering the retribution Pete fears if his personal objectives should prematurely become known to his current employer. He'd profit from reading Chapter 13.

Roy Ricardo

To some extent, Roy was a victim of the way retainer executive recruiting firms do business...a business aimed at meeting the needs of their clients, rather than their candidates. Roy was well-qualified for the ISC job...and he'd certainly have preferred to stay in the drug industry and live near New York, rather than go into the industrial motor business and wind up in Anthracite Valley. But, because he was appropriated first by Doug Abel for the Brute Force search, Roy couldn't be shown the ISC job. Therefore, he was never aware that a better alternative existed. Roy will eventually accept the Brute Force position, because it enables him to move back to the States. However, he'd have been a lot happier at ISC.

Obviously, Roy should have written directly to the chief executives of all the companies that interested him, just as Sam Sage did. Roy's list would surely have included Sherm Summit, just as Sam's did, and Roy would have been exposed to both ISC and Brute Force, just as Sam Sage got a shot at both ISC and Expodex.

Roy went all the way to Argentina to acquire his impressive experience and track record in general management which, added to his proprietary drug marketing experience in the U.S., would have made him an ideal candidate at ISC. Now he goes back to a marketing-only position, and enters a field he would never have chosen voluntarily. An out-of-the-country executive needs the most comprehensive and aggressive job-hunting campaign he can mount. Sadly, Roy's fell short.

Sam Sage

Sam's an extremely savvy executive. He bypassed the allocated-to-another-recruiter-in-the-firm obstacle that kept Roy Ricardo from learning about the ISC position. And all it took was a direct mail campaign that included Sherm Summit, CEO of a company that obviously belonged on Sam's list.

Sam's mailing got action from Mr. S for two reasons:

1. It was very impressive, and

2. Summit had an immediate need.

Because of Mr. Summit's insistence, Sam was finally shown the ISC opportunity, in a *rare* exception to the rule that retainer recruiting firms will show you only one job at a time.

In the end, of course, Sam walked away from the ISC opportunity. He didn't even go to his interview. That was another lucky break for Mark Matthews, because Sherm Summit would have chosen Sam over Mark, on the basis of Sam's far greater experience...all of it impressively successful.

Fortunately for Sam...and for Mark...Sam has mastered all the "Rites of Passage." Career-long cultivation of executive recruiter relationships led to Sam's exploration, with Buddy, of the Expodex opportunity. A classic direct mail campaign broke through to the ISC opportunity. And creative use of personal contacts and networking...coupled with an "underutilized asset" discussion with his old friends at Medica Suisse...led Sam to a "buyable" company and financing for the deal.

A few weeks ago, Sam suffered a severe setback. Today he's happier and more challenged than he ever dreamed of being. Sam's got a once-in-a-lifetime entrepreneurial opportunity. And you can be sure he'll make the most of it.

INDEX

ABOUT THE AUTHOR

JOHN LUCHT *is one of America's foremost executive recruiters. Since 1971, he has been bringing senior executives into major corporations in the US and overseas...as head of The John Lucht Consultancy, Inc. in New York since 1977, and for six prior years at Heidrick and Struggles, New York, where he was an officer. Earlier he was in general management or marketing with Bristol-Myers, J. Walter Thompson and Tetley Tea. His BS and Law degrees are from the University of Wisconsin.*

Please turn the page

. . .If you'd like another copy of
Rites of Passage at $100,000 +

. . .If you'd like to know about other
career-development materials
from The Viceroy Press

. . .If you'd like to convey comments
and suggestions about this book.

Rites of Passage at $100,000 + is available at better book stores everywhere. Visit your local bookseller, and save time and shipping expense.

But if that's inconvenient, you may order by mail. Send $24.95*, plus $3.50 shipping (total $28.45*) for each copy by check or money order to:

> The Viceroy Press Inc.
> P.O. Box 5356
> New York, NY 10185-0043
> (212) 826-3900

If this book has been especially helpful, if you have suggestions for additional content, or if you'd like to be aware of other career-development publications of The Viceroy Press Inc., we'd appreciate hearing from you.

*New York residents please add sales tax (NYC $2.06, outside NYC $1.00). All mail orders must be prepaid.